St. Martin's Paperbacks Titles
by G. Gordon Liddy

WILL
THE MONKEY HANDLERS
OUT OF CONTROL

WILL

THE AUTOBIOGRAPHY OF

G. GORDON LIDDY

St. Martin's Paperbacks

To the memory of
the Honorable Sylvester J. Liddy, R.V.O., K.N.O.
my father

Chapter XII appeared in substantially this form in *True* magazine.

WILL

Copyright © 1980 by G. Gordon Liddy.
Postscript to the Paperback Edition copyright © 1991 by G Gordon Liddy.

Cover photograph courtesy UPI/Bettmann.

ISBN: 0-312-92412-7

Printed in the United States of America

St. Martin's Press hardcover edition published 1980
Dell/St. Martin's edition/February 1981
St. Martin's Paperbacks edition/July 1991

10   9   8   7   6   5

PREFACE

In July of 1973 Stewart Alsop wrote me a letter that said, in part: "It has long seemed to me that your powerful personality played an important part in the episode which has now generated a great constitutional crisis. As my article suggests, I understand the reasons for your reluctance to talk heretofore, but since quite literally everybody else involved in the affair has talked at great length, it seems to me that those reasons no longer hold. In any case, if you wished to put any subject off the record, I should of course respect your wishes. You have played a vitally important role in a major historical development, and it seems to me that by now you owe it to yourself, and indeed to history, to say more about that role."

The article he refers to was titled "War, Not Politics." In the piece he likens the character of some of us who worked in Washington in the early 1970s to the "many brave and good men" who served in the wartime OSS. "Curiously enough, in another time, G. Gordon Liddy would have been regarded as among the bravest and the best. . . . In all secret services, it has to be assumed that any captured agent can in time be broken. But there were a few—a very few—captured OSS agents who remained unbreakable, and they were regarded as true heroes. In the case of CREEP, the stubbornly silent G. Gordon Liddy seems to be the only operative to fall into this category. . . . In wartime, G. Gordon Liddy would have been festooned with decorations rather than slapped in jail. As so often in wartime, his stubborn silence did no good."

I liked the piece, but I'm not ready to agree my silence did no good. If in the end it had been of no benefit to anyone else, I'd have done the same thing. But it did help others, and if the containment strategy—and personal

7

code—that prompted my initial silence had been pursued by all my associates, it would have proved successful, and this book would never have been written. When Mr. Alsop wrote his article in 1973, he had no idea what remained unrevealed. Only now that statutes of limitation have expired can I write what is in this book without risking the liberty of any of my former associates.

For all of that preamble, this is not just a Watergate book. It is not even just a Washington book. I've tried to make it a book of both public issues and personal convictions. In my original proposal to my publisher I said, "I became what I wanted to be." The publisher seized on that, maintaining that what I was, and what I became, and what I then did with it, was what the book should tell.

So I've told it, because I agree with Mr. Alsop and all those after him who carried the same message: I do owe a debt to history. And I do want you to know, as much as a book can convey it, the man I am.

With this book I give thanks to the thousands who have written to me, and circulated and signed so many petitions to the President seeking my freedom, and my debt to history is discharged. I only wish Stewart Alsop and my father, both of whom died with their boots on, were here today to read it.

Oxon Hill, Maryland
11 February 1980

I

Something different: strange, alien, ominous. Sound, that was it; but unlike any other. Sound I could feel. Low, menacing, growing; it poured from the sky, wave after wave coming over the sides of the box down to where I stood, alone and trembling as it washed over me. I stared at the sky. The deep throbbing grew louder and louder. Something was coming; something terrible was coming. I tried to move but found I couldn't, fixed by awe and dread. Suddenly, there it was!

A great, gray snout appeared over the top of the box. It grew and grew—a huge, bloated shape swelling and roaring with incredible power as it came on and on, trapping me in the bottom of the box and blotting out the sky. It was going to get me! Screaming in terror, I ran to the side of the box and pounded hysterically until it opened and I escaped the awful *thing*.

It was 22 November 1932. The box was the backyard of my home in Hoboken, New Jersey, enclosed by the rear of the four-story brownstone, high concrete wall opposite, a six-foot wooden fence along one side and a tall hedgerow along the other. There, eight days before my second birthday, the immense dirigible U.S.S. *Akron*, bigger than the ocean liner *Lusitania*, roared directly overhead at low altitude en route to Lakehurst. I had been walking for six months but, to the concern of my mother, I hadn't yet spoken an intelligible word. I began to speak immediately, to articulate my first memory: absolute, overwhelming fear.

Sound again. The whole stairwell filled with it. Danger! Can't hear mother over the jangling alarm and the screams of my infant sister in her arms. Mother is fleeing the apartment. It's not safe. Something will get us if we don't run! "Mommy pick me up! Pick me up!"

9

But with one arm clutching my sister and the other hanging on to the stair railing, she could not. So I clung to my mother's legs all the way down the fire stairs, yowling in panic, hobbling her every step until she dragged me outside. It was spring 1934. My mother, sister, and I were living temporarily in Washington, D.C., while my father nursed my grandfather through terminal cancer. The surprise fire drill at the Wardman Park Annex gave me my second memory. Again, absolute, overwhelming fear.

The early memories that follow are still fragmented, but the theme is common. Lying on the floor as my paternal grandmother lashed me with a leather harness shouting, "Bad! Bad!" Fear. My mother insisting I not use my left hand as she forced me into right-handedness, and my inability to understand why. More fear. Rounding the corner and coming upon a truck-mounted vacuum, a giant air hose snaking across the sidewalk from a huge bag, suction engine roaring as it cleaned the flues of coal furnaces. Running from the sound and the threat—no, certainty—that I would be sucked inside the monster bag. Fear. Soon my every waking moment was ruled by that overriding emotion: fear.

After my grandfather died in 1935, the front bedroom on the top floor of the Hoboken brownstone became "my" room. It was where I slept at night and, too often, where I lay in the daytime within a tent, breathing medicated steam and burning under a mustard plaster intended to clear my lungs and relieve my cough.

At night, passing cars would send a wand of light across the ceiling and I'd listen to the sounds of steam engines whistling and chuffing in the distance. But night was also the time of the dread "moth-miller." I had been frightened the first time a moth fluttered against my bedroom window on a warm summer night. The light threw a giant shadow on the opposite wall, terrifying me. Frantic screams, then mother explaining it was just a harmless moth or, perhaps, a miller. From that moment on the night was filled with giant "moth-millers" out to get me.

10

I knew it. So my fear grew, each new experience breeding more.

That same summer, my parents took my sister and me on a rustic vacation deep in the woods near Canaan, Connecticut. In the evening we sat around an open fire built within a circle of stones. I returned to the circle the next morning and, curious as only a four-year-old can be, picked up a glowing coal to examine it. It stuck to my palm and burned it badly. Two more fears were added to the seemingly endless list: fire and pain. Pain made me dread each monthly trip to New York for hypodermic injections to combat my respiratory weakness; the only alternative to my father's abandoning his New York law practice and moving to Arizona for the sake of my health. Then came the most frightening menace of all: God.

After I'd spent three years at the Academy of the Sacred Heart, run by rather genteel nuns of the order of St. Joseph, my parents enrolled me in the fourth grade at SS. Peter and Paul parochial school.

The section of Hoboken in which we lived had a large ethnic German and German national population. Families from all over Germany had been recruited by *Nord Deutscher Lloyd* and *Hamburg Amerika* to come to Hoboken to serve the swift German ocean liners *Bremen* and *Europa* that, together with numerous German freighters, docked on the New Jersey side of the Hudson, unlike the ships of Great Britain and France. There were also those families that had come to the United States to serve the giant dirigibles Germany built for the transatlantic run in competition with the great surface ships.

Almost directly across the street from our house was a German Protestant church and, although Irish and Italians were represented in the neighborhood, along with some Jews, SS. Peter and Paul Roman Catholic Church had been founded as an "exclusively German Catholic parish." Its pastor, Father Bogner, was a kindly man my mother loved.

At SS. Peter and Paul our day started with prayers.

We stood at attention in mass formation and began by making the sign of the cross, following the example of a nun. Precisely.

God, we were informed, was omnipotent. Unlimited power demanded and deserved the utmost reverence and deference and left no room for a sloppily performed sign of the cross. An imprecise sign of the cross was an insult to God, punishable by a sudden crack on the head from monitoring nuns. Such punishment was to be received gratefully, otherwise retribution might come from God himself. The retribution of almighty God for a sloppily made sign of the cross was terrible.

Only last year, we were solemnly assured, a lazy, irreverent, careless boy had made a sloppy sign of the cross while saying his nightly prayers. The good nuns, alas, were not present to crack him on the head and, as God was not one to let such a sin go unpunished, the next morning the little boy found his right arm withered, twisted, and paralyzed for life.

There were also certain prayers to be said nightly without fail, especially those for the poor souls in Purgatory. No deceased member of the family was to be left out; it might be just the omission that would condemn the relative to another twenty-four hours of the tortures of Hell. Purgatory was, by definition, no different from Hell except there was hope of eventual release after, say, ten million years of torment. Unless an earlier reprieve was earned by the prayers of the living.

Every night I would cross myself with extraordinary care, then say the prescribed prayers over and over again until I fell asleep. Even if the ritual weren't interrupted by a terrorizing attack from the dreaded moth-miller, I could never be sure I hadn't omitted one; hence endless repetition. Every morning, I woke with dread until I had checked my right arm for crippling deformity.

So the nuns introduced me to *authority*. First, God. And then: the flag. After morning prayers at school, we all pledged allegiance to the flag. This too was led by the

12

nuns and required dignity and precision. We stood at rigid attention, facing the flag in lines straight enough to rival those of the massed SS in Leni Riefenstahl's *Triumph of the Will.*

"I pledge allegiance . . ." we began. At the words *to the flag* we shot out our right arms in unison, palms down, straight as so many spears aimed directly at the flag. It was the salute of Caesar's legions, recently popular in Germany, Italy, and Spain.

Oddly enough, while I worried constantly about executing the sign of the cross correctly, I had no such doubts about my ability to salute the flag. It was more than just the absence of divine punishment for poor performance; it was a positive thing. I *enjoyed* the mass salute and performed it well, unexcelled in speed of thrust and an iron-shaft steadiness throughout the remainder of the pledge. That habit became so deeply ingrained that even today, at assemblies where the pledge is made or the national anthem played, I must suppress the urge to snap out my right arm.

Grammar school introduced me to terrors other than a petty and vindictive God. On the street to and from school there were bigger, older boys whom I feared greatly. Not because they were bullies; to call them that would be unfair; they were just normally aggressive boys. The problem was with me; I was frightened, small, and a coward. I was afraid of nearly everyone. And it showed. I ran blocks out of my way not only to avoid truck-mounted vacuum cleaners, but to avoid other boys who would, I feared, attack me gratuitously.

Yet I loved school; it provided me a means of temporary escape from the constant dread and shame that made life unbearable: it gave me more opportunity to read. My mother had taught me the alphabet before I went to school, and she showed me how to sound out combinations of letters into syllables. At school I raced through Dick and Jane, then sought out other material. I felt like an initiate in a wonderful secret society.

13

Reading was magical and soon I pestered my mother into trips to the children's section of the public library, where I took out every book I could find by L. Frank Baum, Edgar Rice Burroughs, Albert Payson Terhune, Booth Tarkington, and Rudyard Kipling. My father bought me a set of the Book of Knowledge, and in second grade I was introduced to Greek and Roman mythology, the fables of Aesop, classical fairy tales, and elementary science. I lost myself in reading; I remember completing *The Swiss Family Robinson* at the age of seven and bursting into tears because I had loved it so and now it was over.

Total absorption in whatever I read had the blessed effect of freeing me, for the time I was reading, from the gnawing worm of fear—and from the self-loathing my fear produced.

This self-loathing came from the realization that I, of all people, had no business being afraid. The example of my family and the exhortations of my mother were constantly before me. Frequently ill, I was nursed patiently by my mother, who used the occasions to teach me the family history and various tales of personal courage and accomplishment against odds. To keep from boring me by repetition, she would make up stories of high valor, usually about American Indians and their warriors' ability to resist the most horrible tortures without the slightest indication of discomfort. Among her true stories was that of Glenn Cunningham, a farm boy whose legs were burned so badly he was told he would never walk again—and who became our national champion in the mile.

Of family members, my mother's favorite was her older brother, Raymond. He, too, was slightly built, but that hadn't stopped him from being the leader of all the boys in the neighborhood; from fighting off much larger boys who tried to force him from the prime street corner for selling magazines in Washington, D.C.; from becoming an Eagle Scout; from putting himself through Georgetown University and its law school with high grades, and from

14

becoming, finally, a member of that gallant band of supermen who filled the headlines of the day—the "G-men" of young J. Edgar Hoover's FBI.

I learned how Uncle Ray had been there when John Dillinger was slain in Chicago; how he was wounded at the gun battle in which Ma Barker and her gang were shot or captured, and that he hadn't even noticed his wound until after the battle and had not bothered to report it. Uncle Ray, known throughout the FBI as "the Little Guy," carried FBI badge number 19 and was on his way to a fabulous career as one of the Bureau's great Special Agents in Charge.

Uncle Ray's visits lit up our gloomy brownstone and the lives of all who lived there. He would arrive with his constant companion, a stunning 1930s Ziegfeld girl and former Patou model named Marjorie Eziquelle, a Basque beauty who towered over him (and became his wife after her teenage marriage was annulled) and wearing under his arm a Colt caliber .38 Super automatic, then the most powerful handgun in the world. His lean, sandy-haired good looks belied his half-Italian ancestry and surname—Abbaticchio—and his irreverent wit tickled my parents. What impressed me was the way his smile could fade to an icy look that I knew could mean death from the huge Colt, and the fact that he wasn't afraid of anybody—even J. Edgar Hoover. (Ask yourself how many FBI agents traveled openly with a gorgeous showgirl in the '30s and '40s and not only kept their jobs but were promoted.)

Uncle Ray could also be gentle. I was fascinated by the Colt Super auto. One day when I was five, I slipped into Ray's room and found it lodged in the lid of his suitcase. This was a rarity—not only was it something *I* feared, so did everybody else! My curiosity got the better of my fear, an uncommon occurrence. Quietly, I withdrew the pistol and examined it, then managed to get the hammer back and the safety off. Proud of this accomplishment, I walked into the room where the adults sat chatting, to show them what I had found.

Uncle Ray spotted me immediately. He knew the pistol was loaded. Rising, he placed himself directly in front of the muzzle, smiled warmly, then reached down and placed his finger between the hammer and the firing pin. He grasped the piece and gently disarmed me. This gun, he informed me quietly, was his. He would get one for me. Soon thereafter he did—a cap pistol replica of the Colt. He also sent me a case of empty .38 brass from Quantico that for many years I enjoyed playing with.

Uncle Ray and his exploits were only part of the family history my mother recounted to me proudly. Her paternal grandfather, Archangelo Abbaticchio had emigrated from Castellamare di Stabia, Italy, in 1873. He was unable to speak English, and what little money he brought was stolen, so he had to pawn his ring to get to Latrobe, Pennsylvania, where Benedictine monks at St. Mary's Abbey helped him establish a barbershop. He sent for his wife and children, went on to make a fortune in real estate, and, in later life, moved to Washington, D.C., where his son, Raymond, Sr., my grandfather, won fame as quarterback of the Georgetown University football team.

Grandfather played the full sixty minutes (no platoons in those days), weighing 145 pounds, against men weighing over 200 pounds. That was, my mother explained pointedly, when football was football; a few years before my father's time, one of the Georgetown players had been killed in a game. Grandfather played against teams like the Carlisle Indians. Morris Bealle, in *The Georgetown Hoyas*, retold one of my mother's favorite stories (of a typical performance, in 1902) this way:

> Midway of the final period [Ray Abbaticchio, Sr.] was kicked in the left eye by Rain-in-the-Face Johnson, the big Indian fullback.
>
> He was knocked unconscious and it took the team manager 15 minutes to bring him to and bandage the damaged optic. In the meantime the Indians were squawking that the game should go on, but

were told that Georgetown had no more quarterbacks and if they wanted to play they would have to wait. They waited, and the gritty little 145-pound Italian from Latrobe, Penna., played the rest of the game at quarterback with only one eye working.

My mother never made invidious comparisons when she told me these family stories. But I did. Forebears like that, and I was bursting my sickly lungs running away from vacuums, dogs, and other boys! So this was my heritage: all around me, strength and bravery; within me, weakness and fear.

Then there was my father. My mother was immensely proud of him, and with good reason. He was one of two children who survived into adulthood out of five born to an Irish-American couple, James E. and Ann Cleary Liddy. My grandfather, James E. Liddy, had been, I was told, a "stockbroker." His poverty was ascribed to the fact that he was out of work most of the time. This was in part because of a long bout with cancer, and in part because of a hair-trigger temper. He was an extraordinarily able boxer who, it was said, could go three rounds with any man in the world, amateur or professional. As a child I accepted the story uncritically.

Once when I was a teenager, I was asked to fetch something from my father's bureau, which had been his father's before him. I hunted dutifully and came upon a secret drawer. In it was a nickel-plated revolver and several boxes of precisely machined dice. I told my mother who then revealed that Grandpa Liddy had, among other things, been inside man at the legal gambling houses of E. R. Bradley in Florida, where his fighting and gambling skills were particularly valuable. His temper cost him that job too.

So my father was poor and, at age fifteen, found himself with a father, mother, and older sister to support. He went to work on the loading piers of the Lackawanna Railroad in Hoboken, where he quickly learned how to

17

use a cargo hook as a weapon. He was used to fighting. After three children named for relatives had died of infant diseases, his mother had sought to change her luck by naming him for a saint on whose feast day he happened to be born. As it happened, he was born on the feast of the Holy Innocents. The nearest other feast was that of Saint Sylvester. Sylvester was not a name to have in Hoboken. My father always claimed he accepted his name with relief. "Suppose," he would say, "she had named me Holy Innocents Liddy."

My father didn't feel sorry for himself; he felt lucky to get the dock job and he fought hard to hold it. He told me of other youths who had to get up at dawn and walk the railroad tracks with a gunny sack, picking up pieces of coal that had fallen from locomotive tenders the night before. The rule at their homes was, "No coal, no breakfast."

My father won the respect of older men on the docks, and more than one took him aside and told him that "a smart kid like you should get off the docks and get an education." He took their advice. He took a competitive examination for a scholarship to St. Benedict's Preparatory School in nearby Newark, and he won it.

He kept his report cards and I found the one for the fourth quarter of 1916 while still in grammar school myself. The curriculum listed puts current American secondary education to shame. He took Latin, Greek, German, composition, rhetoric, literature, elocution, algebra, Christian doctrine, history, and penmanship. His average, under demanding Benedictine monks and while working after school, was 95.1 percent. Meantime, his older sister, Ann, won a scholarship to Hunter College. To save money, she earned her degree in three years rather than four—and her grades were even higher than my father's.

Toward the end of prep school, my father took a job as a law clerk in the firm of famed Wall Street lawyer George Gordon Battle. Mr. Battle subsidized him so he could leave the docks and enjoy a normal senior year at prep school.

Twice my father had won the elocution medal; now he could go out for sports, starring on the track and baseball teams. He was an outfielder with a powerful arm and a season batting average of .429. When George Gordon Battle offered to put him through Fordham University, he turned down an invitation from Horace Stoneham to try out for the New York Giants.

Sylvester Liddy did not disappoint George Gordon Battle. He continued to work in Mr. Battle's office throughout college and graduated in 1923 with high grades, after being a varsity track man, president of the dramatic club, associate editor of the weekly newspaper, monthly magazine, and the yearbook; a member of the Council of Debate, and winner of the "best actor" award.

He then put himself through law school at Fordham at night while teaching high school English during the day and playing supporting roles in Drama Guild productions of Shakespeare in New York. He formed the Fordham Forum and became its president, then was elected president of his class. Graduating in 1926, he passed the bar examination with ease.

Mr. Battle counseled him to get a job in an established firm large enough to advance a young lawyer of exceptional ability. My father joined the large (offices in New York, Washington, Chicago, Los Angeles, and San Francisco) and venerable (established 1846) Munn & Co., a patent and trademark firm whose clients had included Thomas Edison. By 1929 he was a partner with 2½ percent of the profits; by 1938 the firm was named Munn, Anderson & Liddy. By 1940 he was chairman of the Committee on Trademarks and Unfair Competition of the Association of the Bar of the City of New York and of the Lawyers Advisory Committee of the United States Trademark Association and had won his first knighthood (from the King of Sweden, Royal Order of Vasa, First

Class). He was on his way to international success and recognition. He was forty years old and I was nine.

On my mother's side the legacy was of deep American roots. Her mother was Ada Rebecca Alexander, of the family for whom Alexandria, Virginia, was named; direct descendants of John Alexander, a Scottish sea captain who emigrated to the colony of Virginia about 1658.

In later years I learned something about my great-great-grandfather Columbus Alexander that my mother had neglected to tell me as a boy: before he died a millionaire in 1898, he had led the fight against Washington's Board of Public Works and was the strongest witness at a joint congressional investigation. He came so extraordinarily well prepared that, according to *The Washington Post*, "An attempt was made to connect Mr. Alexander with the burglarizing of the United States district attorney's office, and the carrying away of certain papers of more or less value." The attempt to get old Columbus on that one failed but, as the *Post* noted further, "The affair created considerable excitement at the time." Indeed. *Plus ça change* . . .

Columbus Alexander died in what *The Washington Post* described as his "magnificent home" in Georgetown. Apparently, the *Post*'s present owner agrees; Katharine Graham now lives in the house my mother played in as a girl.

My maternal grandmother died when my mother was sixteen. My grandfather, then a successful lawyer, was shattered by the loss, virtually giving up his practice to grieve. Mother was sent by her aunt to a convent school for girls in Quebec.

When my mother returned from Canada, she went to Georgetown Visitation Convent School and then to work. Her first job was in the passport department of the Department of State. Her family was still socially prominent, however, and she dated the sons of senators and other prominent beaux—until Sylvester Liddy appeared.

The Depression had just arrived and my father, the memory of poverty fresh in his mind, wanted to wait until he had saved $10,000 before marrying. That was a huge sum in 1929, and mother's response was that if she were still free when he had the money, he was to look her up; she had no intention of waiting for him. They married soon after mother's ultimatum. She was twenty-one, he thirty. Nine months later almost to the day, on 30 November 1930, that extraordinary gene pool somehow produced a frail, sickly little crybaby they named George Gordon Battle Liddy.

II

My mother and father saw to it that the Great Depression did not inconvenience their children. I received the finest Lionel electric train for Christmas and, when a very expensive tricycle given me for my fifth birthday was stolen in three days, it was replaced immediately. Even in the depths of the Depression, we had a maid. Her name was Teresa. She was a German national. I loved her.

Teresa's country had been, she said, in deep trouble. Now, however, a wonderful man had risen from the people and was solving all their problems. Weak after having been betrayed and then defeated in war, Germany was strong and proud again. Great roads were being built and, unlike in the United States, everyone in Germany now had a job.

My mother had won an Emerson shortwave radio in a raffle at SS. Peter and Paul Parish, and Teresa and I would listen to programs broadcast from her native land, the volume swelling and receding in cycles.

In those days one frequently heard broadcasts by President Roosevelt. He had a rich, reassuring voice with a calming and encouraging effect. Often I heard commentators repeat one of his best-known sayings: "We have nothing to fear but fear itself." Obsessed as I was by fear, the phrase worked on me.

Listening to Germany touched me differently. First there was the music. I have always been particularly sensitive to music; to this day I must make a conscious effort not to permit it to affect my mood. My memory for it is like a tape recorder; I can play back in my head at will, fully orchestrated, anything I have heard. Indeed, from time to time my mood will throw an involuntary switch in my mind and, unbidden, an appropriate piece will fill me with its sound. The music that poured through the Emerson from Germany was martial and stirring. I lost myself in its strains; it made me feel a strength inside I had never known before.

From playmates who were German, I learned some of the language. One day Teresa was excited. *He* was going to be on the radio. Just wait till I hear him speak! Eagerly, I joined her at the Emerson. First the music, the now familiar strains of a song that started, "*Die Fahne hoch . . .*"—"Raise the banner . . ." It was a rousing, powerful anthem, the Horst Wessel song.

We could tell when *he* was about to speak. The crowd could hardly contain itself. They hailed him in huge, swelling ovations that carried me along. "*Sieg!*" someone would shout, and what seemed like all the people in the world would answer with a roar, "*Heil!*" For *he* was their leader, *Der Führer*, Adolf Hitler.

Hitler's voice started out calmly, in low, dispassionate tones, but as he spoke of what his people would accomplish, his voice rose in pitch and tempo. Once united, the German people could do anything, surmount any obstacle, rout any enemy, achieve fulfillment. He would lead them; there would be one people, one nation, one leader. Here was the very antithesis of fear—sheer animal confidence and power of will. He sent an electric current through my body and, as the massive audience thundered its absolute support and determination, the hair on the back of my neck rose and I realized suddenly that I had stopped breathing.

When I spoke of this man to my father, he became angry. Adolf Hitler, he said, was an evil man who would once again set loose upon the world all the destruction of war. It was just a matter of time. I was to stop listening to him.

The lure of forbidden fruit was too strong; I continued to listen, though less frequently. Teresa had said that Adolf Hitler had raised her country from the dead, freed it from its enemies, made it the strongest nation in the world and delivered it from fear. *Delivered it from fear!*

For the first time in my life I felt hope. Life need *not* be a constant secret agony of fear and shame. If an entire nation could be changed, lifted out of weakness to extraordinary strength, certainly so could one person.

At Mass on Sunday I'd been taught that human beings are created "in the image and likeness of God." But God did not fear; he was all-powerful and could do anything just by thinking about it. Obviously, in my case, an error had been made. But God did not make mistakes. Besides, there was the example of all my relatives. I was of the same blood. The answer was obvious; the error was mine, the *fault* was mine. Since the error was mine, if I were to change, the changing would have to be mine. Alone. I could not *be* changed, there was no one to do it for me.

I knew what I had to do, and I dreaded it. To change myself from a puny, fearful boy to a strong, fearless man, I would have to face my fears, one by one, and overcome them. From listening to the priests at Sunday Mass, I knew that would take willpower. Even Adolf Hitler agreed. He and his people would triumph through the power of their superior will. But I knew from the priests the price would be terrible. God gave us a free will, but to strengthen that will to meet the temptations of life required denial, "mortification," suffering.

Suffering. That was the key. Whatever the consequences of what I was to do, I must accept and endure them—*out-*

23

last suffering to achieve my goals. Wasn't that the message of my mother's stories? Of President Roosevelt? My fears were so many and so gripping that overcoming them, one by one, would build incredible willpower! The world opened up to me. *I could become anything I wanted to be!* The thought took my breath away.

Teresa had told me of the Germans' suffering before their rebirth; my mother had told me how the strength and bravery of the American Indian warriors was born of the suffering of torture. In the Book of Knowledge I had read of the Spartan boy who refused to cry out while a fox concealed beneath his clothing ate the boy's insides—and thus the boy had died a true Spartan. Hadn't Glenn Cunningham suffered as he stretched the scar tissue of his burned legs to run faster? Hadn't my grandfather suffered to return to play football with only one eye? *Had not Jesus suffered the agony of hanging nailed to a cross for three hours before He could triumph over death?*

To face each of my fears and overcome them would require years of psychic and physical pain. But it had to be done. I had seen the fruits of fearlessness and the power of the will. I could no longer live without them. It was 1936, and I was almost six years old.

The first fear to attack was obvious. Time and again that summer I would run at any inkling of that ominous sound from out of my past—the deep, muttering vibration of air around me as a dirigible approached. I knew which one it was—Teresa saw to that—for 1936 was the first operational year of the mighty German *Hindenburg.* She made ten transatlantic crossings that summer, and her schedule was reported, as were those of the ocean liners, in the New York newspapers. Teresa would go to the window or the backyard in an effort to catch a glimpse of her. Whether it was to evade poor weather in the Atlantic or to permit her passengers to see Manhattan from the air and, in turn, to let her huge size and giant swastikas proclaim the might of Nazi Germany to millions of Americans, I don't know, but the *Hindenburg* cruised frequently up the mouth of the Hudson before turning to dock at Lakehurst, New Jersey. When Teresa went to the window, I hid under the bed. There was no escaping the fact that to free myself from fear and cowardice and build an unconquerable will, sooner or later I should have to face the *Hindenburg*.

Since it wasn't certain that the *Hindenburg* would pass directly over my backyard en route to Lakehurst as the *Akron* did four years before, and to ensure there could be no escape, nowhere to hide at the moment of truth, I chose to meet the monster on the grounds of Stevens Institute of Technology, an engineering college where I went to nursery school. Stevens, wide open with great lawns and playing fields, was high on the palisade behind our house and overlooked the Hudson River and the island of Manhattan. Others had the same idea, although, I am sure, for different reasons, and I had a good bit of company as I waited late one afternoon.

First I heard her. That terrible sound could be nothing else. She was still miles away. The *Akron* had been unusual in that her engines were inboard, only her propellers were outside the skin of the airship. The *Hindenburg*'s four giant 1,100-horsepower Mercedes-Benz diesel engines were suspended from the exterior of her hull and could be heard from a much greater distance. On and on came the sound and my resolve seemed to wax and wane inversely with the sound of her engines. I caught myself praying she would turn off before coming up the Hudson far enough for me to see her, and I was condemning myself again for cowardice when she appeared. There was just one word for the *Hindenburg*: awesome.

For twenty-two years the British ocean liner *Mauretania* held the blue riband for the Atlantic crossing, her 68,000 horsepower driving through four gigantic propellers her 40,000 gross tons at 25 knots. Imagine that great ship sailing up the Hudson not *on* the river but in the air *over* it. The *Hindenburg* was bigger. Sail the Washington Monument through the air over on its side, horizontally. The

Hindenburg was more than a third again longer. More than twice the cubic-foot-capacity of the famed *Graf Zeppelin*, the *Hindenburg* was more than half a million cubic feet larger than the *Akron*.

Slowly she swung round toward New Jersey. *She was coming right at me!* The earth trembled and the roar grew louder as the enormous machine went through its ponderous turn. I lifted my head and turned my palms outward to feel the vibration better. It struck my upturned face and palms and seemed to infuse my whole body with the strength of the giant airship. Ecstatic, I drank in its colossal power and felt myself grow—swelling wtih strength. Fear evaporated and in its place came a sense of personal might and power. I stood rooted to the spot as the *Hindenburg* completed her turn and headed downriver, never quite passing over me as I expected, but leaving me thrilled as few other experiences ever have in my life.

The way a telephoto lens distorts by making distant separated objects seem next to each other, so do accounts of the past like this make events separated by time seem to have followed in rapid sequence. My campaign against fear was not a day-after-day affair. My strength of will grew with each success, but I had started out with nothing. I had to gather the nerve for each new battle in my war. And often the conviction would fade, driving me over the same ground again and again. Sure, yesterday I had triumphed over such and such a fear, but that was yesterday —how would I react today? So I had to rerun old tests, while devising new ones.

In between these events, life in the United States in the 1930s droned on at a tempo that, today, seems languorous. The world was vortexing toward war, but my part of it was at a far reach from that current and the movement was almost imperceptible.

I traded bubble gum cards (the gum itself was forbidden, not on grounds of oral hygiene but by class taboo) depicting the violence of the Japanese invasion of Manchuria, the Spanish civil war, and the Italian invasion of Ethiopia, But the pace of my life was still measured by the slow, plodding clop of the milkman's horse and the tinkling of his bottles; the equally slow cycle of the coal man emptying his canvas carrier hundreds of times down the chute before our bin was filled, and the iceman laboring up the same steep steps to fill our icebox. Occasionally there was the doomsday sound of the steam horn of the *Queen Mary* or the *Europa*; the "whap, whap, whap" of a boy on the street hitting a rubber ball on an elastic string stapled to his paddle; the cry of the vegetable vendor or rag collector as his wagon creaked along behind a tired horse; the occasional drone of an airplane engine; the summer visits of the hurdy-gurdy man; and, always, the wail and chuf of distant steam locomotives.

Those were the sounds I would hear as I lay under a "croup tent" breathing steam and trying not to cough because of the pain it caused and the threat that it might bring on another burning mustard plaster to "break it up." Those sounds should be the stuff of nostalgia; but nostalgia for the '30s is something I cannot feel; it's as though my memory of those times were covered with scar tissue from wounds picked up during the war within myself; the nerve endings are gone.

In Hoboken, in the 1930s, I had two sets of friends: those of whom my parents approved and those they did not. Those approved were, in the main, the sons of other professionals who were either neighbors or friends of my parents.

As part of the effort to develop something out of my scrawny body, my parents had acquired the services of a fencing coach, a Belgian who had served as an officer in World War I. Captain Stevens was over six feet tall, and he taught fencing in the European manner; i.e., more than mere technique, he taught the *spirit* of the use of cold steel as a weapon of preference of a man of honor and a gentleman. It was a disgrace, for example, to duck even slightly when Captain Stevens suddenly struck downward

27

with his blade at one's head, which he would do regularly whether that head was protected by the fencing mask or not. The blows were sharp and painful to an unprotected head, although they rarely drew blood. I hated them, and I ducked as best I could, which meant I was in a constant state of disgrace.

There was only one acceptable way for a man of honor to counter such a blow: keeping one's head rigid, one raised one's blade overhead swiftly to parry. The only part of the body permitted to move was the sword arm. Captain Stevens told of the German student societies in which to fail such a test meant expulsion. He spoke of the glory of the *Schmiss*, the facial-scar badge of manhood resulting from a cut received in German student society duels.

As a second step on my journey from cowardice to fearlessness, I resolved never again to flinch from a cutting blow to the head from Captain Stevens's sword. I would parry it successfully or endure the pain without a word. Captain Stevens was fast, strong, and well coordinated; I was slow, small, and awkward. It was some time before I could parry the blow correctly and successfully. In the interim, I took a lot of blows to the scalp. Nor was I able to stop flinching immediately; old habits, especially bad ones, die hard. Eventually, however, I could receive the blow without head motion or facial expression of any kind, and by that time I could parry it.

The next of my fears to be fought was that of height. I did so with the unwitting assistance of my friend Peter Smith. I never confided my fear to him but had always an excuse not to follow him up to the rooftops he liked to explore. Peter was naturally fearless. I resolved to join him on the rooftops. I feigned the same enthusiasm Peter had and bit my lip as we climbed onto the roof through a trapdoor. I had to follow him to the edge to stand and admire the view. A restless soul, Peter wasn't content to stay on one roof. Most were contiguous, since they covered what are now known as "town houses" all in a row. Some, however, were separated by airways that were several feet across and as many as seven stories straight down to a concrete paved alleyway. Insides turning to jelly, I forced myself to follow Peter as he leaped like a gazelle from rooftop to rooftop, often across such chasms, until we had gone as far as the end of the block. When I realized what I had done, I was filled with joy. I still have a photograph I insisted we take from a rooftop. It constituted a diploma, a death certificate for my fear of height.

One of my friends *not* acceptable to my parents was John Fitzpatrick, a classmate at SS. Peter and Paul. Fitz's parents were not middle-class professionals. A second reason: he introduced me to that corrupting item, the comic book.

And a third. I made the mistake of telling them, in an admiring voice, that Fitz regularly played on the waterfront. Anyone who has seen *On the Waterfront*, with Marlon Brando and Rod Steiger, can picture the exact area where Fitz played; it was used for the location shots in the picture. Fitz regaled me with harrowing tales of its perils: the rats as big as cats, mean-looking foreign seamen who chased boys like Fitz sneaking aboard docked freighters to explore the holds; the danger of slipping off the pier to be crushed in the water between pier and freighter. I had, of course, been afraid to go with Fitz to this exotic playground, and my parents didn't want me even to think about it. But I did. Constantly. Since I was afraid to go there, that was where I had to go.

Fitz had told the truth. Walking along one of the cross-supports beneath the docks, about five feet above the stinking, oil-slicked waters of the Hudson, I saw my first wharf rat. It was about eight feet away, calmly facing me, back to an upright support and, I thought, "cornered."

I'd heard of the hazards of "cornering" a rat, especially a wharf rat. It was every bit as large as Fitz had said, about a foot long excluding the tail. Fitz was back on top of the pier, and I was alone. I was so frightened I felt an extreme urge to urinate. Carefully, slowly, I started to back up. I'd taken two steps when I realized that once

29

again I'd given in to fear. The shame brought tears to my eyes. I trembled, thinking of the Spartan boy and the fox. I blinked back my tears and advanced on the rat, shouting, "YAH! YAH!"

The rat jumped into the water and with the grace of a seal swam away calmly. I was triumphant. The rat had been afraid of *me*! I kept going to the end of the support yelling, "YAH! YAH! You yellow rat!" It was a great day. I'd defeated specific fears before, but the rat was the first live enemy I had vanquished. For the moment, I felt like a hero.

My self-congratulation was short-lived. I climbed up to rejoin Fitz, and we decided to explore the hold of a rusted freighter that appeared to be unattended. We were wrong. A seaman who looked like Hollywood's idea of a Marseilles thug spotted us and came running, shouting in a foreign language. Fitz and I scrambled for our lives. To Fitz, it was a lark and he felt no chagrin at all at running; after all, the guy was twice the size of us together. He'd go back another day and hope the man wasn't there to interrupt a fine adventure. To me, however, the incident was mortifying. I shouldn't have run away; it was cowardly, a defeat in my battle. What I thought I would have done with the seaman had I *not* escaped, I can't imagine; but I felt the need to redeem myself.

Two days later I returned alone to the ship and boarded her. I didn't get more than one deck below before I was detected. Again the shouting in a foreign tongue, but this time from someone I couldn't see. I didn't run. I hid. Behind a large roll of cable. After a perfunctory look around, whoever it was must have believed me scared off and he abandoned his search. Shaking, I emerged from hiding and slipped off the ship. I felt vindicated. I'd been terribly frightened, but I *hadn't run*. Again my sense of triumph was cut short. Before I got off the pier a rat ran by in front of me and, startled, I checked my stride. I argued with myself that I had not shown fear, just been startled. But deep inside, I was once again unsure of my feelings about rats.

Busy as he was, my father tried to spend as much time with me as possible. That wasn't much, so he tried to make the most of what was available. He loved trains—the secret reason, I now believe, for my Christmas Lionels. They were nothing, however, to the real thing. In the 1930s, the steam locomotive was still king. Hoboken, New Jersey, was a rail head. Bargeloads of freight cars were pushed by tugboats across the Hudson and joined into mile-long trains to be hauled all over the United States and Canada by mammoth steam engines.

My father often took me down to the railroad station and freight yards where he had worked as a boy. Before the *Hindenburg* encounter I feared the great mechanical beasts, but because of my total trust in the omnipotence of my father I didn't object. I was positive nothing could get me with my father there to protect me.

My father showed me how to distinguish between a freight engine and a passenger locomotive by the size of the driving wheels. In the interest of speed, those of the passenger steam engine were much larger, taller than my head was high. There was a line painted a foot back from the edge of the station platform. So long as we were behind that line, my father explained, we were safe; the engine could go only where the tracks permitted. I was thrilled by the metallic roar, the hiss of steam, and the clanging bell as one of the giants would flash by, shaking the ground beneath me. What extraordinary power they had! Machines could go on forever. They never got tired, never hurt, just kept putting out all that power, day after day, week after week, year after year, world without end, amen. A flash of inspiration struck me. *I would make myself into a machine.*

That year I began to run, not to escape, but for the sheer joy of it. When my lungs began to hurt I told myself over and over again, "I am a machine, a machine feels no

31

pain. I am a machine, a machine, a machine." I heard in my mind the sounds of a locomotive and I drove on until I ran out of fuel—which, I told myself, even happened to machines. I can remember lying on my side on the grass, legs and arms in a grotesque twitching parody of running as I labored to suck air into my lungs, still telling myself I was a machine.

I went to the railroad yards *without* my father and stood *inside* the line on the edge of the station platform, waiting for the locomotive to come. The engineer would see me and blast his steam whistle as a warning. But I knew something he didn't—his steam whistle wouldn't hurt me. It was my friend. I was a machine too! The invisible bow wave of the enormous locomotive would rock me back on my heels and the trembling I felt through the earth synchronized with that of my body; not a trembling from fear now, but of excitement, joy, a sharing of the immense power of that mighty machine. When my father took me down to watch the Lincoln Tunnel being built, I watched with interest but it wasn't the same. We couldn't get close enough for me to absorb the power of the construction machinery.

My father and I did the things other fathers and sons did too. He took me to the big league baseball games and taught me that the best players are the smartest players. It is permissible, my father taught, to make an occasional physical error. It is never permissible to make a mental error, in baseball or anything else. To my father, the intellect was and must be supreme. From my earliest memory to the last day I saw him alive, if I made an error in his presence in English usage (or Latin or German, for that matter), he would correct me on the spot.

Years after I became an adult, my father told me that not once in his life had *his* father ever hugged him or shown him any similar sign of affection. Yet I knew my father had loved his father dearly, acting as his night nurse for more than a year as he died of cancer. As a consequence, my father tried to hug me often, but it always seemed to me that that was just what he was doing; *trying* to hug me, wanting to but not knowing how, as if never having been the object of a fatherly embrace himself, he could not pass on what he had never received.

In fairness to my father, I stress that this is a subjective impression. The fact of the matter is that he *did* hug me, often, and it may well have been that my self-loathing, born of contempt for my weakness in the face of fear, rendered me unable to recognize genuine fatherly affection and to receive it when offered.

My father had a strong personality, yet he had a genius for being assertive without offending others. Early in my life he let me know that he was not interested in any tales I might carry to him about others and had no use for "snitching." He hated lying and taught that it made impossible the mutual confidence necessary for any enterprise among men. "If you don't want somebody to know something," he said, "just don't speak to them about it. Never lie." As for talecarrying, he was blunt. "I am very interested in whatever you have to say for yourself. Others can speak for themselves." A man known for his loyalty to his benefactors, he taught me that a man does "not extricate himself from difficulty at the expense of his associates."

As I grew older and the winning of countless battles with myself produced an increasingly strong personality, my father and I would clash. Yet we loved each other greatly and I have never respected any man more than I did my father. Nevertheless our relationship was, from its inception, almost formal. An example would be the matter of baseball.

Baseball was my father's favorite sport. I enjoyed it well enough, but it was not *my* favorite sport. My father, who excelled at baseball as he did in almost everything he tried, wanted me to excel at it too. It was good for the body and good for the mind. By the time I was eight years old, I resisted playing baseball with him. I'd play stoopball and stickball with other boys on the block and play it well, but I was reluctant to play baseball with or under the direction of my father. I just couldn't play it well enough; that is to say, perfectly.

In the spring of 1940, when I was nine, my father stressed how much he was looking forward to the coming baseball season. Again I expressed my reluctance but my father, the persuasive advocate, talked me into another season of the sport. It was symbolic of our relationship that this agreement took the form of a written contract which both my mother and seven-year-old sister solemnly signed as witnesses. I still have that contract:

CONTRACT

THIS AGREEMENT made this 15th day of March, 1940, by and between GEORGE GORDON BATTLE LIDDY, party of the first part, hereinafter termed "Player," and SYLVESTER J. LIDDY, party of the second part, hereinafter termed "Manager";

WITNESSETH

NOW, THEREFORE, THIS INDENTURE WITNESSETH that for and in consideration of the sum of One Dollar ($1.00) and other good and valuable consideration, paid by the party of the first part, Player, to the party of the second part, Manager, the receipt of which is hereby acknowledged, the parties hereto agree as follows:

1. The Player agrees to play baseball for the coming season of 1940 exclusively for and under the management of the party of the second part as Manager.

2. The party of the second part, Manager, agrees to furnish to the party of the first part, Player, all necessary baseball equipment which may be required for the coming season.

3. The party of the first part, Player, agrees to follow instructions, advice and orders of the party of the second part, Manager, at all times except when the Player is at bat during a regular game and he has a count of three balls and two strikes, he may then use his own best judgment.

4. During the baseball season and during spring training season, the party of the first part, Player, agrees to go to bed every night not later than 8:30 P.M. promptly.

5. The party of the first part, Player, further agrees to eat all his meals regularly and promptly and such foods as Manager may select for him, or if he should be at Camp during part of the baseball season, such foods as the Camp Directors may order.

6. Spring training, weather permitting, is to begin on March 21st, 1940.

IN WITNESS WHEREOF we hereunto sign our names and affix our seals at Hoboken, in the County of Hudson and State of New Jersey, this 15th day of March, 1940.

WITNESS:

Maria A. Liddy   *George Gordon Battle Liddy*

WITNESS:

Margaret Liddy   *Sylvester J. Liddy* [L. S.]

A deal is a deal and on 21 March 1940 I reported to my father for spring training.

35

III

The *Hindenburg* disaster on 7 May 1937 was the catalyst for a major and unhappy change in my early childhood. For some time there had been tension in our household stemming from my father's anti-Nazi views and Teresa's adulation of Adolf Hitler. She was an excellent cook and maid and, for a long time, her skills preserved her job despite my father's discomfort over her Nazi sympathies. It was bad enough that he would come home on warm days to the voice of Josef Goebbels booming sonorously from the Emerson; worse when he found our address was on the German Embassy mailing list for Nazi propaganda. The *Hindenburg*, however, was the last straw.

The problem was that Teresa did not accept the official crash explanation that static electricity ignited hydrogen being vented as part of the landing procedure. She was certain the *Hindenburg* had been sabotaged by the United States. And she said so—not only to my parents and me but to tradesmen and even our guests. Superb cook or not, my father had had enough of her. Teresa, he said, would be happier in the home of German nationals. To me, her loss was a shock. Our first maid had been Scottish, but I was so young I didn't remember her. Teresa had been with us, so far as my memory was concerned, all my life.

My father tried to explain to his seven-year-old son that the Nazis were evil. They persecuted Jews. That made no sense to me at all. Dr. Rosenberg was a Jew. Burton Silver, a playmate, was a Jew. Why should anyone want to "persecute" them? What was "persecution" anyway? The explanation that it was like the way the Romans treated the early Christians seemed a bit remote. Nobody claimed Jews were being eaten by lions in Germany. I was troubled and perplexed. My father was always right, yet I had

never heard Hitler speak one way or another about Jews on the radio, nor had Teresa mentioned them to me. Jews were just someone with a different religion, like Protestants; they worshiped God incorrectly and on the wrong day, were unbaptized and so couldn't go to Heaven, only to limbo with all the unbaptized babies, but no one I knew got excited about it. Indeed, I felt rather sorry for Burton Silver, eventually having no one to play with out in limbo but all those screaming little babies.

After Teresa, we had, in rapid sequence, several disastrously incompetent American maids, and then, for reasons that I suspect had as much to do with my education as with our need for domestic help, my father hired Sophie. Sophie was German—she was also a Jew.

My recollection of Sophie is of a beautiful young woman having a haunted look. She was a refugee from Nazi Germany, still dazed by her rejection by her homeland. I was no more kindly disposed toward Sophie than I was toward her several predecessors, all of whom I considered usurpers of Teresa's position, and reacted by refusing to eat from a spoon Sophie had touched.

When I came home from elementary school with the news that the nuns had explained the recent influx of Jewish refugees by pointing out that the Jews were doomed to wander the face of the earth homeless because they had been responsible for the death of Christ, calling for his crucifixion and saying to Pilate that "His blood be upon us and upon our children," I commented that that didn't seem very fair to me. People like Burton Silver weren't even born then. My father agreed with a snapped "Ridiculous!" and, typically, turned to the law to emphasize the point.

"If I rob a bank," asked my father, "should you go to jail?" He went on to point out that the proposition was called in the law a "bill of attainder" and was condemned specifically in the United States Constitution.

At last my father's argument began to get through to me: Adolf Hitler was using his great gifts and position of power for evil rather than good purposes and was anything but an admirable person. My feelings of resentment against Sophie softened as I began to appreciate her as a victim. My father explained "intolerance" as based upon an unreasoning fear of the different and unfamiliar. That was something I could relate to; I felt I knew all about fear.

On 1 September 1939 my father's prediction finally came true. Hitler invaded Poland. Great Britain and France declared war against Germany immediately and a great debate began in the United States. Most people, while condemning Nazi Germany, remembered George Washington's warning about foreign entanglements and took the position that it was a European war and none of America's business. Franklin Roosevelt, neither the first nor the last President of the United States to break the law as a justifiable means to an end he perceived to be good, ordered J. Edgar Hoover, in the spring of 1940, to join with British intelligence in a secret war against Germany. Well before Pearl Harbor there were active efforts to destroy German naval craft, and an acquiescence in the killing in the United States of those the British thought necessary to eliminate, including at least one United States citizen. Very few knew about this. The Neutrality Law of 1936 notwithstanding, Roosevelt was the elected leader of his people, and in his judgment it was for him to perceive the good of his people. This was, in the words of Cicero, "the chief law"—but Roosevelt was rightly concerned that public knowledge of his breaking the law could have an adverse political effect upon him; hence the secrecy.

Meantime I was gaining self-confidence. My battle still had a long way to go, but I was now able to look back upon a string of victories (including a successful encounter with the school tough guy; I hadn't won the fight, but I hadn't run either), and I became less inclined to suspect I could not repeat them. My health improved and, during my second year at summer camp, I learned to swim by

38

the simple expedient of being taken out in a rowboat to the middle of the lake by older boys who told me I was to be thrown overboard. I was expected to plead for mercy and carry on. I did neither. I was in the state of grace at the time, so I calculated that the worst that could happen was I would drown and, eventually, go to Heaven. I was thrown overboard when I refused to beg and, to my own surprise, promptly swam all the way to shore. When other boys were taken on the rowboat ride, I felt contempt for those who whimpered.

When I was with my father in New York we would lunch at the University Club, and he saw to it that I met his fellow members and had the opportunity to talk with them. It was an extraordinary experience, and I learned quickly that powerful men had certain attributes in common: they were forceful of personality, articulate, exceptionally well educated and interested in everything around them. It was fascinating to watch a number of them together, my father included, like so many magnets forming a field in which they balanced each other off. These men ran the world, and it was obvious that they enjoyed it. I resolved to become like them.

The year 1941 was pivotal for my country, my family, and for me. My father, at forty-two beginning the best years of his personal and professional life, bought us a beautiful new house in West Caldwell, New Jersey. With its fifteen rooms, it looked like a mansion to me.

Once settled in, I was enrolled in St. Aloysius parochial school where I entered the sixth grade in September 1941. Again I was the new boy in school, this time with the additional handicap, thanks to our Packard sedan of being "rich" and, after a few weeks of class, labeled a "brain."

St. Aloysius School was a little over a mile away from my house down tree-lined streets; in good weather I bicycled, and in foul weather I was delivered by my mother in the mighty Packard. It was a happy and idyllic setting haunted only by the remainder of my fears and the need

39

to overcome them. Oddly enough, the first of these to be faced from my new home was my still ambiguous feeling about rats.

Almost as soon as we arrived at our new house in West Caldwell my sister acquired a cat she named Tommy. Tommy had the habit of catching field mice and moles and depositing them at the rear door as a trophy or perhaps a "thank you" for his room and board. One October day in 1941, Tommy left a dead rat on the kitchen steps and I found it. It was not nearly the size of the wharf rat I'd encountered under the Hoboken dock, but a respectable length nevertheless. The carcass was still warm and remarkably undamaged. To demonstrate to myself my lack of fear, instead of using a stick I picked it up with my hands, then looked for a place to bury it. As I walked toward the trees in the back, I saw some old bricks, and I got the idea for a test to destroy forever any dread I might still harbor for rats. I put the rat down and, with the loose bricks, built a small enclosure on the gravel next to the garage. I filled it with broken twigs, bark, and small branches and went into the kitchen for matches. For the next hour, I roasted the dead rat. Then I removed the burned carcass with a stick and let it cool. With a scout knife I skinned, then cut off and ate the roasted haunches of the rat. The meat was tasteless and stringy. Finished, I dismantled the little fireplace and buried the rest of the carcass. As I stamped down the earth over the remnants of my meal, I spotted the cat, Tommy. I smiled as the thought occurred to me: from now on rats could fear *me* as they feared cats; after all, I ate them too.

Sometime later, on a Sunday afternoon, our family was in the living room listening to the radio. I remember I was sitting on the floor, before a crackling fire. Gabriel Heatter interrupted the program with the report of the Japanese attack on Pearl Harbor and the comment that the Japanese were an "excitable people" and that this did not necessarily mean war. The next day, listening to President Roosevelt ask Congress for a declaration of war against Japan, I was sure that those commentators who claimed that the United States would crush Japan in a matter of months were right. It came as a shock, though, when Germany declared war against the United States. I felt betrayed and angry and counted up the years until I could enlist: six. That night, as all America prayed for a quick end to the war, I prayed the war would continue until I was old enough for combat. I knew that if I could only go to war, I would return either completely without fear or dead. Either way I would be free.

In West Caldwell other boys owned or had access to firearms. Generally they were of .22 caliber and usually rifles, although Bob Hedden had a .22 caliber Colt Woodsman semiautomatic pistol. I wanted a gun, too, but my father answered my request with an emphatic no.

For a while, my father's efforts at family gun control worked. I contented myself with a Daisy BB gun. I also manufactured my own black powder from a 3–2–1-proportioned formula of powdered charcoal, sulfur, and saltpeter I bought from the drugstore with the story that my mother needed it for canning. I used it for tiny bombs and for rocket propellant. From time to time I was able to borrow a gun from other boys for "just one shot" but that wasn't satisfactory. Gun control finally didn't work with me any more than it does for anyone who really wants a gun. If I couldn't buy one, I'd make one.

From a neighborhood boy I bought a six-inch-long section of ancient octagonal gun barrel in .22 caliber that included the vital chamber. I sawed off the barrel of my Daisy and attached the .22 caliber barrel by friction fit. It was necessary to cut the Daisy again in order to have the spring-loaded plunger of the BB gun just reach the rear face of the .22 caliber chamber. That way, because a .22 caliber long rifle cartridge is rim-fire ignited, the plunger, when released by the trigger, would both fire the piece and act as a breechblock. It was clumsy, dangerous, and inaccurate, but it worked. I had a gun. The weapon had no front sight and, only six inches long in the barrel,

41

it couldn't be aimed accurately by conventional means, but I learned to sight along the side of the barrel and hit fairly well at twenty yards. It was with this weapon that I first killed.

Squirrel hunting was a popular sport in West Caldwell in the 1940s. I loaded my homemade rifle, cocked the spring, and waited on the steps of the porch. A squirrel was in the top of the pear tree. I raised the rifle. The movement startled the squirrel and he jumped to the oak tree and froze as I stepped off the porch. I sighted along the side of the barrel, aimed for the squirrel's head, and fired.

I missed the squirrel's head and gut-shot him. Bravely, he clung to the tree as long as he could, then started to come down, clutching piteously at branches as he fell, wounded mortally.

I didn't know it, but the shot alerted my mother. She watched the furry creature's descent until it fell to the ground and I shot it again, this time through the head at point-blank range, to put it out of its suffering, then cut off its tail to tie to the handlebars of my bicycle as an ornament.

When I came into the house my mother told me reproachfully that she had seen from the kitchen window the suffering I had caused. I went off and wept. The dying squirrel haunted me. I kept seeing it fall, clutching and clawing from what must have been a terribly painful wound. I was furious with myself—not because I'd caused the pain, though I regretted that, but because I hadn't been able to kill without emotion. How could I expect to be a soldier in the war? I had to do something to free myself from this disabling emotionalism.

I cast about for an idea and found it across the street. Bill Jacobus's father, to help combat the wartime food shortage and to supplement rationing, had built a chicken coop in his backyard. He and his son used to butcher the chickens, then drain, scald, pluck, and clean them for sale.

I asked young Bill if I could help kill the chickens. He

was glad to have the help. He showed me how to grasp the bird in such a way as to have control of both wings and feet, lay its neck on an upended stump, and then decapitate it with one chop of an ax held in the other hand. Bill explained that the shock made the corpse convulse and, if let go, the body would run about, wings flapping, and bruise the meat. I'd need to control the corpse until the shock wore off and the limp body could be hung up by the feet to drain the remaining blood. I should wear my oldest clothes.

Using the ax tentatively rather than making a bold stroke, I made a mess of my first chicken kill; it took me a number of chops to get the head off. The bird slipped out of my grasp and half flew, half jumped about, blood spurting from its neck all over me and everything else in range. Bill was good about it and gave me another chance.

I got better at it, and over a period of time I killed and killed and killed, getting less and less bloody, swifter and swifter, surer with my ax stroke until, finally, I could kill efficiently and without emotion or thought. I was satisfied: when it came my turn to go to war, I would be ready. I could kill as I could run—like a machine.

IV

The big house on Hillcrest Road became the center of our extended family. My paternal grandmother, Mother Liddy, had arrived with us. Shortly before our move the failed marriage of my mother's sister, Paula, brought her young son, Dennis, to us, along with my great-aunt, May Alexander, who was his surrogate mother.

Dennis was five years old and I, eleven. It was Christmas 1941, and I accepted him as a little brother immediately and treated him accordingly; that is to say badly, refusing to let him play with my electric trains because he was "too little," along with similar acts and omissions springing from the asserted superiority usual among young siblings between whom there is a substantial difference in age. My sister, Margaret, fared little better.

The permanent party at our house became seven, spanning three generations. It was a healthy environment; there were rooms enough in the house for everyone to have his or her own and enough left over to accommodate visits from my Uncle Ray, now a Special Agent in Charge at the FBI, his fiancée, Marjorie, and from my maternal grandfather, Raymond Abbaticchio, Sr., known to the family as One Daddy or just O.D., now retired to a life of fishing and collecting antiques.

About this time I was working on my deep fear of electricity. I climbed to the top of a high-tension power line tower, and then I moved out so far on the arm holding the wire that proximity caused my hair to react to the current. I was still not satisfied. Nor did stripping the insulation from a lamp wire and grasping it convince me; the current (110 volts, ac) just made me feel as if my nervous system had gone haywire.

I had one serious problem while at St. Aloysius: my father volunteered to coach the baseball team.

I wanted to make my father's team; I felt I *had* to, but I wasn't good enough at any position I'd ever played before. Then I saw that the others were reluctant to take on the position of catcher in a hardball game. So I became a catcher. I was struck in the head with a bat a number of times and, at 120 pounds, bowled over even more times by bigger, heavier boys as I blocked the plate, but I made the team as a catcher and took satisfaction in picking myself up and going back in there to play hurt. With a convert's zeal I became contemptuous of anyone who didn't want to play hurt; having found that fear can be defeated by head-on attack, it never occurred to me that the reluctance of others to play hurt might be based on common sense rather than fear.

In 1944 I graduated from St. Aloysius parochial grammar school and looked forward to Caldwell High School where most of my classmates would enter the following fall. My father disagreed. He wanted me to have a private preparatory school eudcation and noted that his own prep school, St. Benedict's, was in Newark within commuting distance by the electric trolley that ran through the main street of our town.

The idea was not attractive to me. St. Benedict's was exclusively a boys' school, and I was interested in girls. I knew, also, that at St. Benedict's I would inevitably be compared with my father who had built an outstanding academic and athletic record there and now was the president of the alumni association. None of these arguments was worth much: I was sent to St. Benedict's.

The tide of refugees from Hitler's Germany hadn't been exclusively Jewish. The classes of people on the Nazi hit list were diverse, and one of them was the Christian clergy, especially Roman Catholics whose loyalty to the Pope was believed inconsistent with absolute loyalty to the *Führer*.

The Benedictine order that, from St. Mary's Abbey, Newark, had been operating St. Benedict's Preparatory School for a century, had flourished in Europe since the mid-seventh century. There were many Benedictine monasteries in Germany and, when their monks were threatened by Nazi persecution, the instruction was sent to monasteries in the free world to take in their German brothers for the duration of the war. St. Mary's Abbey had a goodly quota, and by the time I arrived as a freshman in September 1944, they were in place teaching.

In disciplinary matters, St. Benedict's used the demerit system. A whisper in class, or some other breach of the strict code of conduct, brought one or more demerits related to a schedule of punishments ranging from post-schoolday study hall to expulsion. The Germans didn't bother with demerits. Once, when a rather large boy in the rear of the room snickered at the way one of the German monks pronounced an English word, the German looked up calmly and said, "You. Stand up."

The boy stood, a smirk on his face, expecting to receive

45

a demerit. The German walked down to him and, with right-hand lead, knocked him cold. He then commanded the boy sitting nearest the door: "You. *Wasser*."

The boy brought back a paper cup full of water, which the monk threw on the face of the unconscious boy to revive him, then gave him a hand up to his seat, turned walked back to the head of the class and said, "Zo. Un now ve begin again." The Germans really knew their subjects, and there was always an "atmosphere conducive to learning" in their classrooms.

As a freshman I was subject to some harassment from older boys which I accepted so long as it didn't get out of hand. When another boy had a birthday, however, saw the traditional treatment and I realized that with my own birthday coming up shortly, something had to be done. The treatment was to give the birthday boy a series of specialized punches, called "bunnies," one for each year. In my case, that would be fourteen. To give "bunny," two large boys held the victim's arms straight out while others, with a peculiar fist having one protruding knuckle, would drive that knuckle hard into the muscle of the victim's upper arms. It was both painful and paralyzing, making retaliation impossible. I was small so figured I'd have to counter the threat with cunning rather than with force. I devised a plan, took the necessary technical steps, and went to school on my birthday awaiting my trial eagerly. It was not long in coming.

I was approached in the locker room. I removed my suit coat and feigned unawareness until they grabbed my arms, then I ripped my arms upward and away. My would-be tormentors screamed as the flesh of their palms and fingers was lacerated.

That morning, I had taken lengths of adhesive tape and pressed thumb and carpet tacks alternately into the sticky side so that the sharp points stuck out the dry side. The carpet tacks were longer and especially nasty but they had narrower heads; the thumb tacks, with their broad heads, added stability under lateral stress. That done,

46

wrapped the tape around my arms carefully so that I looked like a porcupine with short, very sharp quills. I wore an old white shirt I could throw away, and I packed a replacement in my schoolbag.

The device worked well, though there was less blood than I had anticipated. "C'mon!" I shouted after them, "Try it again!" Shocked and in pain, they would have none of it, backing away from me with incredulous stares. Thereafter the bullies of the school were inclined to leave me alone because it was evident that I would go to unpredictable extremes in my response.

Franklin Roosevelt had become President of the United States in 1933, when Adolf Hitler came to power in Germany. I was two years old. Those giant antagonists died within three weeks of one another in April 1945. I was fourteen. They had been dominating the headlines for as long as I could remember. Their passing was a shock. When, on 8 May, Germany surrendered, there was joy everywhere in the land but in my heart. I was frantic. Could Japan hold out until I could get into the war? Conventional wisdom held it was possible. The tenacious way the Japanese soldier resisted hugely superior numbers and matériel led to speculation that it would take years to conquer the home islands of Japan. In a few months more than two years I could enlist; I still had a chance!

That dream disappeared with Hiroshima and Nagasaki. I remember riding my bicycle through the streets on V-J Day, 14 August 1945. The people were delirious with joy, strangers hugging and kissing in the road, stopping traffic. I was weeping and finally had to go home to conceal it. All my life I had been working to change myself from a weak, fearful little boy into a strong, cold-blooded machine of a man. What good was it being St. George if the dragon had been slain? I was too young in 1945 to know that there is always another dragon.

For nearly a month I was disconsolate, then the resilience of youth prevailed. And a certain doubt. Whom was I trying to fool? I wasn't ready yet to go to war. How

47

could I be sure I'd *ever* be ready? Didn't my palms still moisten when I heard thunder in the distance? Plain thunder? How would I react to the thunder of artillery? The doubt was infuriating, and it goaded me to an extreme plan.

On a Saturday afternoon in September, the western sky blackened and the wind rose. Severe thunderstorms had been predicted over a wide front. Thunder began far away. Soon I could see the glow of lightning in the distance. I timed the intervals between flashes and thunderclap. If they grew longer, the storm would be moving away from me and I would be granted a reprieve. The intervals grew shorter; the storm was heading toward me. I kept swallowing repeatedly as I changed into blue jeans, a T-shirt, and sneakers—and waited.

The wind was getting very strong, but there was still no rain. I left the house quietly by the back door and went around the back of the detached garage into the wooded area to avoid notice by my parents as they glanced apprehensively through the big picture windows at the approaching lightning. Our house sat on the crest of a hill and had been struck by bolts in the past; they feared a fire. I brought with me a four-foot safety belt I'd fashioned by braiding a clothesline rope and fixing a D-ring on one end and a metal snap-link on the other.

The tree I had chosen was a pin oak about seventy-five feet tall. The rain came as I started to climb. It slanted in on the west wind, making the trunk slippery and hard to shinny to the first branches, just beyond reach of a jump from the ground.

After ten minutes of climbing, I gained the highest point that would hold my weight—some sixty feet up—and I lashed myself to the trunk with the belt. By now the storm was very close; there was almost no interval between flash and thunder. The wind was shifting as the storm hit, whipping the trunk, slender at that height, in all directions.

My eyes were closed—against the stinging rain, I told

48

myself, knowing it was a lie. I didn't want to see the great blue flashes of lightning. It was bad enough that through the wind I could feel the air shuddering as thunder shook the universe, and worse still that the flashes were so bright they penetrated my closed eyelids. I was probably up too high. I no longer feared height—that battle had been won—but my weight could be too much for the trunk at this point; it might break off and hurl me to my death below. That was acceptable. Anything was better than what I was anticipating: death by electrocution.

Open your eyes. *Open your eyes,* I commanded myself, O P E N Y O U R E Y E S !

I did. It was chaos. The earth danced as the tree trunk swayed and snapped back against the wind. Water streamed into my eyes and I had to fight to hold them open, not daring to let go of the tree long enough to wipe them.

There was a short, enormous tearing sound that overwhelmed the screaming of the wind, and the world turned strobe blue. K E E P Y O U R E Y E S O P E N ! The instantaneous thunderclap wasn't a rumble; it was an explosion of such short duration and intensity it sounded like a twelve-gauge shotgun blast six inches from my ear. Moments later I found I had been holding my breath. I let it out with an unintelligible shout of pure joy. I was still alive! I had looked it in the face and lived!

With reckless abandon I released one hand and shook my fist at the wildly pitching sky. "Kill me!" I shouted, "Go ahead and try! I don't care! I DON'T CARE!" and I started to laugh uncontrollably as I rode the whirlwind.

The world seemed to recede from me. The lightning remained as bright, but the thunder and wind seemed muted as I laughed and shouted. Their place was taken by music. As sometimes happened when I was moved emotionally, the music in my head started itself. Wagner's "Ride of the Valkyries" would have been more appropriate, but what burst into my brain was Grieg's "In the Hall of the Mountain King."

49

I turned my face up to feel the rain stream against it and run in rivulets under my clothes and down my body. I don't know how long I was up there when the world of sound returned to normal, the music died, and, over my own shouts, I heard another. It was my father, commanding me to come down immediately.

I obeyed, grinning with extraordinary happiness as I made my way to the lowest limb and jumped to the ground.

"What in God's name were you doing?" my father asked. Then, without waiting for my answer as we ran together toward the house, "I just don't understand you!"

"I know," was all I said.

V

At St. Benedict's I tried out for the baseball and track teams, but I was too small. To remedy that, the summer before my sophomore year I started lifting weights, and, in my sophomore year, I made the cut in wrestling.

That Christmas I finally got a real gun. Not from my father; he still couldn't bring himself to buy me one because he didn't believe I was "ready." It came from my Uncle Ray, the FBI executive. Not long afterward I took the single-shot bolt-action Winchester .22 out in the woods after squirrels. I was startled by a shot from my left. A bullet clipped a twig from a tree inches from my head, and three more shots followed as I dropped to the ground and tried to squirm down into it.

I was furious. I jumped to my feet in defiance of instinct, and as rapidly as I could load and fire sent five rounds in the direction from which the shots had come, then listened. I heard nothing. Anger drained from me to be replaced by shame. I walked home in a deep funk.

For years I'd known that I had a violent temper, and I loathed it as yet another manifestation of emotion. In the days when I was ruled by fear, the violence found release only in my dreams. I had them almost nightly. They were in color and vivid; sometimes only one object that seemed to form the theme of the dream—a firearm, or other weapon, or a particular person—would be in color, the rest in black and white.

For years I had one dream over and over: I was in Ireland fighting as a revolutionary and was captured. The other prisoners and I were placed in the "Irish Mail," a device for execution in which a row of prison bars was set about two feet from a concrete wall. Beneath our feet was a concrete floor with a gutter running its length. The power would be thrown on, the bars glow red with heat and the prisoners melt to death, their remains flowing down the gutter beneath their feet. I always managed to escape before death and led the others, always including a tall, beautiful Celtic girl, in battle across a great park-like field. We slaughtered thousands with automatic weapons as we made our way to a stone tower at the far end of the field and shot our way up a circular stone stairway to the very top of the tower. There the two of us, the girl and I, mortally wounded, killed hundreds as they tried to reach us at the landing at the top of the stairs. The girl always died in my arms. I always awakened before dying, only to fight the entire battle over again the next night, and the next, and the next. I last had that dream at about age twenty. It was the simplest of them all.

My temper represented a grave threat to me; it signified a loss of control by the reason and will and a surrender to ungovernable emotion. I felt as if there were a terrible creature within me whom I must never let escape or he'd destroy blindly—friend, foe, and innocent bystander alike. I recognized that he had broken loose when I got up and fired that rifle. I knew that it was unlikely I was being shot at deliberately, that I should have fired one shot into into the air to let whoever it was know that I was there. By acting as I did, shooting without even having a target, I risked killing innocent people.

51

As I grew psychologically stronger the creature was keeping apace. That would not do. It was no good wishing I had more German and fewer Italian genes; I knew perfectly well that with a powerful enough will I could be as *eiskalt* as any Teuton. I must train myself so the more dangerous the situation, the more *Kaltblütig* I became. I had, I knew, a long way to go to achieve that goal.

In my senior year at St. Benedict's I won a silver medal in the school wrestling championship, losing only to the team captain. I won my varsity letter on the cross-country team, and that year we were the New Jersey state champions. By the time I graduated from prep school in June 1948, at seventeen, I had transformed myself. No longer small, weak, and fearful, I was five feet, nine inches tall, physically very strong, and growing more so daily. Psychologically I had gone beyond desirable self-confidence to the excess of arrogance. Having conquered physical and psychological weakness in myself, I was contemptuous of others not as strong, figuring that if I could do it, so could they.

In my long war against specific fears I had, for the most part, been able to choose the time and place of battle. I didn't have that luxury when I was confronted with the test of severe pain. It happened one night during the summer following my graduation from St. Benedict's. After supper I'd gone to the third-floor library to read. I was seated at a large wooden desk in the center of the room, facing the fireplace.

Suddenly, with no warning at all, something seemed to burst deep inside my head. I was seized with indescribable pain. I grabbed my head with both hands and pressed inward fiercely; my skull felt as if it were exploding. Nauseated, I wanted to get to the nearby bathroom to vomit, but the pain paralyzed me. Still holding my head I rocked back and forth, gulping air because the paralysis seemed to inhibit even my breathing. Dimly, my mind absorbed almost completely by the overwhelming agony, I perceived an opportunity to destroy the fear of pain through enduring it. Then that brief thought gave way to another one. In those days, devout Catholics observed the pious custom of "offering up" any suffering they might be enduring—from the mere exasperation of an over-worked mother to the agony of one terminally ill with cancer—as a substitute for the suffering of the "Poor Souls in Purgatory." It was believed that, in turn, the "Poor Souls" would intercede with God to lessen the anguish the living sufferer was "offering up."

In the face of that terrible pain, my will failed, and I offered the torment up, begging the "Poor Souls" to inter-cede with God to end my suffering, even if it meant death.

Nothing happened. Now came shame at my weakness, and, making a virtue of necessity, I resolved to endure and conquer the pain. Never again, I vowed, would I break. This lofty line of thought was cut short as I shot to my feet involuntarily, the top of my head feeling as if it were blowing off. I shifted my hands desperately to the crown and gasped, my mouth wide open like a miler at the finish line. Then, something equally extraordinary and inexplicable happened.

There was an audible snap, which sounded and felt as if a rubber band, stretched taut under the top of my skull, from front to rear, had broken. As if a switch had been thrown, the pain vanished as quickly and mysteriously as it had come, to be replaced by a strange sensation when I sank back into my seat. A delicious warmth started at the top of my skull and flowed down, as if someone were pouring warm, thick syrup over the top of my shaven head.

My next recollection is of waking up hours later in my chair, head down on top of the book. There was absolutely no trace of the pain, or of the subsequent pleasure either. I felt that I had won the final battle. There was no sense of elation, just a quiet recognition that my second last fear was behind me forever. I have experienced great pain since, certainly of longer duration, but never of such intensity. More to the point: I have never since feared pain. Indeed, I have used it purposefully to strengthen my will. But from that day forward I feared nothing but God. And there would even come a day when I did not fear God either.

Within a month I noted another phenomenon, which I am not at all sure was related to that incident, since it could simply be a case of *post hoc ergo propter hoc*. I acquired a second handwriting. I don't mean to say that my handwriting changed. My original handwriting, a sloppy, forward-slanting scrawl based on the Palmer method taught me in grammar school, remained the same. Rather I began to produce, with increasing frequency until in recent years it has become my primary handwriting, a completely different script, characterized by much smaller letters running straight up and down. I can consciously choose either script at will. The oddity is that unless I *do* choose, I find myself writing in either one, for no discernible reason, although the second (and, happily, much more legible) hand has become dominant.

There was no question of where I should go to college. My father, a loyal and active son of Fordham, was confident that the education there, under the Jesuits, would be superior. Once again he was correct. As before, however, I felt I would be measured against my father's record. So be it. *He* had won at prep school, *I* would win at college.

Fordham was a feast for the mind and a challenge to the spirit. To begin with, it was still under the absolute control of the Jesuits, and many of the professors were either Jesuit priests (Fathers) or scholastics (trainees, addressed as "Mister"). As much as I had admired the German Benedictines, I admired the Jesuits more.

That is not to say that I found every Jesuit individually attractive as a personality, or that I did not chafe under their rule; my competitive spirit and self-esteem, several notches higher than justifiable, saw to that. But the Society of Jesus was something special; the shock troop of the Catholic church. So effective an organization was it that even as it was the object of a special effort at suppression by Nazi Germany, Heinrich Himmler used it as the model for his own corps of *Ubermenschen,* the *Schutzstaffel,* the dread, black-uniformed SS, whose hand-picked members swore a special oath of loyalty to the *Führer,* as the highest rank of Jesuits did to the Pope.

No matter what course of study one pursued at Fordham, courses in religion were required during the first two years, and, during the last two, no matter the major, a large dose of philosophy. The most valuable course I took at Fordham was logic, a part of the required program. It honed the mind and thinking process along mathematical lines and prepared us for the Study of Aristotle and Aquinas.

I joined the Reserve Officers Training Corps, disappointed that it did not offer a larger program. The only combat branch taught was antiaircraft artillery, so that's where I went, assuming that if we went to war with the Soviet Union, I could transfer to the infantry or armored branches.

The college was filled with veterans of World War II studying under the auspices of the G.I. Bill. They were respected and envied by those of us who had been too young to fight that war. One veteran was told that if he took one more course that term he could graduate a year early, and then he learned that the only course still open to him was R.O.T.C. He took it and showed up at Wednesday morning drill with the rest of us. The unsuspecting nonveteran cadet company commander chewed him out for having his uniform tie knotted too loosely, saying, "Next time, cadet, you be here in proper uniform! Do you understand me?"

"Yes, sir," was all the older man said, and, as ordered, the next Wednesday, there he was in "proper uniform"— complete with the distinguished flying cross and air medals for all the German planes he had shot down while piloting his P-38 in the European theater; a Purple heart and stacks of battle-starred U.S. and Allied campaign ribbons rising so high on his left breast that his silver wings were almost at his shoulder. He never wore them again, and the cadet commander never again spoke like that to him, or to anyone else for that matter.

The four years passed quickly. In my first year I made the freshman cross-country team, but, when I became ill during Christmas vacation with a reprise of my old respiratory ailment and my parents took me to our family doctor, I was ordered to stop. The good doctor was in his eighties, and, when he spotted the size of my heart in the X ray, he announced that I had an "enlarged heart, known in layman's terms as 'athlete's heart,' " as well as varicose veins.

It is now, and was then among up-to-date physicians, common knowledge that the heart, being a muscle, will grow if exercised by something like long-distance running. It is a normal process and, because its capacity is increased accordingly, considered a benefit. Nor is a degree of varicosity in the lower legs of runners unusual; the calf muscles get very hard and force the softer veins toward the surface. But the old doctor didn't know that, and so I gave up running at his orders.

Upon graduation I was offered Distinguished Military Graduate status if I would accept my commission in the Regular Army, rather than the reserve. Because of a "gentleman's agreement" among the armed forces, I was not told that I could elect to receive a regular commission in any service I chose. Had I been told, I would have taken a regular commission in the Marine Corps and made it my career. As it was, I had no guarantee I could transfer to infantry or armor in the army, so I turned the offer down and took my commission in the reserve. I was not unhappy. In June 1950 North Korea had invaded South Korea, and, although the war was not the one with the Soviet Union I'd hoped for, it was at least an opportunity for combat. In the words of then Marine Corps General "Chesty" Puller: "It may be a lousy war, but it's the only war we've got."

When our grades came in, I totaled up my four-year weighted average. It was 85 and change: a B+. My father had won again but, by God, I was closing rapidly.

I had another and more difficult decision to take at that time—whether to ask a certain young lady to "wait for" me. I was enamored of her, yet something held me back from full commitment. I had read Lindbergh because of my interest in aviation and was very impressed by the logic of his emphasis upon genetics in choosing Anne Morrow for his wife. The young woman was intelligent and beautiful, but I wanted more mathematical ability in the gene pool from which my children would spring. I also wanted size—height and heavy bone structure so that my children would be physically as well as intellectually powerful—and she was of less than average height, with thin, delicate bones. To what, years later, must have been her great relief, I did not ask her to wait for me and we parted friends. Somewhere, I felt sure, I would find the woman I wanted to bear my children: a highly intelligent, tall, fair, powerfully built Teuton, whose mind worked like the latest scientific wonder, the electronic computer. I had worked long, hard, pain-filled years to transform myself; to make a reality of my genetic potential. Now I believed I had earned the right to seek my mate from among the finest genetic material available.

In the summer of 1952 I shared a compartment in a Pullman car with Dick Fleckner, a schoolmate from St. Aloysius who had gone to Fordham with me. After three days of watching America flow by, we arrived at our destination, El Paso, Texas. The Artillery School at Fort Bliss swarmed with three thousand second lieutenants, most destined to be ground up as forward observers in the hills of Korea (where the average life span in that role after discovery of position was approximately three minutes).

Ninety days went by rapidly and the time came when all I needed for my POR (preparation, overseas replacement) qualification was one more written examination and successful completion of the night combat infiltration course. The night before the exam those in the Bachelor Officers Quarters who had been studying with the assistance of a quantity of Mexican beer suggested a sit-up contest to see which officer in the BOQ had the strongest stomach. I couldn't resist such a challege and won the contest.

The next day I felt decidedly ill but took the examination anyway in order not to delay my overseas deployment. It was easy to pass the exam but difficult to hand the paper in as I found to my surprise that I could not stand upright. My classmates drove me to the nearest aid station and left immediately to make the next formation.

Unfortunately, the aid station was not manned by a doctor but by an enlisted man who diagnosed my illness as tarantula bite poisoning. I protested that if one of those big hairy spiders we saw occasionally in the desert had bitten me I would damn well have known it, but the enlisted man insisted that he knew a tarantula case when he saw one and sent me off in an ambulance to the post army hospital.

At the hospital a nurse directed me to take myself and my tarantula papers over to X ray, some three blocks away by wooden sidewalk across the hot sand in between.

Bent over almost double by this time, I dragged myself over to the X-ray room where I proceeded to vomit over the machine. That did nothing to endear me to the operator, but as I passed out I felt him take the tarantula papers from what I was sure was my dying grasp, and I heard him calling for help.

I awoke to find myself elsewhere and in a sitting position. Two people, one male and one female, were trying without success to thread a rubber tube up my nose and down the inside of my throat. "Swallow," they kept commanding and, eventually, I got it down and my stomach was pumped. A real doctor explained that he knew a spider hadn't got me but that he wasn't sure just what was wrong so I was to undergo exploratory surgery as soon as I could be prepared.

I awoke the next day in the intensive care unit with more hoses running in and out of me.

From a cheerful nurse I learned that I was "going to be fine" but little else of what had happened.

Finally when I was in the recovery ward, I was told that I had nearly died and been given the last rites of the Catholic church; and I learned what the problem was: I had blown my appendix when I won the sit-up contest.

It was embarrassing being there in the recovery ward. Everyone else was there as a result of war wounds—men still banging into furniture because they were not yet used to having only one eye, or complaining of pain in arms and legs that were no longer there. Worse, they would ask me questions like, "Where were you when ya got hit?" It was humiliating to have to confess that I was there for appendicitis. In seven days they took out the stitches, declared me unfit for any duty, and sent me home on convalescent leave.

VI

After ten days at home I was eager to return to Fort Bliss, concerned that my class would leave for overseas without me and I'd have to wait for graduation of the next class, three months later, for a combat assignment. Still walking with a slight list forward, favoring the incision, I left my worried mother and confident father for a flight back to El Paso. There, I got the bad news: I was assigned to a training command to work in an office until my incision healed completely.

It was explained to me by the physician that the six-inch incision had cut through four layers of muscle; that they would heal from the inside out and it would take a long time. In the interim, I was not to attempt so much as opening a window—and the job I was given was appropriate to those orders; as officers reported in for papers on their new assignments, I was stationed at the end of the counter, where I took the papers, shuffled them into a neat pile, and stapled them together. Apparently it was not thought beyond my ability to swat a stapler lightly without rupturing myself.

Forty-eight hours later I learned to my rage that my unit would go through the night close-combat infiltration course that evening. Those who passed would receive their POR qualification and orders overseas shortly thereafter. I was now filled with such anger that I recognized it as such and forced myself to consider the situation calmly. The fact was I had passed the final examination, and all I needed for my POR qualification was the endorsement in my file certifying that I had passed the night infiltration test. Without that, I was barred from an overseas assignment in general and a combat assignment in particular.

My course was clear; I would have to pass the infiltration test that evening while I had the chance. My name would be on the class roster, even though not on the list to take the test. If I showed up I could convince the noncoms running the test that an error of omission had been made; after all, I *was* a member of that class. That left the problem of getting physically through the course.

The night close-combat infiltration course was fifty yards long. It took place at a lighted field, and everyone got into a ditch at one end. On the lip of the ditch was a log. Scattered throughout the fifty yards between that log and the end of the course were more logs, ditches, and small areas circled by stone that were not to be entered since they contained explosives detonated to lend verisimilitude. There were also barbed wire and machine guns, set to fire at thirty inches above ground level, using live ammunition. The course was negotiated crawling on one's belly, with full combat pack and M-1 rifle in hand.

There was a time limit. When the lights went out, there would be a pause, then a whistle, and the machine guns would start firing. When time was up, the whistle would be blown again, the guns silenced and the lights snapped back on. Anyone not at the other side failed the test. The immediate question presented to me was: how do I manage to crawl over those obstacles and negotiate the course in the required speed without having my belly pop open and, literally, spilling my guts?

I regarded my waist and found the answer staring me in the face. To hold up our trousers we each wore a tightly woven cloth belt fastened by a polished brass sliding buckle. I had two. I went to the PX and bought two more. An hour before the test was to begin that evening, I stripped and fastened the four belts around my abdomen and cinched them tight, buckles to the sides, so that they held my intestines in place firmly. Then I dressed in the fatigue uniform designated for the test.

When one or two of my classmates remembered that I was on limited duty and asked me what I was doing there, I said, "You know the fuckin' army. Doc says I'm fine; should be able to beat all you bastards to the other side."

"D'int ya say somethin'? Shit you could get hurt, man!"

"Nah. I'm O.K. Really. And what good would sayin' somethin' do? They'd just make me go through it backwards, for laughs."

Three months' experience with the United States Army had prepared my questioning classmates to accept what I told them as gospel. I took my place in line, argued successfully with the sergeant that his list was in error, and made it into the ditch.

There followed a lecture to us all over the loudspeaker, laced with profanity for emphasis to the effect that this goddamn well *was* live ammunition, not blanks, and whoever started that goddamn rumor was an asshole, and whoever believed it and stood up would be a *dead* asshole for sure. No matter what, repeat what, happens, DON'T STAND UP 'CAUSE YOU *WILL*, REPEAT WILL, BE SHOT! STAY THE FUCK DOWN!

The lights went out, a whistle blew, and the machine guns started firing. I wormed my way over the top of the log, sucking in my belly to keep my weight off it, and was on my way.

The belts did their work. They were so tight that their edges bit into my flesh when I pulled my legs forward, but they were also thick and stiff enough to provide a kind of armor. The worst problem I had was when the explosive charges went off near me. The concussion was like someone kicking me right on the incision. The noise was terrific.

The last ten yards were agonizing, but I made it, getting to the end of the course about as quickly as half my classmates. I had to use my M-1 rifle to get to my feet, but in the noisy dark no one noticed. I felt sticky and was concerned that I might be bleeding, but I was elated at passing the test.

My elation was short-lived. No POR qualification came through, and when I inquired, I was told that someone had informed the authorities that I was in no condition to go overseas; that the fact I had passed the test was a fluke and I should be reexamined to see if I had done myself severe injury. I was examined and had not—the stickiness I had felt was just sweat. Nevertheless, POR qualification was withheld until such time as my incision was certified as healed completely. I never found out who had taken it upon himself to do me that "favor," but I suspected Dick Fleckner and, in spite of the fact that I knew whoever it was had acted from the best of motives, I didn't speak to Dick Fleckner for two years.

Most of my class went to Korea. I received the ultimate in absurd assignments: to guard, with 90-mm antiaircraft guns, the skies over New York City from Russian bombers. I argued futilely that since I had been assigned to a combat-ready outfit, I was eligible for transfer to Korea.

By now I had a "critical MOS" (Military Occupational Specialty) as a radar-trained fire control officer. Forget infantry. Forget armor. You're only in for two years and trained for AA radar. Why should the army train you all over again? You wanna go to Korea with AA? Come back in six months. We'll see. But don't hold your breath. You're the guy with the big hole in him, right?

It was clear from the way he said it that he thought the hole was in my head.

So I stayed, and my frustration and resentment grew: frustration because of not being permitted to serve in combat after spending my youth preparing mentally and physically for total war; resentment because I'd been given no useful alternative role. My unit was deployed for show only; the little signs were everywhere and they multiplied as time went on. The first clue that ours was not a serious mission was the matter of settling rounds.

Soon after installation, heavy antiaircraft guns with electronic aiming devices should be fired at high-barrel elevation to settle them into the ground; otherwise they'll shift position after the first shots at an enemy aircraft and the computer calculations will be thrown off. We shouldn't fire settling rounds, said our superiors, because it would be too *un*settling to the surrounding neighborhood—the very people we were supposed to be protecting. In the case of C Battery, 380th AAA Battalion, that was Cropsey Avenue near the Coney Island area of Brooklyn.

Then there was the matter of outrigger stakes. After heavy AA guns have been firmly bedded by settling rounds, their stabilizing outriggers are fixed to the ground by heavy steel stakes to prevent further movement, since even the slightest change of position degrades the computer's data base. To stake the outriggers *before* firing settling rounds is to invite the outrigger-pins to be sheared off when the guns shift from the settling rounds. We were ordered to stake them anyway; regardless of the potential damage and delay that would keep us from getting the guns trained on enemy planes before they could drop their bombs. The reason given: "staked outriggers look neater to inspecting officers."

Finally, there was the matter of the ammunition bunkers. Ammunition bunkers built of sandbags were positioned around each of our four 90-mm guns. They held live 90-mm shells. The sandbags were intended to cut down on the havoc in case one of those shells exploded accidentally. One day we were ordered to remove the sandbags and replace them with bunkers made of cinderblock—a material that would add to the deadly effect of flying shell fragments the lethal element of flying cement block fragments. We complained in vain about the added danger to our men; cinderblocks, we were told, looked neater than sandbags to inspecting officers.

The inspecting officers themselves were the last straw. They were generals whose questions and comments showed they knew little or nothing about antiaircraft artillery. Invariably they were from Washington and it came to me finally that any brass who wanted to take in a Broadway show or the sights of Manhattan would arrange a trip to inspect New York's antiaircraft defenses.

I considered myself a serious man and did not suffer such foolishness gladly. Casting about for a way to vent my anger appropriately, I found it in the device of taking foolish orders at face value and following them to the letter. They wanted to play at being a combat unit with combat orders? Fine. Two could play that game. I studied our standing orders carefully.

Thus it was, one weekend when I was duty officer and in command of the battery, that I was ready as opportunity knocked. Our orders read that the commanding officer was to report immediately, over the military communications channel, any of a number of things of interest to AAA intelligence. Indeed in that number were "unidentified airbursts." Upon sighting any such in our area, we were to report them, together with description and azimuth and elevation from our position.

64

On that dull day I heard a series of mild *crump*'s, and I saw white puffs of smoke in the sky several blocks away. I watched and listened long enough to determine that the two were related, measured the azimuth and elevation from our position, and then, to the utter astonishment and dismay of Eastern Antiaircraft Command Headquarters at Fort Wadsworth, I activated the battle communications channel as prescribed and made a formal report, complete with verifying codeword. The result was glorious.

The army was caught in its own charade. Headquarters *had* to act on the report and had to do so by the book. That the book was ridiculous in its application there and then was beside the point. Headquarters had to play the game, and the rules called for the Fort Wadsworth duty officer to launch a combat situation probe to explain the unidentified airbursts. Down swooped military jeeps and staff cars, followed by police, all with sirens screaming, to the location plotted from the data I had wired into headquarters.

What I had not known was that it was Saint Gennaro's Day, a major feast day for the Italian-American community in that neighborhood. The army, followed by police, carrying out the great Saint Gennaro's Day raid, roared into a block party in progress, disrupting things mightily as they determined that illegal fireworks were being set off. Now the authorities are not especially popular among the Brooklyn Italian-American community to begin with, and Saint Gennaro's Day is a very special event. The army's blunderous assault on the festivities set back the community relations program a solid year—not to mention the effect upon military morale as the army, realizing its gaffe, retreated hastily from the area amid the jeers of the celebrating Italians. I was the wise-ass second lieutenant responsible for all this, so I became notorious among the high command, and they vowed revenge.

Shortly after I arrived at the encampment of C Battery, we received the latest radar and a gun-pointing system, directed by an advanced computer.

The control room looked like something out of science fiction. Multiple radar scopes glowed an eerie green, and their reflection on the faces of the operators made the men look like alien beings. A computer blinked and hummed, and large, lighted plotting pens in glowing glass cases charted the progress of target aircraft on graphs automatically. The battery commander sat at a control console that gave him access to a magnifying periscope slaved to the tracking radar head so he viewed exactly what the radar was following. The whole thing was like a combination spaceship and submarine.

When I first saw this electronic marvel during my familiarization tour, I noticed several charts on the walls. Some were easy to decipher: they plotted areas masked off from radar coverage by high buildings, gave schedules for reporting to headquarters, and so forth. One chart was a mystery. It consisted of rectangles into which were written times, azimuths, and elevations, along with several stars like a restaurant-rating system. I was told that to see what this was for I'd have to wait for a "tracking mission."

On the multidialed wall behind the radar technicians was a prominent switch with a red security cover. It was marked:

BATTLE OVERRIDE

It was explained to me that the vacuum tubes of this sophisticated piece of equipment had first to be warmed up before they could take safely the full power of the 200-cycle generator. In the event of a battle emergency, however, the automatic protective warm-up delay could be overridden and full power applied immediately by throwing the "Battle Override" switch, as everything and everyone become expendable in war. The M-33C cost the government in excess of a million 1953 dollars. I was impressed. So were the troops assigned to man it, and thereby was born a community relations problem.

On our first tracking assignment after that, when it became clear that the target aircraft would not be coming through our sector and boredom began to set in, the tracking radar operator asked, "Lieutenant, you wanna see what that there chart is for now?"

"Sure."

"O.K., Lieutenant, let's hope we have some luck. Should be good; it's dark out now an' they should be home from work just about this time. Look through the periscope."

Mystified, I looked as I was told. I saw the starlit sky as the tracking radar head happened to be pointing upward. The crewmen started to speak again:

"Azimuth: two two one!"

"Azimuth two two one," came the acknowledgment.

"Elevation: four seven!"

"Elevation four seven."

"Slew!"

At the command *slew*, a switch was thrown that slaved the tracking radar head to the azimuth and elevation set in previously. As I stayed glued to the eyepiece of the periscope, the night sky blurred with apparent motion as the high-powered optic moved down and to the left swiftly and then centered with precision on a window in a nearby high-rise apartment building. The room was so high that its tenant had not bothered to pull the shade. It was a bathroom. The light was on and, to the cheers of those viewing the scene through the other two eyepieces of the periscope, an attractive brunette stripped and entered the shower.

"Good ol' Alice; I knew she wouldn't let us down! How ya like that stuff, Lieutenant?"

"Great. Is that what you show the inspecting officers when they ask about that chart?"

"Nah, Lieutenant," came the reply, with barely con-

67

cealed disgust, "when they come around the chart comes down."

I laughed and looked at the chart again carefully. It was filled with "targets."

"They all as good as this one?" I asked.

"Better, most of 'em. We picked Alice 'cause she's always right on time. Takes a shower every night soon as she comes home from work."

"Alice?"

"That's what we call her. We give 'em all names. We don't know 'em but we'd sure like to!"

About a month later, when I was again duty officer, I was called on the field telephone from the front gate and told that a delegation from the neighborhood wanted to speak to the commanding officer. At the moment I filled that role, so I went to the gate to meet them.

The group members were all middle-aged and irate. They accused the army in general and C Battery in particular of sterilizing their daughters. It seemed that the Fire Control Platoon soldiers had been warned during training to avoid getting too close to the magnetron in the base of the tracking radar head because of the possible effects of microwave radiation upon their bodies, especially their genitals. Now they were bragging to local girls about the enormous power of their radar and corresponding danger of their assignments. They pointed to the tracking radar head as the source of all that power and radiation that, daily, they braved in line of duty for God, country, and the citizens of Coney Island.

After that, bored radar technicians had amused themselves by zeroing in on pretty girls on the street, ogling them by high-powered periscope. The tracking head had a mechanical whine, and the girls, looking up, saw the head following them, pointing directly at them, and pouring out, they were certain, all those sterilizing emissions.

I couldn't convince the angry parents otherwise, nor could I promise that the tracking head would never again point toward the street: it would slew automatically toward whatever point the computer called for and choose the shortest distance to get there. There was nothing to do but refer the delegation to Eastern Antiaircraft Command headquarters at Fort Wadsworth, and to forewarn headquarters by reporting the incident immediately.

After the Saint Gennaro's Day fiasco, headquarters was sure I had put those people up to it: another tactic in my psywar against the brass because they wouldn't send me to Korea. This hardened headquarters in its resolve that I would *never* go to Korea, or so I was told in confidence by a drunken staff officer at a battalion party. He also said that my superiors were determined to get even. And soon after they did.

So far as I know, the press never got hold of the story, but in 1954, one of the integrated gun batteries of the 737th AAA Battalion mutinied. Black troops at one of the gun sites in Brooklyn took over the battery area and ran off its white officers at bayonet point. Something had to be done. Fast.

The mutinous battery was reassigned to a different AAA post area a few miles away and all its officers replaced. For the new commanding officer a white Regular Army captain, who had survived the disastrous World War II bombing raid on the Rumanian oil fields at Ploesti, was selected on the basis of his demonstrated courage and experience. He was small physically but his heart was huge. Sparse red hair topped his head, and his cold blue eyes were all business. Soft-spoken and fair, he was tough as they come and not a man to cross.

For the new executive officer the brass selected me. I wanted combat? They'd give me combat. For our third and final officer we were assigned a huge black second lieutenant. He was just twenty-two, about six feet, three inches tall, and weighed at least 220 pounds. A recent graduate of Howard University, he was intelligent, educated, and well-spoken.

As soon as we arrived to take over the mutinous bat-

69

tery, the captain ordered the first sergeant to assemble the enlisted men in the mess hall for an address by their new officers.

The captain spoke first, and in his soft tone of voice he told the men that he was aware of what had happened and that it would not be permitted to happen again. He also assured them that, as far as he was concerned, the past was past and the slate wiped clean. From here on out every man would be judged on his performance as a soldier, black or white, and that was that. He then introduced me as the executive officer.

As the captain had played the good guy role, I took the traditional bad guy role as exec. I told the troops that military courtesy and discipline would be enforced impartially and that certain practices that we understood had been tolerated in the past would not be permitted in the future. Specifically, I said that we had heard that certain individuals had brought liquor on the post and others had failed to show up for morning roll-call formation when the weather was cold or wet. There would, I said, be no privileged characters in the battery. Finally, I tapped the leather holster under my left shoulder. It held a personally owned caliber .38 special Smith & Wesson revolver. I stared at the assembled men and told them that the first man to raise a bayonet against me would be shot on the spot.

The black lieutenant then spoke, firmly and effectively, and the troops were dismissed.

Things were quiet for a while. Unsurprisingly, no one wanted to test himself against the black lieutenant, and the captain's four-row stack of World War II ribbons was respected for the courage under fire it represented.

The first test came on a frigid dawn when it was my turn to hold roll call for the morning report. One of the hard cases decided to sleep in while the rest of us stood in formation in the cold. I got a sergeant and the two of us went into sleeping beauty's quarters, picked up his cot by the head and foot, and carried it out to his place in formation. I then stripped off the covers and, to the amusement of the rest of the battery, let the icy blast of wind off the Atlantic do its work. Very quickly the cold got so bad he couldn't stand it, and he scrambled to his feet, shivering, in his skivvies. I held the assembled formation—all except the late sleeper dressed in heavy overcoats—as the winter wind whipped us all. When the tough guy collapsed, I dismissed the battery. No one ever tried that stunt again.

Soon an inspection turned up several bottles of expensive liquor, which I confiscated. During the next formation, I reminded the assembled men that such violations would not be tolerated, and I emptied the bottles on the sand before the troops. After the men were dismissed I noticed that several scooped up some of the wet sand and brought it to their noses to sniff it, believing, apparently, that I might have substituted water for the booze.

One midmorning a sergeant came to me to say that a private had refused his order. I looked at him.

"How long have you been a sergeant, sergeant?"

"Nine years, sir."

"Are you telling me you don't know what to do?"

"No, sir. I just wanna know if *you* know what I gotta do."

"Sergeant, I think you're taking an unnecessarily long time to make a simple report of an accident that happened to poor Private Benson behind the mess hall."

"Yes, sir. That's exactly right, sir."

"And just what time this morning did this misfortune befall Private Benson?"

The sergeant looked at his watch. "In just about three minutes from now, sir."

"So noted. See that he receives the appropriate first aid. And I'm going to want a repair order for those stairs or whatever it is he's going to fall down or trip over. Identified safety hazards must be eliminated promptly. That's the rule, and we certainly can't go around breaking any rules, can we sergeant?"

"Yes, *sir*! I mean, no, sir, lieutenant, sir." He saluted smartly, turned on his heel, and left, beaming. I had just won over the NCOs.

The last test came following a summary court-martial at which the defendant was found guilty and sentenced to the stockade at Governor's Island. He was permitted to return to the battery to pick up his possessions en route to Governor's Island by jeep. The captain was off post, and I was in command. The corporal assigned to guard the prisoner came into the office.

"Lieutenant, you're gonna have to do somethin' about the prisoner. The driver won't take him. He says he's gonna kill us as soon as we get off the post. Says we ain't never gonna get to Governor's Island."

"What's that you're carrying, corporal?"

"Carbine, sir. Only they didn't gimme no ammunition."

"Sergeant," I ordered, "give the corporal a loaded magazine."

The corporal stood there with the loaded magazine, his face the picture of misery and indecision. "Sir," he pleaded, "that sonofabitch is big as a horse. We all get jammed into that jeep an' he makes a sudden move, I dunno. He could take this thing away from me."

"Is that what he said?"

"No sir. Not exactly."

"Well what, exactly, did he say, corporal?"

"He says he's gonna stick it up my ass, sir. Sideways."

"Corporal, give me that carbine."

I took the .30 caliber carbine from the corporal in one hand and the loaded magazine in the other and went out the door toward the jeep. The driver was standing outside the vehicle looking frightened. Twenty to thirty soldiers were gathered to see what was going to happen. The prisoner was proclaiming loudly that he wasn't going anywhere. As he saw me coming I made a show of putting the magazine into the carbine. The prisoner's response was to reach up and remove a red fire ax mounted on a

72

wooden frame that also supported two buckets of sand. I walked to within ten feet of the man, but still out of range of the fire ax (unless he decided to throw it), and said:

"Soldier, I am giving you a direct order: Drop that ax and get into that jeep."

"Ain' goin' nowhere. Ain' takin' no more orders. Get away from me, man, 'fore I puts this ax in your head." He raised the ax. I jacked a round into the chamber of the carbine and took careful aim at his heart:

"You have just threatened to kill an officer giving you a lawful order in the line of duty. You are armed. I am legally justified in killing you in self-defense. I'm going to tell you just one more time, for the record, so everybody here can hear and testify when they investigate your death. Drop . . . that . . . ax."

The man hesitated, then several of the onlookers spoke:

"Drop it, man. Man gonna *kill* you like he says. Man, he *lookin'* to kill you! That Lieutenant Liddy, man. Look at him; can' *wait* put a hole in you!"

Now the fact of the matter was that only if the man had made some movement toward me with the ax would I have killed him. If he did not move, I intended to shoot him first through one shoulder, then the other, so that he could not use the ax—something (shooting to wound) I would later be taught by the FBI never to do. It wasn't necessary. The fire ax came down slowly, then fell to the ground at the man's feet. I kept the muzzle of the carbine trained on him.

"Walk over to that jeep." I ordered. He obeyed.

"Stop." He stopped. Still keeping the prisoner covered, I backed into the rear seat of the jeep, behind the driver's seat.

"Get in."

He got into the right front seat.

"Now you, driver."

The driver took his position. I made a little speech:

73

"Turn your head around slowly and look at the muzzle of this piece."

The prisoner did, and saw that it was pointed downward, toward the base of his spine.

"Now you better start praying that I don't sneeze, or cough, or the driver doesn't go over any sudden bumps, 'cause my finger's on the trigger and if this piece goes off, it's going to take out your kidney and your spine. All the doctors in the army won't be able to help you then. You live, it'll be in a wheelchair with dead legs and a dead cock for the rest of your life. Now look at me."

His eyes rose from the muzzle of the carbine to meet mine. I looked into him deeply, trying to find his core, holding onto his eyes with mine.

"Now," I said finally, "tell me how you're gonna stick this piece up my ass."

He swallowed, then faced front abruptly, and addressed the driver: "Where my shit, man?"

"We'll send your property along later today," I said. "All right, driver, let's go."

The trip to the stockade was completed without incident or further conversation.

Not long thereafter I was transferred to a 120-mm gun battery in Kew Gardens, Queens. After I served for a short while as executive officer, the commanding officer was transferred and I served for about two weeks as acting battery commander. It was May 1954. Korean war hostilities had ceased, and I and thousands of others were mustered out after two years of active duty. Once again I had not gotten into combat before a war was over, but I didn't feel as bad as I did at the end of World War II. That war we had fought to "end all wars." This time I knew that there will always be another war. I went into the active reserve.

VII

By the time I was mustered out of the army in 1954, my father's career had reached new heights. He had just formed Volvo Import and Volvo Distributing corporations to bring the superb Swedish motor cars into the United States market, and he'd been knighted for the second time by the king of Sweden. In matters of his specialty, trademark law, the New York law firm he headed as senior partner had 308 top U.S. and foreign corporations as clients, including the A&P chain, Fuller Brush, Monsanto, Schiaparelli, the National Biscuit Company, *Scientific American* magazine, and the McNaught Syndicate. In oil his clients included Socony-Mobil, Ohio Oil, Kendall, and Republic. Busy as he was, he found time to serve our hometown as chairman of the Board of Adjustment and the Recreation Commission. He was fifty-four years old and at high cruise.

I, on the other hand, was at loose ends. Having failed to get into combat in Korea, I had now missed out on two wars in a row and had no sense of accomplishment at all from my military service. I was twenty-three, college-educated with an I.Q. measured at diverse times from 137 to 142 and my service obligation completed. And I hadn't the slightest idea what to do with myself. My parents left me alone to sort things out, and I gravitated to the public library. Once more I was back to consuming a book a day. One of them described the work of the Johnson–O'Connor Research Foundation's Human Engineering Laboratory in New York. It asserted that, from a series of objective tests, the laboratory could state with a high degree of certainty a person's strongest aptitudes and predict rather precisely the kind of work one would do best and, presumably, enjoy the most. I had nothing to lose, so I decided to give them a try.

After three days of testing I was given an extensive report telling me such things as that I was "cross-dominated" (left-eyed but right-handed), possessed "the vocabulary of a vice president of General Motors," and was very intelligent. More particularly, I was told my combination of aptitudes indicated strongly that I would do best and be happiest as the editor of a scholarly publication.

I wrote off the testing fee and filed the report. I hadn't trained myself for years to be a warrior, only to spend my life behind a typewriter writing and editing. But I had to do something soon. I was filled with enormous energy but had no outlet for it, and I was so tense I had difficulty with ordinary conversation; unconsciously, my jaw clenched so tightly I was trying to speak through gritted teeth. Curiously, I found that I could sing without difficulty. My voice was strong and had quality enough to bring me some compliments over the years, and I enjoyed both the singing and the music itself. But I was totally untrained. Encouraged by my mother, I went to the Juilliard School in New York City and I passed my audition, but then I was told that Juilliard offered only a four-year degree-granting program. Singing for enjoyment was one thing, but singing for a living was another, so I did not enroll. I did take lessons from a private tutor, however, and as I sang for hours a day, reveling in the power of my voice and the sense of control of that power Maestro Pescia taught me, my tension vanished.

I continued to go with father to interesting gatherings of the able and powerful. Rare was the man, my father pointed out, who could enjoy what such men enjoyed, or have such power to influence events, through singing. I concluded that he was, as usual, correct. I went up to Cambridge with him to enroll at the Harvard Law School, but fall was approaching fast, and I was told I would have to wait until the following year.

Now that I had decided what I wanted to do, another year of delay after the two spent in the army was in-

76

tolerable. At the last minute Fordham, where I'd gone to college and my father had gone to both college and law school, squeezed me in for the fall term.

I threw myself into the study of law, determined that, since chance had sent me to yet another school attended by my father, this time I would surpass him. I continued to study under Maestro Pescia in my spare time, but the pressure of attempting to excel at law school, together with the maestro's insistence on converting me from my natural baritone to a tenor—because the opportunities for tenors as professional singers are so much greater than those for baritones—led me at last to give up the lessons. I still practiced when I could, for relaxation and enjoyment, but now my concentration was on the law. The one thing my father had not done was to make Law Review, possibly because he was also studying for a master's degree in English at the same time. This made it an unequal contest, but still when I made Law Review I felt another weight had been lifted from my back.

In the summer of 1956, just prior to my senior year of law school, one of the most important events of my life occurred. The previous spring my younger sister, Margaret, became engaged. I had been delighted by her choice: Jack McDermott, a very bright and ambitious former naval officer and himself a future lawyer, would contribute to the family gene pool not only his intelligence and psychological strength, but a fair, six-feet, one-inch, 200-pound Celtic physique. Since the tall, fair Celts and Teutons are so similar, and were probably related in antiquity, I was an enthusiastic advocate of the match.

Now one of my sister's former classmates at the College of New Rochelle had invited her and Jack to visit her home in Poughkeepsie. Would I like to go along as a foursome?

My reply was what one would expect from any young man in similar circumstances: "What's she like?"

"Tall," she answered, but that was not conclusive, since at five feet, one inch *anyone* was "tall" to my sister;

77

"good-looking," she continued, "and smart. A math whiz. Works for IBM computers."

I believe my reply was "When do we leave?"

I was sitting in the rear seat behind him as Jack McDermott pulled his car into the driveway at 26 Loockerman Avenue in Poughkeepsie. The property contained two lots, so we weren't sure we were in the right place, and we stopped for a moment to check the address. The front door opened and down the hill toward us walked a beautiful twenty-four-year-old woman. When she reached the driver's side of the car, looming head and shoulders over the roof and having to bend down to confirm to Jack that he had indeed found the correct address, I knew my sister was right; Frances Ann Purcell was tall. She was also slender despite broad shoulders and large bones. She had a model's high cheek bones, gray green eyes, and soft, auburn hair in a shoulder-length pageboy undercurl. It set off her fair complexion and a profile of such strength and regularity as to rival the most romantic interpretation of a Lorelei. I reacted as if I had heard the legendary Rhine maiden sing.

In the course of the weekend I learned that Frances was of Dutch and Irish descent; that her late father, who had died of cancer when she was eighteen, had been a naval officer in World War I and survived severe torpedo damage to his ship in the North Atlantic; that he was six feet tall and weighed 190 pounds before he became ill; that he was a champion athlete at several sports in his youth and a successful lawyer who continued to practice until almost the day he died. Her mother was a charming, powerfully built woman who was one of the first certified instructresses in physical education in the New York State school system.

Frances was, I found, concerned that at five feet, nine inches she was as tall as I and, even after switching to low-heeled shoes, stood taller. I told her to put her regular shoes back on. Far from being sensitive about it, I enjoyed having on my arm a woman six feet tall.

When I learned that Fran's job at IBM was to receive

from brainstorming electronic engineers short, written descriptions of theoretically possible new kinds of computers, for which she would then create a mathematical language, and that she did calculus problems for recreation the way I did crossword puzzles, I knew she was the woman I wanted to bear my children. A Teuton/Celt of high intelligence, a mathematical mind, physical size, strength, and beauty, she had it all. I fell in love.

Three weeks later I presented Frances to my parents, then took her for a moonlit ferry ride across the Hudson from Manhattan and proposed. She turned me down. Frances Purcell was not going to be rushed off her feet. We were Roman Catholics; marriage was for life; she wanted to know me better. There was plenty of time, because I still had to complete law school, pass the bar, and find employment.

So I began a courtship that took eighteen months. It called for long train trips to Poughkeepsie by me and some down to New York/New Jersey by Frances, together with my secret weapon. Fran was a very popular girl and was dated by eminently eligible bachelors who were much closer to her home than I. To keep me on her mind during the long separations, I bought the best tape recorder I could find and recorded a series of love songs from *My Fair Lady*, *Carousel*, and *Oklahoma!*, with some Cole Porter thrown in for good measure. I left the recorder and tape with Frances after extracting a promise that she would listen to it regularly. She did, and I believe my future mother-in-law got sick of the sound of my voice quite early in our relationship.

The tape recorder wiped me out financially. When I wanted to give Frances a gift for Christmas, I lined up with the desperate men at the Presbyterian Hospital on West 168th Street on 21 December and sold my blood. With the proceeds I bought Frances a sterling silver rosary.

During the summer I worked as a clerk in my father's law firm, with the exception of two weeks of active reserve training in the army. I had transferred to the Judge Advocate General's Corps in keeping with my legal training, and during one of those two-week summer tours a curious thing happened; I was given training in clandestine activities. I hadn't requested such training, and no explanation was offered for it. The subject was fascinating, and I didn't object or indicate (as I believed) that there had been a mistake. I enjoyed the course and didn't want to risk removal from the class.

Part of the course consisted in the techniques of surreptitious entry. It was given at an army base in New England where there was also a heavily guarded, barbed-wire-surrounded installation of the ASA (Army Security Agency, a subsidiary of the National Security Agency). When I had been trained in chemical, bacteriological, and radiological warfare, I was issued a certificate of completion, but not for *this* course. And I would not be surprised to learn that there was no record of my attendance. Indeed, we were told not to mention the class to anyone. In later years that training came in very handy.

One summer my father took me to a convention of the national association of Secretaries of State, which he was to address, and something happened which I remembered to my profit for the rest of my life.

We traveled by private compartment in a Pullman car, I in the upper berth, my father in the lower. My father knew many on the train, and the first night out we were invited by several groups for after-dinner drinks in the club car and various Pullman suites. My father always managed to have a full glass in his hand; invariably the same one he was handed upon arrival. I didn't have the good sense to follow his example.

By the time we went to bed, I had the impression that the roadbed of the tracks had deteriorated and the cars seemed to be swaying considerably as a consequence. On top of that I did not feel at all well and was glad to be able to lie down. My father and I said good night, and the lights went out except for the dim blue glow of a night lamp we didn't know how to turn off.

Despite the fact that I was now lying down, I could sense that the swaying of the car was getting progressively worse. I started to moan. The lights went on again, and I heard my father call up to me, "Son, are you all right?"

I was most certainly not, but I wasn't going to tell *him* that. Quite the contrary, despite feeling terribly ill, I rolled over and put my head out over the side of the bunk to reassure my father. He was looking up at me, his own head sticking out into the narrow space between his bed and the compartment wall, his face wearing a look of concern. It soon wore something else.

I never got to reassure my father. No sooner was I hanging over the side of the bunk looking down at him three feet below me than a wave of nausea overcame me and I vomited directly into the poor man's face. The last thing I was conscious of before passing out was his startled cry as he was hit by the full contents of my stomach, dinner, drinks and all.

I awoke the next morning feeling well as can only someone who has long since eliminated all the poison from his system and is very young and fit. I had not the trace of a headache, but my hands shook and I was a bit wobbly on my feet. What had wakened me were the tender ministrations of an elderly black porter. He had already cleaned up most of the mess I had made, and now he got me washed, shaved, dressed, and out of the compartment so he could finish the job by changing the bed linen. The odor of vomit was yielding to the more pungent odor of a strong disinfectant, and, as I left to find my father to apologize, I fumbled with my wallet to tip the porter. He refused, saying that my father had already taken care of him very well.

I found my father in the dining car having breakfast with friends. He greeted me cheerfully and invited me to join them. I played it safe with a cup of coffee and an order of dry toast. My father treated me as if nothing at all had happened, and when I finally got him alone and started to apologize, he cut me off with an irrelevant remark and started a serious discussion about some element of his scheduled address. To the day he died, my father never mentioned that incident to me, nor ever gave the slightest indication that it had taken place. To paraphrase Kipling, I learned about drinking from that. I learned something about my father, too. That man had *style*.

As a law school senior, I was luckier than most members of my class. They had to worry about employment; I was sure of a job with my father's firm if I wanted it, or with the law firm of any number of his friends. Still, I hesitated.

I felt like a man whose body was being prompted by mortal danger to flood with adrenalin, only to have the danger disappear, leaving him super-charged, ready for battle, with nothing to attend but a picnic. I was restless, filled with energy, aggressive, and assertive. I had spent years getting ready to fight and now I was looking for one. The tales of my Uncle Ray's exploits in the FBI came to mind. In peacetime that seemed the most likely place to find the challenge that would prove an outlet for all I had bottled up within me. I decided to speak to Frances.

Frances was not keen about being the wife of an FBI agent. Still, she took the position that should she elect to marry me, she would raise no objection. I came away from the conversation not knowing how Frances would answer when I proposed again. That time was drawing near, and I sought to gain every advantage I could.

As a law student, I couldn't afford an engagement ring, but I knew that there were family jewels I might call on if my mother approved my choice. I spoke to her. She did approve of Frances, and she supplied the diamond ring. I made a date with Frances to join me in New York City. During a stroll along Fifth Avenue I suggested that we pay a visit to the Sacrament at St. Patrick's Cathedral. Inside, I guided us to a pew illuminated by a shaft of light from a high window. For a few moments we prayed silently; I that Frances would agree to marry me. As she stirred prior to rising, I stopped her with a touch on her arm and she looked at me questioningly. From my pocket I withdrew a jewel box and took out my mother's ring. In the shaft of light the diamond flashed even more dazzlingly than I had anticipated. I held the ring in one hand and Fran's hand in the other and whispered to her, "Will you marry me?" She seemed stunned for a moment, then, solemnly, nodded her head. A tear formed in the corner of her eye as I slid the ring on her finger and kissed her.

Before graduating from law school, I applied for the position of Special Agent in the Federal Bureau of Investigation. I was a standard applicant—scrutiny went forward while I took my final examinations, graduated, and threw myself into cramming for the New York bar examination. I passed the bar exam in July 1957, and in September I was sworn in as an FBI agent. I began the thirteen-week training course designed to apply maximum pressure to the candidates as well as to educate and indoctrinate us in the procedures and standards of what was then the best and most successful law enforcement agency in the world. The pressure had a life-saving purpose; better to have a man crack in training school than in the field, where his failure could kill him and fellow agents depending on him.

The underlying theme in all our courses on law, investigation, and forensic science was always to *appear* to go by the "book," the manual of rules and regulations, and to be able to document that appearance. Without being stated in so many words, however, the message to new agents was clear; the Bureau expected us to abide by one primary "do" and one overriding "don't": *Do* succeed; get the job done. To this end we were always to "dominate the situation" and use our "initiative and resourcefulness." No matter what, however, we were always to bear in mind rule number one: *don't* ever, embarrass the Bureau.

The FBI was to be the most important thing in our

lives. It was always ready to assist us in being careful to prevent embarrassment to the Bureau. Going to buy a house? Before signing the contract, better check out your nearest prospective neighbors by running their names and vital statistics through the Bureau indexes to see whatever might be in FBI files about them. A thorough and conscientious agent might run a National Agencies Check on them to learn not only what appeared in FBI files, but also in the files of the CIA, DIA, and NSA. If it came back "no derogatory" from all of them, you were covered. One could never be too careful. How would it look if an FBI agent ended up as the neighbor of a communist? A mafioso? or, God forbid, an unfriendly news columnist?

It followed, of course, that for more important considerations such as dates for unmarried agents—to say nothing of engagements—the woman first ought to be checked out completely; we wouldn't want to bring the wrong person into the FBI family. For that reason FBI agents tended to date and marry female Bureau personnel; they could be presumed cleared, and it saved a lot of trouble. I submitted a memo on Frances and had her checked. She was clean, as I had been sure she would be, but the important thing was that the Bureau would now be comfortable with the idea of our marriage.

The Bureau *über alles* spirit was everywhere. No matter what the facts and circumstances, the Bureau must always win. An example was the matter of carrying a gun. It was emphasized that, upon completion of training and assignment to the field, the Bureau did *not* require that an agent always carry a gun. It was made equally clear, however, that if a situation ever arose in which an agent needed a gun and didn't have one, on duty or off, he was at fault. The Bureau always had its cake and ate it too.

"Suppose," an instructor was asked in one of our classes, "an agent requests bank records of a subject [of investigation] where a subpoena can't be obtained, and the bank refuses. What should he do?"

"One acts as a con man," came the answer, "one uses

one's initiative and resourcefulness to *get those records*. Of course, it goes without saying that in doing so one exercises good judgment at all times so as never to embarrass the Bureau." That was the heart and soul of our training. By the end of the thirteen-week training period, if not before, we were convinced that the FBI was the one protector saving the American people from all enemies, foreign and domestic, criminal and subversive; that the Bureau had never failed the American people and *must* never fail them; that because of this record and the fact that no breath of scandal had touched it since J. Edgar Hoover became director, it enjoyed the unparalleled confidence of the American people; that this confidence was the key to success and must, at all cost, be protected; that thousands of men and women had contributed to the extraordinary success of the Bureau but only one was necessary to destroy it; that when we approached a citizen it would probably be the only time in that person's life he or she met an FBI agent and we had damn well better live up to expectations fostered by our reputation as the best in the world. As Adolf Hitler was referred to throughout the Third Reich as simply *der Führer*, so J. Edgar Hoover was referred to throughout the FBI as *the Director*. There were only a few of us, six thousand out of 180 million, to stand between out country and those who would destroy it. I was truly convinced we were an elite corps, America's protective echelon, its *Schutzstaffel*.

I was surprised to discover that this elite corps had a distinctive class structure. I had always been led to believe that, as the recruiting material specified, prospective FBI agents had to be either law school graduates or graduate accountants with several years of experience. The only exception mentioned were those with college degrees in physics or chemistry destined for the FBI Laboratory, or those with college degrees who were fluent in languages few Americans spoke, such as Chinese and the Slavic tongues. In class I had no difficulty with the law, but there were those who did. And all fell into one category; they had been clerical employees serving for years in low-paying jobs while studying accounting at Southeastern University in Washington, D.C., an instiution of learning virtually unknown outside the FBI. Upon completion of their studies they were permitted to enroll as Special Agents and sent to the FBI Academy.

These former clerks were regarded as especially loyal to the FBI because, unlike those with law degrees or genuine accounting ability, they knew that they could not hope to match their agent salaries outside the Bureau. As a class they were like military officers who rose from the enlisted ranks rather than the service academies. The chief sponsor of this class was the principal sycophant of the FBI and high priest of the Hoover personality cult, Associate Director Clyde Tolson, himself a former clerk. Throughout my time in the FBI I was to find this class distinction divisive and the ex-clerk underclass subversive of the quality of the Bureau.

At the FBI Academy I enjoyed two kinds of training the most: firearms and "defensive tactics." The latter was a blend of the more lethal techniques of several martial arts. It was taught by Big George Zeiss, a huge man, six feet, seven inches tall with a superb physique. From him I learned how to take a gun away from anyone foolish enough to hold it on me close enough for me to reach it, and to tear off his trigger finger into the bargain. 1 learned to kill a man immediately with no more than a pencil; to maim, to blind, and, generally, to employ my body's "personal weapons," against an opponent's "vulnerable areas."

But firearms training was my favorite. The FBI taught me gunfighting with a .38 Special revolver; .30 Remington rifle; .45 caliber submachine gun; and a twelve-gauge shotgun with shortened stock and barrel.

The instruction was given at the grounds of the Marine Corps base at Quantico, Virginia. The first phase was devoted to showing us how good we could hope to get.

The demonstration our instructors put on was spec-

86

tacular. They drew and shot with blinding speed into the lethal area of targets representing a man. They went further—much further: as I watched, they split a bullet by firing at the sharp edge of an ax, the two halves breaking clay targets at either side of the ax blade—then did it sighting backward using one facet of a diamond ring as a mirror. They split playing cards in two—edgeways. One man shot skeet with a twelve-gauge shotgun held in one hand as a pistol. He never missed. Another wrote his initials in a target with a Thompson submachine gun—firing it with the butt resting on his chin. And so it went. When the demonstration was over, they told us any normal man could be taught to be an excellent gunfighter. They would teach us. Then the hard work began.

The FBI preferred gunfighting students who had never held a gun in their hand, since they had no bad habits to unlearn. The instruction started, as it would with golf or tennis, with the grip. The critical placement of the trigger finger was explained and we spent hours practicing with paper matchbooks, pressing backward so constantly and evenly that the paper cover would bend equally on both sides of the matches.

Sighting was taught first by triangulation, and the fast draw was learned ever so slowly. The method was demonstrated over and over until the student could, in slow motion, draw, point, and squeeze the trigger of a four-inch barreled Smith & Wesson or Colt revolver to the satisfaction of the instructor. Then the student practiced that slow motion thousands of times before a full-length mirror to be sure the motion was smooth and correct. The feet were so placed that a stable gun platform was produced and the body so leaned that, if mortally wounded, the agent would fall forward so he could continue to shoot as he died. This practice was all done with revolvers having handles painted red to indicate that they had been deactivated by having their firing pins removed. Gradually the smooth motion would become etched in the neurons of the student's brain. It became second nature and, as it did, faster, then faster yet until the motion in the mirror was a blur and the instructor satisfied.

But it was not enough to be able to draw and shoot fast and accurately. One must be able to reload equally rapidly. As part of the FBI's practical pistol course, which every agent must continue to be able to pass throughout his career, one must, from a distance of twenty-one feet, draw on signal and fire five times into the target. Then the shooter must unlatch the cylinder of his revolver, swing it out, eject the empty cartridge cases, reach into a pocket filled with fifty loose rounds and extract five by touch, reload the cylinder, close and latch it, transfer the revolver to his weak hand and fire five more rounds into the target. When I graduated from the FBI Academy I could do all that in 11.74 seconds.

I wanted to be the best gunfighter in the world. That, I knew, would take years of effort. I was willing. When the class had a forty-minute lunch break, I'd eat a sandwich and spend the rest of the time taking advantage of the unlimited supply of ammunition. Soon the inside flesh of my trigger finger was worn off, and I was wiping my blood from the trigger when I cleaned my revolver at the end of the day. I obtained a product called Nu-Skin, a quick-drying plastic coating that resembled clear glue, and coated my trigger finger with it, then fired until that, too, was worn off. I burned up thousands of rounds of ammunition. It was agonizing but in the end it brought me to such a level of skill that I felt it was all worth it.

That was only part of the FBI program to make a gunfighter. It isn't enough to be *able* to shoot; you have to know *when* to shoot and, even more importantly, when *not* to shoot. As one of the instructors put it: "It embarrasses the hell out of the Bureau if you put a round through a taxpayer. You do that an' you'll wish *you* were the taxpayer."

The problem is the situation in which it takes too long to think about whether or not to shoot. By the time you go through the mental machinations, if it's a shoot situation it's too late; you're already another dead agent with his name up on that plaque on the wall of Hoover's outer office. The FBI's solution was to program agents' minds so that they fired or held fire automatically, without thought, depending on the situation.

To do this a Potemkin village was constructed and peopled with lifelike photograph-figures. The images ran the gamut from John Dillinger cradling a submachine gun to a mother in a mannish suit cradling her baby in the same manner. The village was complete with fireplugs, telephone poles, and garbage cans that could serve as cover and concealment for the agent with the wit to use them, and the entire place was animated electrically.

The figures moved with realistic suddenness. The agent was sent through the village repeatedly, and the figures were moved from one building to another so he couldn't anticipate their appearance. The action was controlled by instructors. Not until the agent shot when he ought to shoot and held fire when he ought to hold fire was he turned loose on the taxpayers with a gun. By that time it was fully automatic. The courage of the instructors was brought home to me when, during a quiet moment, I examined the wooden control tower from which they operated the village's electrical controls and supervised the action. The tower was *behind* the firing line: still it had several bullet holes in it. The instructors took it philosophically: "Better one of us than a taxpayer."

When I left the academy I could see a target, draw, and put a bullet through it in the electronically measured time of $61/100$ of a second. I could also put a bullet through a man sixty yards away with a four-inch barreled revolver; fire a twelve-gauge shotgun rapidly and accurately with either .00 buckshot or a rifled slug and fire the Thompson submachine gun in short, accurate bursts of three or four rounds. I felt as if I had been born with a gun in my hand, and I left certain that I had learned all there was to know about gunfighting. I was wrong.

89

VIII

Frances and I planned to marry in January 1958, following the completion of my training and assignment to the field. Then I learned that unless we were married at the time my orders came through, government regulations would preclude paying Frances's moving expenses, so we moved the wedding up to the first date I would be available: Armistice Day in November 1957. This began a frantic scramble to get everything ready on time, the bulk of that burden falling on Fran and her mother, because the ceremony was to be traditional, formal and well attended.

On 9 November I made it to the church on time, only to be told that I must await the entrance of the bride out of sight in an antechamber off the main altar—a protocol designed to prevent distracting the audience's attention from the bride. Right on time the organ music began and, as I peeked from the antechamber, Frances, beautiful in formal white, was escorted up the aisle by her cousin, James Toomey. If she looked a bit nervous, it was understandable; no one had told the poor girl of the protocol that demanded I be out of sight. She looked for me, didn't see me and was sure I had left her at the altar. When I finally did appear, she took on a most radiant look. It was sheer relief!

The ceremony went without a hitch, and we left the church for the nearby Poughkeepsie Tennis Club for the reception. Later we changed to traveling clothes, and my father was startled to see that under my morning coat I had been, mindful of FBI policy, wearing a gun. "Are you sure," he observed dryly, "that your bride said 'I do' of her own free will?"

Fran and I spent the evening of the ninth through the afternoon of the eleventh of November in a suite at New

90

York's Plaza Hotel, then I sent her back home (while I returned to Washington) with a promise that as soon as possible I would give her a proper honeymoon. Twenty-two years later it can't be said of us that "the honeymoon is over" since I have yet to keep that promise. I am reminded of the fact every November.

My first field office assignment was to Indianapolis. It was the birthplace of the Ku Klux Klan, and to Frances and me it was the Wild West. We drove there, passing through the devastated, stripmined landscape of Appalachia to the beauty of the flat, verdant Indiana farmland, and checked into a downtown hotel, where I became violently ill with intestinal flu. I wasn't even able to telephone the local FBI headquarters to report I was in the city. Fran did it for me and we soon learned what a closely knit band the FBI was. Agents and their wives immediately came to the hotel and made us feel a part of the family. They helped us find an affordable efficiency apartment in the heart of town, and I was soon able to present myself at the office for duty. Frances had been transferred by IBM to the Indianapolis office. Her job was to teach civilian employees of the army how to use the new computers installed at the army finance center to control the worldwide army payroll.

When I appeared at the Indianapolis office of the FBI, I was, to them, a sight to see. In the heart of the Midwest I was wearing a charcoal gray three-piece Rogers-Peet suit straight out of Manhattan. I'm not sure any of them had seen such a thing before, or so they conveyed in a good-natured way. That suit won me my first assignment and nickname. The wife of a badly wanted fugitive had died in Indianapolis, and it was thought that the husband might try to view her body or visit before her interment. The Bureau contacted the undertaker and got permission to set up an elaborate surveillance.

One agent was placed in a closet on the second floor of the funeral home in the living quarters of the undertaker, with a two-way radio. I was supplied with a photograph of the fugitive and was told to wear my suit to the funeral home and act as a casket salesman. "You'll look right in place; nobody out here wears a suit like that 'cept the undertaker."

For several days before the funeral I did my best to sell caskets for the cooperative undertaker while staying on the lookout for the dead woman's husband, a well-known and successful burglar. If I spotted him, I was to push a button discreetly that sounded a buzzer in the upstairs closet where my fellow agent was imprisoned. He would notify other agents by radio, and they would close in and make the capture.

Our man didn't show up at the funeral home, so I became an undertaker's assistant and took part in both the funeral itself and the interment. I kept watch even after everyone had left, until the last shovelful of earth had been filled in over the coffin. The husband never arrived; he was captured some time later in another state. For my role-playing and in honor of my suit, I was nicknamed "Digger" after a radio character who played a comic undertaker named Digger O'Dell. I didn't like it but forced myself to smile, hoping that nonreaction and a new assignment would combine to get me another, more acceptable, nickname. Meanwhile, I put the Rogers-Peet suit into mothballs and bought more appropriate clothing.

One day Frances became ill suddenly, and we found, to our joy, she was pregnant. She had been born very late in her parents' lives and though they would have liked more children, she was an only child. She feared she, too, might have difficulty getting pregnant. *Au contraire.* Her pregnancy did, however, turn out to be difficult. She hemorrhaged severely early in the pregnancy and was ordered by the doctor to spend the remaining months flat on her back day and night, to keep the baby. Dutifully, Fran quit her job and obeyed. I made arrangements with my superior to stay in Indianapolis covering leads so that I could go home at noon to feed Frances and handle the domestic chores.

The treatment worked. After several months the bleeding stopped. By that time I had acquired a new and more acceptable nickname. When I arrived at Indianapolis fresh out of the academy I had, in my naïveté, expected my firearms record to win me assignments close to the action. When I was instead assigned to play left field in the apprehension of one of the FBI's Ten Most Wanted Fugitives—so far from the action I couldn't get hurt, or hurt anyone else—I was crestfallen. I made some discreet inquiries and found out why. Aside from the fact that I was a "first office" agent, still untried and under observation, the Indianapolis office of the FBI had three of the best gunfighters in the FBI, if not the world. One was Special Agent in Charge Harvey Foster. He could, I learned, put five shots into the K-5 (lethal) area of a man-target at sixty yards with a two-inch barreled snub-nosed revolver, and all the bullet holes could be covered with a tea saucer. His exceptional ability with a gun was part of the reason he was one of the most respected leaders in the Bureau.

The other two were the last persons I would have suspected. In the large room where agents had their desks and dictated the results of their investigations, I had seen two men I thought remarkable because of their age. FBI agents have a difficult life and most retire as soon as they can—at age fifty with at least twenty years of service. These two looked to be, in the case of John Paul Jeter, sixty, and Wayne Brantner, seventy. I asked about that when they were pointed out to me and was told that they were special cases who were welcome as long as they wished to stay, but that in the case of Jeter that wouldn't be too long because he was dying slowly of cancer.

Both were big, raw-boned men whose speech betrayed little formal education, especially that of the craggy-faced Brantner. Both, it seemed, were part Cherokee Indian and had been born and reared in the Cherokee Strip area of Oklahoma. Years earlier, when Congress first granted FBI agents the right to carry guns, the problem of firearms instruction arose, and the Bureau turned to the

United States Marine Corps. Marine instruction, however, was more suited to trench warfare than to law enforcement gunfights, which usually came about unexpectedly and at a range of under twenty feet. What the FBI needed were instructors who could teach man-to-man gunfighting. It found them in the likes of Wayne Brantner and John Paul Jeter.

Wayne Brantner's earliest memory was of being lifted to his father's shoulders on the wooden sidewalk in a little town in the Cherokee Strip to watch a shootout between a local card player and an itinerant "tin horn" who had allegedly cheated him. God only knew how old Brantner was—Wayne wouldn't say—but in his early days he was a deputy sheriff out west, as had been Jeter. In the course of their work, both Brantner and Jeter were said to have killed "at minimum" half a dozen men in gunfights. Both ended up as peace officers in small Kansas towns, where FBI talent scouts found them. The rules were waived and they were offered positions as Special Agents if they would share their lethal knowledge and experience with the Bureau. Since the pay of an FBI agent was munificent compared to that of a local Kansas peace officer, they joined up without delay and shared their expertise with FBI firearms instructors. Finally they were pastured out to Indianapolis, their reward the right to stay on as long as they wished. Anytime something dangerous was expected to happen, *they* were the ones who would be close to the action; not some hotshot kid from New York City in an undertaker's suit.

Whenever I met Brantner or Jeter in the agent's room or the hallway, I greeted them respectfully and kept about my business; neither showed any disposition to be bothered with, or by, me. That situation changed the first time we went to our monthly firearms training together.

At these monthly training sessions all agents were required to demonstrate current proficiency with FBI weaponry. When it was my turn on the line I was fast and accurate; but nowhere near as fast and accurate as Brantner. He used a big, five-inch barreled Smith & Wesson .357 magnum caliber revolver, loaded with magnum ammunition rather than the mild .38 Special midrange "wad-cutter" ammunition the rest of us used because it cut neat, round holes in the target. He was so smooth he almost seemed lazy, and when his five shots had emptied out of his big-bore revolver, you could cover the hole in the target with a silver dollar. There was only *one* hole, which looked as if it had been gnawed through the target by a large rat. Brantner watched me as I fired but said nothing.

A short while later it was my turn with the pump shotgun. I took the twelve-gauge, loaded it with .00 buck shot, and faced the row of targets. At a signal I jammed the cut-down weapon into my hip and, working the pump action like a machine while pivoting on the balls of my feet, blasted one target after another to pieces in seconds. A moment after I finished I heard a voice behind me say, "You kinda sudden, boy."

The voice that broke that silence after my performance was Wayne Branter's, and *Sudden* became my new nickname.

When practice halted for lunch, Brantner approached me and said: "You wanta learn how to shoot, boy?"

It was the chance of a lifetime. "Yes, SIR!"

"Paul," Brantner said quietly to the nearby John Paul Jeter, "you reckon we could teach this boy somethin' 'bout shootin'?"

"I reckon," said Jeter. And so began my *real* training in gunfighting.

"Boy," said Brantner, "lemme see your gun." I drew my Smith & Wesson K-38 "Combat Masterpiece" revolver, the same one I had worn in the army, opened the action to be sure it was empty, and handed it to him. Brantner examined it. It had a quick-draw ramp front sight, a wide-spur target hammer, and rear sights click-adjustable for windage and elevation.

"That's a nice toy, boy. Good for target shootin'. Only

you gonna be shootin' at men, not targets. Y'need somethin' t'kill with. Here, try this."

Action open, Brantner handed me the big magnum. We went to the firing line. By that time Brantner had taken off his hand-tooled, leather holster and given it to me because mine was too small to hold the massive magnum. With the line cleared, I reached into my pocket for ammunition to load. Brantner stopped me. In his big, open hand lay five long, gleaming cartridges. "Try these," he said.

I chambered the .357 magnum rounds and holstered, then drew and fired. The action was like oiled glass; I had never fired anything so smooth in my life. The weight of the big revolver took up much of the recoil, but it was sharp and the voice of the piece was an authoritative "DOOM!" rather than the flat "Whap!" of a .38 Special. All five rounds were in the K-5 lethal area of the target, but the group wasn't too good, the result of my unfamiliarity with the powerful magnum ammunition and my consequent poor control of the recoil.

Brantner smiled. "Boy, if you gonna *carry* a big bore, you *practice* with a big bore. Keep it. I got another. You can give it back when you get your own." He glanced at my K-38. "Just one thing: you want me to file off that front sight for you?"

"I beg your pardon?"

"The front sight. You want it filed off?"

"No, sir. I mean, why would I want you to do that?"

"Listen to me good, boy: If you ever pull that gun on a man you're not ready to kill, you'll wish I had, 'cause he'll shove it right up your ass!"

I listened and the lesson sank in. "If you never remember another thing I tell you," Brantner continued, "remember this: you wanna be a gunfighter, you're in the business of killin'. No warnin' shots, no shootin' to wound an' all that other Lone Ranger bullshit. Don't draw 'less you're fixin' t'kill a man, or cover'n him ready to kill him if he don't do exactly what you say when you say it. Don't draw 'less you're right in killin'. Then, by Jesus, DO IT! Don't stop shootin' till you know he's dead. Be surprised how many 'dead' men have enough life left in 'em for one more shot. I'm a hard-shell Baptist an' I believe in a merciful Lord. But lemme tell ya somethin' boy; the merciful man and the careless man both end up the same way in this business—dead. You leave mercy to the Lord. After the sumbitch is dead you can pray for his soul if you want to but, damn it, first things first: kill 'im!"

John Paul Jeter taught me, among other things, how to lay two magnum cartridges along the bottom of the right side pocket of my suit coat to weigh down the lower right side of the jacket. That way, after my gun hand had swept the jacket out of the way en route to my gun butt, inertia would keep it up and out of the way while I completed my draw. I had mentioned to Jeter that I attended bullfights when in Mexico. He nodded and said, "Ever take a good look at the bottom of the cape? It's wet and sandy. They do that for weight and control. Same principle."

Jeter gave me one last bit of advice about gunfighting: "When it's over, don't feel too bad. Jus' remember, he was lookin' to do the same thing to you."

In the months to come I wore Wayne Brantner's big magnum on my side. At his direction I had the belt loop at the right hip on every pair of trousers I owned moved so that the rear of the loop ran exactly along the seam of the waistband. "That way," said Brantner, "the holster can't ride forward when y'draw, an' the butt of that gun will always be in *exactly* the same place when y'reach for it. We're talkin' about shavin' hundredths of a second off, boy; ever' little bit counts."

On Brantner's advice I rejected holsters approved by the FBI having a leather "lip" that rode over the hammer spur to protect one's suitcoat from having a hole worn in it. I had a piece of heavy sailcloth sewn into the lining instead. "Which would you rather have, boy—a hole in your coat or a hole in your belly?"

97

On my twenty-eighth birthday the present Frances gave me was unusually heavy, and I looked at her questioningly as I weighed it in my hand.

"You can give Mr. Brantner back his gun now," she said. I unwrapped her gift, opened the blue box, and found the finest .357 magnum revolver made. I had mentioned to Fran that I was uncomfortable sitting in a car wearing a five-inch barreled gun because the barrel protruded down into the seat and forced the gun up too high. The big framed Smith that was my present had a three-and-a-half-inch barrel. The top strap had been crosshatched by hand by a skilled craftsman to prevent reflection along the top of the barrel, which would interfere with sighting. The grip was of checkered walnut and the finish blued steel with the brightness and perfection of a mirror. It was, simply, the best handgun in the world.

"Happy birthday, darling!" said Frances, her eyes glowing with pleasure. "It was the best life insurance policy I could buy." She was right.

The next day John Paul Jeter checked the action and pronounced it good. "It'll take fifteen hundred rounds through her before she's really broken in. Next time you're at the Bureau, take it in to the gunsmith. He's the best in the world at smoothin' out an action. Tell him I sent you and to do the same thing for you he did for me."

Brantner told me which holster to buy. I sent away to Texas for it. When it arrived, he forbade me to use it as it was. Instead, under his instruction, I coated the revolver with petroleum jelly and wrapped it in one layer of Saran Wrap. Immersing the hard leather holster in warm water until it became soft, I forced the wrapped magnum into it and then carefully shaped the damp leather to the exact contours of the gun. That done, I set it aside for a week. The holster dried, tightening into a glove fit for the new magnum.

Brantner tested the results of my work.

"Watch," he said and held the gun, muzzle down, by the grip. The holster stayed on. "Now watch this," he said. The old gunfighter brought up his other hand and, with one finger, touched the holster. It fell away from the gun. Brantner grinned. "Now you're ready, boy!"

From that day forward I wore Fran's "insurance policy" wherever I went. With me also went every secret of the gunfighter's trade taught me by Brantner and Jeter, constant, uncounted hours of practice, and, still in my twenties, the lightning reflexes of youth. I was armed, too, with something even more important.

"No one," John Paul Jeter had said, "can ever say he's the best there is; no 'less he's fought an' beat ever' man with a gun in the world, an' you couldn't do that in one lifetime. So remember: it's all up for grabs every time you draw." He was warning me against the grave danger of overconfidence.

As Brantner had put it, "You get in a fight situation an' you don't feel that ol' adrenalin pump, you in big trouble, boy."

With Fran's return to health, I was now free to leave the city of Indianapolis during the day, so I was assigned to a three-county territory to the south for which I became the agent primarily responsible. As a "road trip" agent I was assigned a car from the FBI garage, but as low man on the totem pole I drew one of the oldest. Most of the FBI cars in those days were equipped for high speed operation—the famed Ford "interceptor" models. They had a beefed-up transmission; tight, firm, road-holding suspension; premium tires and an engine with special camshaft and pistons that drank in fuel and air through great, multibarreled carburetors, generating unbelievable torque and horsepower, the whole emptying out in a roar behind from exhaust pipes as big around as your wrist.

The car I drew was a "Hoover Special," so called because J. Edgar Hoover, to impress Congress with the frugality of the FBI, kept cars a year longer than anyone else would. Five or six years added up to an awful lot of wear and, despite the best efforts of the mechanics, considerable danger. My ancient interceptor was a screamer, but with an unhappy tendency of the accelerator to stick rather than return to position after I lifted my foot.

Once, in southern Indiana, I spotted a tornado approaching. Deciding that my best course was to outrun it, I floored the throttle. The black Ford leaped ahead with a deep-throated roar and the funnel cloud passed over the road just behind me, tearing a trench through the foliage on either side. I let my breath out since, quite unconsciously, I had been holding it for the sixty seconds I raced the whirlwind; then I congratulated myself mentally for a well-calculated risk. My self-congratulation was premature; as I let up on the gas, the accelerator stayed against the floorboard.

I glanced at the speedometer—94 mph and climbing fast. The road was a narrow, high-crowned blacktop that followed farm section lines; that meant that at any moment it would make a perfect 90-degree turn to the left or right. Cursing Hoover, I reached down to the floorboard for the errant accelerator while trying to look over the dashboard and steer with one hand. I saw barbed wire looming in the distance and the needle of the speedometer against the peg at 120 mph, so I snapped off the ignition instead and began pumping the brakes. The car came to a stop about eight feet from a 90-degree turn, facing a barbed wire fence protecting a field of corn that a small sign said was grown from De Kalb brand seed. Having come within seconds of prematurely harvesting that corn, the fence, the sign and all, I yanked up the accelerator angrily and headed back—slowly—to Indianapolis, where I told them the damn car should be indicted for attempted murder of a federal agent.

Whenever a "road trip" agent had an investigation that required two men, he coordinated with the agent in an adjacent territory. My neighbor was a young, good-looking, powerfully built redhead named Buck Kessler. One day I had a lead that a fugitive might appear at a bar in a rundown neighborhood of Shelbyville. That was in my territory, but the assignment called for two agents. Kessler, who had been working southern Indiana for some time, suggested that if we wanted to stake the place out, we would have to disregard Hoover's concept of how an agent should dress and don clothing appropriate to good ol' boy farmhands. Kessler could pull that off; I couldn't. I still had too many New York mannerisms and hadn't spent enough time out in the sun. I compromised by wearing a lightweight suit and a tie that had been a gift I thought loud enough for southern Indiana. That was a mistake.

Buck and I took a table in the rear of the saloon and violated Bureau rules by ordering a beer; it would have been hard to be inconspicuous ordering milk. We waited and waited and nothing happened. Hunger set in and Buck volunteered to go first for a bite to eat. I stayed at the table. It was then that I learned just how inappropriate my clothing was: a large, dirty man of about thirty, wearing a sweated-through T-shirt, detached himself from a nearby table full of similar friends, came over to mine, and, without saying a word, sat down opposite me.

He leered for a moment, then said, "Me an' the boys"— nodding toward his tablemates—"know what you are."

Damn! I thought, how could he know? I may not have looked like a farmhand, but I sure didn't look like an FBI agent; nor had I been operating in that territory long enough to be recognized.

Beer oozing from every pore, my uninvited guest spoke again. "We know what you are, an' you're gonna give us *all* some. Git your punk ass out inta that alley." He nodded at the rear door. Christ! I thought, the dumb bastards have taken me for a homo and it's torment-a-faggot time in Shelbyville. I was furious, not because I was particularly sensitive to the plight of a homosexual in such a situation, but because I was embarrassed at being taken for one and realized that it was my own fault; I should have listened to Kessler. My anger now focused on the cretin sitting across from me and it fathered a very uncharitable plan.

I affected a frightened but excited simper. "Gee," I

101

said, "I don't know about *all* of you. How about just you? Take a look under the table; I've got something there you'll really like!"

"Put it back in. I know what you've got. Git out in the alley."

"But you really don't know; an' you know what'll happen if I get up without putting it back. Please. Just take a look."

The big side of beef decided to humor me. Anything, I suppose, to get me out in the alley away from any help. He pushed back his seat, leaned down, raised the tablecloth, then banged his head against the tabletop as he found himself staring into the muzzle of a .357 magnum. Then I did a very dangerous thing: slowly and deliberately I cocked the big Smith & Wesson.

"Oh, Jesus!" came the snivel, muffled from under the table.

"All right, sit up!" I commanded. He obeyed, the color drained from his face. I couldn't resist one more jab. Lowering the hammer of the revolver back down slowly with my thumb to prevent an accident, I held my arm motionless, then faked the beginning of a sneeze, taking deep breaths and holding a finger of my left hand under my nose. My would-be terrorizer almost passed out. When Kessler came back in, it was clear from his expression that he was wondering what was going on. I gave him a look and stood up, my napkin covering the magnum, saying:

"Okay, Billy Joe or whatever the fuck your name is, ease over there and tell your friends to follow you out to the alley. Now."

The sweaty T-shirt went over to his friends, whispered animatedly, nodding toward me, and they all rose and went out to the alley. Buck and I right behind them. Outside, Buck followed my lead. We put the lot of them up against the wall, searched them roughly, got names and addresses from driver's licenses, and then, to cover ourselves, displayed pictures of the fugitive. When it was over, I told stupid that if I ever saw him again I'd arrest

102

him as a fugitive from the board of health and I told them all to clear out. They ran. Buck and I decided that the stakeout was blown. We returned home and wrote it up as a negative, reporting the "interview" of the good ol' boys straight—something that was hard to do because we kept breaking into laughter every time we thought about it.

Once I was given a lead to interview someone outside a small town. I found the town to be little more than a filling station and a feed store out on a country road. In my best newly acquired Hoosier accent I said "Howdy" to a group of men loitering on the loading dock of the feed store. They had heard the telltale sucking sounds of the intake on the big interceptor playing counterpoint to the low rumble of the exhaust and, as this high-performance music was coming from what appeared to be a decrepit Ford sedan, eyed me suspiciously.

I displayed my credentials to the oldest man there, who appeared to be the leader, and asked:

"Can you tell me where I can find Fred Hammerly?"

"Yup."

"How would I go about doing that?"

"Stay on this road 'bout three miles till it crosses the crick." As it was obvious that the directions were going to be involved, I whipped out my pen and pad and began to take them down. "Jes past the crick, a section road goes off t' the right. Take that two miles more, give or take, till ya come to a Baptist church. Fred's right t'other side. Whatcha want him for?"

"Just to talk to. No problem."

"Reckon you're gonna have some trouble doin' that."

"Why?"

" 'Cause where he's at is the Baptist cemetery, that's why. Ol' Fred's been dead four years now, give or take."

I expected the group to hoot with laughter, but no one did. They were all quite serious, seeing no humor in the situation. I thanked him and, following the directions, found a small cemetery and located the grave. I could now report him dead in good conscience. Had the man

103

been a fugitive, the Bureau might well have had the body exhumed for identification. The FBI was nothing if not thorough.

Another lead brought me to the home of an elderly widow to inquire about the "character, loyalty, and associations" of someone "being considered for a position of trust and confidence with the United States government which will give him access to classified information," as we were trained to put it and as experience enabled us finally to be able to say in one breath. The little old lady invited me in with the admonition, "Don't mind Oscar."

I looked around the tiny living room and, seeing no one else, asked, "Oscar?"

"He's such a love, but very shy. All I have left, now my husband's gone."

Since I wasn't really interested in Oscar, whoever he was, I started the interview. It was what the FBI calls a "neighborhood" interview, but out there, the old woman was it. If I got nothing from her, I struck out.

I had barely spoken the first few sentences when there was a flash of color to my right and a parakeet landed on my shoulder.

"Oh, my! He likes you! You must be a very nice young man for Oscar to trust you so. Well, if *he* does, *I* certainly should. You just ask me anything you want to know, young man."

At which point the parakeet hopped up on top of my head, I conducted the remainder of the interview quickly as I could, all the while hoping Oscar had sufficient respect for J. Edgar Hoover and the FBI to be able to keep control of his bowels. Oscar proved to be a good citizen, and I escaped unscathed with my information.

Apparently my performance as a "road trip" agent was satisfactory, because I was transferred to the resident agency at Gary, Indiana. This was a vote of confidence; although I was still a "first office" agent I was being sent to live and work a long distance away from "headquarters city," where supervision would be minimal. In a resident agency there was a premium on an agent's "initiative and resourcefulness." Then there was Gary itself: the great steel city of the infamous Lake County. by reputation a hotbed of vice, corruption, organized crime, racial discord, and a target of Soviet bloc espionage. I could hardly wait to get there.

IX

As Frances and I drove north toward Lake County, Indiana, in the spring of 1958, the lush, green flatlands seemed to roll on endlessly into a bright blue sky. From that sky came the first hint of change, a dirty smudge on the horizon, which seemed to grow until, at the outskirts of Gary, it dominated the skyline, then developed into a sooty pall that hung over everything.

Motoring on the main street, I glanced up and stared at something that was, to me, remarkable: an outdoor advertising sign in which the persons shown happily boosting the product were *black*. I had never before seen a black depicted in advertising. Clearly, Gary was going to be something new and different.

As we drove on, the origin of the smoke pall became evident. The main street ended at the gates of U.S. Steel's gigantic Gary Works, its tall stacks disgorging dense smoke from open-hearth furnaces that symbolized the raw economic power of America in the Eisenhower era.

Fran and I spent a few days in a local hotel just a gasp away from the big mill until I found affordable quarters sufficient for our imminent family—a small, square-box one-story house set on a concrete slab in a steelworkers' neighborhood in East Gary that was, on a good day, with the wind right, a good four gasps from the mill. From a small living room an arch led to a combination kitchen and utility room. Off an alcove were two bedrooms, a bathroom, and a closet holding a heating system that featured a blower with a bass note from a loose fan belt and an atonal treble from a bearing that had been begging for years for a drop of oil. Only the bathroom had a conventional door, a gesture toward bedroom privacy being made by stiff folding cloth curtains. We bought a double bed from the widowed mother-in-law of another agent, a set of wooden kitchen table and chairs, one upholstered chair, and a wooden rocker. Dressmaking material laid over cardboard cartons became our end tables, and our biggest investment was a Singer sewing machine so Fran could make herself some clothing and a few things for the baby. Although we had to be careful to cover the garbage cans securely against rats, there were none inside the little house and we were, all in all, content.

The odorous pall of the steel mills notwithstanding, I loved Gary. The six other agents were a cross section of America: fine, competent, good-natured men led by a senior resident agent (SRA), Lewis Fain, a natural leader. As SRA he not only had administrative responsibility for the agency, he insisted upon carrying the largest case load, split between criminal and security matters. Fain was my height but far more muscular, with wrists and forearms so thick they reminded me of Popeye. His sparse red hair was still cropped in the crew cut he wore fighting as an infantryman in the great World War II island battles of the Pacific theater, and his engaging grin immediately took one's mind off his face, which looked as if it had lost the war. I loved the guy from the moment I shook his hand.

In 1958 Gary resembled Mayor Daley's Chicago; it was a city that "worked." Every ethnic group had a piece of the action, public officials made a fortune from graft, and organized crime flourished on prostitution and gambling. The only serious problem was criminal violence.

The money, legal and illegal, in Gary attracted it. Justice tended to be frontier style and swift, especially if an "out-of-towner" was involved. God help the out-of-town stickup man who came to Gary to pull a job. His body

106

would be left for a while on the street corner as an example. Those who left him there would be whoever got to him first: local hoods or the police. Street gunfire was a hazard to innocent civilians—when Frances was narrowly missed in a gunfight outside J. C. Penney's, I gave her a semiautomatic Colt pistol to carry and instructed her well in its use—but the system made things easy for us in the FBI.

Once we got word that a woman who had kidnapped a child in Chicago was believed to be in Gary. We handled it by picking up the phone and calling the police. Within minutes they put out the word: an out-of-town broad had brought a kidnapped kid into town and was causing federal heat. Her whereabouts and that of the child were to be made known to the FBI within eight hours or all the gambling places and whorehouses would be shut down until she was found. Well before the deadline we got a call telling us in exactly what bar and on what stool the suspect was drinking, and that the baby was on the floor in the ladies' room.

When a Soviet agent was coming into town, he would be given whatever room in the hotel we wanted him to have and, when he stepped out, there was no question of our access. We played handball with the police every noon at the YMCA; it was generally a close affiliation. Most of the activities of local criminals did not constitute a federal offense, and they were careful to avoid those that did. The occasional bank robbery or kidnapping was invariably committed by out-of-towners.

We did have one problem. We found that a bookie joint was being maintained in the office of the garage where Bureau automobiles were housed under contract. We explained that this was indiscreet and that discovery could embarrass us. The police saw to it that the operation was moved immediately.

One crime that *was* against federal law was the one that had brought the FBI into the Dillinger case years before—interstate transportation of a stolen motor vehicle. We weren't far from the Illinois line, so we got a lot of those cases. Some of them were big. Because of the number of junkyards in Lake County, the Chicago-based "Pronger gang" came in to buy the remains of totally demolished late-model automobiles. With the wreck they got a valid Indiana title and the only thing they bothered to remove from the yard was the serial number plate, usually spot-welded to the cowl. From there it was easy to steal a matching car, switch the serial number plates, and sell it off at an auto auction.

I was assigned the Pronger case. It took a lot of time and some help from the local representative of the National Automobile Theft Bureau, but I broke it. I did it by working all hours of the day and night and never hesitating to do whatever was necessary, including intimidating used car dealers so that I could cut through the floorboards of their cars to find secret serial numbers on the frames. When I had identified the men I wanted and they became fugitives—even if only from me because I wanted to talk to them—I broke into many an empty house or apartment to search for clues to where they were or what they were doing. That tactic was a simple extrapolation from FBI procedure in security cases.

In security cases the "black bag job"—so called after the valise in which entry tools had been carried in the early days of the program, during the Roosevelt administration—could range over a wide variety of cases. It could be a complex surreptitious entry into an embassy (of friend or foe) in Washington (after surveillance determined that all personnel were off the premises) so experts could open the safe in a manner not detectable and remove for copying onetime cipher pads and similar materials—or it could be what I would do in a criminal case. The former operations were done only after Bureau headquarters had evaluated the feasibility study and given the go-ahead. Most were done for the National Security Agency (the CIA provided the same service overseas) and were deadly serious. Were an embassy employee to return before schedule and there was danger that he would arrive before the agents could get out, he would be mugged on the street by strong-arm men—often those assigned to the Bureau's baseball team—and our government would apologize to his government for the inability of the Metropolitan Police Department to control street crime in the nation's capital.

There were similar operations in the field that were supposed to be undertaken only after the Bureau had weighed the matter and decided. Often, however, an opportunity would arise in which there wasn't time to go through all that red tape. For those situations there was a code phrase. If the submission of the plan for Bureau approval contained the words *security guaranteed,* it meant we did it last night and got away clean—approve it so we can send you the results officially.

Finally there was the "S.I."—the Security Index. This was a list of those individuals, citizens or alien, whom the FBI believed dangerous to have at large in the event of a war or major confrontation with the Soviet Union. There was, of course, an extensive file on each. There was also a file card bearing the person's name, any known aliases, his or her photograph, home address, work address, and occupation. The card was maintained in addition to the file because when the Bureau gave the signal to implement the S.I., the cards would be distributed immediately to FBI agents nationwide (they were maintained in every field office), and agents would fan out all over the United States to arrest the persons listed. They would then be sent to concentration camps until the danger was deemed to have passed, much as U.S. citizens of Japanese ancestry were interned during World War II. It was a matter of high priority to keep the information on the S.I. cards current. Addresses and occupations had to be verified every thirty days. Sometimes the only (or easiest) way to do that was to break into a place, which was done informally.

The first time I saw the security file on novelist Nelson Algren (*The Man with the Golden Arm, A Walk on the Wild Side*), I thought someone was kidding, but it turned out to be another example of the consequence of making FBI agents out of Bureau clerks. For a time Algren maintained a small house near the southern shore of Lake Michigan that was within the territory of the Gary resident agency. Also living there for a time was the author and feminist pioneer Simone de Beauvoir (*The Second Sex*), and both their names were on the mailbox. The agent to whom the Algren case was assigned had risen from Bureau clerk and he was not well read. Thus the Algren file came to be captioned:

NELSON ALGREN, with alias, SIMONE DE BEAUVOIR

When I pointed out that Simone de Beauvoir was neither an alias nor *nom de plume* of Nelson Algren, the agent to whom the case was assigned became very upset. He decided finally not to advise the Bureau (also staffed heavily with former clerks who didn't catch it either) on the ground that it was best to "let sleeping dogs lie." Last I heard, so far as the FBI was concerned, Simone de Beauvoir was just ol' Nelson Algren in drag.

In November 1958 Frances bore our first child, a daughter we named Alexandra after my mother's family. From the beginning we've called her Sandy. I gained investigative experience with the Pronger case, eventually receiving a letter of commendation from J. Edgar Hoover for my work. The bizarre *dénouement*, however, nearly earned me a letter of censure.

One of the members of the Pronger ring that I had succeeded in convicting had been released on bond pending presentence investigation by the probation officer, a not unusual practice. I went to court on sentencing day so I could tell the Bureau the result and close the case. To no one's surprise the sentence was mild, something on the order of two years. What no one but the defendant knew at the time was that he was a severe claustrophobe; he couldn't do time. He wouldn't, either, because he came into court that day prepared, something else only he knew.

As soon as sentence was pronounced, I jotted it down and left the courtroom to go to the clerk's office to check records in an unrelated matter. As I left the clerk's office, I met a hysterical woman running down the hall, pointing behind her and shouting, "They've killed themselves!"

I sought out the source of the commotion and came upon a shaken United States marshal. He said that as he was taking my defendant to the detention cage, they passed a men's room and the man asked if he could use it. Not stopping to hear the marshal's answer, he stepped into the bathroom, and before the marshal could react, he heard a shot.

"Blew his brains out," said the marshal, still in a state of shock. "He's in there, on the floor. I sent for the firemen to pick him up."

An incident like that was bound to get into the press and might prompt an inquiry to Bureau headquarters in Washington. The Bureau did not like to hear developments in FBI cases first from the press, so I went to a phone and called in a teletype for the Indianapolis field office to send to Washington advising of the sentence, the death of the defendant, and the circumstances. That done I thought that for the benefit of my follow-up report I should be able to confirm the identity of the dead defendant personally and returned to the men's room. I nodded to the marshal still on guard outside and entered. It was my man on the floor, all right, only he wasn't dead.

Despite the fact that his blood and brains were dripping off the ceiling onto my clothing and there was a .38 caliber hole in the side of his head and a hole the size of a half dollar in the top of his skull, the man was jerking upward, as if trying to get up off the floor. As I went out to inform the marshal, the firemen arrived, strapped the wounded man to a stretcher, and carried him off to the hospital.

I had, I realized, a problem. I had sent the Bureau wrong information. I called the office and learned that my teletype had, with typical FBI efficiency, already been sent. Embarrassed, I dictated another with the news that the defendant was still alive and being treated in the hospital.

I promised to keep the Bureau informed of his condition.

In keeping with that promise, after what I had deemed with my *Reader's Digest* knowledge of medicine was more than enough time for the man to die, I called the hospital, got the desk, and was told that the man was dead. Having learned absolutely nothing from my first mistake, I proceeded to make another and wired the Bureau that the man was dead. Then, *thinking* I had learned something and deciding to make up for the snafu with a really detailed final report, I called the hospital again, asked for intensive care and, identifying myself, asked the supervising nurse for he official cause of death. With scathing sarcasm she replied that the man was still alive and they were doing all they could to save him and she hoped that, if successful, it wouldn't be *too* inconvenient for the FBI. I mumbled an apology and hung up.

Now I *really* had a problem. One more teletype to the Bureau saying he was alive would sound like the Marx Brothers in *A Day at the FBI*. I forced myself to take stock. *No* one, I reasoned, could live much longer with that massive head wound. I took the calculated risk that he wouldn't make it and sent nothing further to the Bureau. I waited and then called intensive care again. Sobbing and furious the nurse confirmed death. *This* time I had learned my lesson, and I didn't send in my final report until I had viewed the body myself. And that's how I learned about the perils of hearsay.

It was at Gary that the Bureau's programming of me to shoot or hold fire automatically first paid off. Lew Fain had a lead to interview the madam of a whorehouse believed patronized by a fugitive. Bureau rules required two agents for the assignment because of the tendency of brothel personnel to file false charges of impropriety against agents trying to interrogate them. This was their method of discouraging agents from coming to the door, which was bad for business.

We parked three houses away in an alley behind the place, walked around the block to approach from the front, and, at the door, were refused both entry and information. Fain noticed the many cars parked along the driveway leading to a garage in the rear and decided we should record the license numbers on the off chance one of the cars might be registered to the fugitive. If it was, we might be able to get a search warrant. Fain was around the side of the garage out of sight when I suddenly heard him shout, "Liddy! Look out for the dog!" A German shepherd guard had been posted on a long chain fastened to the rear porch where he could cover half the yard. He had attacked Fain as soon as Lew stepped into the yard and, when Lew attempted to defend himself with a chop to the dog's neck, bit him right through the palm.

Fain's warning cry was too late. The dog turned from him and had me by the hamstring before I knew what had happened. I rolled in the opposite direction, drawing as I did, intending to shoot as I completed the turn. My finger was on the trigger and tightening as I swung around but, as the muzzle of the .357 came to bear, it was not upon the head of the dog but of its master. Hearing the commotion he had bolted out the rear door, seen that I was about to shoot his beloved dog, and dived on top of it in an attempt to save its life. My back was turned in that moment, so I didn't see him until my gun was at his head, the trigger almost all the way back and the hammer about to fall.

When my brain registered this new data, my trigger finger froze automatically, saving the man's life. I can take no credit for it. There was no time to think and take a decision. What saved that man was the Bureau's programming. The dog lived too. We had him examined for rabies and, when it was clear he was not infected, gave him back. It was painful having a stick tipped with nitric-acid-soaked cotton run up inside those deep tooth holes in my leg, but I had nothing against the dog; after all, he'd been programmed too.

The two-story office building that housed the Gary resident agency also was home to several other government agencies, and we got to know some of the people who

113

manned them. I saw a Secret Service man I knew walking down the hallway behind a lean, intense young man in a shabby raincoat who moved rapidly, head down, hands in his pockets, seemingly oblivious to everyone and everything around him. The Secret Service agent appeared to have an attitude of deference to the young man in the raincoat so I was curious and asked him about it.

"That was Bobby Kennedy," came the reply. Then I remembered we had a communication advising us that Bobby Kennedy was coming to Gary to investigate corruption, and we were instructed in no uncertain terms *not* to cooperate with him. According to the Secret Service agent, his orders were just the opposite; they were to do all they could to assist.

"What's he like?" I asked.

The Secret Service man shook his head wearily. "You guys are lucky," he said, "not havin' to have anything to do with him. He's runnin' our ass off."

He was indeed. Robert Kennedy wrote a book including his experience in Gary called *The Enemy Within.* Not long after he finished his work there, the Gary I knew was gone. Half the public officials had been convicted, and the old way of life—in which the victimless crimes of gambling and prostitution were tolerated and controlled and numerous ethnic groups coexisted, each with a slice of the pie—had been destroyed. Whether the current state of affairs in Gary is an improvement, I'll leave it to the judgment of those who live there today.

In March of 1960 our second daughter, Grace, was born; we were happy that Grace was a healthy child, but I began to be concerned that I did not yet have a son.

Then orders came sending me back to Washington for two weeks "in-service" training at the FBI Academy. All agents received it every few years to bring them up to date on Bureau policy and the latest investigative techniques, and to share their own field experiences with their brother agents for the good of all.

In Washington I was discreetly sounded out about

whether I was interested in "administrative advancement." I said I was, and it was suggested that I ask for an interview with Hoover since that was a *sine qua non* for such a career goal. I did it immediately.

The ritual was elaborate. I was told to present myself at the "telephone room," a small communications center serving the Hoover complex, fifteen minutes before the time of my appointment. I did so and was then told to wait in the Director's reception room, into which the "telephone room" opened. There I looked over the FBI trophies on display, as well as the wall tablet listing the names of those agents killed in the line of duty.

At precisely one minute before the time of my appointment, Hoover's black majordomo, known throughout the Bureau as Sam, appeared at an inner door and said, "Mr. Liddy." I rose and he led me down a long hall past the closed office doors of the empire of Helen Gandy, Hoover's secretary. As Sam opened a final door and stood aside, he revealed Hoover's large ceremonial office, the only one in which he received visitors. He did his work in a smaller office to the rear closed to the public.

As I entered, Hoover was standing to the left rear of the bare ceremonial desk, waiting for me. He and the desk appeared to be atop an almost imperceptible elevation, the gentle slope of which was concealed by the carpeting. I strode forward and thrust out my hand:

"Mr. Hoover, I'm George Liddy." (I had decided against using "G. Gordon" in the FBI as I abhorred the thought that I might be suspected of a fawning emulation of "J. Edgar.") I grasped Hoover's hand in the viselike grip I knew he expected of a Special Agent and got a viselike grip in return.

"Good to see you, Mr. Liddy. Sit down."

Still holding onto my hand, Hoover steered me to a thickly upholstered, soft-cushioned chair set low and to the left of his desk. The combination of low chair and soft cushion guaranteed that anyone sitting in it would be looking up at the man seated behind the immaculate desk.

I thanked Mr. Hoover for receiving me; told him immediately, as I had been instructed was advisable, that I had no problems I wished to discuss with him; then told him that when, in his judgment, the time came, I would welcome the opportunity to serve the Bureau in an administrative position.

Hoover responded that he was pleased to learn that I had no problems and that I sought administrative advancement. I had expected a homily on the subject, but to my astonishment he launched into a denunciation of Eleanor Roosevelt. During her husband's administration, he said, she had been a most dangerous enemy of the Bureau. Were it not for Hoover's great personal friendship and rapport with Franklin Roosevelt, he said, Eleanor might well have succeeded in interfering with the Bureau's ability to contain the communist menace in the United States. According to Hoover, whenever he found that Eleanor had thrown a roadblock into the path of the FBI, he had only to speak to her husband to have it removed immediately.

I have not the slightest idea why Hoover chose to speak to me about Eleanor Roosevelt, but he took up a great deal of the nearly forty-five minutes he spent with me on that subject. He then spoke to me of the importance of the Bureau and its work to the people of the United States, and he did so in a way that I found particularly inspiring. The man had personal force. His was a dynamic personality, and he was at the peak of his powers. When he made the little sideways movement of his body that I had been briefed to expect as a signal that the interview was over, I shot to my feet, crunched his hand once more, and walked out with my batteries at full charge. Despite my puzzlement over the irrelevant monologue on Eleanor Roosevelt, I don't believe I could have been more impressed had I been a parish priest after a private audience with the Pope.

The first, indeed virtually the only, question asked of me by the older men in my in-service class when I returned was, "How much time did he give you?" When I replied that I had been with Hoover about forty-five minutes, I was looked upon with awe and there were joking references to my probably being made a Special Agent in Charge by morning. When one older man asked me sarcastically what advice I had for anyone else going in to "meet the man," I put on my most earnest look and said: "First chance you get, try to slip in how much you've always admired Eleanor Roosevelt."

Back at Gary, I received news that my Uncle Ray had retired from the Bureau after twenty-five years, to become chairman of the Nevada State Gaming Commission. A package for me arrived from the Bureau. In it was a note that at Hoover's instruction I was to turn in my badge; in its place I was to use the one enclosed. At my uncle's request, Hoover had sent me Ray's badge, number 19; one of the earliest issued in the FBI. I carried it as proudly as any knight ever carried the shield of his father into battle. Indeed, the analogy was carried even further when Ray sent me the snub-nosed Colt .38 special he had carried in the wars of the gangster era.

The news of my having received Ray's badge spread among the agents of the Indianapolis office. Invariably they spoke of what a great agent and leader my uncle had been. It was then that I first noticed consciously the phenomenon that illustrated perfectly how close and familial the relationship of FBI agents was. Although my uncle was still very much alive, now that he was no longer on active duty they spoke of him, as of all former agents, in the past tense, as if dead.

Soon after this I received orders transferring me to the Denver field office. Once again I was told I had been marked for favor because the Denver office was one of the most desired assignments in the FBI. So in July of 1960, with Sandy and Grace in a portable crib erected over the rear seat and with Fran up front, I pointed the snout of our new black Studebaker Hawk west across the plains toward the Rocky Mountains. For me it was a wonderful trip as I engaged the overdrive, watched the rpm drop, then climb again while I blew away everying on the open highway west. It wasn't much fun for Fran, though. She was pregnant again.

X

We took U.S. 30 all the way, slicing through Illinois and Iowa, then diving down to follow the Platte River through Nebraska until it forked south, staying with it into Colorado via Fort Morgan. Even in July the peaks of the Rocky Mountains wore snowcaps that bounced the morning sun back at us when they popped over the horizon. As we changed diapers by the side of the road, one glance upward explained as words never could why this was called Big Sky country. We loved it.

The office quickly found us a small white frame house in south Denver overlooking the front range of the Rockies. Except for mice, which kept startling Fran by running up through the burners of the gas stove and which I dispatched promptly with traps baited with peanut butter, the place was perfect, and Fran exclaimed at how quickly the sheets would dry when hung out in the crisp mountain air.

In 1960 Denver had under way its precedent-setting urban renewal program, and the results were already apparent in a stunning downtown. There were only two major industries then—Coors Brewing to the north and Coors Porcelain (missile nose cones) to the south. Not a particle of pollution marred the mile-high air. The FBI field office, as was the custom in those days, was in the old post office building and its agents formed one of the best teams in the Bureau. One was a man who, having been shot with a 9-mm slug that embedded so close to his spine it was never removed, blew the man who put it there out of a phone booth with all six rounds from a .357 magnum. I relate to people like that.

I did not relate well to the Special Agent in Charge,

Scott Werner. He was a big, handsome man with a full head of distinguished snow-white hair and matching mustache, one of the few men in Hoover's FBI permitted to wear one, probably because he looked so well in it one would take him for a central casting senator rather than an FBI official. Werner was a good administrator, but he was a worrier about petty things. He held a meeting of all the agents every Tuesday morning at which he would harangue us, wasting our time with these concerns.

Because we shared the building with a number of other agencies, we were allotted only three parking spaces. Werner used one of the spaces to park his Bureau car, usually driven for him by an agent.

Tuesday after Tuesday we had to listen to complaining about "outsiders" (read non-FBI) parking in Werner's space. He wanted it stopped, *insisted* that it be stopped. That was, of course, a job for GSA building guards or the local police, not FBI agents, and certainly not agents as dedicated to the serious work of the Bureau as I, a recent recipient of a letter of commendation from, and interview with, J. Edgar Hoover, considered myself to be. One day Werner went too far. He was having a fit over his parking space; we were to see to it that it was never occupied illegally again.

"I don't care what you have to do," Werner raged, "let the air out of their tires—anything—just keep them out of my parking space!"

That did it. The same day, as I was returning to the office, a big, black Cadillac limousine slid into Werner's parking space while his car was out. The chauffeur and his passenger left. I was in the process of letting the air out of the second tire when the returning passenger stormed up to me: "Just who are you and what the hell do you think you're doing?"

"I'm Special Agent Liddy of the FBI and I'm letting the air out of your tires." I said, continuing to do so.

"I don't believe this!"

"Believe it." I said as the second tire went completely flat.

"I demand to see your superior immediately!"

"Yes, sir," I said, getting back to my feet, "if you'll just follow me, I'd be delighted to take you right to him."

I conducted the man to Werner's outer office and said to his secretary, "This is Mr. Whittlesee. He'd like to speak to Mr. Werner immediately."

"I see. Does he have an appointment?"

"No, but I think Mr. Werner should see him anyway."

"What is the nature of his business?" she said, picking up the phone and pressing the intercom button.

"At Mr. Werner's orders, I have just let the air out of his tires. He's very unhappy."

"Oh," she said. Then, doing a double-take, "OH!" she jumped up and went into Werner's office and, a few moments later, ushered us in.

"Mr. Werner," I said, "This is Mr. Whittlesee. He parked his car in your space and, as you instructed, I let the air out of his tires."

Although the bright red color of Werner's face betrayed near apoplexy, he maintained his composure: "I want to apologize, sir, for the actions of my agent. There has been a misunderstanding of instructions. It won't happen again. I hope, however, you can understand our concern. Those parking spaces are reserved for FBI use in case of emergency."

"Well," the man fumed, "why didn't he just say something? I'd have moved the car. But letting the air . . ."

"Quite right," interrupted Werner, rising to usher him out. "I'll have clearer signs and markings put up right away so there'll be no further misunderstandings. Mr. Liddy . . ."

"Yes, sir."

"Please wait for a minute after Mr. Whittlesee leaves. I want to speak to you."

"Yes, sir." Mr. Whittlesee left to get his tires inflated. Werner sat back down. I remained standing to the side of his desk.

"Liddy," said Werner, covering his face with his hands and massaging his forehead with his fingertips, "Liddy . . . Oh, just get the hell out of here!"

I did. For the rest of my stay in Denver, Scott Werner was careful what he said at those Tuesday morning conferences. Years later I was told that after I left he slipped back into the old ways, but with one critical difference: after issuing one of those orders to the assembled agents he would pause to go on to something else, then suddenly shake his finger at them and shout, "That's a Liddy! That's a Liddy!" The men would roar with laughter while mystified newcomers would ask, "What's he talking about?"

"For God's sake," the old-timers would tell them, "just don't obey that order." Then they'd grin and tell them the story.

Scott Werner got his revenge during the search for the body of kidnap victim Adolph Coors III. The Coors kidnapping rocked Denver; that family was the richest and most influential in the state of Colorado. As soon as the crime was reported. the FBI's kidnap plan was activated. Previously prepared messages were fed into the teletype machine sending orders to the Western kidnap squad— designated agents in field offices all over the West—and they dropped everything to board the first available plane for Denver.

As they arrived, a team of construction workers was already at work in the Denver office, cutting it in two, putting in new offices, wiring, and equipment. Because a kidnap investigation is so large, it can tie up an entire field office at the expense of all other investigations. Within days a second field office was created and manned, complete with imported agents and clerical personnel to work exclusively on the Coors case. Some Denver agents were assigned to the regular work of the Denver office until hunters located some clothing and a penknife bearing the initials "A.C. III" on a dump where poachers had for years disposed of unwanted carcasses and an end-of-the-world religious sect dumped its garbage while awaiting periodically an Armageddon that refused to abide by their oft revised timetable.

When the Coors family identified the found objects as belonging to the missing victim, the FBI was faced with a massive task. Because the area where the items were found was visited regularly by bears, skunks, and other carnivorous scavengers, the bones of discarded carcasses and other garbage had been distributed over a quarter-mile area. Teams of agents would have to mark it off, then collect and label hundreds of bones so that pathologists could identify any that were human to determine whether they were those of the victim.

In the meantime someone would have to sit up on that mountain in the 8,000-feet cold, night after night, to guard the area from curious humans and hungry animals. Guests for our first elaborate dinner party, for which Fran had been preparing for days, were just arriving when the telephone rang. Guess who was to get into mountain gear, pack a magnum, and report to the mountain for an indeterminate period of time?

It was days before I returned, after a dentist had made positive identification of the remains of the victim. After brilliant work by the FBI laboratory, which matched dirt samples from within yards of the site of the victim's body with soil from beneath a burned-out auto wreck on a dump in New Jersey, three-quarters of a continent away the killer was caught in Canada by the FBI and Royal Canadian Mounted Police. Aside from covering a few leads, my contribution was limited to shooing a skunk the size of a small dog away from the mountain site. He was about fifteen yards away, and I could see him clearly through the sights of my magnum in the moonlight. He was looking back over his shoulder at me. The magnum was cocked and so was his tail.

I said out loud, "O.K., fella; if you don't shoot, I won't."

He continued to regard me for a moment, then lowered

his tail and shuffled off. I lowered the magnum. A deal is a deal.

During the 1960 presidential campaign I was assigned a lead in an election-law violation case. As Vice President and a former member of congress, Richard Nixon had maintained a home in Washington for years. Prior to the time he had purchased it, the Supreme Court of the United States had ruled that a covenant in a deed running with the land purporting to bar the sale of real property to a member of a particular race or creed was contrary to public policy and unenforceable—a nullity. Nevertheless, the now void restrictive covenants remained as historical residue in most deeds to real property in certain sections of the District of Columbia and nearby Maryland and Virginia. One was in the deed that Richard Nixon signed, knowing, as a lawyer himself, that the clause was meaningless.

The supporters of John F. Kennedy made great political hay of the so-called Nixon Deed. In the case I had, that hay was clearly illegal. Kennedy forces had reprinted the deed, with the meaningless restrictive covenant circled in red and the words *FOR SHAME!* written across the face of the reprint in bright red. Nowhere on the reprint did there appear, as the law required, any indication of who was distributing it. It was circulated heavily in black areas. We were never able to solve that case, but it did serve as my introduction to political hardball, the so-called dirty tricks that, legal or illegal, are a part of every presidential campaign. That experience, and the Democrats' victory through vote fraud in Texas and Illinois (never proved since Nixon chose not to contest the election) peeled away one more layer of illusion that still impaired my vision of the world of politics.

Together with another agent I received a second commendation from Hoover for the capture of an elusive Chicano fugitive; then I found myself in the right place at the right time for the capture of one of the FBI's Ten Most Wanted fugitives.

Ernest Tait was one of only two men in history ever to have been twice on the FBI's Top Ten list. He had once engaged police in a machinegun battle, was a prison escapee, armed and considered extemely dangerous. The Denver office received word that Tait was en route to Denver, there to meet three other men, one a convicted murderer and another a bank robber, for a "big job" the four were to pull in Denver. All the informant knew was that the other three were already holed up in a Denver motel and that Tait was on his way.

In those days there were hundreds of motels in Denver. We split up the town and began the laborious task of searching every one, discreetly, for the three suspects. They were found after we'd checked about 25 percent of the motels in town, and a massive surveillance was placed on them. Slowly, so as not to alert the suspects, the motel was cleared of other patrons. I was a member of the surveillance team assigned to follow the three anywhere they might go, sufficiently closely that we could see whether Tait joined them, but discreetly enough that they would not detect the surveillance and flee, preventing the capture of Tait.

The surveillance was run by radio from the field office communications room and more than a dozen automobiles were used. No one ever stayed behind them long; new, different cars slipping in and out of place constantly. Cars were kept ahead as well as behind the suspects' car, and even on parallel streets on either side so that no FBI car would ever have to turn with the suspects.

The wait was long and tense. There were plenty of opportunities for unintended practice every time they went out and we followed, only to discover that they had gone not for the Top Ten fugitive but for a six-pack and hamburgers. Finally they took us into a residential area. The assistant Special Agent in Charge directing the operation by radio suspected correctly that they were going there because it was a quiet area with little traffic and they could check for surveillance before picking up Tait. When they turned down a particularly quiet side street, he ordered us all to stay far away.

All we could see from a distance was that the suspects' car appeared to stop at a corner where someone may or may not have entered the front passenger seat. Then the car turned around and came back toward us. I was riding shotgun, the front passenger seat of the Bureau car that swung in behind the suspects as they turned onto a three-lane one-way residential street, moved into traffic, and headed east. Like everyone, I had a photograph of Tait with me. Holding the microphone low so it could not be seen, I confirmed that there was now a man sitting in the passenger seat that had been empty.

Back came an order on the radio. My driver was to bring us to the right of the suspects' car in a passing move while I, using the photograph, was to check whether the new passenger was Tait. It didn't have to be said that I was to do so discreetly enough that my inspection would not be noticed by the suspects. With only an old photograph to go on and a second or so at best, the task wouldn't be easy. I would have to take a decision, and my career was riding on it.

The agent driving my car pulled past the suspects' car keeping his eyes rigidly front. I made a discreet glance and radioed: "Suspect is ident."

Back came orders for FBI cars to isolate the suspects' car from all other traffic by moving two Bureau cars directly ahead, two directly behind, and one to each side of them. When that had been accomplished we were all, at a signal, to hit our brakes and sirens at the same time. The purpose of the sirens was to startle and disconcert the suspects in the hope that we could get the drop on them and prevent a gun battle in a residential neighborhood.

My car was the one to the right. As the signal sounded, I didn't wait for the car to come to a halt. I threw open the right front door and jumped out, simultaneously turning and drawing my gun in midair. Having reasoned correctly that the suspects' car would stop before mine did, I landed directly opposite the right front window of their car with my magnum pointed directly at Tait's head. He said, "It's the Man," and his hand froze over a gun lying under a piece of paper on the front seat beside him.

My son, Jim, was born in April of 1961 and I was so elated at finally having a boy that, when I thought about it the next day driving through an unpopulated area, I stopped the car and fired three rounds into the air in a private ceremony of celebration.

Frances and I took the car up into the mountains every chance we got, dragging the three children along. Fran loved Denver and said she hoped we'd never have to leave. I shared her love of that country but I knew I couldn't stay; there was far too much in life I wanted to accomplish than could ever be encompassed by Denver or any other demiparadise.

The good cases continued to come my way. I worked the bombing of A.T.&T.'s microwave repeater towers, and another dangerous fugitive was apprehended just as we were getting him on the Top Ten list. Then I was sent to Casper, Wyoming, to help out an overloaded resident agent. Casper was still enough of an old Western town to have the principal whorehouse situated about two hundred yards from the back door of police headquarters, where it had been in business long enough to qualify as a historical landmark. I took over a fugitive investigation, and when I learned that he frequented that very whorehouse, the resident agent and I went to call on the madam. All we got out of her was some bad breath.

The overworked resident agent wasn't getting any help by having to stay with me, and he wanted to write the lead off as a negative so we could split up and get more work done. I disagreed. The lead had been strong. Either the madam was concealing the fugitive on the premises, or she knew where he was.

"Look," I said, "it's Saturday night, right? And you

were telling me there's a big high school wrestling tournament going on this weekend, right?"

"Sure. They're in town from all over the state. Why?"

"Right after the coaches get those kiddies tucked in bed, where d'you think they're going to head for?"

"Right here. There'll be a line all the way up to the police station. So what?"

"So we come back around ten o'clock tonight and I'll show you."

At ten that evening we slid up to the curb in a Bureau car and parked quietly several yards down from the front of the brothel. Because it had to be used over long distances, the spotlight on the Bureau car had been fitted with an aircraft landing lamp. I had with me a tape recorder with remote microphone. We waited. Sure enough, a station wagon came up to the curb, facing us, and parked in front of the brothel. Out of it piled six beefy men who could only have been high school wrestling coaches. I pointed the spotlight at them and snapped it on. "C'mon," I said, hefting the tape recorder in one hand and the microphone in the other, "just back me up."

We approached the startled men, illuminated brilliantly by the aircraft landing lamp and I thrust out the microphone toward the nearest one:

"KNYX-TV, fellas. Sorry about the light but we need it for our camera crew back there. We're doing a special on houses of prostitution and I wonder if you'd tell our viewers why you chose this particular whorehouse tonight over any numbers of others . . ."

But by now I was talking to myself. Those coaches looked like a circus act as they scrambled back into that station wagon and burned rubber getting out of there.

I was laughing my head off but the resident agent wasn't.

"You know we could get in a mess of trouble with this bullshit, buddy. That ol' bag is connected. How d'you think she stays in business in the cops' backyard?" He was clearly nervous.

"O.K.," I said as we got back into the Bureau car and I turned off the light, "we can probably accomplish the same thing playing it straight. Halfway straight, anyway. Enough to keep us in the clear if there's any comeback."

Another carload drove up. I snapped the light back on and said, "Trust me."

This time I flashed my FBI credentials and a photograph of the fugitive at the startled men. "Special Agent Liddy of the FBI. We're looking for a fugitive and need your help. We think he might be in that whorehouse. We'd appreciate it if you'd look at the picture and if you see anybody who looks like that in there, let us know when you come out. Now if I could just have your names and addresses for our files . . ."

But once again I was talking to myself. As their car sped away, the front door of the brothel opened and the voice of the madam boomed out: "What the fuck's goin' on here?"

I approached her. "You remember us from earlier, don't you? FBI. We're just asking good citizens to help us find a fugitive. All strictly voluntary. We're not having much luck; everybody seems to keep changing their minds about coming in here."

"You're ruinin' my business! I ain't bringin' in no girls from outta state here! This ain't no federal beef. You're harassin' me!"

"Well, that brings up an interesting point. How do we *know* your girls are all local? We can't take *your* word for it; you told us you don't know where this guy is and we *know* that's bullshit. Now, maybe if you told us the truth about this guy's whereabouts, we'd be inclined to believe you about the girls. And we wouldn't have to keep trying to get citizens to volunteer to help us find him. What d'you say?"

She gave us the name of a nearby ranch and we left. The resident agent was right about the madam's connections, though. The first thing Monday morning the Denver

128

office got a complaint from the office of the governor of Wyoming. Meantime, though, the fugitive was apprehended.

In June 1961, when the news came that I had been promoted to Bureau Supervisor at "S.O.G." (for Seat of Government, as we called FBI national headquarters to distinguish it from "W.F.O.," Washington Field Office), Scott Werner and I were happy. Fran was not. Good soldier that she was, though, she swallowed her disappointment and looked at the bright side; she'd be back East where her mother and all her friends lived.

I was assigned to Division 8, the Crime Records Division, headed by an exceptionally able Assistant Director of the FBI named Cartha DeLoach, known throughout the Bureau as Deke.

Fran and I rented a brick house in Arlington that conformed to the regulation that Bureau Supervisors live within quick reach of headquarters. Unfortunately, a house that close did not conform to our budget. The FBI had the power to appoint me, at age twenty-nine, a Bureau Supervisor, but Civil Service regulations did not permit me to be paid accordingly. At about $8,000 a year Fran and I found ourselves living between an executive of the Associated Press on one side and a navy admiral on the other.

The Crime Records Division was a fascinating place. The actual keeping of records on crime was accomplished by just one section. The others handled such things as J. Edgar Hoover's correspondence; all FBI publications; congressional relations; press relations and public relations (though it was denied these last two activities existed); exhibits; requests for information about persons and activities or organizations that attracted Hoover's attention; his visiting schedule; FBI television programs, radio shows, movies, and, very important, ghostwriting for Hoover.

I was first put to work preparing memoranda respond-

129

ing to Hoover's inquiries—in the beginning the more mundane, then, as confidence in my ability grew, matters of increasing sensitivity. The rules were strict and easy to remember: absolutely no errors, of any kind or significance, were tolerated. Everything prepared for Hoover's signature went through the "reading room," staffed by a crew of spinster experts on grammar and spelling. I wasn't there more than two weeks before I got my first letter of censure for an error. It was occasioned by an incorrect initial on an envelope and I noted with amusement a psychological touch: letters from Hoover with good news —a promotion, commendation, or raise—were on blue letterhead; bad news—censure, demotion, transfer for disciplinary reasons, etc.—were on black letterhead.

I learned, too, that no one ever questioned anything Hoover actually said, and few things said in his name. In the latter category was an edict from the reading room that stated that certain English words were being used too frequently in Hoover's correspondence and were, henceforth, banished. It was a scandal when I suggested that Hoover was the only government official whose vocabulary was *de*creasing.

Everyone had to initial his work. As a memorandum passed upward through the chain of command to Hoover, each person reviewing it initialed it, sometimes making a brief comment in longhand. All such writings and initials were to be made only in pencil. Hoover alone was permitted to use ink, and he employed a distinctive blue that made his initials stand out from all the others. They also made all other comments irrelevant. After I had been there awhile, and noted the awe accorded anything written in Hoover's own hand in blue ink, I gave a few old-timers cardiac trouble. I am an excellent forger and Hoover's handwriting is one of my specialties. I'd have one of their memoranda copied over, then write on it in Hoover's hand in bright blue ink something like "Idiotic. This man has been around too long.—H." and leave it in the poor man's in-basket. Finally they knew enough to come to me, trembling, asking, "Please—this is one of yours, isn't it?"

Some of the things Hoover said or noted on memoranda were ambiguous, but no one would ask him what he meant; they'd just make a guess, act, and hope. When a class of new agents was marched through Hoover's office to shake his hand he muttered to an aide: "They've got some real pinheads in that class." The next day, as the class was at firearms training, their lockers were opened and the snap-brim hats all were required to have were measured. The three agents with the smallest hat sizes were washed out.

Each of us had to take his turn in the "nut room." People came into FBI headquarters every day asking to see J. Edgar Hoover. Most of them were tourists in Washington for the only time in their lives, admired Hoover, and wanted to tell him so. Others wanted to offer him advice, or interest him in their latest invention to combat crime— and a very few wanted to kill him. As important as it was to intercept a would-be assassin, it was deemed equally important to Hoover that no citizen disposed to support him and the FBI be offended. Accordingly, walk-in visitors were told we'd "check to see if Mr. Hoover is in." Their names were run through the indexes and the special list of crackpots know as the "nut list," and, if nothing "derogatory" turned up, they were told that Mr. Hoover was, unfortunately, out of the city. They were advised further, however, that special arrangements had been made for them to have an audience with "Mr. Hoover's top assistant, Mr. _____" (fill in the name of the supervisor on duty in the "nut room" that day).

Within a short while I was writing magazine articles for Hoover, and I was assigned to appear at events in and around Washington when an FBI speaker had been requested. Because someone on the way up the administrative ladder is likely at some stage to be a Special Agent in Charge—a role that requires speaking frequently— such engagements were often monitored. I must have done well enough, because my engagements increased in frequency and size of audience, but there was one I thought would send me back to Indianapolis.

I had been assigned to address a local association of handicapped persons on the standard theme of FBI history, jurisdiction, and accomplishments, adding that the Bureau employed handicapped persons wherever it could. I was told that two FBI employees would be present, and I was given their names and assignments.

I gave the talk and, when I got to the part about the handicapped, I thought to dramatize the point by calling out the names of the two employees and asking them to make themselves known. I called the first name. A woman in a wheelchair raised her hand and the audience clapped. It was when I called the name of the second woman that I got in trouble. She was seated next to the employee in the wheelchair and, instead of waving her hand in the air, started to rise. I was horrified. For some inexplicable reason, I assumed that something was wrong with her legs, too.

"No, no, Miss Frobisher!" I shouted. "Don't try to stand; just raise your hand!"

Too late. Miss Frobisher was already on her feet. Embarrassed, I tried to recover and made things worse: "Wonderful!" I shouted. "There's an example of determination we can all be proud of!" and I started clapping my hands. The audience followed in an ovation for Miss Frobisher.

At the tea-and-cookies reception after the speech, I approached the two employees to congratulate them. To my surprise Miss Frobisher was furious. "There's nothing wrong with me, you fool!" she hissed between clenched teeth, "I'm the one they sent to push the wheelchair!"

My office was on the fourth floor of the Department of Justice building; Hoover had his offices on the fifth. So did the then Attorney General, Robert Kennedy. Bobby Kennedy and Hoover hated each other. Headquarters was constantly abuzz with the latest skirmish in their private war. No sooner had I arrived than I was told with great glee of their first clash. Hoover's office was a few feet across a hall from the Attorney General's. Soon after Bobby Kennedy took office Hoover looked down at his desk one morning to find a strange object attached to it with wires trailing off under the carpet. Alarmed, he summoned a technician from the FBI laboratory immediately to find out what it was.

The job was easy for the technician. "It's a buzzer, sir, so when the Attorney General wants to see you, he can just push it and have you step over to his office."

"Rip it out!"

And it *stayed* ripped out. Kennedy retaliated by having a Justice secretary walk his big, hairy dog, Brumus, in the corridor outside Hoover's office. This *lèse majesté* infuriated Hoover. He knew the Attorney General was a physical fitness buff who used the FBI gymnasium in the basement regularly, so he ordered that henceforth no one without FBI credentials was to use the gym, and he posted an agent guard on the door. From that moment on, try as he might, Bobby Kennedy couldn't get into the FBI gym.

Hoover was able to make things like that stick because of the extensive files he had on anyone with political power. The synopsis files on every senator and congressman were kept in an office a few doors down from mine. I used them in my work. It was common knowledge that the Kennedys were powerless against Hoover because JFK's entensive pre- and extramarital sexual activity was thoroughly documented in the sensitive files kept by Miss Gandy. The first entry in JFK's file noted an espionage surveillance observation of a young naval officer leaving the apartment of the target's mistress by the back door as the target came in the front. When the officer was identified it was reported to Hoover, who informed Ambassador Joseph Kennedy of the potentially embarrassing situation. The Ambassador had Franklin Roosevelt see to it that the navy transferred his son out of Washington. Nor were those files limited to politicians or to writings. Anyone

133

with any kind of power or national celebrity was represented and the quality of detail was remarkable: in the tape I reviewed of the lovemaking between the late Sam "Mooney" Giancana and a well-known popular singer, even the squeak of the bedsprings was audible. As we said at the time, in a takeoff of an old joke about Hopalong Cassidy: "Nobody fucks with J. Edgar."

In the fall of 1961 I learned that while things were going well for me at the Bureau, there was trouble at home. We were barely making ends meet financially and Fran was bone-tired from struggling to care for three babies under three years old, even sewing far into the night to make clothing for them and herself. But she always managed a smile for me, and I never realized the extent of her exhaustion until I came in one day to find her in a doorway, gripping the molding on both sides of the wall and crying as she smashed her head repeatedly against the door frame. I took her in my arms and held her. "I'm so tired," she sobbed. "I'm . . . so . . . tired!"

There was more to it than that. She was pregnant again.

XI

The knowledge that Fran would soon have to cope with four children under four years old on little money and less help from me because of the time-demands of my work led us to some basic rethinking—about the birth-control policy of Catholicism and about my job. There was a certain irony to it. Fran and I wanted six children. She had grown up as a lonely only child. I had a sister, and a cousin who was a de facto brother, and I missed the large number of people always present at home.

I was aware also that children can be lost to sickness, accident, or war and six would raise substantially the probability that at least some offspring would survive. Just as important, I recognized that a child can lose itself through failure of the will to achieve and that having six would make it easier to accept and write off such a living death as well.

We *still* wanted six children; but it made no sense to damage Fran's health and lessen her ability to participate in their raising as well as procreation by having all six within six years. Although one of the reasons I had chosen Frances to be the mother of my children was her size and strength, which should have enabled her to bear half a dozen high-performance children, I certainly had not intended to risk damage by pushing her to design limit.

By spring of 1962 I was getting restive at work. I was aware that a large measure of the success of the Bureau was attributable to the astonishing degree of its acceptance by the American people and the cooperation that engendered. I knew I was doing important work in furthering the reputation of the FBI and helping to defeat its critics in what was a part of the COINTELPRO operation. People would tell us things they would confide in no one else, and we could almost always rely on a favorable response to an appeal for discreet assistance. I kept up my ability with firearms by regular practice, but I missed the excitement of the hunt that went with field-work. I was not cut out to be a rear-echelon soldier.

The harbingers of success were there. The FBI has an Inspection Division for ferreting out weaknesses in performance in the field and other headquarters divisions. All major FBI administrators have done a hitch in the Inspection Division. Once a year a special team drawn from other headquarters divisions is assembled to inspect the Inspection Division itself. When I was selected for that special inspection team, it was clearly a good omen.

Early in the summer Fran left Virginia for Poughkeepsie to have the baby in her hometown, where her mother could care for her and the other three children during

135

her convalescence. I remained in Washington to ponder how I was going to provide for a family of six on my small salary.

My father must have been psychic. He had always hoped that I would join his law firm and, having just enlarged it and moved to new offices in the Wall Street area, he made his move, offering me a $2,000 raise to come aboard as an associate. Things were booming. Marathon Oil was part of a consortium that had brought in the new oil fields in Libya and wanted to get into the retail market in Europe as well as expand in the United States. The new M-Marathon trademark would have to be registered all over the world. I told my father I'd talk it over with Fran and let him know.

Our son, Tom, was born in Poughkeepsie in July 1962. When I learned that birth was imminent I took emergency leave, traveled all night, and arrived just in time for the celebration—but too late to have been of any comfort to Fran throughout her labor. We talked over my father's offer. The thought of our family settling down and my practicing law in Manhattan, with the commensurately higher income, appealed to Fran greatly. Still, the consideration uppermost in her mind was my happiness. She knew how much I enjoyed life in the field in the FBI, that I had a good future there and had fond memories of Denver. If I wanted to stay, that was fine with her. The decision, Fran insisted, was mine.

I returned to Washington undecided. Then my father upped the ante; he would lend me the down payment on a new house. I thought about it long and hard. Should I remain in the FBI, the *most* I could aspire to was to become an Assistant to the Director (the number-three spot, after Hoover's crony, Clyde Tolson). Curiously, it did not occur to me that Hoover would ever die. The FBI Laboratory, we used to joke, would break the record and have him back in two days anyway. An FBI without him was inconceivable. I wasn't sure yet just where I wanted to go, but I knew it was farther than that. I felt keenly an obligation to achieve my maximum genetic potential. There was also my obligation to Fran and our four children. She had been a real trouper and would, I knew, stick with it under the most difficult of circumstances— not just when she *had* to, but when it meant my happiness. She deserved a better life and our children deserved the finest preparation for life possible; to do less would be to betray the genetic considerations so important to our marriage. I decided to leave the FBI to practice law with my father.

I resigned in September 1962, after five years with the FBI, and my immediate supervisor, Milton Jones, told me that I would be welcomed back should I change my mind. Deke DeLoach confirmed that I had been slated for a tour with the Inspection Division and said that he understood my decision, and we parted good friends.

With the down payment provided by my father, we bought a new house in Basking Ridge, New Jersey, near a commuter railroad to New York, and Fran and I devoted ourselves to turning it into a happy home. A little *too* happy—by January 1963 Frances was pregnant again.

With the knowledge that by the end of the year we would have five children under five years old we accepted the fact that the rhythm method of birth control just would not work for us. Fran's obstetrician warned her that for the sake of her health she should have no more children for a substantial period of time or, better still, no more at all. This precipitated a crisis in our religious lives that we resolved in different ways.

Frances found a Catholic priest who, in keeping with the change then sweeping through the church in the wake of the Second Vatican Council, told her that it was obvious that her cycle was erratic and that the use of "the pill" with the intention of stabilizing her cycle, rather than preventing conception, was morally acceptable. As a product of Jesuit education I could understand the distinction, but I was troubled by the necessity for it. I began a basic reexamination of the Catholic religion.

In August 1963 Frances's mother died. We went to Poughkeepsie and stayed in her house to settle her estate. I was able to commute to New York on the New York Central Railroad and, if it took more than two hours each way, it afforded me the time to do the homework that had to be done anyway. Adding to the convenience was the fact that Fran's obstetrician was in Poughkeepsie and, in October, our son Raymond was born there. After Fran had recovered, we decided to remain, selling the house in Basking Ridge and remodeling the one in Poughkeepsie.

Fran and I joined a Catholic discussion group for professionals, led by a monk who taught at a nearby seminary. Under his guidance fundamental Catholic dogma was analyzed thoroughly. The problem I had was that to arrive at an acceptance of the dogma I could not rely on logic alone; there was always a requirement for "faith" to resolve what I considered to be a conflict with reason. I was forced, therefore, to confront my last fear: God.

Logic could not take me behind an uncaused first cause, and I could see no logical reason why the name *God* should not be among those one could apply to it, for purposes of discussion if nothing else. From there, however, I was unable to conclude that any body of religious belief assembled by man could logically claim superiority to any other attempt by the finite to deal with the infinite—except, of course, if a divine intervener were to name one as the true faith, but many religions, including the Hebrew, Christian, and Islamic, claimed that distinction for themselves.

Those claims did not persuade me. Looking at the Roman Catholic faith, I was unable to distinguish its assertion of a virgin birth, a return from the dead, and the bodily assumption into somewhere outside the universe of a man and his mother from among similar pagan superstitions. My last fear, the fear of God, died with my faith. I was now alone and would have to live life armed only with my own inner resources. I felt a surge of confidence and resolve like that I had experienced years before when I conquered my fear of lightning. I was free.

I was also concerned for my children. As tormenting and crippling as had been my fear of God, the rituals of the Catholic church had conveyed a sense of invulnerability by being in the "state of grace," and the comforting, timeless universality of the Latin Mass provided a crutch upon which I had leaned in formative years. Could I have climbed that tree to challenge the lightning years ago without the belief in the invulnerability of my soul provided by my "state of grace?" I'll never know. My agnosticism is a poor substitute for the faith I no longer have to give my children. It's sad to realize that those rituals no longer exist to be passed on; like the scent of burning leaves in autumn, they, too, have been banned and are gone with the wind.

I did well in my father's firm. He sent me to Findlay, Ohio, to present to the management of the Marathon Oil company a program for registration abroad of its new trademark, and I worked on the necessary licensing agreements throughout the world. I prepared and argued cases in the Patent Office in Washington but concentrated primarily on foreign matters, especially those associated with the new European Economic Community. Nights I pursued graduate studies at the New York University School of Law under professor Walter Derenberg. I even found time to reorganize my father's filing system. My plan was more efficient but, used to the old ways, he had difficulty with it. Nor was he overly pleased with my secretary. She was a bit young for his taste and could be abrupt when interrupted at her work; but as a native of Berlin able to speak and prepare letters in English, French, and Spanish, as well as her native German, she was invaluable to me and a great help in foreign practice.

Relations between my father and me deteriorated gradually. We were both strong personalities and we differed frequently. There is nothing unusual about lawyers' differing, but when I differed with my father it was not a

139

case of one lawyer arguing with another, point for point and citing cases; I got the distinct impression that he felt I was being an undutiful son. When we clashed, I went home in a bad mood, which did nothing to brighten Fran's day, and my father went home equally disturbed. He had a bad heart and, finally, my sister mentioned that our disagreements were a matter of concern to the family.

I did not get very far arguing with my father, and by 1965 the situation was becoming intolerable. He was then at the very peak of his career. He had just completed a successful term as mayor of his hometown, and he'd been knighted again by the King of Sweden, this time as a commander of the Royal Order of the North Star, an honor so high it is no longer given to nonsubjects of the crown. He should have been very happy. But the disputes with me were spoiling all that. When we thought we were right, neither of us would back off—for anybody. The only solution, I became convinced, was to remove the source of friction: our working relationship. As just plain father and son we could get along fine.

So long as I was going to elect a new life, I wanted something that would be interesting, challenging, allowing full use of my education and experience and capable of carrying me as far as my ability and will would take me. Politics fit that bill, and it had one more very important thing to offer.

By 1965 it was apparent to me that my country was in trouble. We were fighting in Vietnam a "limited war"— a contradiction in terms—in which soldiers were permitted to die but not fight to win. Understandably, many of them, and their families, resented it. The choice was between continuing the status quo; fighting the war properly by going all out to win, giving our men a fair chance at victory and survival; or abandoning the national interest and quitting. I favored all-out war to end the matter as quickly as possible. I was aware of the fact that following the close of World War II when the French were fighting the Viet Minh in Indochina, they were at first highly successful. That was because they were using the Foreign Legion, then manned almost completely by veterans from the most disciplined, ruthlessly efficient practitioners of all-out warfare in history: the *Waffen SS*. It was only after that fact was made public and political pressure forced their removal that the French began to lose.

The conflict over the Vietnam war and especially the tactics used by the antiwar movement were eroding the national will and respect for authority. The young were sinking into the netherworld of the drug culture. Valid demands by blacks for civil rights were often resisted violently by whites, and in response many blacks were adopting violence as an offensive rather than defensive tactic. I never believed in sitting on the sidelines complaining when I didn't like something; the right to complain carried with it an obligation to act to remedy the problem. I couldn't think of a better way to get started in politics and have an effect on what was happening than to be a prosecutor.

Poughkeepsie is in New York's Dutchess County, and Dutchess had two principal political leaders at the time: the sheriff and the district attorney. The county itself was Republican and somewhere to the right of Barry Goldwater. I went to see the D.A. His name was Raymond Baratta, and he was by reputation smart, savvy, and fair. Despite the fact that he was to become a county judge— the next step up the line politically—he was the man to see. We hit it off well and he laid it out for me: everybody in the office would move up one notch, his first assistant, John Heilman, becoming district attorney (there would thereafter be an election, of course, but all were Republicans, so it was assured). Baratta had recently taken on a young man named Rosenblatt who was a scholarly Harvard law graduate. Someone was needed who knew the practical side of criminal law, and my FBI experience suited me for that position. Like all jobs in the district attorney's office, my work would be parttime by description and pay but full-time in fact. If I could squeeze in

141

some private practice of civil law to help buy the groceries, fine; but the D.A.'s office came first.

Frances made it possible for me to take the job by taking one herself as a teacher, her computer background making her one of the few who really understood the so-called new math. She'd drop all five children off at school—the last two at a day nursery—teach, pick up the children, do her housework, prepare dinner for us all, then drive an hour round trip to the State University of New York at New Paltz to earn a master's degree in education at night. It was, of course, to be "temporary," but the good woman is still at it.

After the painful but necessary parting from my father's firm I started to work at the district attorney's office in January 1966. My first task was to try to save a drug case for the Poughkeepsie Police Department. They had a search and seizure problem because of insufficient probable cause in a legal sense. I wrote an eight-page memorandum of law but couldn't keep the search from being declared illegal. It was then I realized that the biggest problem in law enforcement in the county was the fact that the various police agencies had not been able to adjust their procedures to the changes mandated by the Warren Supreme Court. Several officers from different jurisdictions asked me if I'd help by going out to the scene of major crimes with them as an adviser—that was where decisions concerning investigative method were first taken that could make or break a case. I agreed.

I owned a four-wheel-drive jeep and, since most major crimes seemed to be discovered in the middle of the night during a snowstorm, it came in handy. Whenever there was a death in which criminality *might* be involved, I rolled. I went to the scenes of murders, suicides (apparent), and fatal accidents. At autopsies I learned about the effects of trauma on the bodies of men, women, and children. Occasionally I got so involved in cases that I helped run informants to get enough facts to establish probable cause for a search warrant. Sometimes I went on arrests to prevent improper interrogation from ruining a good case. In those instances I armed myself, as I did in the FBI, before going into the office in the morning.

Some police were grateful for my help. Others, especially those embarrassed when I pointed out an error, resented me. The local representatives of the New York State Police Bureau of Criminal Investigation (BCI) for example, were furious when I sent to their crime laboratory evidence they had overlooked in a burglary investigation. When the Poughkeepsie Police Department and I solved that one and a series of other crimes through an informant, they became incensed.

When the informant, whom I was running with a particularly able Poughkeepsie detective named Robert Berberich, subsequently had an automobile accident in which his passenger, a youth with a history of drug abuse, was killed, the deceased youth's father blamed me and had the New York State Commission on Investigation investigate my activities. The angry State Police detectives did what they could to aid my accuser, and so did a few other officers whom I had embarrassed. At the hearing in New York City, where I was defended by my associate in private practice, Peter Maroulis, I was cleared and a member of the commission went so far as to congratulate me, saying, "Mr. Liddy, you're an honest man."

My work was by no means all investigation. I tried cases and loved what lawyers call being "in the pit," on one's own *mano a mano* against the other side with the judge as the referee and the jury deciding the victor.

The process began with the grand jury. The theory is that the grand jury exists to protect citizens from arbitrary prosecution by interposing other citizens between the prosecutor and someone he's accusing. That's a myth. The fact is that because criminal law is so complicated and defense lawyers are not allowed in the grand jury room, prosecutors can and do dominate grand juries. So complete is this domination that a grand jury that attempts to function according to the myth and goes against the wishes of the prosecutor is called a "run away." Recognizing that fact, the rule in Dutchess County was "*you* indict—*you* try the case." That was to protect one prosecutor from having to try a weak case another had rammed through a grand jury. No one likes to go to trial with a loser, especially the other guy's loser. It's bad for the career.

My courtroom methods were unorthodox but effective. Once I prosecuted a man who shot another with a revolver and fled, tossing the gun aside just before he was caught. It was recovered and admitted into evidence against him, a police officer testifying that when found it was fully loaded with the exception of the chamber in line with the barrel, which contained an expended cartridge casing. I watched the jury as the officer testified and saw that I had a problem; most of the jury consisted of people who knew nothing about firearms, and one sweet little old lady sitting front and center clearly couldn't understand how, if the *empty* casing was in line with the barrel, the gun could be fired—something the defendant denied he had done.

When it came time for me to sum up, I knew I had to overcome the jurors' lack of understanding of how a revolver works. I picked up the gun and opened the action to be sure all chambers were empty, then picked up the one empty casing that the officer testified that he had removed from the chamber in line with the barrel, and palmed it. In my hand I had another empty casing of the same caliber, but with one difference; it had a live primer, the little cap in the center that when hit by the firing pin provides the spark that sets off the gunpowder in the rest of the casing to propel the bullet. I made a great show of placing the empty casing into the chamber *next* to the barrel and closing the action. Then I pointed the gun at the ceiling and said, "Watch carefully."

Ever so slowly I began to squeeze the trigger of the double-action revolver. Slowly the hammer started back and the cylinder revolved, bringing the empty-casing-filled chamber into line with the barrel. By now I had the undivided attention of everyone in the courtroom except Judge Baratta, who was presiding. He knew perfectly well how a revolver worked and, suspecting nothing, was nodding.

The jury's eyes followed that slowly turning cylinder as if it were the swaying head of an erect cobra. It was so quiet the click of the cylinder lock going into place was audible. Then the sear disengaged, the hammer fell, and the firing pin hit the live primer.

"BLAM!"

The primer went off. The little old lady sitting front and center threw her arms across her breast and squeaked, "Oh, Jesus!"

The court reporter fell off his stool.

Defense counsel, who had a history of heart trouble, clutched his chest as he rose to object with what he was sure was his dying breath.

Judge Baratta sat bolt upright in startled fury, then controlled it long enough to overrule the objection. As I displayed to my woman juror the evidence that an empty casing is *always* in line with the barrel immediately after a double-action revolver is fired, Baratta glowered at me. The verdict was "guilty," but Judge Baratta didn't wait for it before summoning me to his chambers. *Immediately.* He was chewing on a big black cigar as I entered.

"Goddamn it, Gordon, you almost caused a mistrial out there. I still don't know how the Appellate Division's gonna rule. Why the hell didn't you ask the permission of the court to put on that demonstration?"

"Your honor, if I'd told you what I wanted to do and asked your permission, would you have given it?"

"Hell, no!"

"That's why I didn't ask."

Baratta leaned forward, half out of his chair, outstretched arm pointing at the door with his cigar. "Out! Get out of here! And don't you *ever* do anything like that in my courtroom again, understand? Out!" Ray Baratta never stayed angry at anyone more than ten minutes in his life; but for the moment it was clear that if I didn't get out of there fast, the next person indicted for murder in Dutchess County would be Ray Baratta.

Fortunately, the next time I had occasion to demonstrate something in court I was before a different judge, Joseph Jiudice, trying a particularly vicious assault and robbery case. The defendant was accused of rifling the pockets of the victim after bludgeoning him with a heavy board, which was in evidence. It had taken so long for the case to come to trial that the effects of the blow upon the victim's head were no longer visible. I thought it would be instructive for the jury to have some idea of the damage such an instrument could inflict.

Again during summation, I displayed the weapon to the jury, turning it so they could see its sharp edges and advising them that, as the judge would tell them, they had the right to take it with them into the jury room to examine during their deliberations. I suggested that they do so, and imagine what it would feel like to be hit over the head with it, "*like this!*"

With that I slammed the board down against the wooden railing of the jury box. The blow put a large dent in the solid hardwood, and the startled jurors in the front row jumped back involuntarily. The judge denied a motion for mistrial but, after the jury had announced a verdict of guilty, he said in open court for all to hear: "Mr. Liddy, if you do any more physical damage to my courtroom, you will pay for it out of your own pocket."

Increasingly, drugs were becoming the common denominator of crime in Dutchess County. Not only was there growth in the drug trade itself, but the money needed to fund it was the principal motive behind street-corner robberies and a spiraling rate of burglary that was infuriating homeowners. Curiously, when I started practicing in the district attorney's office. the seriousness of the drug abuse problem among the local youth was not appreciated.

Detective Bob Berberich was doing what he could to

alert parents to the symptoms to look for by lecturing before every civic group that would give him a forum. He was a graduate of the FBI National Academy, which trains the elite of local and state police from all over the United States, and he knew his subject well. We had been working together on criminal cases, our mutual FBI backgrounds forming a bond between us. Because I was "getting some ink," as he called newspaper publicity, he thought that if I would join him in speaking around the country, I might draw bigger audiences and we could alert more parents.

I agreed; I had five children growing up in Dutchess County too. Berberich and I started out on the rubber chicken circuit. He gave graphic, up-to-the-minute local examples of the destructive effects of drug abuse, and he told parents what to look for. I discussed the law and the criminal exposure the young were risking along with the physical hazards of drug use. The combination worked and we got a lot of help from parents who called to let us know where drugs were coming from. It gave police a place to start looking and the names of individuals to target for investigation.

Much of my work in the drug abuse area was grim. Then I met Timothy Leary.

XII

Surprise was all-important. I was worried. Worried and cold. On a midnight in March 1966, still fast in the grip of winter, the raid against Dr. Timothy Leary's huge mansion headquarters on the 1,500-acre Hitchcock estate at Millbrook was an hour overdue. I shivered in a concealing clump of brush some thirty yards from the front of the building, waiting.

For some time the major media had been covering the activities of the unfrocked Harvard don who, as high priest of a psychoactive-drug-based "counterculture" had proselytized the young to "Tune in, turn on, and drop out."

Handsome, articulate, and charismatic, Leary had the ability to influence the young that made him feared by parents everywhere. His message ran directly contrary to everything they believed in and sought to teach their children: "Tune in" (to my values; reject those of your parents); "turn on" (drug yourself); "drop out" (deal with your problems and those of society by running away from them).

So long as Leary came no closer to Dutchess County than New York City (ailing, alien; never thought of without unconsciously blessing the insulating miles between), he was just one more problem of the sick '60s to be dealt with by someone else—like an outbreak of the plague in Bombay. Then one morning the citizens of Dutchess awoke to find the source of the infection in their midst: Timothy Leary was in permanent residence. To add insult to injury, he was at Millbrook, for sixty years a country seat for the nation's ultrarich. Leary's presence did more to arouse the people of the county than all Bob Berberich's and my lectures put together.

Rumors were rampant at the intersection of Main and Market streets, Poughkeepsie's Rialto. Local boys and girls had been seen entering and leaving the Hitchcock estate. Fleeting glimpses were reported of persons strolling the grounds nude. To fears of drug-induced dementia were added pot-induced pregnancy. The word was that at Leary's lair the panties were dropping as fast as the acid.

Sheriff Quinlan's political power was not derived solely from the built-in army of campaign workers afforded him by his deputies and their families. He made it his business to know what the people of Dutchess wanted of their sheriff, and he gave it to them. Concerning Leary, the will of the people was not difficult to divine: they wanted him the hell out of the county. Fast. Quinlan handed the hot potato to his chief deputy, Charlie Borchers. I handled it for the district attorney's office.

Borchers's informants and an intensive surveillance, some of it by air, soon confirmed that a high-turnover, transient population of between thirty and fifty persons inhabited *chez* Leary, and were partaking of LSD and SEX.

The sheriff's office drew up an application for a search warrant. After approval by our "book man," Al Rosenblatt, it was presented to a judge who issued the warrant. It was now in the pocket of Charlie Borchers. At that moment he was shivering beside me in the brush, some twenty to thirty deputies similarly concealed behind us as we awaited the arrival of the sheriff and district attorney so the raid could begin.

The operational plan was keyed to the legal problems involved. Leary's headquarters was the equivalent of an hotel. Informants advised that people, often couples, would arrive, sometimes to stay the weekend. They would be assigned a room for storage of their effects and to which they could retire after participating in the various group activities that took place in the large rooms on the first floor. Group activities included lectures by Leary, community ingestion of marijuana and hashish, and distribution of the "sacrament" of LSD by Leary's then inamorata (later wife), Rosemary, who was referred to as "the Blessed Mother."

We hoped to find not only a central supply of LSD belonging to Leary, but also his guests' personal supplies of marijuana and hashish. It was necessary to strike quickly, with the benefit of surprise, if the inhabitants were to be caught in their rooms so it could be clearly established that any contraband found in the rooms was possessed by each room's tenant.

Clearly, for example, the occupant of hotel room 602 would not be chargeable with possession of contraband found by police in room 24. As the Leary manse had neither numbers on its rooms nor records of room assignments, we would either have to trap the occupants in their rooms, or we would be forced to rely upon the testimony, if any, of guests to establish room assignments and, thereby, constructive possession. To avoid having to depend on testimony, we planned to wait until the occupants had retired for the evening, at which time we would perform a classic "no knock" entry—that is, kick in the front door.

We understood that opposite the front door and at the rear of a large foyer, a broad, central staircase led upward. From it branched hallways off which were individual bedrooms. The plan called for a quick charge upstairs by the bulk of the force of deputies, who were then to fan out and hold the inhabitants in their rooms pending a systematic search. Borchers and I were to lead the charge, he to serve the warrant and I to handle on the spot legal problems that might arise. There was no question, however, about who was going to knock down the front door. Aside from the fact that the warrant commanded the sheriff, not the district attorney, to perform the search, Borchers weighed more than 200 pounds of solid muscle to my 150 pounds of gristle.

The delay was occasioned principally by an unexpected variation in Leary's habits. Surveillance officers reported that Leary, instead of retiring at about 11 P.M., had gathered his guests into a large living room at the right front of the building. The room was dark save for the random flashing of colored lights. The situation continued for some time. Then word came that a projection screen had been set up and, "They're lookin' at movies."

The deputies assumed that the movies were pornographic, and there was some competition for the assignment to move into binocular range to obtain further information.

Presently the lucky scout returned to report in a tone of disgust, "It ain't no dirty movie. You'll never guess what them hippies are watching. A waterfall."

"A what?"

"A waterfall for crissake! It's just a movie of a goddamn waterfall. It goes on and on and nothing ever happens but the water. I kept watching, you know? I figured there'd be, you know, broads jumpin' in and out of the water or something."

"No broads?"

"Nothing! Nothing but water. Them people are crazy!"

Eventually the waterfall party broke up but another hitch developed. John Heilman, the district attorney, who wanted to be on hand with the sheriff, had not yet arrived. There was concern that he had driven onto the estate grounds and, obeying the injunction against headlights, taken a wrong turn and become lost on the fifteen hundred acres.

Borchers and I waited for word in a frozen silence broken only by muttered curses uttered through chattering teeth. Finally, at nearly 1 A.M., we were told that the D.A. had been found and would be arriving shortly.

The shivering deputies had been moving about in a vain attempt to keep warm. Their movements were audible. So was the sound of an approaching car, its automatic transmission locked in low gear and whining in protest. I pointed to my watch and raised my eyebrows in silent query to the heavy man at my side. He nodded his head in reply. "Fuck it," said Charlie Borchers. "Let's go."

Charlie didn't have to kick the door in. It was unlocked. It opened on a large foyer bare of furnishings. The equally bare floor was strewn liberally with excrement. A stairway loomed ahead. From atop the banister post glared the stuffed head of a tiger, a plastic flower clutched incongruously in its jaws.

Borchers and I started up the stairs, the thundering herd of deputies right behind us. We hadn't cleared more than ten steps before my worst fears were realized: in the light of a hall lamp we saw Leary, Rosemary at his side, descending to meet us.

Rosemary was wearing a diaphanous gown. Leary was wearing a Hathaway shirt. Period. Since the stairs were

151

steep and we were craning our necks upward as Leary bounced downward, our first view of the good doctor was, to say the least, revealing.

There was a brief confrontation on the stairs as we met, and Leary, quite understandably (and civilly, all things considered) asked whether ". . . someone would mind, awfully, telling me just what is going on?"

Borchers said he had a warrant to search the premises. As he spoke, Borchers gestured to the deputies, who had paused momentarily behind us, to keep on going. Dutifully they streamed past us on both sides en route to their assigned floors, halls, and rooms.

Some of the deputies were to arrive in time and some, it became obvious, would not. Doors started popping open onto the hallway half a stairway above us and men and women in various stages of undress emerged. Some were resentful of the intrusion on their sleep or other bedtime activities, and a smattering of "Oink, oink!" and "Fascist pigs!" could be heard above the rumble of the deputies' heavy-booted deployment. Others looked upon the unfolding event as a "happening" and, grabbing guitars and with good humor ignoring the commands of the deputies to "Return to your rooms, everybody! Return to your rooms!" proceeded to join the fun by improvising on the spot some surprisingly good folk songs in keeping with the spirit of the occasion:

> "Oh, they're busting Doctor Leary
> Cause the evening, it was dreary
> And the fuzz had nothin' better else
>   to do.
> We got sheriffs out the ass
> Cause they're lookin' for our grass
> And they hope to find a ton of acid
>   too!"

"I think, Doctor," said Borchers, surveying a scene that, from the viewpoint of textbook police procedure

152

could only be described as deteriorating, "we might do better in a little more private place."

For a moment Leary said nothing. His eyes sparkled and his smile broadened as he became more amused at our increasing discomfort.

"Certainly," he said finally, "we'll go to my room."

Leary did an about-face and, his arm around Rosemary's waist, led us upward to the second floor and into a suite of rooms directly over the scene of the late, late waterfall show.

Leary may have been amused momentarily, but Rosemary was not. She was outraged. We had no sooner arrived in Leary's front room when she spied a deputy leaning over a small, ornate brass urn sitting on the hearth inside a fireplace. "Don't you dare touch that!" she shouted, rushing across the room toward the offending deputy, "That's my sacrament!"

While my attention was fixed on Rosemary's sacrament, the district attorney walked into the room flanked by our book man, Al Rosenblatt.

None too happy at the folk-singing disorder through which he had made his way to the room, the district attorney made his presence known by barking, "I want the warrant read to this man *now*, and I want some pants on him! We have matrons with us!"

Borchers started to read in a rapid monotone: "State of New York, County of Dutchess . . ."

Meanwhile, back at the fireplace, I joined Rosemary and the deputy. Both were clutching the brass urn and glaring at each other, motionless, like two basketball players awaiting a jump-ball signal from the ref. "What should I do with the sacrament?" asked the deputy, slowly but forcefully removing the urn from Rosemary's grasp.

I looked inside the container. It was nearly filled by a dried, ground, vegetable matter that was unmistakably a good grade of marijuana. "Mark it with your initials and the date for identification," I said, "and take it along."

My attention moved from the evidence to Rosemary, who was still, of course, in her diaphanous gown. Furious, breathing deeply and sputtering, at that range she would have taken J. Edgar Hoover's mind off John Dillinger.

My reverie was broken abruptly by a voice behind me shouting: "Pants! The district attorney wants pants on this man!"

I wrenched my gaze away from Rosemary in time to meet the glance of Borchers. He had finished reading the warrant to Leary and had handed him a copy. The chief deputy rolled his eyes skyward and walked off toward a connecting room. As I, too, wanted no part of the developing pants crisis, I muttered something to the D.A. about checking on things downstairs and left the room.

The deputies were making progress. As I went downstairs the folk singing had tapered off, the search was progressing, and people were being led out of the central area for interrogation in side rooms.

Once again on the first floor, I entered the waterfall room. It was dark. A threadbare rug lay on the floor. By the dim light filtering in from the foyer, I could see that there was excrement on the floor here. Its odor mingled with the still strong scent of burning marijuana. It was a moment or two before I realized that the sheriff was also in the room. He was over against a wall, poking at something with the toe of his shoe. "Christ, Liddy," he said, "they've even got a dead dog in here."

I stared at a dark mass on the floor. As my eyes became accustomed to the dark, I could see that it was, indeed, a dog, lying on its back, paws in the air. A few more prods by the sheriff's toe, however, revealed that the animal was still alive. With a groan the pooch rolled over, staggered to its feet, then lurched out of the room. It was on a contact high!

By now there was considerable activity in the foyer, which lay between the waterfall room on one side and a room of nearly equal size on the other. To no apparent purpose, a large number of deputies was crossing the foyer, to and fro, in what amounted to a slow-motion parade.

I observed this phenomenon for a moment, noting that as each deputy made his crossing, he would glance covertly up the stairway. My curiosity aroused, I investigated.

A walk into the foyer and a quick glance up the stairs and the mystery was solved: on a stair just above eye level sat a young woman (later identified as a writer for a woman's magazine there to do a story on Leary, to whom the raid was a bonanza). She was wearing a night-gown hitched up above her knees, wide-spread thighs supporting a lapboard and pad upon which she was writing intently.

Appearances to the contrary, things were being accomplished. His men were reporting to the sheriff the finding of apparent contraband and, when the circumstances were of interest, they reported those too. Some were outrageous; others had the deputies laughing so hard they could hardly gasp out the story.

In the latter category was the tale of one of the first deputies through the door behind us. Young, eager, and exceptionally fleet of foot, he bounded to a top-floor hall where, obedient to the letter of his instructions, he burst through a bedroom door. Landing in the approved pistol-course crouch, massive .357 magnum revolver thrust out before him, he was ready for anything. Well, *almost* anything.

By the light of a single candle flickering from the top of a Coca-Cola bottle, he saw a young man and woman, nude, upon an ancient mat. She was on her back. He was at his apogee, about to plunge to her perigee, when the officer shouted: "FREEZE!"

For one stunned moment, the man hung there, suspended, as the forces of Eros did battle with those of Smith & Wesson. Smith & Wesson won.

"You're . . . *you're kidding!*" the wretch squeaked.

Then, eyes fixed in horror upon the muzzle of the huge handgun, to the complete dismay of the poor girl beneath him, instead of coming he went.

Not at all funny was the report of another deputy. Grasping a bedroom doorknob tightly, he thrust the door open and jumped in at an angle to his left. The maneuver was fortunate as it prevented the door from opening all the way.

This time it was the officer who froze. "The baby! My God, look out for the baby!" screamed a woman. So genuine was the note of fear in her voice, even his lungs stopped expanding in mid-breath. Surprise was followed by shock and anger at what had nearly happened. Still motionless, the deputy watched as a distraught woman darted behind the door to pick up a sleeping infant. It had been lying in a bundle of rags behind the door. Had the heavy door been opened completely, the baby would have been crushed.

By this time, I thought, the combined forces of the sheriff's and district attorney's offices should have been able to get a pair of pants on Leary, so I walked back upstairs.

I was wrong. As I reentered Leary's suite, he was struggling to get into a pair of trousers that were clearly several sizes too small.

"But I got them out of his own bedroom," a deputy was saying to Rosenblatt. "Well, the man obviously can't get into them," replied an exasperated Rosenblatt.

"I told the officer at the time," said Leary, "that these trousers belong to my son."

"There," said Rosenblatt, "they belong to his son. Anyone could see that! Now . . ."

The command, whatever it was to be, was never given. At that moment, Rosenblatt's elbow, sweeping upward with his arm in a gesture, struck a framed picture resting insecurely halfway up the wall. It fell. As luck would have it, there was at the time a young man sitting cross-legged directly underneath the picture, his back against the wall.

Unaware of the falling frame, the youth was more surprised than hurt when it nicked the tip of his nose in passing. But because the nose is a very vascular area, it bled copiously.

"They've shed blood!" screamed a girl. "Human blood!" We were right back to pandemonium.

"Violence!" "Police brutality!"

Rosenblatt rushed about assuring everyone unnecessarily that he had not intended to injure the boy as hippies pointed to him as the near-slaughterer of an innocent.

Somehow in all this, the sheriff's department had managed to get a pair of trousers on Leary. As if in fear that Leary would Houdini out of his pants again at the first opportunity, the district attorney ordered me to interview him immediately.

"Let's get out of here, Doctor," I said. "You know this place. Why don't you find us a corner where we can have a little quiet?"

Leary's answer was to lead me away to a small room on the second floor. It was about fifteen by ten feet in size. A single box was the only furniture. The floor held the usual assortment of droppings. I gestured toward the box, inviting Leary to sit down.

"I believe," said Leary, "that one increases one's understanding and ability to communicate when one's ass is in contact with the ground."

"Well," I replied, eyeing the excrement and hitching up my trousers a little higher than usual as I seated myself gratefully on the box, "to each his own."

"Doctor, my name is G. Gordon Liddy and I'm assistant district attorney of Dutchess County. I want to question you about what's been going on here, but first I want you to understand that you don't have to make any statement, and any statement you do make may be used against you in a court of law. You also have the right to a lawyer. You understand?"

The law of the state of New York did not then require that these warnings be given prior to interrogation. They were, however, the standard prelude to questioning by special agents of the FBI. As a former FBI agent, I gave them as a matter of routine and had advised the sheriff's officers to do the same.

Leary wasn't buying any. "I'm aware of my rights, Mr. Liddy," he said, "and I choose to exercise them. I intend to contact an attorney, probably from the Civil Liberties Union, just as soon as you people clear out of here, if you ever do. In the meanwhile, I'm hoping you'll understand if I say nothing to you in response to your questions."

"Certainly, Doctor," I said, rising to leave.

"Sit down, sit down," said Leary. "It isn't often these days I get a chance to talk to a civil Philistine." I paused, curious. There was also a chance that Leary might make an admission against interest.

"This raid," said Leary, "is the product of ignorance and fear."

"This raid," I replied, "is the product of a search warrant issued by the state of New York."

We sparred like that for a few minutes, he trying to get me to see the error of my ways, I trying to pick up something I could use against him. Neither of us was very successful.

"The time will come," Leary said finally, "when there will be a statue of me erected in Millbrook."

We were both smiling. "I'm afraid the closest you'll come is a burning effigy in the village square." Leary rose and, by mutual acknowledgment, the interview was over.

I returned downstairs, heard some activity in the kitchen, and poked my head through the doorway. Deputies were removing trays of ice cubes from the refrigerator to be carried away for later analysis against the possibility that the frozen liquid was not water but LSD.

"How we gonna keep these things frozen?" one deputy asked another.

"What difference does it make, dummy, if it's frozen or not?"

"For crissake, we gotta keep the evidence in the same shape we find it!"

"Sure. We're gonna scratch our initials in the ice and if it melts, there goes the I.D."

"Don't be such a fucking wise guy."

I left this discussion of the techniques of maintaining the chain of evidence to return to the waterfall room. From somewhere a small table and two chairs had been produced and placed facing each other on either side of the table. A number of couples were assembled in the foyer awaiting interrogation. I sat behind the table and the first couple was brought in. The deputy separated them and seated the male first.

I gave him the same warnings I had given Leary. Then, quickly: "Where are you from?"

"D.C."

"District of Columbia?"

"Yeah."

"Where's she from?" nodding toward the girl.

"Baltimore."

"When'd you come up here?"

"Today ... yesterday. It's after midnight."

"How'd you get here?"

"Car ... and it's mine, not stolen. You can check."

"We will. Where'd you pick her up?"

"In Baltimore. Her pad."

"Did you go anywhere else?"

"Huh?"

"Did you make any other stops or drive straight through?"

"Just for lunch, gas, on the turnpike."

"So you admit," I said, bearing down, "you traveled directly here, with a woman not your wife, crossing several state lines?"

"Yeah. Sure. So what?"

I was being clever now, employing an old police technique: Get the suspect to admit to a violation of law not in your jurisdiction and "give him a break"—a promise not to turn him over to other authorities for the foreign offense in return for information helpful in one's own jurisdiction. In this case I was going to hit him with the Mann Act—the so-called White Slave Traffic Act, intended to break up interstate prostitution rings by making it a violation of federal law to transport a woman across state lines for "immoral purposes." It was a law never intended to apply to what the Department of Justice referred to discreetly as "personal escapades."

"And when you arrived here," I continued in my best Efrem Zimbalist, Jr. manner, "you had sexual intercourse with her, didn't you?"

"Jesus Christ, man; you guys never gave us the chance!" So much for my cleverness.

With a sigh I dismissed them both and asked a deputy where the bathroom was. There was one off the kitchen. Once there, I found the usual equipment and raised the lid and seat together with the toe of my shoe. There was no telling what godawful disease these people had and I was not going to contract one if I could avoid it.

The raised lid revealed a large, multicolored eye painted directly above the waterline at the back of the bowl. From the viewpoint of the average standing man, its azimuth and elevation made it a perfect target. I was trying my luck and thinking that nothing more could go wrong, when it did.

"WHAM! whap, whap, whap, BAM!" The sound of gunfire.

"Sweet Jesus, no!" I thought. "Not that!" In my mind's eyes I could see the headline:

MASSACRE AT MILLBROOK!
Police Guns Mow Down
Flower Children
Who Offered No Resistance

I got myself together as quickly as I could and dashed out to the foyer. Everyone else in range had the same idea. In shocked silence we discovered the source of the "gunfire." Coming to a halt in the driveway before the front door was a convertible, its top down in the frigid weather. Three college-age boys were on the front seat. As the first struggled drunkenly to get out of the car, a second set off another string of firecrackers and cherry bombs: "Whap, whap, whap, BAM!"

Laughing joyfully, the three staggered up the porch steps. "*Party! Party! Party!*" shouted one as they tumbled through the front door.

The astonishment of the three to find themselves suddenly in the midst of a platoon of jackbooted, heavily armed sheriff's deputies was matched only by the equal astonishment of the deputies themselves.

The would-be party guests, however, were finding things less and less fun. One, who had been driving the car, was fairly sober. He kept trying to make his companions realize the seriousness of the situation. "Listen," he was saying, "if there ever was a party here, there's none now. We've gotta get out of here!"

"Naw, ish a costume pardy. Lookit alla cowboys!"

"Shut up, for Christ's sake. They're cops!"

"Cops?"

"This joint is busted, man, busted!"

"Geesuz!"

The deputies did nothing to relieve the boy's sense of impending doom. One gave me the high sign, and I returned to my interview chair in the waterfall room. A moment later, the soberest of the three was hauled before me.

"Your name?"

"Sir, please, I can explain . . ."

"Your *name!*"

"My name? Mm . . . Mitchell Masters Gibbs the Third. Sir, you must believe me. We meant no harm. We're up

161

from Princeton for the weekend. There was a dance at Bennett (a now-defunct junior college for the daughters of the very rich, situated in Millbrook). After, we had a few drinks . . ."

"A few?"

"Well, quite a lot, actually."

"I can see that."

"Yes. Well, we dropped the girls off at the campus and someone said there was always a party at Leary's. We had trouble finding it . . ."

I gave him Broderick Crawford in *Highway Patrol*: "You realize you could be indicted—*right now, mister*—for mopery with intent to creep, in the nightime, on a raided premises, in the *first degree*? Do you know what you could *get* for that?"

"Oh, God, my father . . ."

"God the Father, Son, and Holy Ghost together couldn't clear *this* beef, kid."

"No, no. You don't understand. I mean my real father. He's president of _____ Steel. He's never going to understand. Never!"

I hadn't seen such abject misery since the Monsignor caught the kid next to me in the choir with his hand up the gown of a neighboring contralto. I relented.

"Mister, you're lucky. I think you'd be convicted after the jury got its first free lunch from the county. But I also think we've got a criminal intent problem here. You'd be sprung two years later by the court of appeals. A lot of work for nothing. So I'm going to have a deputy drive the three of you back to your motel. But none of you better ever come back here again until the statute of limitations on mopery runs out. You understand?"

He never said another word, just nodded his head vigorously in assent and turned to follow a deputy out the front door.

The mopery episode pretty much concluded the festivities for the evening. Early morning, I should say—it was almost daylight when the last cruiser pulled away.

When we sorted out the haul, we found that we were long on scientific journals kept by Leary in the course of his experimentation with psychedelic drugs, but short on the drugs themselves. We did come up with quite a few checks from weekenders who hoped to deduct as a "charitable contribution" to Leary's foundation what were actually payments for drugs and instructions in their use.

There was a second raid a short time later that produced substantially more in drugs. Save for a chaotic ten minutes when a goat, tethered insecurely outside the kitchen door, broke loose and ran into and through the house pursued frantically by deputies, its hilarity was limited.

Leary did indeed secure the services of an ACLU attorney. He was Noel Tepper, a clever opponent. Tepper demanded and received a suppression hearing in county court before Judge Baratta. One of the few former district attorneys I know with a sense of humor, even Baratta was going bananas by the time Tepper put his fifth Hindu on the stand to describe the alleged religious significance of the seized material.

Fortunately for Leary (and Judge Baratta, who otherwise would have been studying Hindu religion for a year), the Supreme Court of the United States decided *Miranda* v. *Arizona* in June. *Deus ex machina*. Everyone was off the hook.

The warnings I and every other interviewing officer had given on the night of the raid did not include the offer of free counsel should the suspect be unable to afford one. Neither was there obtained what the Supreme Court described as a "knowing waiver" of the right to remain silent. None of the statements disclosing who was rooming where, so necessary to establish possession, were any longer of legal value. We did, however, have a chance at Leary for maintaining a nuisance, or some such misdemeanor, so the makings of a bargain were there.

Judge Baratta, ever the practical man and now haunted by Hindus from Noel Tepper's seemingly inexhaustible

163

supply, approved a compromise. Everybody won, nobody lost. Leary went scot-free; but his stay in Dutchess County was over forever. Off Leary went to other pursuits. So did I.

XIII

By 1967 the national controversy over the Vietnam war had arrived in Dutchess County and added to the divisiveness engendered by the civil rights movement. When Martin Luther King, Jr. announced his opposition to the war and his intention to sponsor massive demonstrations against Vietnam as well as racial inequality, the tension began to build. There was talk of a "long, hot, summer" among the student left at Bard and Vassar and colleges across the county, as well as in the black community, and in numerous police departments.

I was involved deeply in the intelligence work trying to get an accurate picture of what was coming, working principally with Bob Berberich of the Poughkeepsie city police. Day after day, as summer approached, reports came in of agitation in the black community for a demonstration in Poughkeepsie. It would not, the reports insisted increasingly, be peaceful. Details included the alleged stockpiling of incendiary devices such as Molotov cocktails and of firearms on rooftops and in cellars in the lower Main Street area, as well as plans both to close off the ghetto to nonblacks and to march out from it into upper- and middle-class white neighborhoods.

I was ready too, but for a different reason. I knew that when the whole student left, antiwar, civil rights, and anything-goes-so-long-as-it's-against-the-United States movements had coalesced and reached a backwater like Poughkeepsie, the kettle that had been simmering for years was about to boil over nationally. I believed a time of great challenge was at hand for the nation and for me personally. For some years, as I watched all this develop, had been building my willpower in a manner that was a continuation of the technique of resisting physical pain I had used as a teenager to win a place on a championship cross-country team despite scarred lungs. It was a technique recognized in the East, but not well known to Western civilization. I had begun by using lighted cigarettes, then matches and candles, progressively increasing the time I exposed my body to pain as I built up my will, much as one might build muscles by lifting increasingly heavy weights. By 1967 the exposures had become long enough to start leaving small permanent scars. Still I persisted, always using my left hand and forearm so as never to incapacitate my right—my gun-hand. Then I made a mistake.

I burned the underside of the second joint of my left index finger so badly it required surgical attention. Fortunately, the surgeon was from India and familiar with the practice, although he found it unusual in an Occidental. He told me that it would take a year before I could fully straighten my left index finger, and then only after repeated exercise to stretch the scar tissue that would form in the angle of the joint. I had, it seemed, nearly cooked out the joint and lost a tendon. If I was going to continue the practice, I would have to be very careful.

Since my will was now so strong I could endure a long, deep, flesh-charring burn without a flicker of expression, I wasn't concerned. I thought I'd gone as far as I reasonably could and saw no need to try to go further; I was ready for anything.

When the Poughkeepsie riot arrived, it started right where reports said it would—in the lower Main Street black ghetto. It began with milling about in the street, the lighting of gutter fires, erecting street barricades of junk and garbage, and a lot of emotionally charged talk of "breaking out" to march into the neighborhoods of "whitey." The police first patrolled the area heavily, breaking up concentrations of people and, finally, sealed it off in

165

an attempt to keep the trouble confined. Politicians and the press combined to downgrade what was going on to a "disturbance." For a while it was a police/black stalemate. Then, as more and more alcohol and fiery speech were added to the mix, the surge outward began. The police resisted and cleared the street.

Again the response came from the place predicted by Berberich's reports: the rooftops. From there assorted missiles, up to and including furniture, were hurled down upon the police. A fire started in the street was extinguished quickly by some blacks who protested to others that it made no sense for blacks to burn down their own homes. The police, I with them, took cover behind police cars as the missiles rained down from above. When some police reported that others a good distance away were receiving small arms fire, I listened but could hear no shots. Just then one-half of a heavy metal shear, a scissorlike device used in duct construction, hit the street a few feet away with such force it was embedded in the asphalt point first. There was another shout of "incoming fire," and the police began shooting at the rooftops and upper-floor windows of the tenement houses that lined the north side of the street. Searching the rooftops and windows, I could see no one. As the police were reloading, I and several senior officers shouted, "Cease fire." That ended the shooting. Once again my FBI programming on the use of firearms had stood me in good stead, my magnum unused.

The Poughkeepsie riots of 1967 ground to a halt soon after that, but the experience prompted me to look ahead —somewhat grimly. I felt increasingly that something had to be done to arrest the tide of national disorder and weakness—and I became more and more convinced that the power of political office was needed to do it. The next logical step up in Dutchess County was to district attorney. But a local D.A. has very little impact in national terms, and if he pursues his job vigorously he's likely to make certain enemies who can cut off any progress to higher office. I decided to try to leapfrog local and state involve-

166

ment, trying directly for Washington where I could do some good. Besides, even if the progress from D.A. to family court judge, to county court judge, and so forth until a congressional opening occurred when someone died was a sure thing—which it was not—it was a *slow* thing, and at thirty-seven I wanted to change the way things were going in the United States *now*.

As it happened the congressional seat for New York's Twenty-eighth District was now open because the incumbent was abandoning it to try for the Senate. I was a Republican, and working for that seat entailed opposing Hamilton Fish, Jr. for the GOP nomination. Fish, son of Franklin Roosevelt's old adversary, had the inside track—and the money. I was making $8,000 a year; it was an indulgence for me to pursue politics while Frances held the family together working as a schoolteacher. The Twenty-eighth District consisted of Dutchess County and a lot more (all told, it was nearly the size of Connecticut). How could I find the wherewithal to mount a primary campaign?

The answer—or part of an answer—came from out of the blue. A man from the Washington-based United Republicans of America, dedicated to helping conservative thinkers secure Republican congressional nominations around the country, approached me with an offer of help. The group promised $5,000 in cash, goods and services, plus the help of a strong direct-mail machinery. They made the campaign seem possible.

But I wanted to talk it over with Fran first. Five children, a job, and working on her master's at night so she could earn more. Wasn't this enough of a burden for her without adding the demands of an election campaign? I told her the opponent, Ham Fish, was the party's designated choice, and that precipitating a primary would irritate some important GOP figures. The party stalwarts felt they owned Dutchess after having gone undefeated in that county for more than fifty years. It was uphill, I told Fran; steep uphill and loaded with roadblocks, too. But Fran,

167

who had backed me throughout our married life, was will
ing to do so once again. I decided to go for it.

The first thing I did was visit the Republican count
chairman, Jay Rollins. I told him what I wanted to do. I'r
not sure Rollins took me seriously, or believed I had th
stomach to go through with it, but to his credit he told m
it was an open party and I was free to seek the nominatio
without being thought disloyal, a position for which h
later took a lot of abuse.

Next I contacted members of New York's Conservativ
Party, a potent force in state politics because it had th
third line on the ballot. I wanted their nomination; the
wanted to know my stands on the issues. I was strong o
national defense, supported the Vietnam war in that
wanted to go all out to win it; was against gun control
was accepted by the sportsmen whose clubs for huntin
and fishing made up the New York State Conservatio
Council (I was their firearms legislative counsel and the
had awarded me their Golden Fish award), and no on
had to ask my stand on the drug counterculture, civil dis
order, and conventional crime—my record as a prose
cutor spoke to that. Still, I had a tough time with th
Ulster County delegation because I wouldn't advocat
elimination of the income tax (I didn't know where th
money would come from to run the government), no
would I condemn labor unions, because I believe that the
contribute to industrial and political stability and thei
abuses are curable by legislation.

The Conservative Party offered me its nomination o
condition that I not repeat what a prior Republican pri
mary candidate who had received it had done when h
lost: send out letters to Conservative voters asking then
not to vote for him, but for the winner of the Republica
primary. This was important to the Conservatives becaus
a low vote on the Conservative Party line might caus
them to lose that line to the Liberal Party, and to forfei
credibility generally as a political force in the state.

I told the Conservatives that if I didn't get the Republican nomination but still believed I had a chance to win by running on the Conservative line alone (if, for example, I'd received a high vote in the Republican primary and I had sufficient resources to mount a winning general election campaign), I'd consider it. But I also told them that if I saw that my active candidacy (my name could not legally be removed from the ballot at that point) would have the effect of electing a Democrat, I wouldn't go through with it. I'd nominally endorse the Republican winner and stay out of it, promising only not to send out the letters they found so offensive.

I got the Conservative nomination. It was a boost because it carried heavy weight with conservative Republicans, who, despite their distaste for the liberal policies of Governor Nelson Rockefeller and Senator Jacob Javits, hadn't quit the party to join the Conservatives, and who would be a force in any primary election because they would vote their convictions.

John O'Shea, an independent insurance agent and one of the most organized men I know, agreed to become my campaign manager, and Vincent Cuccia, who had been assistant D.A. under the legendary Frank Hogan in Manhattan, signed on as treasurer. We were off and running. The campaign was hard work, great fun, and taught me a lot about politics.

My opponent, Ham Fish, would not debate me. I didn't blame him. Why should he help me get voter recognition outside Dutchess? Learning that he was scheduled to appear on a radio talk show with a big audience and telephone call-ins, I got hold of the Democratic candidate, John Dyson, and invited him up to my headquarters to have some fun. As soon as the show started, Dyson and I, using separate extension phones, got poor Ham on the line and proceeded to have a three-way debate of the issues.

On another occasion, Fish had arranged to be the guest speaker at a festival in a small Dutchess County town under complete party control. No one there wanted to see or hear from me. I got there early to see what I could stir up. I found that the festivities were to be carried live over the largest radio station in the county. A remote unit had been set up on a front porch of the main street into town, which commanded a view of the parade route and the area where the speech would take place. I knew the radio guys and it was easy to persuade them to help me even things up a little.

The radio men dutifully reported the parade with Fish and let its listeners hear the school band that provided the music. While things were being set up for Ham's speech, we got out some old tapes and, using the sounds of a frenzied crowd attending some long-forgotten football game and a voice-over while blending in some taped martial music that made the Marine Corps band sound like the Camp Fire girls, the announcer started in:

"Listen to that crowd, ladies and gentlemen! Just listen to them! Someone's coming! They're going wild! Wait a minute . . . I can almost see who it is . . . it's . . . GORDON LIDDY! Listen to that crowd!"

Over the radio it sounded to Dutchess County like Adolf Hitler entering Nuremberg in 1934. The fact was that the crowd consisted of the two radio guys and me, sitting on the porch having a ball. When I spoke it sounded like I was addressing Yankee Stadium at halftime during the Super Bowl as far as the public was concerned. People started to feel sorry for Fish.

The funny moments sustained those of us in the campaign through the long, hard work that is the guts of American politics; door-to-door canvassing, hundreds of meetings for coffee in living rooms, speeches at night before a hundred in a firehouse or a thousand in a high school auditorium; endless traveling, the serious, earnest question-and-answer sessions on what's wrong with the country and how to put it right. Every spare moment she had, Fran accompanied me and I won many a vote that was really for her.

The only serious faltering in the campaign was by the

mail-order machinery the URA had promised. After the immensely successful first two mailings, the third was canceled and the fourth mailed so late much of it arrived after the primary. To this day I believed that failure cost me the win: Fish beat me, 51 percent to 49 percent, but I took Dutchess, stunning the county GOP organization.

But I was not the Republican nominee.

Now I had to confront the decision of whether to campaign actively on the Conservative ticket. The Conservative Party urged me to press on, but since their campaign fund was all of $300 and the election was five months away, I judged that my running would only ensure that Fish would lose to Democrat Dyson. I privately concluded I should not run.

I still was in the grip of my original motivation, however: to get to Washington where I could affect things on a national scale. Could I use my apparent deciding-vote status to make that happen? I went to see the new county GOP chairman, George Reid. Reid was honest, well-intended—and troubled. It was his job to get Ham Fish elected. This meant unifying the party and controlling the loose cannon called Gordon Liddy.

I told Reid that I was considering running on the Conservative line, but that "for the good of the party," I might endorse Fish and accept appointment to the imminently vacant office of Dutchess County district attorney. I chose that phantom goal because I knew that the assistant attorney, Albert Rosenblatt, wanted it enough to fight for it. That should line up my opponents' sights on the wrong target.

Reid jumped at the chance to offer me the appointment as district attorney, something he sincerely believed he could deliver but that I, knowing the feelings of the party pros, guessed he could not. Reid even went so far as to take me to Washington to see the Republican House Minority Leader, Gerald Ford.

I had already met Mr. Ford when he had appeared in Dutchess to speak on behalf of the party. He needed transportation and someone had gotten the use of a twin-engined private plane (Ford would not fly in a single-engined plane). I had learned to fly in 1967, and my friend Bob Schwalb, a pilot of exceptional ability, let me talk him into serving with me as the two-man flight crew to fly Ford back and forth to Washington. Ford quickly endorsed my being named district attorney, something that alarmed me because I thought that with Ford behind it I might actually get the appointment.

I needn't have worried. Rosenblatt picked up all his political IOUs and went to work to block Reid. I endorsed Ham Fish, though I declined to send out mailings to Conservatives in violation of my promise, and I sat back waiting for Rosenblatt to make it impossible for George Reid to keep his promise. I intended then to call upon Reid to get me a post with the Republicans on Capitol Hill—something I was now sure he could deliver through the intercession of Gerald Ford.

Enter Harvey Dann, a prominent insurance agency owner over in New York City who had been a classmate of John Mitchell and who lived in the Quaker Hill section of Pawling. We had never met, but he invited Frances and me to dinner at his home for a "little chat about your future." Curious, I accepted.

Dann said that he was a friend and supporter of Ham Fish, and he was impressed by my plurality over him in Dutchess. To Dann, that meant that I had a good organization and knew how to lead it. He had learned that I was interested in becoming district attorney. He thought that hardly worth my effort. He had, he said, a much better idea; he was deeply involved in the effort to elect Richard Nixon President in November. What, he wanted to know, did I think of Mr. Nixon?

I told Dann that Fran and I had met Mr. Nixon when he spoke in the county a year or two previously, and I had been impressed by what he said, his skill in saying it, and his personal warmth. I supported Richard Nixon and intended to vote for him.

172

Dann asked whether I'd be willing to do more than that. I asked what he had in mind.

According to Dann, the drive to elect Nixon was in trouble in the state of New York. Although Nixon had the ostensible support of Rockefeller, the Governor was seeing to it that most of the party resources were being used to ensure the reelection of Senator Javits and to build a larger Republican congressional delegation from the state, as well as elect local and state candidates. The Nixon effort was dying on the vine. Dann's classmate, John Mitchell, Nixon's national campaign manager, had given him the task of building a separate effort for Nixon in the mid-Hudson Valley region. Similar efforts were under way in other areas of the state.

Dann wanted me to take charge of the Nixon separate effort, called "Citizens for Nixon/Agnew" in the mid-Hudson area centered on Dutchess County and to devote my primary election organization and personal following to that task. I would have to be interviewed at Nixon campaign headquarters in New York City, but he was sure I would pass muster and be given the assignment. If I took it and brought Nixon a plurality in our area, and he won the election, I would, Dann assured me, "land on your feet." And he would see that John Mitchell knew about my work. I believed in the Nixon candidacy and in my ability with my supporters to do the job for him. I also believed that my performance would give me an IOU. Yes, I would land on my feet—and those feet would be in Washington, D.C.

I took the job and threw myself into the Nixon campaign, opening storefront headquarters, getting them manned, buying advertising, organizing for election day, and generally taking care of the myriad details that go into a successful campaign. I even had some fun with the advertising. One of the themes of the 1968 Nixon campaign was the slogan, in atrocious English, "This time, vote like your whole life depends on it." I put up huge billboards carrying that slogan, but then had sign painters modify it so that the mid-Hudson area had the only Nixon ads that were grammatically correct:

as if
"This time, vote ~~like~~ your whole life depends on it."

I had a friend rent a rebuilt Stearman biplane for me—one of the fabric-covered, double-winged, radial-engined old-timers with open cockpits, used to train pilots for the military in World War II. It was bright red. My friend and I lay on our backs and, using white water-soluble poster paint, printed a big *NIXON* underneath one bottom wing and a big *AGNEW* under the other. Then, wearing leather flying jackets, helmets, and goggles against the November cold in the open cockpits, we took off on election day for the two cities in Dutchess County: Poughkeepsie and Beacon.

My friend knew me well enough to be worried about his license so I made sure I had the controls when we got over the targets. I buzzed the main streets of both cities. At Poughkeepsie, I couldn't resist climbing out, then rolling into a screaming, redline dive directly down at the windows of Ham Fish's campaign headquarters on the top floor of a corner building on Market Street. I pulled out with a roar of power from the big Pratt & Whitney radial engine after scaring the shit out of Ham's staff, then flew back to the airfield with a grin so big my gums damn near froze from the prop wash. Calls were coming into the FAA in a stream but, as I had figured, the complainants kept identifying the plane as a World War I fighter with *NIXON/AGNEW* on the wings, and the harried FAA kept answering, "Lady, there ain't no airplanes registered *NIXON/AGNEW*; you gotta gimme the *numbers*!"

A quick hosing off with cold water destroyed the evidence, but some reporters caught me coming back into town still carrying my helmet and goggles. When they accused me of breaking the law, I laughed and told them that the election law forbids electioneering within 100 feet of a polling place. "Hell, I always pulled up a hundred feet when I flew over a polling place."

Nixon took Dutchess with a 15,000-vote plurality. Not long thereafter Chairman Reid came to see me. He was embarrassed because he couldn't deliver on his promise of the district attorney job. He suggested that we go to see Gerald Ford about a job in Washington.

The question was, what job should we talk about? I'd done my homework and was ready with the answer: Special Assistant to the Secretary of the Treasury, for Enforcement. It was a sub-Cabinet-level post, which didn't require Senate confirmation. What I didn't know was that it was a post also wanted by Eugene Rossides, one-time Columbia football star turned lawyer and spokesman for the Greek lobby. He wanted the job upgraded to the rank of Assistant Secretary and joined with the position of Assistant Secretary for Tariff and Trade Affairs. As a close political ally of the once-more victorious Senator Javits, he got what he wanted.

In Washington Reid explained his problem to Ford, and Ford unhesitatingly tried to live up to *his* word by asking how he could help. We told him the problem. Ford, an old pro if ever there was one, was quick to see that since the Rossides job had been upgraded to Assistant Secretary, there was no reason why I couldn't still become Special Assistant to the Secretary, as I had wanted. Ford called Rossides while we sat in his office. He stroked Rossides skillfully, calling him "Mr. Secretary" and invoking Rossides's residual renown as a football player as only another football player could. Then Ford applied subtle pressure not lost on Rossides, who had not yet been confirmed by the Senate. Ford was, after all, the House Minority Leader and many a Treasury official (including me) would eventually be up on the Hill to testify in favor of the new administration's programs. Ford sent me to see Rossides.

Rossides, short, bald and powerfully built, was a curious mixture of assertiveness and insecurity. He was unhappy about my title as Special Assistant to the Secretary, preferring that I be called some kind of assistant to *him*, but I had it wired and we both knew it. He sent me on a courtesy call to Under Secretary Charls Walker and to the office of Senator Javits, and then the job was mine. Since the old "for Enforcement" position had been merged with his, mine was to be "for Organized Crime" to satisfy the technicalities.

I went home and gave Fran the good news. We decided that I would go to Washington alone at first so the children could complete the school year without interruption, then she would come down to help house-hunt. My supporters were delighted, and the Dutchess Republican organization relieved, when I went off to Washington.

It was March 1969. The nation was at war not only externally in Vietnam but internally. Within the previous thirty months 28 had died in Watts; 40 in the race riot in Detroit, which required federal paratroopers to restore order. In the past year 125 cities had been hit by riots, including the nation's capital, and the army had to be called out. Snipers had shot at police in Cleveland as violence was increasingly directed against them as a "revolutionary" tactic. The Democrats reaped the fruits of their permissiveness as their own national convention was trashed by a radical mob. Huge "peace" demonstrations led to such scenes as army troops fighting off protesters assaulting the Pentagon. Like the millions who had voted for Richard Nixon, I was fed up with the double standard of the left. I had learned long ago the maxims of Cicero that "laws are inoperative in war" and that "the good of the people is the chief law." That "anything goes" concept so beloved of the left-liberals cuts both ways.

Looking back now from a decade later many people think of that time as the era of the "flower-child" and wonder how we could think of them as a war-like enemy. As a reminder that we weren't simply dodging flowers in those days, I offer these lines, spoken by Mark William Rudd, leader of The Weatherman faction of the Students for a Democratic Society. He delivered them in 1969 at a national "war council" of the Weathermen in Flint, Michigan:

> ". . . We have to start tearing down this fucking country. We have to have a revolution in this country that's going to overthrow—like bombs, like guns, like fire bombs, by anything and everything. . . . The most important thing that the Weathermachine should be right now is to create a consciousness, a political consciousness and the best way to create this is by doing and performing some kind of exemplary action, like offing some pigs, creating chaos in the streets, blowing up pig stations, blowing up banks. Once the Weathermachine begins this and starts the ball rolling, then the Weathermachine will not have to be involved as much. Other white revolutionaries are going to get involved and try to destroy the system that we all hate so much."

That, to me, is war. I was ready. And willing.

XIV

I wanted to start to work immediately, so I imposed upon the hospitality of Al and Paula Beitel, my uncle and aunt in Chevy Chase, Maryland, while looking for an apartment within walking distance of the Treasury. I found one on Rhode Island Avenue, Northwest, at Fifteenth Street. I should have looked a little longer.

Only when I'd moved in did I notice all the hooker traffic and furtive meetings in hallways. When I went outside to say good-bye to my Aunt Paula, who had hauled my gear down in her car, I *really* found out where I was living. Walking toward the car, I heard a scuffle to my rear and, turning, saw two black men mug and rob a white man. Well, I'd come to Washington to fight crime, hadn't

I? I charged the two muggers, thinking that if I took care of one, the victim could handle the other.

To my surprise, both muggers, no doubt astonished, fled. I took off after them, thinking to flag down a police car along the way. No police were to be found. They crossed Fourteenth Street and stopped running a few yards from the corner. I didn't know then that Fourteenth Street, Northwest, is Washington's red-light district, riot corridor, and heroin heaven all rolled into one. I found out.

In a moment I was surrounded by guys off the doorsteps of ravaged row houses. About seven looked as if they wanted to play; the rest were spectators. I knew this would be one fight I wasn't going to win, so I decided to get in the first blow. As mugger number one said, "You followin' me or sumpin', mister?" I answered, "Yeah!" and hit him with a sucker right-hand lead to the jaw. He went down and the fight was on. It was off again pretty quickly when someone hit me hard from behind.

I wasn't out, because I remember what happened, but everything suddenly seemed in slow motion and voices sounded far away. My arms wouldn't do what my brain told them and my legs gave way. On the way down I took a kick on the left shoulder. I tried to get up but couldn't. A hand dipped into my pocket and my wallet was gone. Simultaneously the crowd vanished into the row houses and the police arrived. They helped me to my feet and, after explaining, I led them into the building. By that time the quarry had fled through the back door so I went back to my apartment to clean up.

The next day I submitted a memorandum advising Treasury that I had lost a fight and their building pass. My shoulder hurt, so I went to the aid unit for some aspirin. They asked me why, in triplicate, and when I explained they refused to give me any until my shoulder was X-rayed. The film revealed that my left clavicle had been sheared off near the end, and I was sent to an orthopedic surgeon. I explained to him that I was living alone and couldn't dress in a cast so he devised a harness that had me looking like Quasimodo for the next six weeks.

I decided that for so long as I was living in that neighborhood I'd better carry a gun. I learned that the Washington police wouldn't give a gun permit to someone at Treasury because that was up to the Secretary; if he wanted his agents to carry firearms, he had by regulation the power to arm them. The Secret Service, Customs, IRS, and the Bureau of Alcohol, Tobacco and Firearms all came under Treasury and each had certain agents authorized to carry a gun. All I needed was to become a "Treasury agent" within the meaning of that law, get myself some credentials that would satisfy any police officer who might notice I was armed, and I'd be all set.

It was very clear to me that I, as Special Assistant to the Secretary of the Treasury for Organized Crime, was a Treasury agent within the meaning of the regulation authorizing the carrying of a gun, so I put something to that effect in the file. But what about credentials? My building pass wouldn't do; every clerk and secretary had one. That proved to be no problem either.

When I was originally briefed I was shown a stock of gold badges and imposing credential covers bearing the seal of the Treasury in gold on simulated morocco leather. For insertion inside there were blank credentials. These bore beautifully engraved and scrolled UNITED STATES TREASURY DEPARTMENT. Under this example of the best work of the Bureau of Engraving and Printing, which produces our currency, was a splendid, light blue rendering of the main Treasury building. Across the face of the building could be printed any name and title desired. The lower portion bore the seal of the Treasury, a signature line for the "holder" and a countersignature line for the Assistant Secretary for Administration. There was space for a photograph and the legend:

whose signature and photograph appear hereon is an accredited representative of the Department of the

179

Treasury of the United States and as such is authorized to conduct official inquiries on behalf of the
United States Government.

The credential said nothing about firearms, but it was
so impressive-looking nobody would challenge it. These
credentials and badges were phony. They were for the use
of the Central Intelligence Agency.

Everyone knew that the Treasury had many different
law enforcement agents of one kind or another, but few
knew—or cared—what they actually were. This made
"Treasury agent" an ideal cover for CIA officers operating
within the United States. The Treasury, on request of the
CIA, would make up a credential and issue a gold badge
in any name desired and any photograph supplied. I
promptly had my photograph, name, and title made up
into one of the credential sets and was equipped to carry
a gun anywhere in the United States. The Lord helps those
who help themselves.

When I first came down to Washington, I was traveling
light and brought only three guns with me: my .357 magnum Smith & Wesson, a snub-nosed Colt .38 Special, and
a big Colt 1911 government model .45 caliber semiautomatic pistol. Within days of moving into the Windsor
House I had occasion to use one, when there was a knock
on my door at two in the morning.

Not expecting visitors at that hour but aware the place
was crawling with pimps, hookers, hopheads, and what
have you, I picked up the .45 auto.

An unloaded gun is worthless and *every* gun should
always be treated as loaded, so mine always were. I eased
the slide back to make sure there was a round in the chamber, thumbed back the hammer, and slipped on the safety.
I held the gun muzzle down, as I approached the door,
first turning on the hall light so I would be illuminated
brightly, then reaching forward to open the door from a
distance. A huge black man loomed in the doorway. He
saw the big Colt and froze.

"Good morning," I said, "what can I do for you today?"

The man's eyes bugged out. He just couldn't get them off the massive .45. "Er, ah, 'scuse me," he blurted finally, "could I, er, ah, borry a stamp?"

"Sorry, pal; this window's closed." I snapped the safety off the Colt with a click that echoed down the empty hallway.

"You wanna be careful, wanderin' around a place like this at night," I said, swinging the muzzle of the .45 up to cover his belly. "Don't you know," I called after him as he bolted for the stairwell, "this is a bad neighborhood?"

But he was long gone, and I was laughing so hard my shoulder was killing me.

At Treasury, I was sent to monitor the Capitol Hill deliberations of the Committtee for the Reform of Federal Criminal Law. Among many other things it was considering new gun-control legislation and the staff was loaded with antigunners. Our interest was official, because Treasury's Bureau of Alcohol, Tobacco and Firearms had investigative and regulatory jurisdiction of the subject. There I met two who shared my thinking on the issue: Wally Johnson, an aide to Senator Roman Hruska, and Donald Santarelli, one of three newly appointed Associate Deputy Attorneys General.

The three of us were of one mind concerning gun control: we were against it and recognized that the shooting sports constituency was a vast, politically oriented group that could form a vital element in support of Richard Nixon's new administration. But this required the administration's backing the right of law-abiding individuals to own and use firearms for hunting, competitive shooting, and self-protection. We wanted to resist the push by entrenched liberal bureaucrats at the IRS who were working for more restrictive laws aimed ultimately at the disarming of American citizens.

I have long opposed gun-control legislation on philosophical and practical grounds. Philosophically, I think it wrong to take away a property right of all the people, exercised currently by about 100 million citizens, on the ground that a tiny minority have abused that right, or on the even more specious ground that members of the majority *might* abuse it sometime in the future. I cannot imagine a more liberal position.

Practically, gun control is useless as a deterrent to crime. In the late '60s a survey to determine how many crimes had been solved in New York City during the more than fifty years its strict Sullivan Law had been requiring licensing and registration revealed *not one* crime solved through tracing the serial numbers on a gun registered under the law. Were one able to wave a magic wand and make all firearms in the country disappear overnight, about 95 percent of all crime in the United States designated as "serious" by the FBI would be unaffected. Registration, licensing, and other attempts to regulate firearms possession have as much chance of being effective as Pope Innocent III's attempt to ban the crossbow in the Middle Ages. As one professional criminal put it to me:

> On my mother, when I go on a piece of work I don't look to hurt nobody. But God forbid something goes wrong and I gotta do what I gotta do and the sucker's got a piece. I mean it ain't all that cut and dried you know—he could end up whackin' *me* out. I hope they take away *all* them guns from *all* them legitimate schmucks. Me? Forget about it. I'll always have a pistol when I need one.

Because of his new position at Justice I got to know Don Santarelli well; we liked each other immediately, and Santarelli proceeded to fill me in on the players in the new administration. As a result I cannot say that I wasn't warned, early, about John Dean.

Dean, together with George Revercomb and Santarelli, was an Associate Deputy Attorney General. The three of them operated under the supervision of Richard Kleindienst and had access to John Mitchell. Santarelli advised me to be careful of what I said around Dean. When I asked why, he explained that Dean was an "idea thief." If one mentioned a good idea in Dean's presence, one remotely in Dean's area of official interest, before one's memorandum was out of the typewriter, Dean's would be on the appropriate desk, crediting himself with the idea. "A word to the wise," said Santarelli. As I can attest from this and other instances, not listening to Santarelli's evaluations of people is a mistake; he can sniff a phony from farther away than a bloodhound can smell a dead sock.

Don and I quickly agreed to coordinate informally on the firearms issue so that Justice and Treasury would stay in step.

The second major item on my agenda at Treasury was the problem of drug abuse. In September 1968 candidate Nixon had promised to "move against the source of drugs." President Nixon wanted to make good as soon as possible and the Departments of Justice (which had direction of the Bureau of Narcotics and Dangerous Drugs) and Treasury (which controlled the Bureau of Customs) were given the lead to do something effective, fast. That led to the formation of the Special Presidential Task Force Relating to Narcotics, Marijuana and Dangerous Drugs, which led to Operation Intercept and, eventually, the Paraquat program.

Dick Kleindienst and Gene Rossides were appointed cochairmen of the task force. I was one of twenty members from a broad range of cabinet departments along with key agencies and bureaus assigned to develop a program for the President. By 6 June 1969 the report was ready.

It zeroed in on Mexico as the source of much of the problem; the idea was to get Mexico to do something effective about the growing of marijuana and opium poppy which were finding their way into the United States in great quantities. Although for diplomatic reasons our report paid lip service to the Mexican efforts—more so than we would have but for the Department of State—

the fact was that the United States was not at all satisfied with the Mexican effort and we were determined to do something about it. As our report said:

> Despite this country's encouragement, and the efforts of Mexican authorities to aid in the effective control of illegal trafficking in marijuana and dangerous drugs, Mexican resources and efforts continue to be inadequate. . . .

> For a number of years the Mexican Government has employed light observation planes and helicopters on spotting missions, but it would appear that these operations to date have not been of sufficient scope to cover adequately the vast land area where these crops can be found. The use of broad remote-sensing techniques in states involved, with subsequent crop identification by agricultural experts, would appear to be more efficient and effective. If the Mexican Government has such a capability at the present time, it is not being used for this purpose. *On the other hand, there is no question that the United States is capable of undertaking such missions.* (emphasis supplied)

The last referred to a idea I submitted for the use of sophisticated aerial reconnaissance to spot the Mexican drug crops. We knew that Mexico had no such capability and wanted official Mexican acquiescence in our doing it. Regarding what should be done with the crops once located, here was the heart of what we wanted to do:

> . . . the Task Force is impressed with the potential effectiveness of chemical crop destruction utilizing aircraft.

Right there was the genesis of the Paraquat program, but:

Before embarking on such a program, it would be necessary to obtain the agreement of the Mexican Government.

We rushed to get the report out by 6 June because there was a bilateral meeting between the governments of Mexico and the United States scheduled for 9–11 June to deal specifically with the problems of illicit traffic in narcotics and other dangerous drugs.

When the United States and Mexico met and these recommendations were raised, the Mexicans, using diplomatic language of course, told us to go piss up a rope. The Nixon administration didn't believe in the United States' taking crap from any foreign government. Its reply was Operation Intercept.

Operation Intercept was billed as a program to shut off the flow of drugs from Mexico by maximum application of the right to search persons and vehicles crossing the border for contraband. As part of the effort to convince people that that was what it was all about, I was sent on a speaking tour of every town on the entire 2,000-mile U.S. border with Mexico to explain what was going to happen and why, to citizens whose lives and economy would be disrupted.

When Operation Intercept was executed in the fall of 1969, the result was as intended: chaos. We produced a world-class traffic jam. In anticipation, most of the task force was on the West Coast where Kleindienst had an aging Corvair airliner (used by the Immigration Service to ferry illegal aliens back deep into Mexico) standing by for an aerial look at thousands of vehicles backed up for miles on either side of the border at San Ysidro/Tijuana. It was the biggest mess any of us had ever seen, and we took perverse delight in our handiwork.

Operation Intercept has been called a failure—but only by those who never knew its objective. It was actually a great success. For diplomatic reasons the true purpose of the exercise was never revealed. Operation Intercept, with its massive economic and social disruption, could be sustained far longer by the United States than by Mexico. It was an exercise in international extortion, pure, simple, and effective, designed to bend Mexico to our will. We figured Mexico could hold out for a month; in fact they caved in after about two weeks and we got what we wanted. Operation Intercept gave way to Operation Cooperation.

I got along well enough with Gene Rossides. In 1969 he took me with him to meet Egil "Bud" Krogh, Deputy Assistant to the President, who was then passing on presidential messages in the area of law enforcement. Krogh was young, intelligent, and intense; he was clearly dedicated to Nixon and, best of all, open to reasoned argument and suggestion. I saw quickly what he was looking for and in the next week, when Rossides let me try my hand at language to represent Treasury's point of view, I got a substantial amount into the official piece verbatim.

On another early occasion Rossides let himself be talked into considering backing a proposed law to require all ammunition for nonmilitary use be serialized and a record of each round kept by Treasury's Bureau of Alcohol, Tobacco and Firearms. I tried to explain to him that there are millions of rounds of .22 caliber ammunition alone manufactured each year and that the cost of keeping such records would be astronomical. He said something about computers. The argument that such a program would do no more to reduce crime than handgun registration had done in his native New York City didn't persuade him either. Finally I walked into his office with a handful of .22 cartridges and poured them onto his desk. "O.K.," I asked him, "where are you going to put the numbers?"

He picked up a tiny cartridge and looked at it. "Yeah," he acknowledged finally, "I guess you're right."

Although airliner hijacking had been a problem for some time, the companies had resisted suggestions to improve security because of the costs involved. But when three huge jets worth tens of millions of dollars were blown up by the Palestine Liberation Organization (PLO), White House telephones sizzled with screams for help from the airlines. I was assigned to the task force that developed the "Air Marshal" program, and when the question arose concerning what armaments they should carry, the matter was referred to me.

I recommended the .357 magnum with high-velocity hollow-point ammunition. There was political resistance to use of dumdum bullets, and I had to explain that they were far less dangerous to the innocent than solid "ball" ammunition because dumdums expanded and stayed in the target individual, expending all their energy in knocking him down, rather than going through him to hit an innocent bystander. I cited Nazi experiments using live Jews that determined one 7.9-mm solid bullet from a Mauser rifle could pass through and kill up to sixteen humans lined up in a row, and noted that while a stray solid-point round through the fuselage wouldn't result in explosive decompression of the aircraft, it might well sever a vital control cable or hydraulic line.

My recommendation was adopted, but the Bureau of Customs wanted to protect the appearance of their new guns from the corrosive effect of salt air in coastal areas so they specified heavy nickel plating—so heavy that it had an ironic result: many of the guns were so thick with the nickel there wasn't room to chamber ammunition properly and they had to be returned to the factory.

Gene Rossides gets uncomfortable around people who are right too often when they disagree with him. A forceful personality himself, he finds it difficult to coexist with others equally or more forceful. Nevertheless he had some very good qualities. His best was that he was a fighter for what he believed, be it the special interests of the Greek lobby or, as in 1969 and 1970, that Joseph Califano had made a mistake during the Johnson administration when he took the Bureau of Narcotics from Treasury and put it under the control of the Department of Justice. Gene wanted it back.

Rossides was right on the merits. From the federal point of view the drug problem is one of smuggling. The rest is really in the purview of the state and local police. While the Bureaus of Narcotics and Customs, both of which had federal drug law enforcement responsibilities, were under Treasury, their tendency to let natural competitiveness boil over into a feud was controllable. Now that they were under different Cabinet departments, their constant feuding, which actually reached the point of shooting at each other from time to time, engaged the attention of the Attorney General and the Secretary of the Treasury rather than just an Assistant Secretary.

But right on the issue or not, Rossides had a problem: Justice wanted to keep the Bureau of Narcotics and Dangerous Drugs (B.N.D.D.) and that meant Rossides was going up against John Mitchell. In the Nixon administration, no one could win against Mitchell. We made our best case and lost. It was not a total loss, however; Treasury's backing the Bureau of Customs position to the hilt did wonders for that organization. Even more was done for it when Rossides brought in New York lawyer Miles Ambrose to be Commissioner of Customs. He was a big, highly intelligent man and a natural leader. He, too, was a forceful personality and he, too, made Rossides feel uncomfortable.

As Ambrose got more and more good press and the obvious devotion of the men of the Bureau of Customs, Rossides brooded. He was upset when it became known that he had personally approved the comic opera dress uniforms of the White House police force so much derided in the press; he kept insisting to everyone that he had not approved of the hats.

Contributing to Rossides's anxiety was his knowledge that he had annoyed John Mitchell in his attempts to regain B.N.D.D. after the matter had been resolved against him. He started telling visitors and Treasury people alike that he had intended all along to stay only one term. Nor was his anxiety alleviated by his knowledge that John

Mitchell had been one of my political patrons. Because I, too, annoyed Rossides. I wouldn't be his yes man, especially on the firearms issue, and some of the things I did that were natural to my personality caused others to talk about them, and for them to talk about anything other than what Rossides did or anyone other than him, added to his pique and insecurity. Rossides resented that in Ambrose and he resented it in me.

One such instance occurred during the so-called Vietnam Moratorium in the fall of 1969. A number of my colleagues and I had to work late so we went to supper nearby. As we returned to the main Treasury building's Fifteenth Street entrance, I had just put a fresh cigar in my mouth when we found our way into the building blocked by a stream of people, four abreast, walking down the sidewalk carrying lighted candles as a symbol of protest. Leading the way for my comrades, I shouldered into the stream and across the path of a large man. I was disgusted by this display of support for the enemies of our country and expressed it by seizing the man's wrist and pulling his candle flame up to my cigar to light it.

"There, you useless son of a bitch," I growled, "at least now you've been good for something!"

Another incident occurred during a meeting of the working group of the Cabinet Committee on Heroin. The Johnson administration had extracted a promise from Suleyman Demirel, Prime Minister of Turkey, to eliminate all opium poppy cultivation in that country by the end of 1971. Rossides and I agreed that the United States should use all its economic power to force Demirel to make good on his promise—something Rossides's ethnic background and identification with the Greek lobby did not exactly make him reluctant to do. The Department of State, aware of Rossides's visceral anti-Turkish feelings, cited the shakiness of the Demirel government and said at one of our meetings that instructions to our ambassador to push Demirel harder would destroy the ambassador's usefulness.

I argued that if Demirel were going to renege, it didn't matter whether he fell or not; indeed, a new prime minister might prove more amenable. I had no use for our ambassador because I believed he had fallen victim of the occupational hazard of ambassadors and was representing Demirel more than the United States. When the State Department representative at the conference asked me, dripping hauteur, "and just what, Mr. Liddy, do you propose we do with our ambassador should what you propose destroy his usefulness?"

To State and Rossides's outrage I replied disdainfully: "Have you considered locking him in a room with a Luger to do the graceful thing?"

State prevailed on the issue and we were prohibited from applying economic pressure on Turkey. Demirel fell anyway, and the deadly poppies continued to grow.

When I was invited to a meeting at the White House between the Nixon administration and prominent members of the shooting sports and firearms manufacturing constituency, Rossides was furious. It also upset him that I was on such good terms with Santarelli at Justice and Krogh at the White House. He brought in another New York lawyer and started trying to ease me out. I was quite willing to go; I even knew what I wanted to do: replace the retiring director of the Bureau of Alcohol, Tobacco and Firearms, which came under Treasury via the Internal Revenue Service. I wanted to curb that Bureau's harassment of legitimate firearms dealers and gun collectors, and its pressing for more antigun legislation to justify an increased budget, and generally to shape it up.

But I was soon passed the word from John Ehrlichman that when the time came, the White House candidate for the post was Jack Caulfield, a former New York City police officer who was an aide to John Dean, by now, midsummer 1970, the new Counsel to the President. I wasn't going to make the mistake Rossides did over the issue of B.N.D.D. When I got the word I withdrew my name from consideration, wished Caulfield good luck, and meant it.

Months later I was sent to see Assistant Attorney General Robert Mardian, who had a deputy slot open. Mardian said he had someone else in mind for that post and tried to interest me in another position that he described as "super-confidential," so confidential, in fact, that he couldn't tell me anything about it. I declined to apply for the pig in a poke, but Mardian apparently believed that he had to hire me and so, without my even knowing it, almost had me on the payroll before I finally convinced him that I just wasn't interested in the lesser position.

Fran had been unable to sell the Poughkeepsie house, so she rented it and brought the children to Washington in February of 1970. We leased a house on Legation Street just a few blocks south of Chevy Chase, and west of Connecticut Avenue. From our point of view it was a bad neighborhood. A few blocks away, hippies living communally in single-family houses would demonstrate their devotion to nature by such symbolic gestures as beating old Volkswagens to death at the curb with sledgehammers in a haze of marijuana smoke. The area was mixed black and white with the blacks sharing the strong antiwhite bias of the times. Closer to home the houses were occupied by career Democrat-liberal bureaucrats who hated Richard Nixon and had a laissez-faire attitude toward the raising of their children.

The trouble started in the local school. My three sons wore crew cuts and Nixon buttons. That led to some offensive remarks by some of the bigger boys, which led to the bigger boys' being beaten up by my two older sons, Jim and Tom. The schoolyard soon became generally respectful of my sons (and, if the truth be told, of my daughter, Alexandra, who is fearless and could hold her own in those days in a fight with her brothers). But when one more kid challenged Tom and went down under his fists, Fran and I were called in by the school authorities who informed us sniffily that, until our children had enrolled, there had *never* been a fight at Murch School. We were asked to tell our children to follow the school policy that

191

if any one picked on them, they were to report that person to the authorities and "not resort to violence." I was having none of that.

To Fran's distress, I replied that in the late 1930s French children were taught that philosophy while German kids were taught to be fierce in battle. Given the destruction of the numerically superior French armies by the *Wehrmacht* in about thirty days, I preferred the German approach. Murch School would just have to live with it.

Frances, who was a teacher in the same school system, was mortified by my decidedly undiplomatic way of expressing myself; but as word got around that my children remained free to defend themselves, the taunts pretty much ended—few were willing to pay the price of swift, certain, and punishing retribution.

But certain older children, teenagers in nearby high schools, many of them larger than I, took to clandestine warfare. Eggs were tossed at the house or broken over the roof of Fran's convertible to bake on in the sun; tires were deflated at night and the grounds of the house damaged; we'd be awakened by firecracker attacks late in the evening. I was aware that with the amount of serious crime in the District of Columbia the police would have no time to worry about who was throwing eggs at my house. I don't believe in being a victim, and I do not suffer fools gladly. I decided to do something about it.

My first move was to observe the pattern of attack. I noticed that the vandals took advantage of the cover offered by the alley in the rear of our house. It was seven feet below the grade of the backyard, so deep that the garage was cut into the rear of the yard, its roof on a level with the grade of the yard. The attackers roamed the alleys in search of "fun," smashing and overturning garbage cans, throwing firecrackers into yards, and so forth. If one listened carefully, one could hear them coming; they made no effort at stealth, it never occurred to them that the tables might be turned.

192

When I was ready I waited until I heard them a distance away in the alley and moved into concealment in the shrubs of the backyard. As they approached they discussed their plans. They would halt below the garage and, on the count of three, let fly with the eggs. As they approached the garage I slipped toward it and, as they reached the count of "two" jumped off the garage roof into their midst. Panicked, eggs dropping all over the place, they fled up the alley. I ran far enough after them to see which way they went and planned an ambush of my own. Across the street was another alley they frequented. There I waited in the shadow of another garage until one of the egg throwers came along. I grabbed him in a restraining hold I had learned years before in the FBI. He was about my size and struggle as he might, he wasn't going anywhere. The others swarmed around, offering my captive encouragement. It didn't help. I held him immobile and demanded his name and address, informing him that the only way he was going to get home was for me to take him there to speak to his father.

The young man refused to give his name. Another said he had a knife and I'd better let his friend go. I told him that he'd better not produce a knife or I *would* let his friend go—then take the knife from him the hard way, break it, and take him and the pieces to *his* father. At that my captive yielded and I took him home, explained to his incredulous parent what had happened and that I intended to defend my property from vandalism and wouldn't hesitate to use reasonable force to do so.

But the vandals didn't believe me. About a week later another egg hit the house, so I took to patrolling the alleys on my own. Now *I* was hunting *them*. That spoiled all their fun and, I assumed, one complained to his parents. One evening as I was cleaning my gun collection, which was spread out for that purpose over newspapers on the dining room table, many of the pistols disassembled, I received a telephone call. A neighbor wanted to talk to me about my nocturnal activities. I told him fine, come on over. Figuring he was the father of one of the vandals, I wanted to talk to *him*.

A few minutes later a man came to the door, and Fran showed him into the living room. I came in through the dining room double door, the dining room table in plain view. My self-invited guest shied at the sight of the Bulgarian crown Lugers, the Colts, Smiths, Browning, and other firearms and I apologized for the gun oil I was wiping off my hand with a rag.

The man accused me of "terrorizing" the young people in the neighborhood. I told him about the vandalism and said I wasn't about to take any of that crap from a bunch of snotty-nosed teenagers. He acknowledged that there was no excuse for vandalism, said that was the first he had heard of it, but that the problem was one for the police, not individual initiative. I replied that the theory was fine but the practical application nil in view of the District's crime problem and the shortage of police; that I didn't believe in worrying about enemies, preferring to let them worry about me.

My visitor was a career bureaucrat. He told me where he worked and at what. I told him that I worked at Treasury, and he made the unwarranted assumption that I, too, was a career bureaucrat and threatened to "go to your superiors in Treasury" if I didn't agree to discontinue defending myself and instead rely on the police. I thought of Rossides, laughed, and told him to go ahead. His bluff called, my visitor proposed a compromise; he believed he knew the parents of the people I was complaining about. Would I give him the opportunity to go to them and try to solve the problem that way?

I would, so long as the vandalism stopped. If it didn't, I was going hunting again. We shook on it.

The vandalism stopped for a while, then started again. I called my erstwhile visitor and told him I was going after them. He asked for one more chance and I gave it to him. The vandalism stopped and that was the end of it.

In August 1970 we moved to a new house between

Forts Foote and Washington on the Potomac River in Oxon Hill, Maryland. Just two blocks from the river, it was a beautiful area, but even more beautiful were the people. Here were no bureaucrats; our neighbors were almost all military officers. Suddenly the kids' crew cuts were right in style. My neighbors liked Richard Nixon, who was showing himself to be hard-nosed when it came to Vietnam and national defense. We loved it there and joined the nearby Tantallon Country Club.

In October 1970 I attended the ceremony at the Great Hall of the Department of Justice when Richard Nixon signed the Organized Crime Control Act, one title of which I had drafted. The President and I chatted, and I found him to be warm, engaging, and looking very well. The ceremony was covered by television, and that evening, as I watched that coverage, I was shocked at the way the President appeared on the screen. Richard Nixon was just not telegenic. The same man who had appeared so warm and well to me in person looked tense and almost ill on television. It was remarkable.

My problems with Gene Rossides were now coming to a head. He had neither the political clout nor stomach to deal with me himself so he enlisted the aid of Under Secretary Charls Walker. I knew Walker because I had prepared him for his appearance on CBS's *60 Minutes*, during which he was grilled by Mike Wallace about the Nixon administration's policy on firearms. One of the areas of concern was the fact that Treasury had forced IRS to recall all prints of a film that, under the guise of explaining the gun control act of 1968, was spreading virulently antigun-ownership propaganda. The suppression had been my work, and I told Walker how to defend it by pointing out the gross errors in the film.

Walker asked me to try to get along with Rossides. He, too, knew that I wasn't alone in the Nixon administration. At about the end of the year Secretary Kennedy resigned to return to his banking career, and Governor John Connally became Secretary of the Treasury. He was a very impressive man and I looked forward to discussing the gun control issue with him because I believed that as a Texan and sportsman himself he would have it in reasonable perspective.

My meeting with Secretary Connally was canceled by Rossides and Walker sent for me. He was going to take advantage of the change in Cabinet officers to ease me out of Treasury. I was, he said, to be made Enforcement Legislative Counsel of the Treasury and, to get Rossides and me apart, I would report through the General Counsel, Judge Samuel Pierce. I was to understand, however, that this appointment was just to enable me to find a different place in the administration or private life, whichever I chose, from a position of strength. I could take as long as I reasonably wished to find something new, but I was finished at Treasury; there just wasn't room there for both Rossides and me.

Don Santarelli counseled me to stay at Treasury as long as I could because "someone we can trust is needed there and you're more valuable to us there than anywhere else."

I accepted that and conferred with Judge Pierce. He was a big, smart, good-looking black man who had come from the same New York law firm in which my father had clerked so many years ago under the man for whom I was named—the late George Gordon Battle. I told Pierce frankly of the situation concerning Rossides, Walker, and me, and he said not to worry. He took people as *he* found them, and all he cared about was how I performed my job under him.

It was a pleasure to work with Pierce. Not only was he intelligent, he had the ability to get things done in remarkably quick time. He was especially good with the White House staff. We got on very well.

Through Judge Pierce, I was able to keep my hand on the firearms issue and that infuriated Rossides, who would complain to Walker about it, who would in turn speak to Pierce. But Pierce was not the kind of man to be intimidated. Anyone who has been able to overcome what a black man has to to rise as high as Judge Pierce isn't about to be pushed around. He assigned me to do a legislative analysis on the alternative proposals being floated about in connection with the Lockheed loan guarantee, but I continued to work at developing an objective standard to apply domestically in proposed "Saturday Night Special" legislation. The old "sporting use" criterion of the Gun Control Act of 1968 had put the United States in violation of the General Agreement on Tariff and Trade. Rossides didn't like that, but because of the technical expertise involved, I was the only game in town for Treasury. Even I couldn't have done it without the help of experts—and good friends—Michael Parker, Neal Knox, and Ashley Halsey.

In March 1971 Ash Halsey, who had been editor of *The Saturday Evening Post* in its glory days and was now editor of *The American Rifleman*, official organ of the National Rifle Association, invited me to address the NRA on the occasion of its 100th annual convention. After an exchange of correspondence to clarify what was wanted, I cleared what I was to say—a recapitulation of Nixon administration policy of record—with the late Cal Brumley, then Assistant to the Secretary for Public Affairs. On 4 April I gave the talk. It was well received and did the administration a lot of good for the 1972 election. The speech was reported and when my name appeared in print, Rossides had an anxiety crisis. Judge Pierce called me in to tell me that Rossides and Walker were now insisting that firearms be exclusively Rossides's area of responsibility. Pierce wasn't going to give in, but he was no longer sure how long he could hold onto me and suggested that I ought to check with my sponsors for instructions. Then, to demonstrate his continuing faith in me and his refusal to be intimidated by Walker, Pierce gave me a copy of John Ehrlichman's letter to Secretary Connally concerning expected events within the next eighteen months that would force a response from the administration. He asked me to prepare a reply for him.

I looked at it and said: "This is sure to involve gun control. In view of what you've just said about Walker and Rossides, what do you want me to do?"

Pierce smiled. "You put in there anything you think belongs in there. Don't worry about Walker and Rossides; I'll take care of them." I tossed him a salute and left with what I knew would be one of my last assignments from Pierce, and I did so with regret. Judge Pierce had everything I admire in a man: brains, brawn, and balls.

I drafted a seven-page memorandum for Judge Pierce in answer to the Ehrlichman inquiry, and every subject in it was one claimed exclusively by Rossides. Because one of them was gun control and I wanted to be sure I coordinated with Santarelli in accordance with our long-standing agreement, on Saturday, 24 April, I went to see him at the Department of Justice.

The atmosphere in Washington was tense; just how tense I didn't realize fully until I got to Justice. Half a million demonstrators were in town, the vanguard of an announced huge mob of left-wing types who had vowed to shut down the nation's capital on the greatest holiday of the Communist world, May Day, 1 May.

My credentials got me through the GSA guards at the side door and, as I started on my way toward Santarelli's office, I discovered just how sharp the struggle had become with those who had lost the 1968 election and wanted to reverse that result by any means. The corridors of the Justice Department building intersect at acute angles. At those angles, where they could sweep two corridors at once, there were uniformed infantry behind crew-served automatic weapons—belt-fed light machineguns. Any of the mob who managed to overwhelm the GSA guards and enter the building to "shut it down" would be cut to pieces by machinegun fire. Nobody fucked with John Mitchell.

When I reported to Santarelli what Judge Pierce had told me of Walker, Santarelli replied, "It looks like your usefulness at Treasury is at an end." He said he'd check

ith John Mitchell to find out where I should go. His
meeting with Mitchell resulted in this memo:

Egil Krogh   June 15, 1971
Deputy Assistant to the President

Donald E. Santarelli
Associate Deputy Attorney General

Gordon Liddy

Wally Johnson and I rode home with the Attorney General after the testimonial dinner. The Attorney General was most explicit in his response to
our inquiry about the Liddy status to the effect that
the decision had been made to take Liddy aboard at
the White House on the issues of narcotics, bombing
and guns, and the Treasury Department performance
on those subjects and that the decision to do so
should be implemented immediately. When we indicated that it seemed to be languishing, he was very
strong in instructing us to follow through with you
to see that it occurred. When I told him I thought
you needed more muscle to accomplish it, he said
why did you not come to me with that information
sooner. He then added that you should go to whoever it is you need to to accomplish that end and
that you had his support in doing so. He concluded
the discussion with the admonition to "get it done."

XV

Bud Krogh welcomed me into his opulent office in the Old
Executive Office Building and moved from behind his desk
to sit near me. He apologized for not having me on the
White House staff sooner and for not being able to offer
me a raise in pay, or any significant "perks." I told him

I was just damn glad to be there. He grinned and said, "Walker and Rossides had a fit" when they learned of my White House staff post, and that to "keep peace in the family" he'd had to agree that I was not to have any voice in firearms matters. From now on, Treasury would be told, the action man on firearms would be Krogh's assistant, Geoff Shepard. I would make my contribution by reviewing whatever came over from Treasury for Shepard and giving him my comments, either orally or by memorandum. I was to keep up my contacts with the gun people but caution them not to let Treasury know I was still in the picture. I agreed to that. I was interested in results, not who got credit.

There were a number of other things Krogh said I could do for the White House. The drug problem was one area where my experience would be useful. Then Bud grew very serious. There was another project starting up that he was in charge of, with someone else, and where "I'm going to really need your help."

Krogh got up saying he wanted to introduce me to somebody, and I followed him into a nearby office. A prematurely balding young man who had compensated by permitting his blond hair to grow long in the back was seated behind a desk going over some papers. Krogh introduced him as David Young, late of the staff of Henry Kissinger. I was presented as a new staff assistant who would be working on "our project." I, of course, had no idea what the project was. We left quickly and returned to Krogh's office, where he explained that the "project" had started as the declassification of old documents, but that the publication by *The New York Times* on 13 June of what had been dubbed "The Pentagon Papers" had greatly upset the President, and an intensive investigation of the man believed responsible, Daniel Ellsberg, was being conducted by the departments of Defense, Justice, and the FBI. A lot of investigative agencies were involved and these efforts were to be coordinated by the White House; he and David Young were in charge.

Krogh said that while Young could devote full time to the project he, himself, had too many other responsibilities. He wanted me to work on the project for him, bearing in mind that David Young was equally in charge with him and I would serve under his direction also. New office space was being provided, but until then I would share space across the hall.

On 10 July *The New York Times* did it again: it published the United States negotiating position for the SALT talks and seriously undercut our bargaining position vis-à-vis the Soviet Union. Then we heard that a full set of the Pentagon Papers, including those that *The New York Times*, to its credit, had not published, had been delivered to the Soviet embassy in Washington.

On 24 July President Nixon conferred with John Ehrlichman and Bud Krogh about the devastating problem of leakage to the press of the highest classifications of national security information. Krogh came from the meeting shaken and soon afterward spoke to me. The President, Krogh said, was absolutely furious, as was Henry Kissinger, about the "deliberate" leaks. Krogh and Young were to orchestrate a government-wide search to find the leakers and root them out. It had the "absolute highest priority." Daniel Ellsberg, who had been made a hero by the press, was now the symbolic personification of all the leakers. He had been indicted on 28 June, and it was mandatory that the prosecution succeed. Krogh, Young, and I were to supervise and coordinate all this for the White House. I had my marching orders.

The only identification my office bore was the standard placard saying "Room 16" on the wall beside its door, and even that was almost hidden by a potted palm. It was cleared out and three inner offices and one outer office created with incredible speed. We were in it before the paint was dry. The outer office was narrow, then one reached the front wall of the other three. The office to the right, on the corner, was assigned to David Young. The one in the middle was mine, and the one on the left became a conference room. It was supplied with a long table, chairs, a large blackboard, and, in the left corner as one entered, was placed a large metal object resembling a safe. Wires running from it led to an off-green telephone. The object was not a safe, but it did indeed have a combination lock. Only the Secret Service had the combination, and each day an agent opened it and inserted into the mechanism an IBM card bearing the day's code. The phone was a KYX scrambler and over it we could speak securely to any U.S. installation of significance in the world. We used it mostly to talk to the CIA at Langley. It sounded as if we were speaking to each other from opposite ends of a long drainpipe.

To the right as one entered, in the outer office, were a desk for a secretary and a file safe for our work papers. On the ceiling was a small half hemisphere that, when activated, projected ultrasonic waves throughout the area. If a mouse so much as stirred in the room at night, the Secret Service came running. In spite of the special security devices we were prohibited from leaving any documents out overnight. A special lock was placed on the door by Secret Service technicians, and we were each issued a registered key.

From his staff Bud Krogh assigned a classically blond, precise, and efficient German-American to Room 16. Her name was Kathleen Chenow. The CIA came over to give us the highest clearances and take our oaths not to compromise them. One, for example, was so high that just the *first letter* of the identifying code word was classified SECRET while the word itself was TOP SECRET and the information protected so classified the Holy Ghost could only give it to God the Father on a need-to-know basis. I was briefed on "Project Jennifer": the attempt, by means of the Glomar Explorer, to raise the Soviet submarine sunk in the Pacific. It is the only one I can reveal to this day—because it is already blown—but my clearances included the high-technology satellite intelligence systems and matters of similar seriousness. I received them because my work on the new project required access to Pentagon files. Nevertheless, the top drawer of the file safe in Room 16 was forbidden even to me. It was, I believe, where David Young kept results of the Kissinger-ordered and other exceptionally sensitive wiretaps.

With Young so deeply involved in trying to locate the source of the SALT leak and Krogh maintaining his office upstairs, I was the only one left to do what obviously needed to be done: we just couldn't "wing" such an extraordinarily complex and sensitive assignment, so I undertook to organize the unit.

The first thing required, I believed, was our own sensitivity indicator to distinguish our product from that of the agencies we were coordinating and other White House sources. As history was to prove, compromise of the kind of documents we were generating would be disastrous. Our organization had been directed to eliminate subversion of the secrets of the administration, so I created an acronym using the initial letter of those descriptive words. It appealed to me because when I organize, I am inclined to think in German terms and the acronym was also used by a World War II German veterans organization belonged to by some acquaintances of mine, *Organisation Der Emerlingen Schutz Staffel Angehörigen*: ODESSA.

On the blackboard, in German for clarity and added security, I diagrammed the new ODESSA organization. The only exception to the German was the use, common in the Nixon White House, of the Greek letter and mathematical symbol, pi, as a symbol for the President. As I diagrammed, something puzzled me. I knew how the Nixon administration operated; at the apex of power there was very little room and the jockeying for position was intense. Anytime something important was going on, those with power, derived from proximity to the President, were careful to be represented, either in person or by a trusted proxy.

The Ehrlichman presence was Krogh. Kissinger was represented by David Young, even though Young tried to

203

disassociate himself from Kissinger by saying that he had not been assigned his role by "Henry," as he called him; he said he had quit as Kissinger's appointments secretary because he had gotten to the point where he could no longer "lie all day for Henry." I owed my position to John Mitchell. The only other power not represented was Charles Colson. It was inconceivable to me that Colson would not have a presence in such an enterprise. As these thoughts were going through my head, Kathleen Chenow entered to tell me there was someone in the outer office inquiring about reviewing some of our holdings on Ellsberg. Dave Young was busy. Would I see him? I walked out and was introduced to Howard Hunt.

E. Howard Hunt presented himself as a consultant working for Charles Colson sent down to Room 16 to review whatever we had available on Ellsberg. The empty space on my organization chart was filled. All the heavy hitters were accounted for.

Hunt was about my size, twelve years older, and a brief conversation revealed two things about him: he was knowledgeable in the area of intelligence operations and had a command of the English language one associates with brains and a first-class education. I had heard of him from Bud Krogh and, after conversation confirmed his expertise in the field of intelligence, I accepted him. We clicked immediately and I did what I could to help him. I agreed to have lunch in the near future and returned to my work as he left for his own office on the third floor.

Fran became lonelier and lonelier as I worked until late at night and through the weekends. The leak problem was still the top priority, but I also worked on firearms and heroin matters. I had to correct Treasury when it sent over proposed testimony or legislation. The drug problem entailed meetings with State and CIA. State, remembering well my comment about the ambassador and the Luger, was particularly unhappy to see me, and I pressed CIA on the problem of the Golden Triangle area of Burma. Richard Helms pointed out, quite correctly, that that area was under the control of local warlords and "not responsive to the central government," and it would be futile to lean on Burma. When asked if we could send in clandestine forces to defeat the drug warlords who were running the opium trade, Helms said that would be impractical, given the assets at our disposal and what it would take. "These are very tough people who know that country as does no one else. You send people in there and the most likely thing to happen is that they'll just disappear." When asked what *could* be done, he said, "We could rough them up a bit, say from the air." But I don't believe that was ever approved. If it was, and we did it, it was closely held.

By far the bulk of my time was devoted to the problem of the Ellsberg prosecution and leaks. Added to that was an instruction to try to find, in Defense Department files, cables from the time of the assassination of Diem that would shed light on what, if any, was the American complicity in that episode. The Nixon administration believed that John F. Kennedy had ordered Diem slain. I checked the cable traffic at the Pentagon. My contact there was the late Fred Buzhardt, then General Counsel. I had no difficulty getting access to the regular traffic, but when I found that cables from the critical period seemed to be missing (the volume of the cable traffic dropped noticeably, particularly on the prospective coup of Minh against Diem) and asked to see the Joint Chiefs of Staff back-channel traffic, I ran into a stone wall. Buzhardt wasn't the problem; it was Secretary of Defense Melvin Laird.

I reported my difficulty with Laird to both Krogh and David Young. Krogh said that Ehrlichman would turn Laird around and give me access to the Joint Chiefs' back-channel traffic, where I believed I might find the "smoking gun" cable—to coin a phrase—but even Ehrlichman couldn't break down Laird. I had to abandon the project. At the same time Hunt was trying to find the same kind of cable by going through the traffic at State. He, too, determined that the key cables were missing. I am convinced, from the content and tone of the traffic that I did see, that the United States either ordered, or at least acquiesced with prior knowledge, in the murder of Diem—but I can't prove it.

I also saw trouble coming in the Ellsberg matter. I read the indictment with an experienced eye and believed that it had been drafted in haste and poorly. Arrangements were made for me to see Robert Mardian to set up a steady flow of the latest FBI reports to us. Mardian had a large office in the building across from the Department of Justice that housed the Internal Security Division. Its walls were covered with political memorabilia. Mardian didn't just frame autographed photographs, he would include the transmittal note. He said that I should have taken the job with him, that he now could reveal what it was he wanted me to do. He had, he said, established a unique organization, an intelligence evaluation group with representatives from every major U.S. intelligence agency. All he had to do, he boasted, was to make a request of this group and the most sensitive of information would be at his fingertips. He took me where it was operating and gave me a tour. When it was over, it was obvious to me that Mardian had been "had."

The group was a typical bureaucratic con job. Its members owed first loyalty to their own organizations, were not really high-level people and would give Mardian only what their superiors wanted him to have; on anything else they would stall. Mardian didn't know it but the real coordinating group was ODESSA—and even we had problems, such as that with Laird.

The only good thing to come out of the Mardian meeting was my introduction to the man who was coordinating the investigation of Ellsberg et al., and analyzing the results for Justice. John Martin was a career trial lawyer and former FBI agent. He gave me access to everything he got as soon as he got it, and together we analyzed the law and the reports, and ordered additional investigation. It became apparent to me right away that the performance of the FBI in the Ellsberg investigation was seriously deficient. An example was a report that Ellsberg had a foot-locker full of photographs stored at a Bekins warehouse on the West Coast. The report was old, and only after we insisted did the Bureau try to retrieve the footlocker, only to find that Ellsberg's friend David Obst removed it a few days before.

I conferred with Mardian about the problem with the FBI. He told me that Hoover had discontinued clandestine activities, reportedly in 1965, but Mardian boasted that he had hired "one of his top boys for that hot stuff." He liked to speak elliptically, but he made it clear that he had on his staff at least one black-bag man—that is, a surreptitious entry specialist—although he never admitted having had him employ those talents. He also boasted of having hired the man who did Hoover's accounting work and who "knows where all the bodies are buried—boy, if he ever talked!" None of that bragging did me much good. I arranged to have access to the Internal Security Division building without any record being made of my presence— an exception to an otherwise strict rule—and I spent a lot of time there with John Martin, for whom I had great respect. To get a handle on the FBI situation, I conferred with many of my old comrades in the Bureau, including some now with the Domestic Intelligence Division. The picture I received of the Ellsberg investigation was bleak. Hoover, I was told, was a friend of Ellsberg's father-in-law and did not have his heart in the investigation. Further, Hoover was in poor shape physically and mentally, a result of the natural process of aging. The wife of a government employee, a nurse, was said to be giving him massive injections of some substance to keep him going. Hoover's feud with William C. Sullivan, the assistant director in charge of the FBI's Domestic Intelligence Division, had wrecked the division by causing people to choose sides or just be fearful of the fallout. Things were going from bad to worse.

Gone, I was told, were the good old days of individual initiative—at least in Domestic Intelligence. My friends and I swapped examples of "getting the job done," and I was told that the halcyon days lasted through the civil rights investigations. In 1964 the Bureau paid $18,000 for the location of the bodies of three slain civil rights activists who were buried in an earthen dam in Mississippi, but the best results were those in which agents' imaginations were employed. Typical was the time when the governor of a Southern state refused to cooperate in the investigation of the Ku Klux Klan infiltration of his own state troopers. After the FBI burned a cross on the governor's lawn, the outraged governor cooperated with the Bureau forthwith. Alas, those days were no more.

To verify these recent rumors about the FBI, and to determine just how helpful they were ever going to be in solving our leaks problem, I decided I had to speak to Sullivan. I did that, and immediately afterward prepared the following "Memorandum for the File." These memorandums were routinely read by Krogh and Young and, when they thought it appropriate, relayed to Ehrlichman:

THE WHITE HOUSE

WASHINGTON

August 2, 1971

MEMORANDUM FOR THE FILE

FROM G. GORDON LIDDY

I met today with Mr. William C. Sullivan, Assistant to the Director of the FBI, and the following is a summary of the main points of the conversation.

I explained to Mr. Sullivan the charter to Mr. Ehrlichman from the President in the matter of overview of the general problem of gratuitous disclosure of the private acts of government. I explained the functions of Messrs. Krogh and Young, and myself in responding to them.

I told Mr. Sullivan that it had come to our attention over the weekend that the investigation of the security leak problem in general, and the Ellsberg case in particular, was not being conducted on a "Bureau Special" basis, and I further advised Mr. Sullivan that there had been instances where cooperation had been insufficient, no matter what the level of investigation. As an example, I cited the initial refusal of the FBI to develop the names of all guests in a motel in the Boston area during a critical period. Sullivan took notes and then stated that the intensity of the concern of the President was known to him and from that point of view the case was being conducted on a "special" basis. He advised, however, that he was experiencing difficulty in acquiring the necessary manpower. For example, he stated that his request to be permitted to assign men from outside the Domestic Intelligence Division to the Ellsberg case had been initially denied by the Inspector concerned. Sullivan continued that he believed he would be able to overcome this roadblock.

I told Mr. Sullivan that I understood my mission to be one of helping to solve the problem and not to add to it. I said that I did not want to initiate any action that would cause difficulties between FBI personnel and the Director; and therefore, I was attempting to get things moving by approaching him informally. I left the impression with him, however, that should the informal approach fail to achieve the wishes of the President, I would do whatever is necessary.

Sullivan stated that he thought my role would be most helpful to the Bureau, and he was grateful for the approach that I was taking. At this point Sullivan related some of the difficulties under which he was laboring.

(1) Hoover, as a result of a minor misunderstanding which occurred in Denver, Colorado, terminated all FBI liaison with the CIA. As a result, whatever liaison that is conducted is done on a clandestine basis, to the detriment of the government and the respective missions of the FBI and CIA.

(2) The top FBI expert on Soviet espionage is currently "chasing fugitives" as a result of leaving a safe drawer open in his office, again to the detriment of counter-Soviet espionage efforts on behalf of the government.

Observations and Conclusions

Sullivan appeared very insecure in his position, almost frightened. He gave the impression of a man doing his utmost to do his duty as he saw it, but under attack from above and below. So long as this situation exists, the operations of the FBI and, therefore, the interest of the United States, will suffer as Sullivan occupies a position of day-to-day control of all FBI investigative operations.

At Sullivan's direct request I had lunch with Charles Brennan, Assistant Director in charge of Domestic Intelligence. Brennan was frank. He stated that he and Sullivan were both under attack from above and below. He related that Hoover attempted to transfer him to a Bureau Field Office and that it was necessary for the Attorney General to countermand the order personally. Brennan feels that Hoover is out to get him and Sullivan and that only the protection of the Attorney General can save either. . . .

From Brennan I learned that not only is the Ellsberg case not being conducted as "Bureau Special," but absolutely nothing is being done by the FBI on the SALT leak, the U-2 leak, or the Jack Anderson leak.

According to Brennan, were the Ellsberg case to be escalated to "Bureau Special" as the Berrigan case, he would need an additional five supervisors and the Washington Field Office would have to assign more men; probably from outside those presently assigned to Domestic Intelligence work.

Brennan then brought in Section Chief Wannall and Bureau Supervisor Waggoner. Waggoner has the Ellsberg case assigned to him and Section Chief Wannall is his immediate superior.

Wannall stated that he was experiencing the following problems:

(1) needed information from DOD is difficult to obtain and slow in coming.

(2) it would be unfortunate to prohibit the FBI from arranging to interview those who might be prospective candidates for interview by DOD. To do so would place the FBI in a position of being cut off from leads as they develop.

(3) Wannall asserted, and was joined strongly in his assertion by Brennan, that the FBI clearly cannot do a good job on the Ellsberg case, or on the expanded problem of leaks, unless/until it receives authorization to interview press personnel. It is for this reason Wannall stated that the bulk of their investigation has centered on background investigations and the xerox incidents. At this point Brennan interjected that the prohibition against inter-

viewing press personnel originated with Assistant Attorney General Robert Mardian. Brennan stated that Mardian now denies this, and he expects to receive from Mardian momentarily a memo with language he will be able to interpret and assert to Hoover as "carte blanche" to conduct any investigation deemed logical, including interviewing members of the press.

Wannall stated that if I am to have access to any of the material in his Section it will be necessary that he see instructions to that effect from Hoover. He also stated that it was the FBI policy to regard the security leak problem of other agencies as their own business, and not something for the FBI to clean up.

I replied that in a normal climate such a policy would be logical. I pointed out, however, that the situation was anything but normal and that the President was vitally interested in seeing to it that the practice of gratuitous disclosure of sensitive material was halted. I told all present that they could conclude, therefore, that it is proper for the FBI to broaden the scope of its investigation as requested.

Brennan stated that for this to be accomplished it would have to be done on a "Bureau Special" basis, and Hoover would have to order it specifically. He suggested that an appropriate vehicle to bring about the foregoing would be our response to the reply to the letter from the President to Hoover requesting investigation of those listed on an attachment as key figures in the leak problem.

Observations and Conclusions

A decade ago I worked with Waggoner in the Denver office of the FBI. He was a good man known for cutting through red tape, getting right to the heart of the problem, and producing results.

Wannall impressed me as being what is known in FBI slang as a "torpedo"; i.e. an informer for the higher ups and a hazard to his immediate superior. Strictly a book man, Wannall occupies a key position as Chief of the Section in control of the Ellsberg case. He can be expected to do nothing without the specific instructions of Hoover. He will be a bottleneck.

Waggoner as Bureau Supervisor in charge of the Ellsberg case will be able to be no more effective than Wannall, as his superior, will permit.

Brennan impressed me with his grasp of the problem and his enthusiasm for solving it. It must be understood, however, that Brennan works under the handicap of being known by his subordinates to be in disfavor with Hoover and having a Hoover agent directly underneath him. It is also my impression that Brennan has covered his flank via a close alliance with Mardian, who is probably his pipeline to the Attorney General.

Blind Addendum

I learned from an excellent source within the Bureau that for sometime now the Bureau has not conducted any clandestine operations. These highly productive, very confidential techniques have been terminated because any activities which could cause the slightest criticism of the Director or any additional negative effect on his image are now proscribed.

I think any further discussion of this particular aspect should be oral.

I soon had evidence that this memo had not stopped at Krogh's and Young's desks, or even Ehrlichman's. A few days later I had another meeting with Mardian. After this encounter I made another file memo for Krogh and Young in which I cited two interesting moments in Mardian's conversation, the first concerning my original memo, the second concerning Hoover and the President:

Route of Liddy memo of August 2, 1971

In the course of the general meeting when Wannall's name came up, Mardian looked directly at me and said, "you know, the Torpedo." I got the message; Mardian had read my memo dated August 2, 1971. This was confirmed privately after the meeting when Mardian stated that the Attorney General had seen the memo and Mardian related the contents thereof to me. He advised that the Attorney General was displeased with Messrs. Sullivan and Brennan of the FBI telling them that "this problem is well known to and receiving the attention of the President of the United States. You don't need to program Liddy about it." Mardian continued that the Attorney General was not angry with me nor in fact did Mardian exhibit any displeasure. If anything, he was rather gleeful about his immediate access to what was obviously intended to be an in house memorandum.

Alleged veiled threat against the President by Hoover

At the conclusion of the general meeting, in private conversation with me, Mardian discussed the serious problem of the deterioration of the FBI under the recent leadership of Hoover. According to Mardian sometime ago a special study of the FBI was conducted by the Directors of the CIA, DIA, NSA, and the Secret Service. Many, not all, of the problems and deficiencies of the FBI which have risen in the past five years were set forth in the memorandum along with suggested solutions.

It was through this memorandum that the President and subsequently Mardian himself first learned of the serious deterioration of the FBI capability and performance. According to Mardian, Hoover had even "threatened the President of the United States." He said that he was present in the office of the Deputy Attorney General after Hale Boggs had made his blast at the FBI and Hoover and that Kleindienst had stated that a Congressional investigation of the FBI would be welcomed. Hoover called Kleindienst and Kleindienst held the phone in such a way that Mardian could overhear the conversation. Hoover was angry. He said that it was all very well for Kleindienst to "welcome the investigation," but that "you understand that if I am called upon to testify before the Congress, I will have to tell *all* that I know about this matter." Mardian stated that he knows what Hoover was referring to and recognized the implied threat to the President in the remark. According to Mardian, however, Kleindienst obviously did not perceive the threat and this was apparent to Hoover. Hoover, said Mardian, therefore telephone the President and repeated the same remark quoting himself to Kleindienst. The President, according to Mardian, recognized the threat. Support for the broad Congressional investigation of the FBI thereafter was withdrawn.

Mardian was not explicit to me about the nature of the threat, but soon thereafter I was led to believe that it implied Hoover's revealing what he knew about the telephone taps secured for Henry Kissinger.

There was occasional relief from all this. As I worked at the White House, one heard talk of the election that was just a year away and nostalgic storytelling of the triumphs of 1968. I got awfully tired of stories about "giant rallies" with all the balloons going up in unison. Finally, I had enough of it. "Hey, you guys," I said one day, "you want to see a *real* rally?" Curious, they asked what I was talking about.

One of the advantages of living in Washington is the availability of the museums, art galleries, and libraries. One of my favorite haunts had been the National Archives, and I subscribed to the little schedule of motion pictures to be shown at the theater there. I had taken my children to see Leni Riefenstahl's cinematic masterpiece *Triumph of the Will*. I called the National Archives and set up a special showing for the White House staff. About fifteen people attended. At the climactic end of the picture, as thousands stand to sing the rousing Horst Wessel anthem following scenes of hundreds of thousands of storm troopers and SS in the mass formations of Albert Speer's gigantic spectaculars, the last notes drifted off, the picture faded, and the lights came up. There was a moment of stunned silence. Then from the rear of the audience came an awed, "Jesus! What an advance job!"

Hunt continued to maintain a separate office, but he was so intimately involved in what we were doing that I assumed it was only because there was no more space available in Room 16. We became fast friends and our families visited each other. Howard's wife, Dorothy, had a strong personality and herself had an intelligence background. She worked in the Spanish Embassy, and I suspected she had been placed there by the CIA. Even on social occasions, when Howard and I would be alone together, we'd talk about the Ellsberg case and how the information we were receiving was not helping to resolve the central problem: who was Daniel Ellsberg? Romantic rebel of the left and lone wolf? Or part of a spy ring that had deliberately betrayed top secret information in unprecedented quantity to the Soviet Union? His motivation was crucial. We didn't know what we were dealing with. Indeed, there was some question about whether he had given the material to *The*

216

New York Times, or whether the *Times*, learning he had it, and while Ellsberg hesitated, had bag-jobbed Ellsberg, who then acquiesced. When this suspicion came up, based on statements by the *Times* counsel about the difficulty they had gone to to get the material, I suggested to Mardian the *Times* be wiretapped, something permitted by the state of the law at the time in such circumstances. The suggestion didn't trouble him, although I don't know that he ever acted upon it.

Hunt said that Colson wanted to destroy Ellsberg's status as a hero of the left-liberal establishment because his continuation in that role might lead others to emulate him. I was more concerned with his possible link to the KGB. Howard suggested the desirability of a CIA psychiatric profile, and I agreed immediately. Ellsberg had, according to FBI reports, a long psychiatric history and had studied in England at Cambridge University, the place that had proved so fruitful in the recruiting of Soviet spies from among the British intelligentsia. We needed to know much more about him and the CIA profile sounded like a good place to start.

The study was prepared with the aid of materials Hunt and I assembled from the FBI data that were submitted to us through the Internal Security Division. The CIA effort was disappointing and we called them in for a conference.

At that conference Hunt stressed the Colson goal and I the investigative aim. We knew from what was clearly a masked FBI wiretap report that Ellsberg used to telephone his psychiatrist, Dr. Lewis Fielding in Beverly Hills, at all hours to tell him the most trivial intimate details of his life, sometimes as they were occurring. The CIA psychiatrists agreed that he might well have told Fielding not only what he had done with respect to the Pentagon Papers, but who, if anyone, were his accomplices and to what extent he was involved, if at all, with Soviet intelligence.

The CIA tried again but the second profile wasn't much

help in my drive to learn whether Ellsberg was a loner or a Soviet agent. Hunt and I arrived at the same time at the same conclusion: Fielding's files on Ellsberg could be of immense value.

I contacted John Martin and he said that the FBI had already approached Fielding and been rebuffed. I thought a bag job in order and mentioned it to Howard, asking him if he had any experience in West Coast. By that time John Ehrlichman had said he thought that the two of us could handle it. I went to John Martin and, without telling him what I wanted it for, got what information there was on Fielding's home and office that we didn't have in the White House. While I was at it I got a complete description of the Ellsberg home in Massachusetts, too, in case we decided to see what we could find there.

Hunt and I mentioned the matter to Krogh and wrote up for him the suggestion for a vulnerability study of the Fielding office on the West Coast. By that time John Ehrlichman had said he thought that using the name ODESSA as a sensitivity indicator might draw inquiries from the curious and be counterproductive, so it was abandoned. But to Hunt and to me the unit was always ODESSA, despite that fact that the press picked up the "Plumber" sign Dave Young put outside his door after the unit had been disbanded. One of the last memos to appear under the official indicator "ODESSA" said, in part:

THE WHITE HOUSE

WASHINGTON

August 18, 1971

MEMORANDUM FOR: BUD KROGH AND
                   DAVID R. YOUNG

FROM: GORDON LIDDY

SUBJECT: ODESSA STATUS REPORT . . .
RAND MALPRACTICES

With respect to the McNamara Study, Rand, on
the initiative of its President, Harry Rowen, chose
not to follow certain of the regulations governing the
care and custody of Top Secret material. For example, certain Top Secret documents were deliberately
not entered in the Top Secret document account-
ability system.

According to General Counsel of the Department
of Defense, J. Fred Buzhardt, investigation to date
has disclosed that, in violation of the eighteen-month
rule, over 600 Rand-affiliated persons retain Top
Secret clearances, whereas only six qualify under the
rule.

Other evidences of Rand's supervening pertinent
security regulations and, as characterized by Buzhardt, lying to DOD representatives in an attempt to
cover up, has persuaded him to conduct a personal
investigation at Rand, Santa Monica. The results
thereof will be included in a future report.

CASE DEVELOPMENT; *U. S. v. ELLSBERG*

Ellsberg can be tied to the xerographic reproduc-
tion of Top Secret documents in Los Angeles, California, on October 4, 1969. It can be demonstrated
that for sufficient periods of time, Ellsberg had access
to and custody of the McNamara Study. Moreover,
he has made a number of admissions against interest.

There are, however, major problems of proof for
the Government. These lie in making the connection
between Ellsberg's activities and the publication of
excerpts from the task force documents by *The New
York Times*. Department of Justice officials advise

that the calling of additional witnesses before a Federal Grand Jury in Boston is imminent, and investigation continues in an attempt to improve the quality of the Government's case.

ADDITIONAL PROSPECTIVE DEFENDANTS

Anthony J. Russo, Jr., a former research analyst with Rand Corporation and colleague of Daniel Ellsberg, can be demonstrated to have been present during the xerography of Top Secret documents on October 4, 1969, at the office of Linda Sinay in Los Angeles. Russo, however, was granted immunity by a Federal Grand Jury. Nevertheless, he refused to testify and, as of August 16, 1971, Russo was in jail for contempt of court.

It may also be possible to prosecute Cornelius Sheehan and his wife, Susan Sheehan, for unauthorized retention of Department of Defense documents and unlawful conversion of Government property, arising out of their xerography activities in Boston during March 21-23, 1971.

As Sheehan is a reporter for *The New York Times*, the Attorney General has directed that no prosecution be undertaken without his specific authorization. Development of a case against the Sheehans continues and is expected to be augmented by the Grand Jury hearings to be held shortly in Boston.

CIA PERFORMANCE TO DATE

Although the psychological study of Ellsberg prepared by CIA was disappointing, it must be remembered that there was but little relevant material available from which to prepare it. A proposal to obtain a rich lode of material of this nature for an in-depth study is currently being considered by Mr. Ehrlichman.

CIA has been understandably reluctant to involve itself in the domestic area but, responsive to the President's wishes, has done so. Overall performance to date is satisfactory.

DOD PERFORMANCE TO DATE

While DOD has been somewhat uncommunicative with us on a day-to-day basis, General Counsel Buzhardt seems to have a thorough grasp of the problem from both the viewpoint of his own department and that of the White House. He and his investigators have been working diligently. There remains considerable amount of work to be done by DOD, and responsiveness could be improved. Overall performance is satisfactory.

ASSESSMENT OF FBI PERFORMANCE TO DATE

The FBI investigation has been characterized by a lack of a sense of urgency; substandard lead setting and the stifling effect of internecine administrative bickering. What ought to have been a classic example of the all-out "Bureau Special" investigation, in the tradition of the great kidnapping cases of the past, has failed to materialize. Tested against the FBI's own historically high standards, performance to date has been unsatisfactory.

POLITICAL EFFECTS OF DISCLOSURE OF THE ODESSA OPERATION

In the absence of a clear understanding, on the part of the public and of the Members of Congress, of the damage done by the gratuitous disclosure of the McNamara Study (CIA damage assessment attached, Tab C), disclosure of the ODESSA operation would lend itself to charges of "witch hunting"; "cover-up"; and "repression."

Rather than being on the attack, we would be forced into a defensive posture—the last thing we want. Given their current bias, the media would have a field day at the President's expense.

We concluded, therefore, that ODESSA must be closely held. The only overt program should be that involving criminal prosecution under the appropriate Federal Statutes. The remaining malefactors should be identified and dealt with no less severely, but by alternative means.

CAVEAT

Although the foregoing has been gleaned from extensive and recent data, it must be borne in mind that there has not yet been a major breakthrough in the investigation. For this reason, the drawing of conclusions of any but the most tentative nature is untimely and ill-advised.

Shortly after this memorandum was written the word came back from Ehrlichman via Krogh: The survey of the Fielding place was approved.

Howard Hunt had mentioned to me that the CIA had provided him with physical disguise and flash alias documentation in connection with one of his missions for Chuck Colson, and I suggested that the same be provided me for the trip to Beverly Hills.

In fact it was not Colson but John Ehrlichman who secured this cooperation from the CIA. In a telephone call to General Robert Cushman, Deputy Director of Central Intelligence, Ehrlichman said that Hunt had been taken on as a security consultant by the White House, and that he might be turning to the Technical Services Division of the CIA from time to time for help. The CIA, said Ehrlichman, should think of Hunt's having "pretty much carte blanche." Cushman duly reported that at the next CIA Morning Meeting.

(The CIA's willingness to cooperate was not interminable, however. Eventually the following memorandum went to Cushman from his assistant:

MEMORANDUM FOR: General Cushman

Attached is the report on Howard Hunt's latest requests for TSD support.

I see two problems:

1. Hunt has brought a stranger into the picture who is now privy to TSD's role in this affair. The White House should have cleared this with us and—we must be told who the fellow is. He could embarrass us later.

2. Hunt's use of unique clandestine equipment in domestic activity of an uncertain nature also has potential for trouble. The Agency could suffer if its clandestine gear were discovered to be used in domestic secret operations.

I will instruct TSD to clear all of Hunt's requests with this office. Also, I think it would be desirable to obtain Ehrlichman's assurance that Hunt's latest caper is ok. Even then, this does not relieve the Agency from its vulnerability if associated with domestic clandestine operations against Americans.

Karl

27/8/71

(DATE)

Scribbled at the bottom of the file copy of this memorandum is a note, presumably in Cushman's handwriting, that he had called Ehrlichman, and Ehrlichman had agreed to "call a halt on this." In fact, however, Hunt and I continued to call on and receive CIA assistance well into 1972.)

In any case, it was still before Cushman's call to Ehrlichman, so Hunt made his own phone call and it was successful: shortly thereafter we left for a CIA safe house, actually an apartment in Washington's "New Southwest" urban redevelopment section. There I was introduced to a "tech," a man from CIA's Technical Services Division. He was "Steve" and I was "George," from the alias I was to adopt, "George F. Leonard."

The apartment was spare, an "efficiency" that was clearly the home of no one. What there was in it appeared to be primarily equipment of "Steve's" trade and a little extra clothing.

The alias documentation I was furnished was for a citizen of Kansas. I received a series of identification cards that purported membership in record-buying clubs, libraries, and other "pocket litter" as well as a Kansas driver's license, Social Security card, and, ironically, a life membership in the National Rifle Association. "Steve" then gave me a sheet of lined notepaper with the name *Steve* on one side and a telephone number where he could be reached: 532–4574. On the other side was handwritten almanac-type information about Kansas I was to memorize for use in casual conversation should it become necessary.

Next "Steve" gave me a very small Tessina 35-mm camera of Swiss manufacture. It had a built-in spring-powered film advance and shutter-cocking mechanism. The speed of the shutter and the aperture of the lens were preset and the camera fit into a special pocket in the bottom of a pouch filled with pipe tobacco. The pouch had a small, round grill through which the camera could take pictures when the shutter release was pressed through the pouch. The film was high-speed black-and-white. "Steve" told me the camera had been set to have an exceptional depth of field. He had me practice with it until I was familiar with its operation, then asked me to sit down on a straight chair.

As I sat in the chair, "Steve" produced a full wig, dark brown in color and cut rather long. He fitted it to my head and then, using barber's tools, gave me a "haircut" so that it appeared natural around the ears and at the neck. That done, he gave me a pair of glasses in fine West German frames. The lenses were extraordinarily thick and convex, of the type used by persons suffering from severe tunnel vision, and likely to be remembered by observers to the exclusion of one's features. I put them on. The lenses had no effect at all on my vision. "Steve" then asked me to try out a "gait-altering" device. It consisted of a lead insert covered with denture material so that it would be smooth and comfortable, intended to be worn inside the shoe at the heel. All these things, together with a brush for the wig, were placed into a small shaving kit and handed to me. I folded his written information on Kansas and put it into the kit with the rest of the materials, and Howard and I left.

On 25 August Hunt and I flew to Los Angeles and checked into the Beverly Hilton, which was, according to our map, only a few blocks away from Dr. Fielding's office. We then walked to the vicinity of the office, located it, and returned. The next morning we had breakfast with someone Hunt wanted me to meet—Morton "Tony" Jackson, a prominent Beverly Hills attorney and sometime radio broadcaster who had served with Hunt in the CIA. Hunt introduced me under my alias and indicated in conversation that we were on a drug control mission. After the meeting Hunt told me that he wanted me to know Jackson because he was a "solid" guy to whom we could look for support in an emergency.

After breakfast, Hunt and I disguised ourselves and went to Fielding's office to photograph it from all angles. To allay suspicion he posed me in the foreground of the photographs like a tourist. In the rear we found a private parking lot adjacent to an alley and commercial lot and on the other side was a commercial parking garage. In a space in the private lot marked "Dr. Fielding" was a Volvo sedan. We photographed it, being careful to include the license plate.

The Fielding office building had glass doors in the front and to the rear at the side opening on the private lot. We photographed potential escape routes and then rented a car to drive to Fielding's residence. There we photographed the front and rear of the apartment house, the latter from an alley, and I went into the building to locate the apartment exactly. I found it on the upper floor at the rear where its windows overlooked the alley. Now all we had to do was survey the target again at night, the actual conditions under which the entry would be made, but that would have to wait until dark, so we returned to the hotel.

By the time we reached the hotel I was having considerable difficulty with the gait-altering device. I was limping, all right, but the damn thing was killing me. I took it out and decided to go for a normal walk in the park to get some sun. I still had on the brown wig. I sat down on a park bench and let the sun warm me. I hadn't been there five minutes when a huge young man, who appeared to be an American Indian, started walking nearby, passing me, coming back, glancing at me and hesitating, as if undecided about something.

"Jesus!" I said under my breath, "I'm being cruised by a seven-foot Navajo. It's gotta be this fucking wig." I got up and returned to the hotel to put away the wig, complaining to Hunt. He roared with laughter and I never wore the wig again.

That evening Howard and I returned to the Fielding office building. Lights were showing on the top floor, which was a residential apartment, and cleaning equipment was in view in the hall on the ground floor. I took the tobacco pouch in my hand and said, "Let's go." Hunt and I entered the building as if we were the landlords. We looked over the first floor, which consisted of offices, then I slipped into the stairwell and went down to the basement to check it out. When I came back, we went upstairs.

On the second floor, as we looked for Dr. Fielding's office, we were spotted by a Hispanic cleaning woman. Hunt spoke to her in Spanish, telling her we were doctors

226

who had to leave an urgent message for Fielding. She opened his office door and, as Hunt held her in conversation, I used the tobacco pouch camera to photograph the interior of Fielding's office. He had a small foyer, at the right of which were files equipped with locks I saw I could defeat easily with a torsion bar and pick. A small office and a small waiting room with a separate exit completed the layout. When I came out, Hunt diverted the cleaning woman for another moment while I took a close-up photograph of the exterior lock on the office door. Hunt tipped the woman, and we left for the hotel garage and our rented car.

Hunt and I checked the office premises from the car at fifteen-minute intervals for several hours to observe the pattern of police traffic and the progress of the cleaning woman. A police car came through the alley and across the rear of the building once, slowly, then kept on going down past the parking garage and out onto the street. The cleaning woman left at midnight and, we were surprised to learn when we checked, she left both the front and rear glass doors unlocked. We had all the information we needed and took the "red eye" flight back to Washington, arriving at 6 A.M.

"Steve" met us at Dulles Airport and was given the 35-mm film. So the CIA developed and printed all those first photos of the Fielding layout. Howard and I went home for some sleep, then met at the White House to draw up a plan for the entry operation. That done, I waited for Hunt to go get the developed film from "Steve." When he returned I found that the tobacco pouch camera had not worked well—the lens wasn't fast enough for the available light; I wouldn't have used it again.

Bud Krogh took the plan and the next day said we "had a go" on the entry, but with one change: neither Hunt nor I was to go in. That would have killed it as far as I was concerned, but Hunt said he could call upon some loyal Cuban-American friends from his Bay of Pigs days who were trained by CIA in clandestine work, including surreptitious entry. He made a phone call and reported that his men were agreeable. The mission was on.

We decided that the Labor Day weekend would give us optimal opportunity to go in unobserved, as well as three days for the operation, and set it up accordingly. The Cubans would fly out separately and check into the Beverly Hilton, which we had determined had a line of sight from certain of its rooms to the Fielding office building and thus would be ideal for use of a transceiver. Because of my poor experience with the CIA's small 35-mm, we budgeted a complete set of Minox miniature photographic equipment: everything from an automatic "C" camera, much smaller than that of the CIA, to special attachments for taking photographs at an apparent right angle; a waist-level finder, mini-tripod, copying stand, flash unit, all developing equipment and chemicals so we wouldn't be dependent on the CIA; even an attachment to affix the little camera to one eyepiece of a binocular so it could take long-distance shots when sighted through the other lens. I don't think there was a Minox accessory available we didn't plan to acquire. A gun would be too noisy without a silencer, and none of mine, including a sterile (that is, nontraceable) CIA 9-mm assassination piece I now owned, was threaded to receive one, so I brought to the office a folding Browning knife—deadly and quiet.

On Wednesday, 1 September, Hunt and I waited in Room 16 for Bud Krogh to appear with the operational funds. He was late, and we were concerned about possibly missing our plane; yet when he turned the money over to me, Krogh insisted that I go out and exchange the bills for others so that they could not be traced. I went immediately to two banks, the first to convert the hundred-dollar bills into twenties, the second to convert most of them back again for ease of transport. The two banks were near the White House, so I was back quickly for last-minute instructions. Krogh had only two: call him at home as soon as the operation was over, and "For God's sake, don't get caught!"

Hunt and I flew to Chicago where we stayed overnight and then bought the radio transceiver equipment at two different stores. This time I too brought my own camera. It was a 35-mm Retina IIIC of German manufacture that I preferred because it was a range-finder model and equipped with an 80-mm Schneider lens.

Hunt and I flew to Los Angeles under operational aliases and checked into the Beverly Hilton, asking for and receiving rooms we had requested because they would give us line of sight to the Fielding office building. We had four transceivers with us, 5-watt, 6-channel TRC 100B models sold by the Radio Shack chain. We tried them out and found that they were useful over the necessary distance without difficulty, but that the channel for which we had a crystal was the same one used by a local cab company. We debated getting another set of crystals but put off the decision until evening to see how much traffic there was on the channel we had. It proved to be relatively little, and, as the channels were citizen's band, we stayed with the one we had as it offered good cover for our transmissions.

I bought virtually all the Minox equipment at the Camera Exchange in Beverly Hills, and then Hunt and I divided up the task of purchasing, from a number of different shops, the items we would need for the entry. Hunt got a footlocker-like suitcase and several other items, such as a length of nylon line that, when knotted, could be used as an emergency escape rope. I bought the necessary tools at several hardware stores and together we assembled the kit with tools, photographic equipment, and a large roll of opaque black plastic I bought from a photographic supply store in Los Angeles. It was for use in blacking out the windows of Fielding's office. Hunt bought service uniforms for the Cubans.

The Cubans turned out to be fine men. There was Bernard Barker, who had dual nationality, spoke accentless English, and had survived eighteen months in a Nazi prison camp; Felipe De Diego, a handsome businessman and Bay of Pigs veteran, and Eugenio Martinez, power-fully built veteran of many dangerous secret missions into Castro's Cuba for the CIA.

That night, 3 September, Hunt telephoned Fielding's home and determined he was there. Then we drove the Cuban men to Fielding's office building. Two of them were in service uniforms and Hunt's and my CIA disguises. We checked the area, found it quiet, and Hunt left to place Fielding's home and automobile under surveillance. We allowed Hunt enough time to get into position and be able to call us on the transceiver were Fielding to have left home, then proceeded with the mission.

I parked my car behind the building in the rear public lot where I could see the complete length of the alley through the rear-view mirror and the front windshield. I adjusted the rear mirror so I could slump down in the front seat and the car would appear empty from the outside. The antenna of the transceiver was nearly invisible in the dark. The disguised men took the suitcase, which Hunt had plastered with authentic "Rush" airfreight labels addressed to Fielding at his office, and had no difficulty "delivering" the footlocker, the Spanish-speaking cleaning woman obligingly letting them into Fielding's office for that purpose. After the cleaning woman went home, Barker, Martinez, and De Diego left for the rear glass doors, which we expected to be unlocked. They soon returned. To our surprise, all the entrances to the building were locked tight. The men got into the car and we had a council of war. I decided that it would be too risky to break the rear glass doors. The interior of the entrance was well lighted and the damage would be detectable easily, even from a distance. I sent one of the men to reconnoiter. He was back quickly to report that there was a window on the ground floor overlooking the private parking lot so covered by overgrown shrubbery that it would hide the men as they broke in and keep the damage concealed. I checked it out myself. Not only was the concealment excellent, but a nearby central air-condi-

230

tioning unit was generating ambient noise to help mask the sound of the breaking. But there was a problem. The same shrubs and noise concealing my men would prevent *them* from detecting the approach of others. Someone was needed to cover and protect their backs.

Although I was forbidden to participate directly in the mission, I was the only game in town and believed so peripheral a role would not be breaking my agreement with Krogh. I drew the Browning knife from the case attached to my belt and unfolded the blade.

My plan was to try to distract and mislead anyone who started nosing around by either pretending to have car trouble and looking for help or, if the situation demanded, as in the case of police, by fleeing ostentatiously to draw them off, confident I could elude them. I can run for miles, and there were numerous deeply shadowed hiding places in the area from which I could pause to warn the men inside with the transceiver. Only if there were no other recourse would I have used the knife, but use it I would, if I'd had to; I had given my men word that I would protect them.

For the period of the actual breaking and entering, I posted myself in a narrow space between two buildings concealed by more shrubbery from which I could see clearly the area of the break-in, all of the private, and much of the public parking lot. My view of the alley, however, was restricted.

Only by listening hard could I hear the glass break over the noise of the air-conditioner. I gave the men time enough to enter, then slipped out of hiding and walked like a late-working tenant over to my rented car and resumed that post because it offered a superior view of the area and I believed the radio reception from Hunt would be better. There were no transmissions.

Presently Hunt drove up, passed me, circled, then parked and entered my car. He was quite agitated, saying that Dr. Fielding had gotten out of pocket. Hunt wanted to know where "the boys" were. I explained the situation to him and pointed out that if Fielding were coming to the office at this unlikely hour, he would have arrived before Hunt himself and I had seen nothing of the Volvo sedan.

Hunt calmed down and returned to his car to patrol the area. He returned shortly, again agitated, saying that it was too risky and urging that I order the men out of Fielding's office. I didn't share his concern and said so. We compromised on a radio call to see how things were going and get an estimated time of leaving. I tried a call but couldn't raise the men inside. Hunt then tried his transceiver with a similar lack of result. Although the instruments cost under $100 each and were not nearly as powerful as the $700 units used by police, they should have had sufficient power. It never occurred to me that the men inside might have the gain turned too low. I swore I'd do no more operations without professional grade equipment, and to hell with the budget.

Hunt wanted one of us to go in and bring the men out, but I forbade that as contrary to our orders from Krogh. While we argued, the issue became moot as the men emerged from behind the shrubbery. Hunt intercepted them and ordered them back to the hotel. We all returned in accordance with the original plan.

Hunt arrived first, and by the time I got there he was cooling a bottle of champagne. The Cubans arrived next. Barker spoke for them. They had brought out the suitcase and put it in the trunk of one of the cars. The files had been resistant, and they'd had to damage them to get them open. To allay suspicion, they had then ransacked the office, strewing pills on the floor to make the entry appear the work of junkies looting physicians' offices in a search for drugs. All well and good, but what did they find?

"Nothing, Eduardo," said Barker to Hunt. He held up a piece of paper on which I'd written the name "Daniel Ellsberg" and given to him just before he entered—the

232

first time they knew the name of the target file. "There's no file with this name on it."

Hunt was unbelieving. "Are you *sure*?" he asked. They were. The men had brought out photographs of the damage inflicted and described every drawer and file in the office. They had been through every one and there was no file on Ellsberg. We were quite disappointed, but at least the operation had been "clean": in and out without detection. We decided to celebrate that, at least, with the champagne.

The three went out to a pay phone to reserve a flight to Miami on the first plane, and I called Krogh to report. He was so relieved that nothing had gone wrong, he wasn't concerned that we hadn't found anything. I told him I'd brief him when we got back.

Hunt had determined that there was no available direct flight to Washington so we planned to get out of there as quickly as we could by flying to New York and taking the Eastern shuttle down to Washington. Then a thought occurred to me and to Hunt at about the same time: perhaps the Ellsberg file had been taken to Fielding's home for storage as a closed case; the office was small and quite possibly that was Fielding's practice with inactive files. We decided to suggest an entry of Fielding's home to Krogh when we returned, then realized that we really hadn't done enough of a survey of the Fielding apartment to make such a recommendation. We would get some sleep and, before returning the cars and flying out, make the necessary survey.

After some rest, Hunt and I motored out to the Fielding apartment. I used my 35-mm Retina with the 80-mm Schneider lens for some outside photographs, then decided to do a close reconnaissance. I entered the building, which had exposed halls covered only by a roof, approached the apartment door, and, with the Minox, used the measuring chain to take close-up photographs of the lock on Fielding's front door. Next I wrote down the type and brand name of the lock, then walked to the rear and looked over at Fielding's patiolike porch. There were no sounds from inside so I eased over the side and saw that the porch could provide an escape route to the rear alley because the jump wasn't very far.

Meanwhile Hunt was doing recon work of his own in the area, and we finished quickly, turned in the cars, checked out, and left.

The next day, Sunday, 5 September, we were back in Washington at about noon. Hunt went home and I went to the office to draw up notes for a report to Krogh. On Tuesday, 7 September, I reported to him on the operation. I showed him the Polaroid photographs Barker had taken of the damaged files to prove that they had indeed been entered and searched, and told him of the fact that we had had to use an alternative entry method. Although Krogh was relieved that the operation had gone undetected, he was disturbed when I showed him the photographs of the damaged files and reacted somewhat like one unfamiliar with violence when combat scenes appear on television; he could accept it intellectually, but the harsh reality of what sometimes has to be done was something for which Krogh was not prepared. I was completely candid with him in my report showing him everything: the suitcase, tools, even the knife I had carried. He asked me, incredulous, "Would you really have used it—I mean, kill somebody?"

"Only if there were absolutely no other way. But yes, I would, if necessary to protect my men. I gave them my word I'd cover them." Krogh was visibly taken aback by that but said, "Hang on to those tools and things, we may need them again later on." Encouraged by that comment, I worked with Howard Hunt over the next day or so to draw up an entry proposal for Fielding's apartment but, when I submitted it, the word came back from Krogh: "not approved." I couldn't blame Krogh or Ehrlichman or, if he was consulted, Nixon for that judgment. The file might no longer exist, and there was no information that it was in fact in the Fielding apartment. In view of the risk factor, the decision was reasonable. But we were back to square one on Ellsberg.

XVI

I wasn't discouraged by the failure of the Fielding job to produce results—in that line of work there are as many dry holes as there are in the oil business—nor, apparently, was the White House. In September of 1971 I was engaged in a project attempting to bring a fresh approach to the federal drug enforcement effort when Howard Hunt approached me on the next Ellsberg neutralization proposal. According to Hunt, Daniel Ellsberg was scheduled to speak at a fund-raising dinner to be held in Washington, and Chuck Colson thought it an opportunity to discredit him. The dinner would be well attended by media opinion-shapers and the speech would get wide coverage. Could ODESSA drug Ellsberg enough to befuddle him, make him appear a near burnt-out drug case?

Hunt and I studied the matter and developed a plan to infiltrate enough Cuban waiters into the group serving the banquet to be able to ensure that one of our people would serve Ellsberg at the dais. One of the earliest dishes on the menu was soup. A warm liquid is ideal for the rapid absorption and wide dispersal of a drug, and the taste would mask its presence. Hunt was certain that he could provide men from the Miami Cuban community who'd worked at major Florida hotels; the drug, a fast-acting psychedelic such as LSD-25, he said he could get from the CIA together with a recommendation of the dose necessary to have Ellsberg incoherent by the time he was to speak.

This time the plan went through Colson, not Krogh. We waited and waited for an answer to the proposal, but when it finally came in the affirmative, our superiors had waited too long. There was no longer enough lead time to get the Cuban waiters up from their Miami hotels and into place in the Washington Hotel where the dinner was to take place. The plan was put into abeyance pending another opportunity.

I had maintained my association with Miles Ambrose and was impressed at how well he was running the anti-smuggling activities of the Bureau of Customs. We discussed the power of the grand jury and how it could be used by the federal government to suppress the domestic illicit drug trade. From these conversations I developed a proposal for a new attack on the problem and presented it to the White House in a memorandum to John Ehrlichman called "Breaking the Connection." The proposal was not adopted as such, but it led, ultimately, to the formation of the Drug Enforcement Administration.

My time was spent not only on drug and leak matters but anything of a law enforcement nature that was of a White House level. Much of it continued to concern firearms and supervision of the activities of Treasury in that area. I continued my close association with Howard Hunt, often lunching with him at his club in Georgetown, and it was again through Hunt that ODESSA received its next assignment. Daniel Ellsberg had been associated in the past with Morton Halperin and the Brookings Institution and, according to Colson as relayed by Hunt, either or both of them were believed to be using Brookings for storage of substantial additional amounts of classified documents at least as sensitive, if not more so, than the Pentagon Papers. Further, the Brookings security vault might have evidence shedding light on the identity of any of Ellsberg's criminal associates in the purloining of Top Secret Defense files; whether Paul Warnke and Leslie Gelb were among them; and whoever delivered the classified documents to the Soviet Embassy. Could we get into the vault, say, by using a fire as a diversion, and retrieve the materials?

The problem appealed to me because I recognized it as

236

one turned down earlier by Jack Caulfield. He had mentioned it to me, with much rolling of eyes and nodding of the head in the direction of Colson's office, as something too "far out" for his imagination and too risky for his nerve. I thought it could be done and so did Hunt. The problem was that the cover under which our men went in there had to be first-rate, and that meant costly. We devised a plan that entailed buying a used but late-model fire engine of the kind used by the District of Columbia fire department and marking it appropriately; uniforms for a squad of Cubans and their training so their performance would be believable. Thereafter, Brookings would be firebombed by use of a delay mechanism timed to go off at night so as not to endanger lives needlessly. The Cubans in the authentic-looking fire engine would "respond" minutes after the timer went off, enter, get anybody in there out, hit the vault, and get themselves out in the confusion of other fire apparatus arriving, calmly loading "rescued" material into a van. The bogus engine would be abandoned at the scene. The taking of the material from the vault would be discovered and the fire engine traced to a cut-out buyer. There would be a lot of who-struck-John in the liberal press, but because nothing could be proved the matter would lapse into the unsolved-mystery category.

Hunt submitted the plan for approval, but this time the decision was swift. "No." Too expensive. The White House wouldn't spring for a fire engine.

Early in October, Bud Krogh called me in and gave me yet another sensitive assignment. The President wanted advice on what to do about J. Edgar Hoover. I was to consult my sources in the FBI, prepare a thorough study of the problem complete with recommendation, and list the pros and cons of taking the decision recommended. I spent the better part of the month acquiring information, then wrote the following memorandum:

October 22, 1971

MEMORANDUM FOR: BUD KROGH

FROM: GORDON LIDDY

SUBJECT: *THE DIRECTORSHIP OF THE
FBI*

History

The FBI was born in another age. Six years after
the doughboys came home from France at the end
of World War I, America was still rural. Outside of
her cities, paved roads were few. The automobile
was just making its impact felt upon our society. The
United States had entered World War I with something like 600 machine guns in its entire armed
forces. The Germans had thousands and they terror-
ized the farmboy turned doughboy who returned
home with tales of its awesome power.

The criminal element quickly exploited the new
technology and married the machine gun to the
automobile. Roving mobile bands swept into town
and staged bank robberies which were the mecha-
nized equivalent of wild west raids. The hinterlands
were in terror of the Dillingers, the Barkers, the
Floyds, the Nelsons, Bonnie and Clyde. There are
towns in Indiana today with concrete pill boxes in
their main square built in the 20's and 30's as miniature Maginot lines to defend against what was
called "autobanditry."

Since 1908, there had existed in the Department of
Justice a small unit known as the Bureau of Investi-

gation. It was incompetent and corrupt. J. Edgar Hoover, a young Justice Department lawyer, himself in his 20's, was called upon by then Attorney General Harlan F. Stone to serve as the 5th Director of the Bureau of Investigation to clean it up and turn it into the response to the criminal challenge demanded by the public.

Hoover met the challenge. He fought technology with technology, virtually inventing practical forensic criminal science and the crime lab[1] and organized practical mass identification procedures built upon the new fingerprint technology.[2] For patronage hacks, he substituted young lawyers and accountants, depression hungry and eager to do a job. Hoover knew each man by name. There was mutual trust and respect. By the late 1930's, skill and dedication brought success and with success spread the fame of Hoover and his "G-men."

The organization was paramilitary in nature. Discipline was strict and one thing became crystal clear: the new FBI was created in the image and likeness of J. Edgar Hoover, and thou shalt not have false gods before thee. One who found this out was Melvin Purvis, the small, brilliant nemesis of John Dillinger. By the mid 1930's, Purvis' fame rivaled Hoover's. On the back of breakfast cereals, children were offered "Junior G-man" badges so that they could be just like Melvin Purvis and the FBI. Hoover crushed him. FBI history was rewritten, giving the credit to agent Samuel P. Crowley.[3] Years later, Purvis died a suicide.

---

[1] November 24, 1932.

[2] June, 1930.

[3] Who was hardly in a position to disclaim it. Crowley died under the guns of "Baby Face Nelson" four months after the death of Dillinger.

Master of modern law enforcement, master bureaucrat and charismatic leader, Hoover had good instinct and judgment. At the height of his fame he resisted the opportunity to form a national police force because he judged it to be wrong for America. Instead he formed the FBI National Academy[4] to train state and local police to FBI standards.

With World War II came a new challenge—Axis espionage.

Again, Hoover exploited the latest in technology—primitive but effective concealed sound recording equipment and disguised motion picture cameras. The FBI had its own continuous wave back channel communication system from office to office and even Hawaii. Fingerprints were put on the then brand new IBM card sorting equipment in the D.C. National Guard Armory. The greatly expanded FBI could, at the end of World War II, claim correctly that there had been not one successful act of enemy sabotage carried out in the United States in World War II, as contrasted with the Black Tom explosions and other sabotage during World War I.

The cold war was made to order for Hoover and the FBI,[5] and it went into the 1950's lean and hard. Masterful feats of clandestine counter-espionage were accomplished, and the FBI was rightly to be feared by foreign intelligence agencies.

The Korean War brought another expansion, but an internal change was taking place. No longer were all

---

[4] July 29, 1935.
[5] The FBI had been investigating the activities, *inter alia*, of the Communist Party, U.S.A., since it entered the domestic intelligence field pursuant to secret instructions from President Roosevelt issued September 1, 1936.

agents recruited from skilled professionals such as lawyers, accountants, scientists and linguists. Moreover, the cult of Hoover had begun to flower, and a lot of good men were leaving. It was becoming more difficult to replace them.

Much is made in the popular press of the so-called "petty tyrannies." This is misplaced concern. Crack FBI agents accepted the 24-hour discipline and the small annoyances. They knew that the inflated auto recovery figures, the meticulous records they were forced to keep on informant contacts that were unjustified by production, the professional image, etc., all helped Hoover when he went before Congress for appropriations.[6] They were also aware that in the clandestine war against ruthless enemies every bit as professional as they were, lack of discipline could be deadly.

The "petty tyrannies" could be tolerated because of one great psychic reward. The FBI agent knew that he was a member of an elite corps. He considered the discipline under which he labored tougher than the U.S. Marines and its reasons for being analogous to that of the Corps. The country knew it too, and respected the agents accordingly. The burden was bearable and morale high because the FBI agents knew in their hearts "We're Number One."

Things Start to Go Wrong

In the early 1950's there emerged the phenomenon of the "Bureau clerk." These were young men without the education prerequisites brought in to the Identification Division for the most part as clerks and sent off to earn an accounting degree from such dubious institutions as Southeastern University in

---

[6] And the highest pay in law enforcement for the agents —beginning salary today is $14,000.

Washington, D.C. They then became Special Agents and earned a salary they could not hope to approach outside the FBI. Reached at an early age, they became true believers in the cult of Hoover.[7] Jealous of the more competent professionals, and unwilling to disagree with Hoover on anything,[8] as they rose administratively by currying favor through flattery, the Bureau started to decline.

Hoover's assets, however, continued to increase. The Crime Records Division of the FBI is without doubt one of the finest public relations organizations ever put together.[9] It has a legitimate purpose. The extraordinary reputation of the FBI and its agents, fostered by the Crime Records Division with its motion pictures, books, magazine articles, television and radio shows, speech program, press and Congressional contacts, mean that an FBI agent will be given information by a citizen that the citizen would not entrust to any other agency. When the FBI agent says the information will be kept in confidence, he is believed. The media impact is such that when a citizen is con-

---

[7] And competitive ritual sycophants, baking cakes for Hoover's birthday; soliciting ever more flowery service club testimonials, etc.

[8] The most absurd manifestation of which led to a rewriting of the history of the Trojan War. For a speech on communism, a draft sent to Hoover for approval compared the U.S. Communist Party with the legendary Trojan Horse. The draft came back with the marginal notation in blue ink, "They're not horses, they're snakes!—H." The draft was "corrected" and thus was born the Trojan Snake.

[9] By Louie B. Nichols, who went on to become Vice President of Schenley Industries. After Nichols left the FBI, Hoover remarked, "I never want another man to have such power in this organization again."

fronted with a real FBI agent, the agent is at a tremendous psychological advantage.

But here, too, things started to go wrong. More and more the Crime Records Division spent its time building up and protecting the reputation of Hoover. Hoover and the Bureau became synonymous. To attack one was to attack the other. So long as the Crime Records Division could keep Hoover away from the press, it could work wonders. But, contrary to the widely held impression, Hoover is not a reticent man. In recent years he has become even more of a hip-shooter; lately even departing the carefully prepared scripts for his Congressional appearances. Thus, the Berrigan problem, the Martin Luther King incident, the Ramsey Clark quote, and so on.

The concern with image, the cultism, has finally taken its toll. Virtually any genuine innovation or imaginative approach is stifled for fear of outside criticism. That which occurs is often done by field agents on their own initiative, with great pains taken to prevent Bureau Headquarters from learning of it. The morale of the FBI agents in the field has deteriorated badly, not because of the rule on haircuts and no coffee at the desk, etc., but because in his heart the FBI agent can no longer say, "We're Number One."

The Present Situation

The greatest decline has been in the performance of the Domestic Intelligence Division. As previously reported, all clandestine activities have been terminated. Liaison with the intelligence community has been disrupted and key men either forced out or relegated to posts where their skills cannot be exploited. Should the Peoples Republic of China be admitted to the United Nations, the establishment of its delegation will bring a quantum increase in the presence on U.S. soil of some of the finest espionage agents in the world. Thus, the Domestic Intelligence Division, the one most badly deteriorated, will be presented with a heavy increase in its task at a time when it cannot perform competently the task at hand.

Relations between the FBI and the Department of Justice, never good but for a short period after the advent of this Administration, are again deteriorating. Hoover refers openly to Assistant Attorney General Robert Mardian as (inaccurately) "that Lebanese Jew." He has reportedly threatened the President. Recently there have been articles in *The Washington Post, The New York Times, Time* and *Life,* which indicate that officials and/or former officials at the highest level of the FBI are now divulging to the press the serious shortcomings of Hoover and the Bureau.

So long as anti-Hoover press stories concerned themselves with the so-called "petty tyrannies" there was no real problem. Such stories are not new, and are disregarded as the mutterings of disgruntled former junior employees. It is quite another situation when clandestine techniques are discussed openly and the security of the United States against foreign espionage and sabotage is called into serious question.

Years of intense adulation have inured Hoover to self-doubt. He remains realistic, however, and on June 30, 1971, his most trusted confidante, Clyde Tolson, stated to a reliable source, "Hoover knows that no matter who wins in '72, he's through."

Hoover has had a long, honorable and remarkable career. His accomplishments are truly great. But the situation was probably best stated by Alfred Tennyson in "The Idylls of the King":

244

> The old order changeth, yielding place to new,
> And God fulfills himself in many ways,
> Lest one good custom should corrupt the world.

J. Edgar Hoover should be replaced as Director of the FBI. The question is when?

Timing

One foresees no real problem with accomplishing the change following the 1972 election. The question then resolves itself as to whether the step should be taken before that time.

There are a number of reasons arguing against removing Hoover as Director of the FBI during 1972:

1. The change should have attached to it no hint of partisan politics, virtually an impossibility in a presidential campaign year. If the removal does not become an issue, the question of succession will. It is in the category of a Supreme Court appointment and carries with it the necessity of a confirmation hearing in the Senate.

2. 1972 will see the trial of the Berrigans and Ellsberg commence. The removal of Hoover in the course of those trials would, at least, lend weight to what are sure to be defense contentions of a conspiracy to justify Hoover's accusation against the Berrigans.

The most compelling reason against taking action in 1972 is the probability that issue-starved Democrats can be counted upon to exploit the matter even to the point of irresponsibility.

The question can, therefore, be refined further: should J. Edgar Hoover be removed as Director of the FBI between now and the end of the year?

1. Hoover could resist and make good his threat against the President. I am unaware of the nature of the threat and, therefore, cannot comment on the acceptability of the risk involved.

2. Removal of Hoover will not gain the President any votes on the left. The anti-Nixon bias of the left is visceral, not rational. On the other hand, some of the right could be alienated if the successor named is not acceptable.

3. The succession could become an issue unless someone is named who would be acceptable to both the left and the right, a difficult person to identify.

4. We would be presented with the problem of finding a suitable successor in a short period of time.

5. Even were the Peoples Republic of China admitted to the United Nations tomorrow, in all probability it will be a considerable period of time before it is ready to staff its delegation.

6. Hugh Sidey is wrong,[10] there will be no "convulsion" in the FBI if Hoover is not replaced immediately.

---

[10] "The crisis in the FBI finally demanded his [the President's] action. The aging J. Edgar Hoover would have to be eased out before the end of the year or Nixon would face a major convulsion in the FBI. . . ." *Life*, Oct. 22, 1971, "Heady Days Of Presidential Power."

[11] *See*: "F.B.I. Is Said to Have Cut Direct Liaison With C.I.A." *NYT*, Oct. 20, 1971 (Tab A); "Deterioration of the FBI" *Wash. Post*, Oct. 11, 1971, (Tab B); "The File on J. Edgar Hoover" *Time*, Oct. 25, 1971 (Tab C).

1. Sullivan, and possibly others, are talking to the press. The information is accurate, substantive and damaging.[11]

I think we must assume that there will be no let-up of truly damaging disclosures.

• Maxine Cheshire states in the *Washington Post* for October 21st that "a former FBI official [Sullivan] took copies of enough records with him when he left to write a book. Now he is looking for a journalist collaborator."

• I am informed reliably that Sullivan "wants to be vindicated." At 59 and out of office, there is no payoff for him in remaining quiet. Others may follow Sullivan's example.

• Evans and Novak in their column of October 11th said that there was "more to come."

• *Life* is believed to have another major story in the works.

• Sullivan has been "keeping book" on Hoover for some time. He is a skilled writer who authored Hoover's book on Communism.[12] His book could be devastating should he choose to expose such matters as the supervisor who handled Hoover's stock portfolio and tax matters; the painting of Hoover's house by the FBI Exhibit Section; the ghost writing of Hoover's books by FBI employees; the rewriting of FBI history and the "donation" by "admiring" facility owners of accommodations and services which are often in fact underwritten

---

[12] *A Study Of Communism*, Holt, Rinehart & Winston, New York, 1962.

by employee contributions; and the dismantling of the nation's counter-espionage capability.

• In the past, when the FBI was performing its mission in an outstanding manner, aggrieved former high officials held their tongues in the belief that to go public would hurt mission performance. Now that performance has fallen off, Sullivan (obviously) and others may well believe that the way best to protect the FBI is to attack so that the problem can be remedied.

2. There will be no upheaval in the FBI should Hoover be replaced immediately. The vast majority of agents would approve. A few old cronies, such as Clyde Tolson, could be expected to resign in a huff with, perhaps, some public comment.

3. Immediate removal would guarantee that the President would appoint the next Director of the FBI, something akin in importance to a Supreme Court appointment opportunity.

4. The Hoover incumbency would be undercut as a factor in the forthcoming Berrigan and Ellsberg trials.

5. The matter would be over and done with now and removed as a potential issue for the 1972 campaign.

6. Inaction, plus further disclosures in the press, could lead to charges that the President knew, or ought to have known, of the serious deterioration of the FBI, and failed to act out of concern for his re-election.

7. Short term, a prompt removal could enhance the President's image as an action oriented President and confound his critics.

8. Long term, the action could be compared

legitimately to the resolute stand taken by President Truman in the Douglas MacArthur case which, unpopular at the time, is now viewed as a plus in his presidency.

9. The country is, in my judgment, ready for the change. The situation is somewhat analogous to that of China.

Methods

1. The most desirable method would be for Hoover to ask the President to find a successor as the "unfounded" personal attacks upon Hoover are, in his judgment, harmful to the national interest in general and to his beloved FBI in particular. This might be brought about through a Mitchell-Hoover conversation.

2. A second amicable method would be for the President himself to express the above sentiments to Hoover. He might well cooperate on that basis, were things handled adroitly.

3. The President could simply announce now that on January 1, 1972, he will not take the affirmative action of seeking to exempt Mr. Hoover for another year from the mandatory retirement provisions of the law, stating that he cannot in good conscience do so as neither he nor the country has the right to expect so much of one man, and that he wishes to announce whom he shall nominate as a successor now so that there should be not the slightest element of partisan politics involved in the changeover.

Comment

Hoover is in his 55th year with the Department of Justice.[13] Even his secretary dates from the first

---

[13] Since July 26, 1917.

world war.[14] There is no dishonor, express or implied, in asking a man in such circumstances to give up the burden of office.

Recommendation

After weighing all of the foregoing, I believe it to be in the best interest of the Nation, the President, the FBI and Mr. Hoover, that the Director retire before the end of 1971.

Shortly after I submitted the memorandum, first Krogh, then Ehrlichman telephoned me. "The President," said Krogh, "says it's the best memo he's seen in years and wants it used eventually as a model of how to write a memo for the President." John Ehrlichman said, "Gordon, I thought you'd like to know your memo on Hoover came back with A+'s all over it. Good job." But A+'s or not, as he had so many other challenges in the past, J. Edgar Hoover managed to survive.

The ODESSA unit as such was winding down. I was being given more and more to do for the Domestic Council (the White House equivalent of the National Security Council, but for domestic affairs, headed by John Ehrlichman); Hunt was performing tasks for Colson and drug-related work for the Domestic Council and David Young was off with John Dean interviewing prospective nominees to the Supreme Court of the United States. I had just about concluded that the White House was disenchanted with in-house clandestine activities when I received word Bud Krogh wanted to see me in his office.

He wasted no time. "John Dean wants to pitch you on something," he said, "and I think I ought to be there when he does. Do you mind?"

"Hell, no. I work for you. You have every right to be.

---

[14] Helen W. Gandy, who became Hoover's secretary on March 25, 1918.

Besides, with Dean, it's always best to have a witness anyway. Do you know what he wants?"

"Yeah, but I think I should let him speak for himself. He'll be here in a minute.

I had had relatively few dealings with Dean, most of the matters that concerned us mutually being handled through Jack Caulfield. We had both, for example, been asked to recommend whether the President should attend the opening of the Kennedy Center in view of the expected left-wing slant of the Bernstein *Mass* that was to be presented, and we both had recommended against it. Caulfield had let me know that he had obtained, for Dean, Xaviera (Happy Hooker) Hollander's appointment book and other materials, but said they were useless to either Democrats or Republicans because so many prominent members of both parties were represented in them they would cancel each other out in a political "balance of terror." Caulfield had approached me a number of times to join in forming a private security services company that would "do for the Republicans what Intertel does for the Democrats," and he'd shown me a half-million-dollar plan called "Operation Sandwedge" with both offensive and defensive capability for use in the 1972 presidential campaign. But since I was not interested in going into that line of work with Caulfield, I'd declined.

Dean entered and sat down with a bare minimum of social pleasantries. His clothing was young lawyer conservative in contrast to the length of his hair, which he'd combed forward to cover a receding hairline. The rest was piled up on top of his ears and hanging shaggily down over the collar of his suit coat, its light blond color similar to that of a competitive swimmer who spends five hours a day in a pool full of heavily chlorinated water. No glasses adorned his youthful, ferretlike face.

He got right to the point. "Gordon, it may be necessary for you and Jack [Caulfield] to go into the closet for awhile."

"How's that?"

"There's an election coming up next year. We've had a taste this summer of how the other side can be expected to operate. We've got to be able to counter that with an absolutely first-class intelligence operation." Dean was leaning forward intently, elbows on his knees, his left fist grasped in his right hand. He was serious as cancer. Krogh remained silent, letting Dean do the talking. I put what Dean had said together with his mention of Caulfield and asked, "You mean Sandwedge?"

"No. We're going to need something much better, much more complete and sophisticated than that. Bud tells me you're quite knowledgeable in this area."

The Sandwedge proposal Caulfield had shown me flashed through my mind. It had an offensive as well as defensive capability, and the offensive specifically included black-bag jobs—surreptitious entries—and electronic surveillance. Dean was telling me that was considered inadequate.

"Well, knowledgeable enough to know that if you're talking about what I think you're talking about—all-out, full capability, offensive and defensive intelligence service with sophisticated clandestine collection techniques and covert actions, you're talking about a hell of a lot of money."

Dean shot it right back: "How's a half a million for openers?" He was offering me the entire Sandwedge budget for start-up costs. The man was serious all right; that was serious money.

"Well," I said, "you're talking the right numbers, anyway. Half a million is just about right for openers, and it'd probably take another half before we're finished. That doesn't bother you?"

"No problem," Dean said levelly.

I told Dean I wasn't sure that it'd be wise for me to "go into a closet," that I wasn't there under the same circumstances as Caulfield—not that low a profile. If I disappeared all of a sudden, people would ask questions.

"You can't do it from here," Dean interjected.

"No," agreed Bud Krogh, speaking for the first time.

I told them I could understand that, but that I'd need some kind of cover.

"Well," said Dean, "you give it some thought, and we'll give it some thought. But what do you think of the idea?"

Dean was asking me for a decision, but I wasn't prepared to give him one without knowing something else. That the coming election year would be like no other was apparent. The riots and violence of the past summer with its attempts to shut down the government of the United States; the wholesale theft of top-secret documents by Ellsberg and the support for those taking such extreme measures by the traditional backers of the Democratic Party among the media—*The New York Times, The Washington Post,* and the networks—made it plain that we weren't in for a campaign in '72; it would be war. The need for what Dean was proposing was obvious, and I certainly had no reluctance to go to war. But it would be an undeclared war and what I would be doing was clearly illegal. I had no intention of failing any more than I would intend to be killed in a shooting war; but the risk was there and in the event of failure, I would have to be prepared to accept the consequences. It was all too prevalent a ploy in the White House for juniors to invoke the name of the President to advance some idea of their own without the knowledge of their superiors. I was willing to go to war for the President, but not for John Dean.

"I am willing," I said, choosing my words carefully, "to serve the President in any way I can, but there are a number of different ways I can serve him. I'm here because of John Mitchell, and I work for John Ehrlichman. I want to be sure that this is how *they* feel I can best serve the President. So before I decide, I'd like you, Bud, to run this past Ehrlichman and you, John, to check with John Mitchell. If *they* both agree, then I'm your man."

Krogh nodded his head in assent and Dean got to his feet hurriedly, said, "Fair enough," held out his hand to shake mine, and left as quickly as he had entered. Bud Krogh rose and shook hands too, saying "O.K., Gordon, we'll get back to you."

I left and looked up Howard Hunt, finding him in his third-floor office. I told him of the offer Dean had made and the first thing Hunt asked was, "Do they have any idea what something like that costs?"

I quoted to him John Dean's ". . . half a million for openers," and he said, "Good. They're in the ball park at any rate. In that kind of work the cheapest commodity there is, is money. You going to do it?"

"If Mitchell and Ehrlichman agree, and we can work out a satisfactory cover. If it's a go, can I count on your help and that of our friends in Miami? I'll need it."

"With that kind of budget I don't see any reason why not. No more Mickey Mouse radios, huh?" Hunt needled.

"Deal." I grinned. We went out and had a drink on it.

A week or so went by and Krogh sent for me again. "How," he asked, "would you like to be General Counsel for the '72 campaign?"

"I'd love it."

"Good. Dean says they need help on the election laws and things like that over there and you'd be right there to run the intelligence operation."

"Sounds ideal. Has this been run past Ehrlichman and Mitchell?"

"Yes, and they agree."

"O.K. Where do we go from here?"

"Check with John Dean. I think you ought to see John Mitchell. He'll be heading the campaign. Jeb Magruder's sort of sitting in for him now. Do you know him?"

"No."

"Nice guy. Better see him soon too. And Gordon?"

"Yes?"

"I'm sorry I was never able to pay you what you're worth here. Don't do it for less than thirty thousand. I'll be sure they know about the financial sacrifice you've been making."

I thanked Bud, told Howard Hunt the good news, and returned to Room 16 to speak to David Young. He would have to know I was leaving and, despite the fact that we had very different personalities, we had in common that we were from the same area of Dutchess County and had developed a rapport. The ice was broken during the summer one day when Dave had looked gray and so concerned I asked him what was the matter.

"I've got to see the Secret Service. I got a note this morning when I came in. It says the security check last night found a top-secret document unlocked in my desk. I don't know what it could be; everything's accounted for."

Off the poor guy went to see the Secret Service. If true, it was a major security breach and all the more embarrassing because ODESSA was charged with enforcing tight security on the rest of the government. A few minutes later Young returned. He had a folder under his arm marked TOP SECRET-SENSITIVE and he was the most relieved man I could imagine.

"What's so funny?" I asked as he started to laugh.

"I'd forgotten all about this," he said, brandishing the folder. "I brought it over with me from Henry's. You know, it's not true he hasn't got a sense of humor. We used to kid him all the time and he got a kick out of it. Look at this. We had it made up, then waited till he was on *Air Force One* in conference with the President, and had the Marine guard interrupt and give it to him with the word that it was urgent. He took it in there with the President and opened it to see what was important enough to interrupt the President of the United States."

With that, Young opened the folder. Each page consisted of a photograph similar to the first, which was a publicity still from a movie starring Frank Sinatra and a certain famous movie star whom the then single Kissinger had been dating. The lovely woman was lying on a chaise at the side of a pool wearing the most minuscule of bikinis and looking up at Frank Sinatra. Under the photograph was the caption: "If you can't do better than last night, Frank, I'm going to go back to fucking Henry."

I told Dave Young of my new assignment. He told me that I'd like Jeb Magruder, but that I shouldn't agree to take the post for less than forty thousand a year. "You can get it." He insisted. "Who else could do it—or for that matter *would* do it?" Then he gave me one more bit of advice. "Don't go over there until your title and salary are approved. Once you're over there, you'll have no bargaining position left."

He sounded, I thought, like Henry Kissinger and Kissinger knew more amout negotiating than anyone since Metternich. I decided to follow his advice.

John Dean took me to meet Jeb Magruder in his office. I found him prepared to discuss the areas in which he needed legal advice and aware of the fact that my primary role would be to run the intelligence operation for the campaign. He admitted to knowledge of neither law nor intelligence operations, was pleasant and eager to have me move over to the committee. Too eager. I told him I had first to have my position as General Counsel approved and a salary of thirty thousand dollars. He told me there "might be a problem in those areas." When I asked him what that might be, he said that "we operate without formal titles here" and "Bob Haldeman has a rule: no one is to make money on the campaign. So we only pay whatever it was you were getting over at the White House." He asked me how soon I could come over, and I told him that I wouldn't until the matter of title and salary had been settled.

"But I just explained . . . ," he said, and I interrupted to tell him that I didn't want to make any money on the campaign, but that I didn't want to continue losing it either, and that an exception would have to be made. I told him further that to accomplish what was expected of a General Counsel I would have to be able to represent myself as such and that was that. We had definitely gotten off on the wrong foot. Magruder was known to be a chairwarmer for John Mitchell, and there were a number of people over whom he did not have control, such as Fred LaRue, Mitchell's good friend and eyes and ears on the committee, and Magruder didn't want the General Counsel to be another. I, on the other hand, wasn't going to have a nonlawyer like Magruder telling me what to put in a legal opinion intended for other lawyers, nor did I expect someone who knew nothing about intelligence work to be calling the shots in that area either. I knew that I had to resist him from the onset. The battle thus joined, I consulted Dean after we left.

Dean said he understood and would arrange a meeting, Magruder excluded, with John Mitchell. He asked me to prepare an agenda for the meeting and I did. It included the areas of legal interest raised by Magruder as well as intelligence, but it started out with the most important things to me—organization and the chain of command.

On 24 November 1971 John Dean and I conferred with John Mitchell in the Attorney General's inner office in the Justice Department building. Mitchell said that the identity of the campaign chairman had not as yet been settled but that, although he didn't want it, "It'll probably be me." We went over all the legal areas but never got at all to intelligence. Primed by Dean, he brought up the matter of title and compensation and went along with me completely, then indicated that he could spend no more time with us, and Dean and I took our leave.

I was pleased that in the matter of salary and title I had won a victory over Magruder in what I knew would be a prolonged conflict, and I thanked Dean for his support. Then I asked him if we would be coming back again to discuss what I understood to be my principal mission, intelligence. Dean said that in view of the lead time I had said the creation of such an organization entailed I should start work as soon as possible and that I should be prepared to present a program to Mr. Mitchell for his approval.

I explained to Dean that organizing the intelligence operation would take much of my time and I'd need help

on the legal work of the committee. He promised to ge
me all the volunteer legal help I needed and gave me th
name of a prominent local Republican lawyer to see abou
organizing it.

I returned to Room 16 and, heeding David Young'
advice, resisted going over to 1701 Pennsylvania—whe
Magruder called to ask when I'd be there—until he finall
told me that Haldeman had approved an exception to th
salary rule, the matter of my title having already bee
decided against him by John Mitchell. On 6 Decembe
1971 I moved from the White House to the Committe
to Re-elect the President.

XVII

I was assigned an office across the reception area fron
Jeb Magruder in Committee to Re-elect the Presiden
headquarters at 1701 Pennsylvania Avenue, N.W., whicl
was diagonally across the corner from the Old Executiv
Office Building in the White House complex. Other neigh
bors were Robert Reisner, who was Magruder's executiv
assistant; Robert Odle, the office manager, and Herber
"Bart" Porter, who was running the surrogate speake
and celebrity program; and around the corner in the rear
just outside Rob Odle's office, sat Magruder's secretar
and, behind her, Jeanne C. Mason, secretary to Rob Odle

After settling in, I spoke to Magruder about my pri
mary task, organizing the intelligence service. I told hin
that I anticipated spending a million dollars and neede
immediate funding for start-up and recruiting costs
Magruder did not challenge that estimate but said that
would have to present a budget of that size to Joh
Mitchell for his approval. He suggested that it be a de
tailed justification for the amounts sought and accom
panied by a flowchart showing the rate of expenditure b

258

month from then until the end of the campaign in November 1972.

I pointed out to Magruder that according to Dean a half a million had been approved already by Mitchell for start-up and that I couldn't wait for approval of a formal budget before I started spending for organization and recruiting. There was too much lead time involved, and I wouldn't know what capabilities I could promise in the submitted budget until I knew what personnel I could count on.

Magruder agreed and authorized me to draw funds on an as-needed basis from Bart Porter who, he said, kept discretionary funds in a safe in his office.

It was at this point, not much more than three minutes into my first private conversation with Magruder, that I realized I was going to have trouble with him. With the authorization of immediate funds for recruiting and start-up of the intelligence operation, Magruder said I should be prepared to undertake investigations on request. I had no trouble with that; it was a modest request for service. It was what came next that bothered me.

"When you get going," Magruder said, "you're going to be asked to make reports to Gordon Strachan. Do you know Gordon?"

I confessed I did not.

"Well," Magruder continued, "he's very young and inexperienced but he works for Haldeman in a very low capacity. He wants to be cut in on the basis he represents Haldeman. If he calls, just say yes to what he asks, but put him off. Try not to give him anything. It's nothing intentional but he's just unreliable."

Jesus Christ, I thought, I'm not with this guy three minutes and he's poisoning the well of another guy in the White House I don't even know. It wasn't hard to figure out. Magruder had been a Haldeman staffer and so was Strachan. Magruder, now removed from proximity to Haldeman, was afraid Strachen was going to move up at his expense. I wasn't going to get involved in that crap.

"Jeb," I said, "no one's given me any instructions yet on who gets copies of what. In this line of work I can tell you that the fewer the better. But if I get orders from competent authority to give something to this Strachan guy, I'm going to have to do it. You guys'll just have to work that out yourselves." Our meeting ended on that sour note, and the very next one was to cause even more trouble.

Magruder called a meeting of key people in his office at which he introduced me as General Counsel and then proceeded to tell all in the room that "Gordon will also be in charge of 'dirty tricks.'" I was annoyed by that gratuitous security breach and waited after the meeting to tell him that any more such talk could blow my cover. I explained that I was going to be running a sophisticated intelligence service, not a "dirty tricks" campaign and that compromise could be dangerous. I did not intend to tell Magruder what I was doing or how I did it; he would just have to accept that the work product would go to John Mitchell. What Mitchell did with it was his business; if he wanted to share it with Magruder, Strachan, or anyone else there would be nothing I could do about it, but I thought that the fewer people on the distribution end the better. I telephoned John Dean, related the incident, and told him he'd better zip Magruder's lip.

Bart Porter was bright and energetic. He had been told by Magruder that I could draw funds from him. He asked for no accounting, only that I sign for the money I drew. I told him that I would return anything left over from each draw and give him an envelope, sealed, containing receipts to be placed in his safe. Should anything happen to me, the sealed envelope was to be given to John Mitchell and to no one else.

My first trip was overt. Magruder said that there was considerable anxiety among the staff at the selection of San Diego as the convention site because the press had already reported that left-wing extremists were distributing printed plans for disruption of the convention and soliciting nationwide for demonstrators. I asked Howard Hunt to accompany me on an inspection of the San Diego facilities and we flew to Los Angeles, intending to take the morning plane to San Diego. When I called the office I learned that John Dean and some Secret Service men were en route. Hunt's presence with me would cause speculation so I left him in Los Angeles to consult Tony Jackson for personnel leads and flew alone to San Diego to attend a meeting between members of the campaign staff and San Diego organizers. On my first day there I sat in on a meeting at which the donation of $400,000 in services by ITT, mostly through its hotel subsidiary, was discussed.

John Dean brought up the fact that there was an antitrust suit pending against ITT by Justice. Those speaking for the San Diego organizers said that there was no connection between the offer and the antitrust suit; having the convention in San Diego would be good for the ITT subsidiary and that was the only reason for the offer. Dean said that even though there was no *quid pro quo* expected by ITT from the administration in the antitrust matter, the mere fact that there were no strings attached was insufficient—the administration could not afford even the *appearance* of a deal. He was right and I supported his position. We both opposed the acceptance of the ITT offer vigorously, and I have no idea who eventually overruled us.

While there I went over to the Sports Arena and inspected the building and surrounding area. From a security point of view it was a disaster. A broad, flat plain swept up to the arena vast enough to be used for location shots in filming Napoleon's retreat from Moscow. There was no way short of deploying crew-served automatic weapons backed up by mortars that that plain could be held against determined hordes of violent demonstrators. When I returned I wrote a memorandum urging the selection of

261

another site. Retaining San Diego was just asking for trouble, and we'd already been promised plenty of it by the left.

Fran and I spent New Year's Eve at the Hunts' and I conferred with Howard there and subsequently in our old ODESSA conference room in the White House compound. We worked out a rough consensus of what the operation should entail: planting of our operatives in the staffs of Democratic candidates; surreptitious entries for placing of electronic surveillance devices and photographing key documents such as lists of donors and drafts of position papers with an eye for interstaff rivalries that could be developed into disruptive strife; the capacity to neutralize the leaders of anti-Nixon demonstrations; the exploitation of sexual weaknesses for information and the promotion of ill-feeling among the Democratic candidates to keep them as divided as possible after the nomination.

With that as an outline, Hunt and I worked up a list of needed personnel specialties, then set to work recruiting. Hunt agreed to take primary recruiting responsibility and that of administering the delivery of funds. He wanted a salary of $3,000 per month and, since I was getting $2,500 a month, I didn't argue. We flew first-class and stayed at the most expensive accommodations in the finest hotels, entertaining potential recruits at places like Chasen's because they must believe that money is no object to their employers if they are to accept the risk of that kind of employment under believable assurance of complete support in the event of trouble. Our two priorities were a "keyman" or expert locksmith and a "wireman" or electronics expert, and I wanted to get people into the campaign headquarters of Democratic candidates as soon as possible.

During one of our trips to California Hunt attempted to recruit one woman suggested by Jackson, and I a woman suggested by Hunt's candidate. The woman I was working on, Sherry Stevens, was ideal as a plant. She was flashily good-looking, young, had secretarial skills and experience, and appeared able to attract men sexually if she wished, possibly even the candidate. At dinner Miss Stevens seemed reluctant, balking at the risks involved, and when I told her that her identity would be revealed to no one and she could just walk away anytime if she feared exposure, she pointed out that *I* would know her identity. I told her that no one could force me to disclose anything I chose not to reveal. She didn't believe me and I was casting about for some way to convince her when I noticed she smoked. I told her to light her cigarette lighter and hold it out. She did and I locked my gaze upon her eyes and placed my hand, palm down, over the flame. Presently the flesh turned black and when she smelled the scent of burning meat, Sherry Stevens broke from my gaze and pulled the lighter away from my hand. She seemed frightened badly so I took pains to calm her, wrapping an ice cube against the burn with a napkin and returning to my dinner. Pale, Miss Stevens said she was sure I would never betray her, but excused herself as a candidate, invoking a just remembered plan to marry a Swiss airplane pilot in September of 1972. When I told her that I'd be glad to have her services through August, at a very generous rate of pay, she refused and, expressing concern for my hand, asked to be taken home.

At her apartment Miss Stevens gave me more ice cubes for the burn and appeared even more fearful, saying she hoped "you won't go down in flames" if she didn't offer to sleep with me. I told her that if I became offended every time someone didn't offer to go to bed with me, I'd end up being offended by an awful lot of people. "My God," I said, waving the napkined hand, "is that what you thought all this was about? Weren't you listening to what I was saying?"

"Well, I wasn't sure."

"*Be* sure. I want you for the job. No strings attached."

She promised to think it over. Back at the hotel I learned that Hunt had done better, getting a preliminary commitment. When I didn't do my customary hundred pushups the next morning, Hunt asked why. I showed him my hand and explained how it came to be that way. "That way" was, by now, a huge blackened, water-filled blister covering my palm and rendering my left hand virtually useless. I located a nearby physician in the phone book and had him lance the blister, treat the burn, and bandage it, then Hunt and I returned to Washington to make our plans in more detail.

Back at the committee I explained the burn to the idly curious as the result of an accident in which an entire pack of matches went off in my hand. Hunt and I developed our plans over the next month and kept at the recruiting. We had difficulty getting a keyman, even after Hunt traveled afar to interview candidates from CIA retirees and paid others to do so, and we both interviewed a man whom we brought to Washington and put up at the Hay Adams Hotel. We had the same difficulty in finding a wireman. I needed information on state-of-the-art equipment so, shortly after he joined the committee as physical security chief on 9 January 1972, I questioned James McCord. He was ex-FBI and ex-CIA, where he had been a "tech," specializing in that field.

He was intimately familiar with the techniques used by the Soviets in intercepting microwave-transmitted telephone calls in Washington from special antennas on the roof of their 16th Street embassy just a few hundred yards from the White House, as well as with U.S. techniques, now rendered useless through disclosure by Jack Anderson, for intercepting car-to-car and other transmissions by Soviet leaders in Moscow. A short time later he approached me and demonstrated the extent of his knowledge rather practically by providing me with the transcript of an automobile telephone conversation of Robert Strauss concerning Democratic Party fund-raising. With a portable X-ray machine he demonstrated the only way to detect a sophisticated listening device that could be built into furniture or planted in other deep concealment. The cost to produce the bug, which he characterized as precision

264

My mother,
at about the time
of her wedding.

Jean Raeburn

My father.

My father's father
in his usual stance—
a fighting one.

The frightened,
sickly child at 9½.

Frances, when her
last name was still Purcell.

John Lane Studio

In my cross-country
warm-up suit, with
my father.

Frances and me, November 9, 1957.

Three shots—
one with no mustache at all,
then a little one, then
(just after my release from
prison) with the mustache
of today.

I introduced myself to this man as "George Liddy." "G. Gordon Liddy" felt to me uncomfortably imitative of "J. Edgar Hoover."

Opposite page, bottom: Some of the handguns once owned by the author and on dining room table when neighbor came to complain of his anti-vandal activities in northwest Washington, D.C., in 1970. *Left rank:* .45 Colt semi-automatic carried by author's grandfather in World War I; 9mm parabellum Browning with 14-round capacity and adjustable sights; two 7.65mm Colt hammerless semi-automatic pistols and two European 7.65mm semi-automatic pistols bearing German *"Waffenamt"* World War II markings. *Center rank:* Smith & Wesson .357 magnum revolver, 3½" barrel with quick-draw ramp front and adjustable rear sights, wide hammer spur and grip filler, given to author by his wife on 28th birthday; two .25 caliber semi-automatic "holdout" pistols: top is Pieper-Hendaye; bottom, Colt with grip safety. *Right rank:* two Lügers in caliber 9mm parabellum: top, Bulgarian Crown model with Cyrillic markings and grip safety, bottom, DWM; Smith & Wesson .38 caliber "Combat Masterpiece" with 4" barrel, quick-draw ramp front and adjustable target rear sights, wide hammer spur and grip filler; Colt "Detective Special" revolver in .38 special caliber, 2" barrel and grip filler; Smith & Wesson revolver in .22 Long rifle caliber, 2" barrel with adjustable rear and quick-draw front sights.

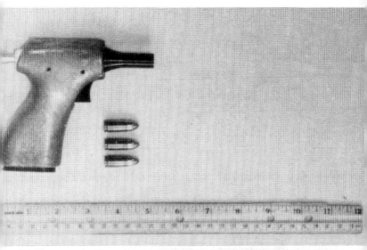

Sterile assassination pistol, caliber 9mm parabellum, issued by the Central Intelligence Agency. Manufactured of steel, aluminum and plastic, it may be carried submerged in water. Barrel unscrews readily for cleaning and even easier concealment. Piece bears no markings of any kind.

Left to Right: Raymond, Thomas, James, Grace and Alexandra

Son-in-law Brian

Daughter-in-law Sali

handwork within the knowledge and competence of a handful of men, he estimated at $30,000 per unit.

Hunt enlisted the aid of Bernard Barker and we traveled to Miami to interview men for our counterdemonstrator and antiriot squad, along with several prostitute candidates for use at the Democratic convention. The men were exactly what I was looking for: tough, experienced, and loyal. When I got through talking to them, some with the aid of interpretation, the leader spoke to Barker in Spanish. He looked at me and held out both hands with his fingers spread and curved like talons. Nodding his head at me he said something to Barker that included "*El Halcón*." Barker laughed. Afterward I asked Barker what the man had said. "He called you a falcon," said Barker, making the same clutching gesture, "the bird other birds fear." It became my code name.

Howard Hunt and I interviewed about a dozen men. Afterward Howard told me that between them they had killed twenty-two men, including two hanged from a beam in a garage. Our experience with the prostitutes was not good. Hunt and Barker kept recruiting dark-haired and -complexioned Cuban women. They were very good-looking, but their English left something to be desired. I was not sure they'd be suitable for the purposes I intended: posing as idly rich young women so impressed by men of power they would let themselves be picked up at parties and bars by Democratic staffers who, in the course of boasting of their own importance, would disclose valuable information. Hunt took the position that what the seduced men had to say would be tape-recorded anyway. I wanted to be able to call upon the memories of the women for what was said at locations other than those we had bugged. I was also affected by my own bias. Because *I* would be more attracted to Northern Europeans, I assumed fair women would be more successful and rejected those selected. Finally, having despaired of seeing other than the dark and sultry type from the Cubans, I retained, sight unseen except for professional photographs, two stunning

Anglo-Saxon women recruited by Barker's associate Frank Sturgis.

As Hunt and I refined our plans and we both traveled, paying for their time those we attempted to recruit, setting up extra phones and lines between Hunt's office and that of Barker in Miami, increasing Barker's office equipment and staff, and paying Hunt himself, I continued to draw money from Porter. Each time I'd return the unused portion, as much as a thousand or as little as three dollars, together with an envelope with receipts sealed into it against a possible accounting, should my employer want one.

On 10 January I realized the danger of this practice when I was sent to audit the records and accounts of Jack Caulfield's operative "Tony" in New York City. Caulfield told me that "Tony's" contract was being considered for renewal, and he wanted an independent audit by someone familiar with clandestine activities.

We found "Tony," later identified at Watergate hearings as Anthony Ulasewicz, at Apartment 11-C, 321 East 48th Street, Manhattan. Caulfield had described the place as "a very elaborate pad—beautiful, wait'll ya see it. My guy Tony's puttin' the make on one of the Chappaquiddick broads. The joint's wired for sound. He gets her in the sack a few times, wins her confidence, and we get the facts."

When "Tony" opened the door, I couldn't believe what I saw. First there was "Tony" himself; a big, overweight middle-aged man who in his best day would not exactly rival Redford. Still, Casanova himself was an ugly man, and maybe "Tony" had something only a woman could appreciate. The apartment itself was something else. It was small, so small that the "bedroom" was nothing but a tiny converted alcove with a pitiful, homemade wall erected across its opening and a curtain for a door. The wall, in which he was trying to hide a tape recorder, was covered in the fake brick sold at Montgomery Ward stores in poor neighborhoods to dress up aging kitchens. A white

shag rug was on the floor, and the windows were hung
with red imitation velvet drapes. The decor was strictly
better-grade Juárez whorehouse circa 1951.

Whatever his failings as an interior decorator or se-
ducer, "Tony" kept first-rate records. He received a
salary of $36,000 per year, and every cent spent over and
above that was accounted for in meticulous detail. His set
of records was a time bomb, waiting to go off; everywhere
he had gone, and virtually everything he had done, could
be reconstructed from them. I approved the audit on the
spot and urged him to destroy the records and not generate any more like them.

Hunt and I finally had our plans made in fullest detail.
I told him of the need for a cash flowchart and that I'd
like to have our diagrams also put in chart form for my
presentation to the Attorney General. The problem was
security. Neither Hunt nor I was very good at chart-draft-
ing, and I didn't want something homemade-looking for
use in presenting a million-dollar proposal.

Hunt was up to the challenge. He took our own crude
but legible diagrams to professionals: the CIA. Magruder
arranged a meeting with John Mitchell in the Attorney
General's office for 27 January and invited John Dean
to sit in. Several days before, Hunt had me stand at noon
on the corner of 17th Street and Pennsylvania Avenue,
where the CIA delivered to me a wrapped set of three-by-
four charts of professional caliber.

I'd been working day and night because the legal work
that was supposed to be nominal, just enough to serve as
convincing cover, had turned out to be substantial; but
my sense of purpose as I realized the opportunity I'd been
handed pumped me so full of adrenalin I never felt tired.

I knew exactly what had to be done and why, and I
was under no illusion about its legality. Although spies in
the enemy camp and electronic surveillance were nothing
new in American presidential politics, we were going to go
far beyond that. As far as I was concerned, anything went
if it were merely *malum prohibitum* (about which more

267

later). There was a law of physics that every action has an equal and opposite reaction; I was ready to break that one, too, in reaction to the radical left and the whole drug-besotted 1960s "movement" that was attacking my country from within.

My mind reached back twenty years to the interior of my fire-control van and the red switch that stood out in such stark contrast to the olive drab walls. That switch had a spring-loaded cover on it that had to be lifted to gain access to the switch itself. The bright red color and the protective cover were precautions to ensure that the switch would be thrown only after conscious and deliberate thought, because to throw it was to risk blowing the entire system; it was to be used only during a wartime emergency to circumvent the protective staging of the system. The sign under the switch read BATTLE OVERRIDE.

The experience of the past ten years left no doubt in my mind that the United States was at war internally as well as externally. In August 1970 the Army Math Center of the University of Wisconsin was added to the list of bombings. A father of two died in the blast and three others were injured. Two years before Daniel Moynihan had warned of the "onset of urban terror"—a bit late, I thought, in view of the thousands of bombings, burnings, riots, and lootings of the '60s, to say nothing of the murders of police just because they were police, the killing of judges, and the general disintegration of the social order.

Moreover the antiwar movement threatened to prove the vehicle for these radical elements to gain enough acceptance to achieve political power (six years later it was Senator George McGovern's son-in-law who was to get the bail of one of the Math Center bombers reduced so he could be freed). The events of the 1960s offended me gravely. To permit the thought, spirit, life-style, and ideas of the '60s movement to achieve power and become the official way of life of the United States was a thought as offensive to me as was the thought of surrender to a career

268

Japanese soldier in 1945. It was unthinkable, an unspeakable betrayal.

I remembered the rioting, burning cities, the bombings and killings, and the attempts to close down the nation's capital by mob violence; the American actress in the capital of our enemy broadcasting appeals to our combat troops to commit treason; the cooperation and approval of great newspapers in the theft and compromise of masses of classified documents. I remembered the crew-served automatic weapons in the halls of the Department of Justice, and I knew that what had happened to Richard Nixon in 1960 and to Lyndon Johnson in 1968 could not be permitted to happen again. With an ice-cold, deliberate certainty I knew exactly what I was going to be doing in 1972 and it was damn well about time: we were going to throw the Battle Override.

XVIII

In his offices at the Mullen Company across the street from the Committee to Re-elect Headquarters, Howard Hunt announced the recruitment of Virgilio "Villo" Gonzalez, a Cuban émigré locksmith. Although Hunt would continue to try to obtain an ex-CIA man with covert-entry experience, who could act as number one man with Gonzalez as backup, he assured me that if worse came to worse Gonzalez was up to the job. "He's ex-Batista secret police and hard as nails. He'll never talk. Hell, he hardly ever says anything now."

The only key person not yet recruited was the electronics man. McCord had been useful in furnishing technical information, but I didn't want to use anyone from the committee because I wanted to promise John Mitchell a "double blind" or double cutout protection of the committee from the intelligence operation in the event of discovery. But the rest of the necessary men and women were in a standby status, some being paid to remain available.

I was so confident of the ability of the group recruited that when I happened to meet Bud Krogh on the steps of the Old Executive Office Building, I thought of a proposal I'd made months before. I'd asserted that key foreign drug-smuggling operatives, who were well known should be recognized as killers of American children and subject to being killed themselves. By us. State had been horrified at the idea of such direct action as assassination and the suggestion had gone nowhere, but Bud had not seemed to object in principle. He had been traveling abroad quite a bit and had an appreciation of the difficulties involved in combating the drug barons with mere diplomacy. I was also very grateful to him for all he had done to advance me in the administration. I patted him on the back and said, "Bud, if you want anyone killed, just let me know." He smiled and said, "I will." I reacted to his smile by saying, "I'm serious."

"I know you are," said Krogh, his smile gone. "I'll let you know." In January, 1972 promised to be the best year I'd ever had. Even Treasury, numbed by my being named Counsel to the Committee to Re-elect the President, appeared to have accepted defeat; proposed testimony by Rossides was now being sent directly to me by his deputy for review when it concerned any of my known areas of interest. I considered the upcoming interview with John Mitchell a mere formality. After all, this program was a White House initiative and I had done, in my own estimation, a good job of planning and organizing. I was eager to get the meeting over with so we could get into action.

That was my attitude on 27 January as I stepped into the limousine that was to take Magruder and me to the Department of Justice for our 4 P.M. meeting with John Mitchell and John Dean. The only fly in the ointment I perceived was the presence of Magruder. More important than my dislike of him, I didn't consider his presence

:cessary or proper. The fewer who knew my proposal,
e better from the point of security. Mitchell was looking
me to produce and I had accepted the responsibility.
would choose the targets, the missions, and the methods.
itchell was the consumer. I was just going to show him
:actly what he was buying with his million bucks.

As we were riding, Magruder asked about my hand
:ain and, to shut him up, I abandoned the matchbook
ory and told him the truth, that I had burned it inten-
onally in a recruiting effort. As I had been doing things
:e that for years and was used to it, I failed to realize the
fect such a thing would have on someone like Magruder.
e was shaken, and that made me even more contemptu-
is of him.

We met John Mitchell in his small, inner office behind
e great ceremonial one so familiar to the public from the
ays of Bobby Kennedy. At my request there was an easel
t up. I greeted the Attorney General and, as Magruder
ated himself in front of the desk with Dean, I set up my
arts in the order I wanted to display them.

The plan was given the overall name of GEMSTONE,
ıd although most components bore the names of a pre-
ous or semiprecious stone, some were named for min-
als. I explained that the proposed service was what had
:en requested by John Dean and that it had full offen-
ve as well as defensive capability. Then I got down to
oecifics. I started with operation DIAMOND.

DIAMOND was our counterdemonstration plan. At the
me, we still expected the convention to be held in San
iego. I repeated my objections to the site, then pointed
ut that the best technique for dealing with a mob had
:en worked out years before by the famed Texas Rang-
rs. They were so few that law enforcement types still tell
ιe story of the town that telegraphed Ranger headquar-
:rs for help in suppressing a riot and were startled to see
 solitary Ranger ride into town. "There's only one of
ou?!" they cried, and the Ranger replied quietly, "There's
nly one riot, ain't there?"

271

The Texas Ranger technique was to linger on the fringes of the disturbance, watching until they could identify the leaders, then work their way through the crowd to leaders and beat the hell out of them until, leaderless, the rioters became easy to disperse.

I pointed out that we would be dealing with skilled and determined urban guerrillas who had been distributing manuals for violent guerrilla tactics against the convention, including homemade bombs; that the Sports Arena area would be impossible to hold against a well-led mob attack; and that I proposed to emulate the Texas Rangers by identifying the leaders through intelligence *before* the attack got under way, kidnap them, drug them, and hold them in Mexico until after the convention was over, then release them unharmed and still wondering what happened. Leaderless, the attack would be further disrupted by fake assembly orders and messages, and if it ever did get off the ground it would be much easier to repel. The sudden disappearances, which I labeled on the chart in the original German, *Nacht und Nebel* ("Night and Fog"), would strike fear into the hearts of the leftist guerrillas. The chart labeled the team slated to carry out the night and fog plan as a "Special Action Group" and, when John Mitchell asked "What's that?" and expressed doubt that it could perform as I had explained, I grew impatient. I was getting no support from Dean and Magruder. Both were sitting there, watching Mitchell intently, trying to gauge his reactions. I expected that from Magruder, but not from Dean. This was, after all, what he had asked me for, and I looked for an indication from him to Mitchell that this was what they were getting.

With Magruder and Dean out to lunch, I felt obliged to impress Mitchell with my seriousness of purpose, that my people were the kind and I was the kind who could and would do whatever was necessary to deal with organized mass violence. Both Magruder and Dean were too young to know what I was talking about, but I knew that Mitchell, a naval officer in World War II, would get the message if I translated the English "Special Action Group" into German. Given the history involved, it was a gross exaggeration, but it made my point. "An *Einsatzgruppe, General*," I said, inadvertently using a hard *g* for the word *General* and turning it, too, into German. "These men include professional killers who have accounted between them for twenty-two dead so far, including two hanged from a beam in a garage."

Mitchell gazed at me steadily, took another puff on his pipe, removed it from his mouth and said, "And where did you find men like that?"

"I understand they're members of organized crime."

"And how much will *their* services cost?"

I pointed to the figure on the chart. It was substantial. "Like top professionals everywhere, sir," I said, "they don't come cheap."

"Well," said Mitchell dryly as he brought his pipe back up to his mouth, "let's not contribute any more than we have to to the coffers of organized crime."

I didn't know Mitchell well enough to be able to tell whether he was being sarcastic or just objecting to the amount I had budgeted. I looked to Dean and Magruder for a clue. I found none. They just sat there, staring at Mitchell, like two rabbits in front of a cobra. Mitchell said no more, so I went on to the other operations.

RUBY concerned the infiltration of spies into the camp of Democratic contenders, then the successful candidate himself. COAL was the program to furnish money clandestinely to Shirley Chisholm of New York to finance her as a contender and force Democratic candidates to fight off a black woman, bound to generate ill-feeling among the black community and, we hoped, cause them difficulty with women. Once again Mitchell interrupted me. "You can forget about that. Nelson Rockefeller's already taking care of that nicely."

For each operation I explained what would be done in detail. EMERALD outlined the use of a chase plane to eavesdrop on the Democratic candidate's aircraft and buses when his entourage used radio telephones. I turned in the information intercepted from Robert Strauss as an example of what could be done on a much larger scale with proper funding.

QUARTZ detailed emulation of the technique used by the Soviet Union for microwave interception of telephone traffic, and I explained in detail the way it was done by the Soviet Embassy.

For use in gathering information at the Democratic National Convention at Miami Beach, Hunt and I had an option to lease a large houseboat moored within line of sight of the Fontainebleau. This would enable it to be used as a communications center for CRYSTAL—electronic surveillance. It was an opulent barge, with a lush bedroom featuring a large mirror over the big king-sized bed. We'd get our money's worth from the houseboat. It would double as headquarters for SAPPHIRE because it was from there that our prostitutes were to operate. They were *not* to operate as hookers but as spoiled, rich, beautiful women who were only too susceptible to men who could brag convincingly of the importance of what they were doing at the convention. The bedroom would be wired for sound, but I disagreed with Hunt's suggestion that movie cameras be used. That wouldn't be necessary to get the information, might cost us the women recruited who might object to being filmed *in flagrante*, and, as I pointed out to Howard, there wasn't room to install them overhead anyway. Mitchell listened to that impassively, as did Dean. Magruder, however, wore a look of eager interest.

I presented a plan for four black-bag jobs, OPALs I through IV. They were clandestine entries at which microphone surveillances could be placed, as well as TOPAZ: photographs taken of any documents available, including those under lock. As targets I proposed the headquarters of Senator Edmund Muskie's campaign on K Street, N.W.; that of Senator George McGovern on Capitol Hill; one for the Democratic National Convention at any hotel, because we had access to just about anything we wanted through all the Cuban help employed in the Miami Beach hotels. One entry would be held in reserve for any target of opportunity Mitchell wished to designate as we went along. I looked at him questioningly, but he just kept sucking on his pipe, suggesting none.

Next I presented plans for GARNET: counterdemonstrations by groups that would attract media attention and be perceived by most Americans to be repulsive as they advocated the candidacy of Democratic candidates of our selection. The groups would also carry out disruptive tactics at fund-raising dinners and other affairs.

The largest disruption operation, however, was reserved for the Democratic National Convention itself. We had paid well to acquire the entire blueprints for the convention hall and all its support machinery. The plan I outlined, TURQUOISE, called for a commando team of Cubans—veterans of raids into Castro Cuba—to slip at night from apartments rented across the street to the rear of the hall, where the air-conditioning units were, and sabotage them by destroying the compressors and introducing a destructive grit into the bearings of the blowers. Even John Mitchell smiled as I asked them to imagine those Democrats, already hot under the collar from so much internecine fighting over the nomination, when, in the 100-degree Miami summer weather, all the air-conditioning went out, damaged beyond quick repair, and the temperature inside the hall reached 110 or more degrees.

I closed the presentation with a summary of the many different offensive and defensive intelligence-collection and disruption operations the plan made available, and with a final two charts. One, BRICK, summed up GEMSTONE cost breakdowns by units (RUBY, COAL, DIAMOND, etc.) and the total of nearly one million dollars. The last was the flowchart, which looked roughly like a ski jump with a rise at the other end, running from day of approval, with the high outflow for equipment purchase, the valley of preconvention operations, and the rise as they increased in intensity at the time of the Democratic convention.

When I had finished, Dean and Magruder remained silent. John Mitchell made much of filling and relighting his pipe and then said, "Gordon, a million dollars is a hell of a lot of money, much more than we had in mind. I'd like you to go back and come up with something more realistic."

"Yes, sir," was all I said. I was disappointed and felt that I had been misled by John Dean. It was he, after all, who had said that half a million would be "for openers" and that the half-million-dollar Sandwedge program with its black-bag and electronic surveillance capability had been thought inadequate. He had said nothing throughout the presentation, or now, in support of the program I had gone to such pains and great expense to prepare.

As I restacked the charts, John Mitchell continued, "And Gordon?"

"Yes, sir?"

"Burn those charts; do it personally."

"Yes, sir."

I walked out of Mitchell's office with fire in my eyes. Before we even reached the car, in which John Dean was to join us for a ride back to the White House, I unloaded on both of them. "Thanks for all the help. What the hell does he mean, 'realistic'? You're the one, John, who said there'd be 'half a million for openers.' I've got top people committed and standing by on the basis of a budget of a million, in good faith. What's going on?"

Magruder was solicitous. "Mr. Mitchell," he said, "sees more of the picture than any of us. It may be that contributions aren't up to what they were expected to be by now and there just isn't the money for intelligence and dirty tricks they thought would be available. These things happen in campaigns. You've got to be flexible. You're going to have to cut out the most expensive stuff."

"It's clear," chimed in Dean, "that he wants a less

broad-gauged program. Jeb's right; you're going to have to cut it back."

"All right," I answered, exasperated. "but I want a figure I can rely on. I've got to tell my people something. I want to know exactly what budget to plan for."

We dropped Dean off at that point before he could respond, but Magruder said, "Cut it in half. If they said half a million for openers, they may have that amount. Try half a million."

I went home to Oxon Hill that evening with my elaborate CIA-prepared charts and, as ordered by Mitchell, burned them personally in the ground-floor fireplace of the family room.

When I reported this news to Howard Hunt, he was annoyed as much by the fact that we didn't have a decision yet as by the fact of the budget cut. "We can't keep these people on a string forever, Gordon," he protested. "They're not used to this kind of treatment and it certainly isn't something that breeds confidence. The minute we start saying that we have a money problem, these people are going to take a walk."

I apologized to Hunt and asked him to keep the people in line as long as possible, and we went to work quickly on a new plan calling for the expenditure of no more than $500,000.

We cut the big-ticket items first. McCord's radiophone interception operation, which called for an expensive plane capable of staying with a jet airliner, was the first to go. So did the ground microwave program and the air-conditioning sabotage plan. Operation COAL was out because Mitchell had said it was being taken care of by Rockefeller. We pared here and there and finally brought the figure down to half a million. Mitchell hadn't liked the charts, so I decided to use regular bond paper to duplicate them in miniature. Hunt and I did what we could do in his office, then I went looking for someone to type up the budget, which, this time, I had stated in meticulous detail.

277

By now, my office was on the floor above, Fred Malek having joined the campaign and taken over my old quarters. The matter was so sensitive I did not want to expose it to my secretary because there were no euphemisms used. I wanted someone who would not be shocked and who could keep her mouth shut. While on the main floor I had made friends of other secretaries, showing some of them who worked late hours how to defend themselves against attack, including how to kill a man with no more than a pencil. Some of the women had been shocked by that, but one had not. She was Jeanne Cress Mason, formerly of the ultrasecret National Security Agency, the code-makers and -breakers for whom the FBI had performed so many embassy break-ins. She typed that budget as if it were a grocery list and paid it even less attention, having learned to be professionally incurious at work.

To avoid the curiosity of others, however, I had brought the work to Mrs. Mason after hours and, now that she was finished, I thought she looked particularly tired. I knew she suffered from time to time from severe migraine and asked her if she felt ill. She shook her head in the negative and said, "No, only disgusted."

"What's the matter?" I asked her, thinking I had misjudged her reactions to the harsh realities of clandestine action.

"Oh, it's just Jeb and the old Ava Gardner thing. You won't believe what he wants me to do."

The reference to Ava Gardner wasn't surprising; Jeanne Mason bore a striking resemblance to Gardner in her prime and was a remarkably beautiful woman in her own right. People used to kid her about it and she tired of it, dressing and wearing her hair as differently from the way Gardner did as possible.

"Try me," I said.

"That worm actually called me in and said he'd see that I got to go to the convention, if I'd help him play a trick on Frank Sinatra."

"Frank Sinatra?"

"Yes. He's one of our celebrities and he'll be at the convention. Jeb said, 'You know he's never gotten over Ava Gardner. He's still in love with her. I want you to put your hair up and dress just like her, then we'll spring you on Frank. Everywhere he goes, there you'll be. It'll drive him out of his mind.' He was laughing. He thinks someone else's pain is funny."

"What'd you say?"

"I told him to his face I thought he was sick and walked out."

"He is sick. Forget about it. He won't have the guts to ask you again."

That took care of the miniature charts and the detailed budget for the second meeting with Mitchell, but I still had no flowchart. I took the problem home with me and had a brainstorm: the flowchart had to do with the timing of the expenditure of money only; it said nothing about what it was for. Fran was an artist; she ought to be able to do a flowchart. I told her what I needed, but not what for, and within half an hour she produced a flowchart as good as that the CIA had drawn up for the first meeting.

I was now ready for the meeting with Mitchell and advised Magruder. In the meanwhile the advertising people told me they wanted to form a special corporation, an advertising agency, just for the 1972 Nixon campaign. I formed November Group, Inc., under the laws of the state of New York, where it would be operating. As I was doing so I started to receive disturbing telephone calls from Nixon/Agnew headquarters in various states. The callers all told the same story: a young man, small, dressed in Ivy League fashion and wearing wire-rimmed glasses, was approaching headquarters personnel and telling them he was authorized by national headquarters to conduct a "counter campaign" against Democratic presidential hopefuls. He solicited local GOP support. I sent out a memorandum to all Nixon/Agnew headquarters titled "Matter of Potential Embarrassment" and asked their cooperation in tracking the man down. I believed him to be a Democrat *agent provocateur*.

Magruder called. My second meeting with Mitchell was set for Friday, 4 February.

Once again we met in Mitchell's inner office. Dean had not arrived, but Mitchell told me not to wait. I handed him and Magruder each a thin sheaf of standard bond-sized papers: the miniature charts, budget, and flowchart.

The items eliminated from the initial proposal were all so expensive that with some cutback of SAPPHIRE (the houseboat was out, but the hookers were in) and of demonstration sizes and the number of OPAL and CRYSTAL operations, Hunt and I were able to retain a substantial amount of the initial program at the reduced cost of $500,000.

John Dean has since said that he entered at the very end of my second presentation. He was not that late. He came in after I had handed out the new, smaller charts and explained to Mitchell and Magruder what had been cut out, but he was there in time to hear that programs DIAMOND (removal and detention of violent demonstration leaders); CRYSTAL (electronic surveillance); SAPPHIRE (the prostitute program); OPAL (the covert entry operation); and RUBY (the agents-in-place program), could be retained in reduced form.

This time Mitchell did not order the destruction of the charts when he handed his back to me; nor did he ask me to come up with something "more realistic." He just said he'd have to "think about it" and let me know. It was at this point that John Dean interposed his objection. It was not, as he has so often said, that such matters should not be discussed in the Attorney General's office, but that (addressing himself to John Mitchell): "Sir, I don't think a decision on a matter of this kind should came from the Attorney General's office. I think he should get it from somewhere else—completely unofficial channels."

John Mitchell nodded his head soberly and said, "I agree"; at which point Jeb Magruder chimed in with "Right." Dean hurried away before I could chew on him for what I believed to have been a suggestion that would only delay a decision further. But I landed all over Magruder.

"Why the hell," I said to Jeb, "am I constantly being put in the position of a salesman for something somebody has already ordered? I'm not going to continue being put into an embarrassing position like this with my people. I've promised them an answer. If they think we're indecisive they're gonna want out and at this point, frankly, I don't blame them. Now I want a fucking decision and I want it fast!"

Once again Magruder was conciliatory. "What John said was unfortunate, but he has a point. Don't worry; I'll follow through on it and get you a decision."

"When?"

"Soon, Gordon, soon."

Weeks passed and there was no decision forthcoming. Howard Hunt said that he had experienced the same problem often in the CIA: enthusiasm of top officials waning and projects dying on the vine. He was not sanguine that anything would ever come of GEMSTONE.

My reaction was that until I was told it was off I was obligated to be ready to go, and there were signs that the concept was still alive. Not long after my communiqué on the "Matter of Potential Embarrassment" went out, Jeb Magruder called me into his office to tell me that the subject of my inquiry was not a Democrat after all but a young man hired by Bob Haldeman, through Dwight Chapin, who was just following orders. I told Magruder I didn't like it; I was supposed to be running the whole clandestine show and someone like Haldeman's man would just stir up everyone and make them alert, if nothing worse.

Magruder had anticipated my reaction and was ready. "No problem, Gordon," he said. "Everyone's agreed you're to be in charge. They just want you to take him over, give him guidance so he keeps out of trouble. He's not into any of the rough stuff. Strictly 'rat-fucking.' "

By this time I knew that *rat-fucking* was a University of California fraternity term for glorified Halloween pranks. I told Magruder I'd talk to the guy, identified as "Don Simmons" but later revealed to be Donald Segretti, and Hunt and I arranged to meet him in Florida where we'd "Mutt and Jeff" him (the old good cop, bad cop routine).

Hunt and I met Segretti in a sleazy motel in a rundown section of Miami. We were wearing slacks and pullovers to blend into the neighborhood; Segretti stood out like a herpes blister on a debutante in his three-piece suit. We grilled him on what he'd been up to, then extracted a promise that he'd keep in touch with Hunt, and gave him the name of a secure local printer. Then I took Segretti aside and told him to be careful to do exactly as Hunt ordered because Hunt (introduced as Ed Warren) was, "like so many professionals after a while, dangerous. He sometimes kills without orders. The least he might do would be break both your knees." Shaking, Segretti swore to stay in line.

If Mitchell and Ehrlichman had indeed approved the original intelligence organization concept and Haldeman had people of his own working clandestinely, the problem, I thought, was not one of second thoughts but of indecision and quarreling over money. Then another incident added to my conviction that GEMSTONE was still very much alive. When Howard Hunt was told by Robert Bennett, his employer, that Hank Greenspun, a Las Vegas newspaper publisher, was believed to have documents in his office safe that would "blow Muskie out of the water" and I passed that information on to Magruder, the reaction was swift. Hunt and I were authorized to check on the feasibility of cracking the safe and retrieving the documents.

Although I was still drawing money from Porter, Hunt and I decided that in the absence of a go-ahead on the creation and funding of GEMSTONE, we ought to make an alliance of convenience with Howard Hughes, known to be an enemy of Greenspun. Hunt had excellent connections with Hughes Tool and the Summa Corporations through his employer, Robert Bennett, whose Mullen Company represented Hughes and who was embroiled in the campaign to prove the purported authorized biography of Hughes by Clifford Irving to be a fraud. According to Hunt, Greenspun probably had documents in his safe that Hughes would like to retrieve. By prearrangement, Hunt and I flew to Los Angeles and stayed in a suite obtained for us by Hughes at the Beverly Wilshire Hotel. It is in the old section, very 1940-ish and huge, appropriate to anyone doing business with Howard Hughes. Each of us had his own bedroom, bathroom, dressing room, and we shared a spacious living room.

There we conferred with Bob Winte, a Hughes security man. I suggested that we mount a joint operation. I believed Hughes would go along with it because Winte had already obtained for us the floor-plan of Greenspun's office, with the position of the safe marked clearly. It was a safe I believed easy to crack and I proposed that Hunt and I do so with a Cuban team while Hughes provided transportation and cover for us in Las Vegas. Key to the plan was a Hughes jet transport to be on standby in the desert. We would crack the safe and take everything in it without examination, head straight to the waiting jet, and fly to a Hughes-controlled Caribbean destination of his choice. There we would examine our findings jointly with Hughes' representatives and divide the materials on the basis of our separate interests. Winte said he would seek approval and seemed to think the matter a mere formality. When, a short time later, Hunt told me that Hughes had declined on the basis of the cost of the jet, I didn't believe it and concluded that the real reason was that

Hughes figured there was something in the Greenspun safe that he didn't want us to see. From Hughes's point of view, we represented the government.

Another series of events that led me to believe GEM-STONE would be approved was the fact that Magruder had the committee turn over to me a project of its own called SEDAN CHAIR, which they had been running for some time, the funding also going through Porter. It was an operative posing as a chauffeur loyal to Muskie who in fact photographed every document given him for delivery or mailing and turned it over to the committee. Magruder explained that he wanted all such activities centralized in me. I had Hunt meet the operative's control, code-named "Fat Jack," and we took over the operation. Next I learned that Ken Reitz, who was running the youth program, had some sort of clandestine operation going on. That made *three* operations: Haldeman's, the committee's own "Fat Jack," and the Rietz kiddie corps program. Somebody high up had had to give the O.K. for the latter two and I suspected Haldeman. Was it any wonder that his rival, Mitchell, wanted to capture overall control of the clandestine operations through me? I couldn't conceive of Mitchell's agreeing to be campaign chairman with Haldeman running clandestine operations out of Mitchell's shop and on campaign money. If Mitchell was going to pay the piper, he was going to call the tune.

Bob Bennett continued to be helpful. Hunt came to me and said Bennett had a nephew we might use as a plant. He was at Brigham Young University and thinking of getting into the campaign to gain credits. Again Magruder approved the expenditure of funds from Porter and the youngster, Thomas Gregory, was also placed in the Muskie camp. Gregory became RUBY II in GEMSTONE terms, "Fat Jack" having already been designated RUBY I.

By this time I'd drawn nearly twenty-five thousand dollars from Bart Porter, and it was this funding through

Porter that enabled Magruder to exert a control that I didn't think he should have. But without a budget of my own, Magruder was in a position to call the shots. I began to suspect he was delaying a decision on GEMSTONE deliberately, to maintain this control over intelligence operations. He was, after all, a Haldeman man.

At about that time Magruder sent me to see Hugh Sloan, treasurer of the finance committee. Sloan gave me an envelope with about a thousand dollars in it, and on Magruder's instructions I gave it to Howard Hunt. What it was for was none of my business so I didn't ask, but I learned later it was to finance Hunt's trip to the bedside of Dita Beard where, using our CIA-provided physical disguise, he interviewed her for Colson about the authenticity of her controversial memorandum concerning the ITT contribution to the convention.

Finally I hit Magruder on the lack of the promised speedy decision by Mitchell on the second GEMSTONE proposal. It was then he told me it had been rejected as "too expensive." Once more I went back to Hunt with bad news, but he agreed reluctantly to help me cut the budget in half again, as Magruder now suggested. We retained the four OPAL clandestine entries for electronic and photographic surveillance; retained the two existing RUBY agents in place and provided for two more; retained the two SAPPHIRE prostitutes for use against Democrats in Miami along with some counterdemonstration forces— and that was about it.

Because this time I would not have the opportunity to present the plan to the Attorney General myself—Magruder was to pass it to him for decision—I decided that since Magruder would see it first anyway, I'd make a virtue of necessity and consult him on it. Any advocate was better than no advocate at all.

Magruder approved the drastically revised plan, even to the point of agreeing to my demand that moneys spent to date not be charged against the new $250,000 budget. He had only one suggested change: that the prostitutes to be used at the Democratic convention next summer be brought up to Washington from Miami and put to work immediately.

I told Jeb that bringing whores to Washington was like shipping cars to Detroit, with all the free stuff being given away on Capitol Hill they'd just be a couple of more grains of sand on the beach. Besides, the budget was bare bones; there wasn't a nickel left over for their transportation and payment for all those months until summer. Magruder replied that they could be paid through Porter if necessary. Again I stressed that it just wasn't practical to bring hookers to Washington.

Magruder didn't want to let the subject go. If he could justify a trip to Miami, could I fix him up with our girls? Jesus, I thought, the wimp can't even get laid with a hooker by himself. I saw an opportunity to turn Magruder's lust to advantage. If GEMSTONE were approved, I told him, he'd be paying for them anyway and could take his pick. From the look on his face as I left his office, I had the feeling that if Magruder had anything to say about it, GEMSTONE would be approved.

On a brisk February day shortly thereafter, Howard Hunt and I had lunch with a man he introduced to me as Dr. Edward Gunn, a physician retired from CIA and an expert on "the unorthodox application of medical and chemical knowledge." I took "retired" to be in quotes since that is a standard technique and Hunt introduced me under my operational alias, "George Leonard." We lunched at the below-ground-level restaurant in the Hay Adams Hotel on the corner of 16th Street, N.W., just across Lafayette Park from the White House.

The purpose of the luncheon, Hunt had explained to me previously, was to take advantage of the expertise of Dr. Gunn in preparing, for the approval of Hunt's "principal," a plan to stop columnist Jack Anderson. Even with each other, Hunt and I often, when discussing the most sensitive of matters, used the term *my principal* rather than identify our superiors. I, at least, had several. Hunt, to my knowledge, had only one: Chuck Colson.

Anderson, Hunt reported, had now gone too far. As the direct result of an Anderson story, a top U.S. intelligence source abroad had been so compromised that, if not already dead, he would be in a matter of days. That was too much. Something had to be done.

The conversation at lunch was in the hypothetical terms usually employed in such circumstances. We did not mention Anderson's name explicitly. Hunt urged the use of LSD on the steering wheel of the "target's" automobile to cause him to hallucinate at a public function and thus be discredited. Dr. Gunn shot down that idea on the ground that CIA experience with the drug had demonstrated the unpredictability of individual reaction.

I took the position that, in a hypothetical case in which the target had been the direct cause of the identification and execution of one of our agents abroad, halfway measures were not appropriate. How many of our people should we let him kill before we stop him, I asked rhetorically, still not using Anderson's name. I urged as the logical and just solution that the target be killed. Quickly.

My suggestion was received with immediate acceptance, almost relief, as if they were just waiting for someone else to say for them what was really on their minds. There followed a lengthy discussion of the ways and means to accomplish the task best. Hunt, still enamored of the LSD approach, asked Dr. Gunn whether a massive dose might not cause such disruption of motor function that the driver of the car would lose control of it and crash. Dr. Gunn repeated his earlier negative advice on the use of LSD. Besides, though LSD *can* be absorbed through the skin, our hypothetical target might be wearing gloves against the winter cold, or be chauffeur-driven. The use of LSD was, finally, dismissed.

Hunt's suggestion called to Dr. Gunn's mind a technique used successfully abroad. It involved catching the target's moving automobile in a turn or sharp curve and hitting it with another car on the outside rear quarter. According to Dr. Gunn, if the angle of the blow and the relative speeds of the two vehicles were correct, the target vehicle would flip over, crash, and, usually, burn. By this time I was sure Gunn had guessed the identity of the hypothetical target, since he asked whether he was local and suggested, if he was, that we use the method he had just described at Chevy Chase Circle, a route Anderson did travel. Chevy Chase Circle, he pointed out, is notorious as the scene of fatal auto accidents and its configuration ideal for use of the technique.

I argued that Dr. Gunn's method would require the services of an expert to ensure success, and one might not be available to us. Dr. Gunn looked surprised, as if it had not occurred to him that we would not have available all the resources of the CIA.

Other methods were discussed and discarded. "Aspirin Roulette," for example: the placing of a poisoned replica of the appropriate brand of headache tablet into the bottle usually found in the target's medicine cabinet. That method was rejected because it would gratuitously endanger innocent members of his family and might take months before it worked.

I came up with the suggestion we finally agreed upon as the one to be recommended. It was a lethal adaptation of a technique long in use by the FBI during surreptitious entries. When an embassy safe, for example, is to be penetrated so that crypto material may be photographed for use by NSA, everyone who might have access to the office is followed while the penetration is in progress. It is not begun unless a wiretap or other positive means has established that the embassy personnel will be away for a sufficient period. Should someone return unexpectedly, however, he would never get into the embassy door. He would be assaulted, his wallet and watch removed, and, while he was unconscious as the latest victim of the outrageously high rate of street crime in Washington (which is not within the jurisdiction of, and therefore not the fault of, the FBI), the entry team would make good its escape.

I submitted that the target should just become a fatal victim of the notorious Washington street-crime rate. No one argued against that recommendation and, at Hunt's suggestion, I gave Dr. Gunn a hundred-dollar bill, from Committee to Re-elect the President intelligence funds, as a fee for his services. I took this to be to protect Dr. Gunn's image as "retired."

Afterward Hunt and I discussed the recommendation further. It was decided to include the suggestion that the assassination of Jack Anderson be carried out by Cubans already recruited for the intelligence arm of the Committee to Re-elect the President.

"Suppose," said Hunt, "my principal doesn't think it wise to entrust so sensitive a matter to them?"

I am asked frequently whether I believe in "blind obedience" to orders from legitimate authority, the code that permitted many Germans to carry out genocide. I do not. While there is a presumption of regularity that must obtain in any orders from legitimate superiors without which no government could function, I believe in individual responsibility, free will, and the rule of reason. There is a point beyond which I will not go, and that is anything my conscience tells me is *malum in se* (evil in and of itself) or my judgment tells me is irrational. I have no problem with doing something that is *malum prohibitum* (wrong only because of the existence of a law prohibiting it).

An example of *malum in se* would be the sexual assault of a child. In every society such a thing would be recognized as wrong. It would require no act of the legislature forbidding it to inform people that it was wrong. An example of *malum prohibitum*, on the other hand, would be the statute prohibiting driving through a stop sign without coming to a complete halt. Absent such a law, to do so would be a morally indifferent act.

Common sense tells us that minor problems require and justify but minor responses, and only extreme problems require and justify extreme solutions. In the case of killing it is well to remember that the Ten Commandments, translated correctly from the original Aramaic, do not contain the injunction "Thou shalt not kill." It reads, "Thou shalt not do murder." Quite another thing. There are circumstances that not only justify killing but require it (when one is charged with the safekeeping of a child, for example, and the only way to prevent its death from another's attack is to kill that other person). These are all situations that require informed and responsible judgments.

There are other ethical doctrines that may be applied. In World War II some bomber pilots were concerned when they knew that, for example, the ball bearing factory that was their target was across the street from an orphanage and their bombing altitude meant that it was very likely the orphanage would also be hit. In such a situation the principle of double effect comes into play; the unintended secondary effect of the destruction of the orphanage is permissible. The classical example is that of the driver of a loaded schoolbus going down the one-lane mountain road with a sheer thousand-foot drop on either side rounding a turn to see a three-year-old girl on a tricycle in the middle of the road. He is going too fast to stop. The choices are go off the road and take thirty-five children and himself to certain death to spare the three-year-old, or run over the three-year-old and save the thirty-five. I'd run over the three-year-old. I also fail to see any distinction between killing an enemy solider in time of declared war and killing an enemy espionage agent in a "cold" war, or even killing certain U.S. citizens. For example, were I back in my ODESSA position and were given the instruction from an appropriate officer of the government, I would kill Philip Agee if it were demonstrated (as it has often been argued) that his revelations have led directly to the death of at least one of his fellow CIA officers, that he intended to continue the revelations, and that they would lead to more deaths. Notice that this

290

killing would not be retributive but preventive. It is the same rationale by which I was willing to obey an order to kill Jack Anderson. But I would do so only after satisfying myself that it was: a) an order from legitimate authority; b) a question of *malum prohibitum*; and c) a rational response to the problem.

I thought about the damage Anderson was doing to our country's ability to conduct foreign policy. Most of all, I thought of that U.S. agent abroad, dead or about to die after what I was sure would be interrogation by torture. If Hunt's principal was worried, I had the answer.

"Tell him," I said, "if necessary, I'll do it."

XIX

While waiting to learn whether to kill Jack Anderson, I grew impatient with the lack of a decision on the third GEMSTONE budget submission and decided to do something about it. Word was around the committee that John Mitchell, beset with marital difficulties and after reluctantly managing another presidential campaign, would return to his lucrative private law practice to cash in on the second Nixon administration. That would leave me without what is called in New York political and police circles a "rabbi." I was impressed by Chuck Colson's coldly pragmatic approach to politics and his skills as an infighter and concluded I might kill two birds with one stone.

I approached Hunt and laid it out for him. I wanted him to introduce me to Colson. There I would not only seek to gain an ally in the second Nixon administration, I'd ask Chuck to kick some ass and get us a decision on GEMSTONE. Hunt was obliging and, in the latter part of February, arranged an appointment; he made the introduction, then withdrew to the rear of the room while I spoke to Colson. I told him that I hoped I'd be working with him the following year because his approach and mine were similar, and I used that to lead into the problem of a decision about GEMSTONE.

Colson didn't want to hear a thing about GEMSTONE and cut me off with "All you need is a decision, right?"

"Right."

"O.K." With that Colson scooped up his phone and got Magruder on the line. "Gordon Liddy tells me he can't get a decision out of you people on an intelligence program. I don't want to get into a debate of the merits; it just seems to me that after all this time somebody ought to be able to make a decision. Let's get on it."

That was all there was to it. Joan Hall, Colson's secretary, appeared to remind him of something and out we went.

It was now nearly March and I had long since been fed up with Magruder. Hugh Sloan had increasingly been asking me for advice and was appreciative of the counsel I gave him. Maurice Stans, a brilliant, self-educated, and self-made millionaire leader in the accounting industry and former Secretary of Commerce, had become chairman of the finance committee on 15 February, and things were really beginning to hum down there. I considered moving downstairs as counsel to the finance committee but was still undecided when I happened to find myself in the elevator lobby with Magruder one noon. He approached me and, in the presence of a number of other people, leaned his arm on my shoulder (he is taller than I) and once again brought up a subject of conflict between us.

At his request I had written a legal opinion concerning the primary election laws in certain key states. Magruder had complained that he couldn't understand it and that I'd have to "simplify" it. I had replied that the opinion was written by a lawyer for a lawyer—John Mitchell—and that to "simplify" it would be to degrade it. John Mitchell, I assured him, would be able to understand it.

Now Jeb raised the issue again.

"Gordon," he said in a voice loud enough to attract the

attention of the others in the elevator lobby, "I'm really not satisfied with your work on the primaries. You're just going to have to redo it." He stood there, leaning on my shoulder as the others stared, waiting for my answer.

I gave him one. "Jeb, if you don't take your arm off my shoulder, I'm going to tear it off and beat you to death with it."

Magruder snatched his arm back as if my shoulders had suddenly become red-hot, turned, and ran into an elevator. I took another. Later I heard that he was telling everyone I had threatened to kill him. That did it. I decided to get out from under Magruder and conferred with Hugh Sloan about becoming counsel to the finance committee exclusively.

Sloan was enthusiastic. A brand-new election law would take effect on 7 April, and he believed the finance committee would need exclusive counsel soon. When Sloan raised the matter with him, Maurice Stans agreed. I had no hesitancy in taking the job on because GEMSTONE was still unapproved and, I believed, if approved, would not demand the time from me that it would have in its original state. John Mitchell had become chairman on 1 March and brought Jack Caulfield with him as an executive assistant. I was encouraged. There was now no question of the decision "coming out of the Attorney General's office." I was still in my upstairs office, awaiting an interview with Maurice Stans before moving in as counsel to the finance committee when Jack Caulfield came to see me. He had a tape of a telephone conversation he had had with a former Secret Service agent on the West Coast and wanted it transcribed. Because I had a secure secretary, I accommodated him. When he came back for the transcript, he was furious and I asked him what the problem was.

"That fucking Magruder. He couldn't stand my being close to Mitchell and reviewing memos as his assistant so he's cut me down to bodyguard status. I went in to see the son of a bitch and asked him to settle it like a man out back in the alley and he started shaking. He won't fight. He's yellow."

"Tell me something I don't know. What are you going to do?"

"I dunno. I'll work out something. But I really had a chance to make a contribution, and the little prick fucked me right out of it. Don't people around here know what kind of guy he is?"

"They know, there's just nothing anyone can do about it. He's Haldeman's boy." I told Jack I was moving out myself to the finance committee and he congratulated me.

At lunch with Hunt I brought up the matter of killing Jack Anderson. He told me to forget it, from which I concluded that the decision from Colson, I assumed, was negative. I inquired no further. A short while later Magruder called me into his office to deliver another whining complaint about Anderson. One of my first assignments from him had been to check out a rumor—which proved impossible to substantiate—that Anderson had been involved in a land fraud on Maryland's Eastern Shore. Another was that he had sent someone to break into our committee headquarters but was thwarted by our security. I checked that one with McCord and he knew nothing about it. I was in no mood for any more of Magruder's petty carping about Anderson, so I tuned him out; but one sentence came through loud and clear: "Gordon, you're just going to have to get rid of Jack Anderson.'

For serious reasons of state I had just offered to kill Anderson for the White House and been turned down. Now *this* pipsqueak wanted to put out a contract on him for no more reason than that he was a general pain in the ass. I was in the corridor leading to the elevator lobby when I spotted Bob Reisner, Magruder's assistant, coming the other way and had an inspiration. If I mentioned Magruder's request to Reisner, the young man, who was very straight, would report it to Jeb without fail. Once Magruder knew that someone like Reisner knew about his request he'd call it off and, I sincerely hoped, never mention Anderson's name to me again.

I stopped Reisner in the hall and said, "Bob, you'll never guess what your boss has just ordered me to do."

Reisner looked puzzled and said, "What?"

I stared for a long moment and then gave him my best we're-all-upstairs-over-the-saloon-in-Gary-Indiana-at-night-wiping-our-fingerprints-off-the-machineguns look and said: "I'm on my way to knock off Jack Anderson."

"W-what?"

"You heard me."

"Jeb said *that*?"

"Told me to get rid of 'im, plain as day."

"Oh, well I'm sure he didn't mean *that*!"

"Yeah? Well, where I come from, kid, that means a rub-out." I spun on my heel and left. I could hear Reisner running down the hall behind me to get to Magruder, so I lingered in the lobby, letting several elevators go by. Sure enough, minutes later, there came poor Reisner, running back after me.

"Oh, Gordon, I was afraid you'd be gone. Jeb said he most certainly definitely did *not* mean it that way. Just forget it. Don't do *anything*! He was just *kidding*!"

Grinning inwardly, I fought to be stern as I said, "Damnit, he better learn how to make up his mind. That stuff's nothing to kid about." An elevator arrived and I left.

Stans was all business, no nonsense, knew his own mind about what he wanted to do and wanted you to do. For all that, he was gracious and we talked for a few minutes about matters of mutual interest. Stans was a noted hunter and sportsman who had taken the biggest game in the United States and Africa. We chatted about favorite rifles and calibers. I told Stans nothing of GEMSTONE or intelligence work because he had no need to know and I wasn't at all sure he would have taken me on if he had thought I would have had to divide my attention between work for him and work for what he referred to as "the people upstairs," the Committee to Re-elect, for most of whom he had rather low regard. He thought them spendthrifts of the money he worked so hard to collect.

Still without approval of the much modified GEMSTONE plan, I continued to provide services on an *ad hoc* basis. If the job required money I drew it from Porter. Typical of these assignments was a reported kickback scheme in connection with the Democratic National Convention, and in mid-March I ran an investigation in Miami that included pretext phone calls and tape-recorded conversations. On 15 March I sent an interim memorandum to Attorney General Mitchell, and it came back wtih a note, "need more information," from John Dean.

My transfer to the finance committee became effective on Monday, 27 March. Maurice Stans demanded performance but gave you all you needed to do your job, then left you alone to do it. Stans gave me an office near Sloan's and a secretary par excellence, Sally Harmony. I told her that I'd be involved in clandestine activities and wouldn't hold it against her if she chose not to take the job. Her reply was one she was destined to repeat before the Senate: "I can keep a secret." She was superbly skilled, beautiful, and a slave driver. She made it her business to know what I had to do and when, then never let me forget; but she made it easy by being the most organized person I'd met since J. Edgar Hoover. I repaid Stans's thoughtfulness by promptly devising a way for people of wealth with stock that had appreciated greatly in value to donate it to the finance committee with no tax consequences to either the donor or the committee, even though the committee got full benefit of the long-term capital gain.

Herb Kalmbach and I got to know each other, and I soon formed a high opinion of him as a lawyer and as a man. He was the kind who, were the ship sinking, would put *your* mother into the lifeboat before his own. My relationship with Hugh Sloan continued to be good, and I wished I'd made the move sooner.

About 1 April I received a telephone call from Bob Reisner. He relayed a message from Magruder that "You've got a 'go' on your project." I gave Hunt the good news, but there was little I could do at the moment. The new federal election law would take effect on 7 April, and it required disclosure of the identities of donors. The finance committee had a backlog of people who were willing to give, but only on condition that their identity would not be made public. That required that their donations all be picked up in a matter of days and everyone in a senior position on the committee, including me, was pressed into service as a collector.

In the days before 7 April, I arranged the setting up of enough committees to spread out $50,000 from Howard Hughes and collected the checks in the offices of Hunt's employer, the Mullen Company. I flew to New York to pick up another $50,000 from one of the Rockefellers, then on to Detroit, Buffalo, St. Louis, and Chicago to pick up checks or shares of stock, or to have large shares broken up into smaller lots by transfer agents. I had no time for GEMSTONE and relied on Hunt to alert the teams against the time we could start operations.

As soon as the new election law deadline had passed, I went to see Hugh Sloan with my budget. I showed it to him, told him I was authorized $250,000, and I'd need $83,000 immediately. Sloan, exhausted by the last-minute collection rush, barely looked at the budget sheet, waved at the disorder in his office, and asked me to come back later.

No sooner had GEMSTONE been approved than Magruder called me up and told me that the FAT JACK operation I had inherited from Porter under the nom de guerre SEDAN CHAIR, and any other operations I had working against Senator Muskie in his campaign for the Democratic nomination, were to be shifted to use against the McGovern campaign. "But don't forget Kennedy," he said. "Anytime Kennedy decides he wants it, he can have it, and the feeling is he may be playing possum. Keep thinking about Kennedy."

Hunt was able to shift Thomas Gregory out of Muskie headquarters into McGovern's, but we couldn't transfer the FAT JACK operation, at least not right away. I instructed that he be kept on the payroll in hopes that he would be taken on as a volunteer. At my instructions McCord had rented an office suite adjacent to that of Muskie's on K Street, Northwest, from which I had intended to launch one of the OPAL entries. McCord, Hunt, and I had already surveyed it, and McCord had done a good job in selecting the site. We had a lease on the place and hoped that after the nomination the winner might take over the old Muskie space for some auxiliary purpose. Democratic National Committee headquarters in the Watergate complex was expected to become the campaign headquarters of the winner.

Sloan came up with the $83,000 in hundred-dollar bills, paper-clipped together into bundles of $1,000 each and stuffed into a large manila envelope so I wouldn't be seen carrying "the green," as he called it, from his office to mine. In my office I had a five-drawer steel security file safe. The bottom drawer contained all the blueprints for the Miami Convention Center. Now in the top drawer I placed a series of manila envelopes, 9 inches by 12 inches in size. Each envelope was labeled with a different GEM-STONE code, such as RUBY, SAPPHIRE, etc. I separated out the money for McCord's equipment needs and put that into one envelope for delivery to him, then apportioned the remainder according to the budget in the individually labeled envelopes as a means of controlling the use of the funds. Sally Harmony sat outside my office, so when I performed these tasks I closed and locked the door. It was not that I didn't trust her, I was just practicing standard "need-to-know" security.

The erosion of the GEMSTONE funds for Magruder's *ad hoc* assignments finally led me to try to free myself from his control. He called me in for another one, and I refused, telling him that now that John Mitchell was campaign manager I'd perform as outlined in the approved GEMSTONE plan and submit the results directly to Mitchell or they could find someone else. Newly ensconced at the finance committee as the result of my own efforts, I thought I could make it stick. I was wrong.

Fred LaRue called to summon me to a meeting with him and Magruder. The balding, soft-spoken Mississippi millionaire was a close friend of John Mitchell's and served as his eyes, ears, and troubleshooter; a summons from him was a command performance.

Soft-spoken or not, LaRue was tough and he wasted no time. "What's this," he asked me, "I hear about you threatenin' Jeb on an elevator an' sayin' you don't want to run the intelligence program?"

I knew then that Magruder had run right to Mitchell or LaRue to snitch. "You're right," I said to LaRue, "next time I won't threaten him; I'll just kick him in the ass." Then I turned on Magruder and, referring to his habit of carrying his tennis racquets around the office, said: "You come to play tennis with me, mister, you better bring more than your racquets. You better bring some balls."

Magruder, shrinking back as if I were about to hit him, looked relieved when LaRue said, "All right, that's enough of that kind of talk. What's the problem here?"

I told him that I couldn't get along with Magruder and that was why I'd moved to the finance committee.

"He cut his own deal!" Magruder chimed in, sounding like a kid accusing a bigger brother of taking more than his share of cookies.

LaRue ignored him and kept speaking to me. "It's obvious you two aren't the best of friends, but you're both forgetting the only thing that's important around here an' that's to get the President re-elected. Now with you downstairs, the only time you two have to have anything to do with each other is in connection with the intelligence program. That's your job and it's an important one an' it's been decided that you'll work through Jeb, so you're both gonna have to forget about your differences and remember what we're all here for—to re-elect the President. Now, can you two understand that?"

LaRue was right and I knew it. At his urging Magruder and I shook hands and the meeting was over. I had lost my try for independence.

With GEMSTONE approved and Hunt not yet able to replace Villo Gonzalez as number one keyman nor find an ex-CIA wireman willing to take the job, I had run out of time for recruiting. I had been using McCord right along for advice on technical matters and for such tasks as fronting the lease of space adjacent to Muskie headquarters, but I had never intended to use him on an operation. Now I had no choice and would have to chance it, if I could persuade him. I approached him, offering an increase in pay to $2,000 per month and another $2,000 for each entry. He agreed.

The first target I selected for an OPAL entry was McGovern headquarters on Capitol Hill. We had Gregory in there to give us the layout. I surveyed the exterior myself by driving past it and then down the alley beside and behind it in my green 1971 Jeep. The four-wheel-drive quarter-ton was easily maneuverable in the tight space of the alley because of its short wheelbase; could go over curbs with ease; and, in the event I had to make a fast getaway, had unsuspected speed from a 160-horsepower aluminum V-6 engine originally developed by General Motors for Buicks—just the kind of fine machinery I have always appreciated.

In following instructions to be ready for Kennedy, Hunt and I selected a mass of photographs from the Black Star service that depicted every aspect of Chappaquiddick, as well as some showing Kennedy sailing off Hyannis aboard his yacht a day or so later. Taken with a telephoto lens, some prints showed him with a neck brace and some without. In all, he appeared to be in excellent health and spirits. We paid a substantial amount for the large number of glossies, and then Hunt turned again to his professional art studio—the CIA. Their political section drew up a devastating series of anti-Kennedy political cartoons. The cartoons and the glossy prints went into my second file safe drawer to be produced in the event I was asked what we were doing about Kennedy.

The OPAL budget was high. In addition to their salaries, both Hunt and McCord got a month's pay each for every entry, $3,000 to Hunt and $2,000 to McCord. On a time basis, Barker was allotted between $800 and $1,000 and the other men lesser amounts according to lost income. There were also the first-class air fares to and from Miami, hotel rooms, food, car rentals, and so forth. It all added up to a budget of $10,000 per entry. Because I received my $30,000 salary specifically for running the intelligence operation, my services as counsel being only a cover, I neither budgeted nor received anything for myself from GEMSTONE.

Even at those figures, the budget was tight. There was no room for anything else if the money were not to run out before the end of the campaign or even earlier, because it was being doled out on the basis of the expenditure flowchart. As a result, when there were extra expenses, such as more money for FAT JACK for photographic work, printing for Segretti, photographs of Kennedy, and so forth, that were not in the GEMSTONE budget, I found myself robbing Peter to pay Paul. I'd take the cash from an envelope holding the money for an operation to be carried out sometime later with the intention of trying to scrimp some on an earlier one and hope to make it up. I put IOUs into the envelope such as "$500 for Kennedy photographs" so I'd know how much to replace and where, should I ever get ahead.

I gave the bulk of the $83,000 to McCord with instructions to get the $30,000 transmitter as quickly as possible, and he used the rest of the money to buy a van, small transceivers, and other sophisticated electronic gear, and to pay for the K Street offices and other expenses he had. Once having come from Porter on an *ad hoc* basis, all sums now came from the GEMSTONE budget. As a matter of principle, the Cuban men did not want money for working for their adopted country, nor for working toward what they hoped would be the eventual freeing of their native Cuba with American help. However, Hunt had proposed, and I agreed, that the men not lose anything either. They all worked, and when they did anything for us it cost them lost wages and commissions. Hunt and I calculated their losses generously and recompensed them.

Sloan wanted an accounting, and I gave him one right after he gave me the $83,000. When I started to detail what I was using the money for, however, he said that wouldn't be necessary and hurried me out nervously. That was the only accounting ever requested or made.

Near the end of April Magruder sent word that he wanted to see me. I thought he had another unbudgeted project in mind and was in a cold mood when I entered. My assumption proved incorrect.

Magruder asked, "Gordon, do you think you could get into the Watergate?"

I knew just what he meant. I had targeted the DNC headquarters for later, when and if it became the headquarters of the successful Democratic candidate at their convention, so I said, "Yes. It's a high-security building, but we can do it. It's a bit early, though."

Magruder understood and replied, "How about putting a bug in O'Brien's office?"

Larry O'Brien was by now involved in gearing up for the Democratic convention and was spending most of his time in Miami. Our Cuban agents were studying how best to bug him there, and I'd been laying out money for information, buying off hotel employees, etc., so I said, "For that, it's a bit late."

"O.K." he said, "so he's in and out. There's still plenty of activity over there. We want to know whatever's said in his office, just as if it was here; what goes on in this office."

I thought the reference strange. Were I the Democrats, I'd want to bug John Mitchell's office down the hall, not

Magruder's. I thought of the $30,000 device I had ordered from McCord and said. "All right, we can do that."

"The phones, too."

"That's easy."

"And while you're in there, photograph whatever you can find."

I was disturbed by this turn of events because it was not the situation I had agreed to, nor outlined in GEM-STONE. My deal called for *me* to choose the targets and the timing. Once again, control was being taken away from me. In the intelligence business it is the consumer who tasks the agency with the requirement, but the professionals determine how and when to get it. That custom was being broken. This time, however, I couldn't blame Magruder. It was clear from his facial expression and manner of speech that he was just relaying orders. In an attempt to salvage the original agreement—that of my picking the time and place of the entries—I said, "O.K., Jeb, we'll do it, but remember, this burns up your optional entry right at the beginning. There are funds for no more than four, and the other three, if you remember, are already set."

Magruder didn't bite. "Get in there as soon as you can, Gordon. It's important."

I saw McCord and gave him the target. He promised to check out the interior of DNC quickly to get the layout. When I asked him if he'd have the listening device in hand soon, he assured me that he would.

J. Edgar Hoover died on 2 May and was laid out in state in the rotunda of the Capitol. His presence there attracted leftist activists like ghouls to a graveyard. An anti-Vietnam rally that week took place on the Mall, and police reports described the participants as marching under the Vietcong flag. Daniel Ellsberg and other radicals were slated to participate in another such rally, and once again Magruder called on me.

He alluded to the rally that had taken place. "The President is really pissed about that [Vietcong] flag being

303

used on the Mall. They're gonna do it again. Do you think your guys could break it up and get it?"

"Get what?"

"The flag. Colson wants to give it to The Man."

I told Jeb I could probably bring up a team of Cubans from Miami to break up the rally, or at least cause a noticeable disturbance and sign of opposition. If there was a V.C. flag, a coordinated attack focusing on it should be able to succeed, but I had an objection: to bring up a contingent from Miami, feed, house, and return them would cost a lot of money—money I just didn't have.

"What about all the money you got from Hugh?" Magruder parried.

"Damn it, Jeb, that's all budgeted. GEMSTONE's down to a quarter of what I was promised to run it when I agreed to do this. I'm already running short with all these extras, like that bullshit pamphlet on Muskie you guys unloaded on me. If Chuck wants a V.C. flag for the President that badly, let *him* pay for it."

My reference to the Muskie pamphlet was just one of many little pet projects of someone or other I always ended up having to take care of. That particular one had been a phony attack on him as anti-environment, supposedly prepared by grass-roots opponents. I'd been stuck with the distribution of a pile of them and it had cost GEMSTONE money. I finally got it done through Segretti.

Magruder seemed to think Colson's whim of capturing the V.C. flag for the President was of sufficient importance to authorize me to draw $3,000 from Porter for a quick trip by some Cubans. When I'd shifted from Porter to Sloan as my source of funds, I'd asked Porter if he needed an accounting; when he said he didn't, I suggested he might want to shred the envelopes I'd given him. I signed for the $3,000, brought up some Cuban heavyweights under Barker, and they went to the rally. This time there was no flag in evidence. They disrupted Ellsberg's speech and punched out some radicals sufficiently hard for Barker to have injured his hands and Frank Sturgis to have been detained by police; but the cops were sympathetic and let him go. The men returned to our headquarters at the Mullen Company to report. So the trip wouldn't be a total loss, Hunt and I drove the men to the area surrounding McGovern's headquarters, and Hunt announced it to be the site of an upcoming entry operation. We checked the alley and rear doors and noted escape routes. Then, on the way back, I took us past the Watergate and said this place would come first, then permitted the men to return home. I had a thousand dollars left over from the money I drew from Porter and, though sorely tempted to replace some of the cash unbudgeted matters had consumed from the GEMSTONE budget, returned it instead to Porter the next day. After all, *he* hadn't used up any of my budget.

That was my final money dealing with Porter. In total, I'd received a little over $30,000 from him.

Sloan asked to see me and showed me a package of signed traveler's checks. He explained that they were a donation left over from the 1968 campaign and that to ask the donors to exchange them for cash at this late date would be embarrassing. The money was needed because it was "green" and that was hard to get now that the new election law was in effect. Could our people turn the traveler's checks into cash? It would have to be very discreet and divorced from the finance committee.

I told Sloan I'd try, and Hunt and I flew to Miami and conferred with Barker. He said he could arrange things through a Cuban banker who would process the thousands of dollars in traveler's checks in such a way that our problem would be solved. Barker was good as his word, and in a short time I was able to turn over the cash, less the expense of the trip to Miami, to Hugh Sloan. From his point of view it was a good deal, but it turned out not to be from mine. Barker, I learned, had had to pay the banker well for his services, and, of course, I had to reimburse him from the GEMSTONE budget.

Sloan approached me again, this time with a $25,000 cashier's check from a Minnesota businessman, Kenneth

Dahlberg, made out to himself and dated 10 April. He told me that it represented the contribution that somone else made prior to 7 April but converted so as to become anonymous. He also had four checks made payable to Manuel Ogarrio, drawn on Ogarrio's account at the Banco Nacional in Mexico City on 4 April in the amounts of $15,000, $18,000, $24,000, and $32,000. Because the Dahlberg check was dated after 7 April, although representing prestatute money, and the other checks were on a Mexican bank, he asked me if I could convert them to a total of $114,000 in cash.

I mentioned again to Sloan that I'd have to deduct the costs involved because this service was unbudgeted, and he agreed readily. This time Barker's service took an embarrassingly long time, so long that it took two trips to Miami to retrieve the proceeds, which I finally got directly from Barker in the safety deposit vault of his bank. He was apologetic, having elected to try a different method of conversion. When I turned the money over to Sloan, I deducted not only the expenses of converting the $114,000 but also the unreimbursed GEMSTONE budget withdrawal to cover the fee Barker's banker charged for the first transaction. The total I placed in the GEMSTONE treasury came to $2,500, made up of twenty-five one-hundred-dollar bills. They were well worn. Unfortunately many of those given to me by Barker and turned over to Hugh Sloan were not; they were brand new, serialized consecutively, and they sat in his safe, ticking away like a time bomb.

XX

On 7 May I was called to a meeting in the offices of the Committee to Re-elect and learned, in the strictest confidence, that within twenty-four hours the President would take forceful action to end the Vietnam war. The President's action, I was told, would generate fierce opposition from the radicals who were insisting upon U.S. surrender. My assignment, and that of the others attending the meeting, was to immediately generate as much support from the public, the press, and Congress as possible. This program was to be given the highest priority.

I called Howard Hunt and told him that I wanted our Cuban people to organize public demonstrations of support in the Miami area. Money was no object. There went the GEMSTONE budget again.

On 8 May President Nixon announced he was mining the harbor of Haiphong and resuming the bombing of North Vietnam. All hell broke loose on the left. There was a general meeting attended by John Mitchell and addressed by General Alexander Haig, who briefed us on what was being done militarily. After his briefing Haig asked for questions. I don't believe he expected any; these were political, not military, people.

But I took him at his word. "General," I asked, "why haven't we bombed the Red river dikes? If we did that, we'd drown half the country and starve the other half. Those few railroad lines coming in from China'd have to carry nothing but food; there'd be no room for ammunition."

Before Haig could answer, John Mitchell jumped in: "We don't need any amateur military advice. Let's not have any more of that."

Once again it was emphasized, by both Haig and Mitchell, that the most important thing any of us had to do was to influence opinion in favor of the President's initiative and counter the media manipulation against him by the radical left. I coordinated all information on the campaign to influence public opinion and Congress. On Monday, 15 May, I sent John Mitchell a confidential memorandum entitled "Reaction to the President's Vietnam Response." It was all-encompassing, but concerning the work of the Cubans in Miami I reported:

307

Earlier reports mentioned plans for a rally on Saturday evening, May 13, at Bay Front Park, Maimi, Florida. Because of differences of opinion in the Cuban community and some internal jealousies, it was thought best to cancel the rally and to substitute a motorcade on Saturday afternoon.

Accordingly, on the afternoon of Saturday, May 13, a motorcade of 200 automobiles and 60 trucks was assembled at the Central Shopping Plaza, 37th Avenue and 7th Street, NW, Miami. The vehicles were placarded with signs such as "Nixon—We Back You 100%" and "Free the POWS Now," as well as a number reading "Tell It to Hanoi." The motorcade lasted two and one-half hours (2:00 P.M. to 4:30 P.M.); starting at the Central Shopping Plaza, the route went south on 37th Avenue to the Tamiami Trail, then to Biscayne Boulevard and then all the way back up Flagler to 32nd Avenue. As the motorcade proceeded with lights on, more than 200 more vehicles joined the caravan, having a total of nearly 500 vehicles (automobiles and trucks).

The reactions of the street crowds on the way was very favorable. The route took the caravan through areas populated heavily by Cubans, and there was much shouting of "Viva Nixon." Traffic was nearly paralyzed. The police were sympathetic and helpful. At one point when the caravan stopped while police cleared traffic, one store took the popular music off its outdoor phonograph speakers and played "The Star-Spangled Banner."

Persons on the scene stated that *Miami Herald* coverage was biased against the motorcade in that it published no photographs with strong pro-Nixon sentiment, but only those which could be taken two ways; e.g., "Free the POWS now." The *Herald* report (Section B, page 1) should not be relied upon as an accurate description as the actual event and the reaction thereto was far more favorable to the President.

The next day Howard Hunt called on the phone. He wanted to discuss something that "Chuck just laid on me." I met him and he referred to the fact that Alabama Governor George Wallace, when campaigning for the Democratic presidential nomination in Laurel, Maryland, had been shot and critically wounded the day before by a would-be assassin named Arthur Bremer. Bremer, he said, lived in Milwaukee, and Colson wanted Hunt to search his apartment to find out what he could about Bremer's background and motivation and, possibly, to plant some documentation there linking Bremer to the radical left. Hunt was apprehensive about the assignment and asked my opinion of the chances for success.

I told Hunt that if Colson knew the name and address of the assailant, he must have gotten it from the Secret Service or the FBI, and that if they knew it, they were already all over that apartment. Whatever was there of interest would by this time be sealed in evidence containers and the place under guard. Hunt replied that he had told Colson that the place would probably be under guard, but that Colson had argued that a good entry team could get in anyway. I told Hunt that the risk was enormous and the chance of gain slight, pointing out that in the unlikely event he was successful and got into the place to plant his material linking Bremer to the radicals, when it was found thereafter by the FBI, they'd be suspicious immediately because it hadn't been there when they searched the place themselves. That was enough for Hunt. He informed me later that Colson had called the assignment off.

The sterile CIA 9-mm parabellum pistol I had acquired was designed for use by insurgents to assassinate Communist cadre members abroad. I intended it for use in the event Bud Krogh or other of my White House superiors

309

tasked me with an assassination. The Jack Anderson matter would be a good example. But the CIA pistol was unsilenced. I needed a silent weapon, recalling that I had had to resort to the Browning knife in the Fielding operation. The CIA 9-mm was not threaded for use with the preferred Maxim-pattern silencer, nor was the 7.65-mm Colt semiautomatic pistol I had, which had been delivered by Colt directly to the OSS, the predecessor of the CIA.

To fill this need I acquired a 4-mm German-manufactured Walther LP (for *luftpistole*) air pistol. It was silent, powerful, virtually recoilless, and, with target sights, superbly accurate; at ten meters (about thirty-three feet) every shot would go inside a dime. Using a pointed lead projectile coated with easily obtainable pure nicotine, lethal delivery would be silent, swift, and sure. In the basement of my house in Oxon Hill, where there was a second fireplace to act as a backstop and I had sufficient privacy and range, I practiced until I was as familiar with the Walther as with my favorite Smith & Wesson, then took it to my office at the finance committee and put it away in the file safe, replacing the CIA 9-mm, which I took home.

The GEMSTONE budget was really short now, so I welcomed Howard Hunt's suggestion that we have Gregory admit McCord into McGovern headquarters without bringing up the Cubans to act as guards. If we could cut down the ten-thousand-dollar budgeted expense for penetration of McGovern's headquarters, some of the GEMSTONE funds expended for unbudgeted tasks could be made up. Gregory arranged a tour of McGovern headquarters for McCord, who posed as his out-of-town uncle. That was successful, and McCord reported that the place had an alarm attached to the rear door that operated on a delay. Ten seconds were available to shut off the alarm after the door opened. He studied the offices of Gary Hart and Frank Mankiewicz, where we wanted to put in microphones, and reported that the job could be easily done within five minutes. All Gregory had to do was admit him after everyone else had left for the evening.

Gregory had been staying late so that he could give us the tally of McGovern contribution receipts on a day-by-day basis, as well as contributor lists, schedules, and any copies of position papers before they were made public. Now Hunt asked him to hide in the furnace room and wait until the building was empty, then let McCord in. It didn't work. He was discovered, had to do some fast talking, and leave. He got nervous but had the presence of mind to phone McCord and tell him to abort.

With Gregory so jittery, Hunt changed plans. He'd bring up only two Cubans—Barker and Martinez—and have them play a reprise of their successful Fielding entry in Beverly Hills. This time they would arrive at McGovern's with a heavy package crate for delivery. McCord would be their supervisor, and all three would be dressed in deliveryman uniforms. McCord would slip away and plant his bugs in the five minutes it would take for Barker and Martinez to deliver the crate and get a complicated set of receipts signed for "properly, according to the new rules."

Just as that plan was to go into effect, Gregory reported that there had been an attempted burglary at McGovern's and that the place was now guarded by a Burns Agency man posted inside the front door twenty-four hours a day. This called for still further plan modification because Gregory was now even more frightened. We'd have to get more Cubans and a credible package.

The new plan called for the purchase of a very expensive and complex electric typewriter. McCord would be the salesman who had come along to insure proper installation. The typewriter itself would be bugged, just so we'd have *something* in there should McCord not be able to get loose long enough from the Burns man to plant bugs in the offices of Mankiewicz and Hart.

Although we were now concentrating on McGovern, Muskie had not yet given up and we did not neglect him. Segretti was disrupting his fund-raising activities, and he continued to have difficulty with negative press stories about his wife, the same kind of thing that had occasioned his breakdown in the snows of New Hampshire. We knew this was a vulnerable spot and when *Newsweek* reprinted excerpts from a nasty article against Mrs. Muskie in *Women's Wear Daily,* I had been ordered by Magruder to exploit it. With so much else to do, I hadn't got around to it.

I was trying to think of what to do with the *Newsweek* article when I suddenly recalled what the Democrats had done to Richard Nixon in 1960 with the "Nixon Deed." I took the page from *Newsweek,* got a brush and red ink, and outlined the most derogatory portion, then wrote in big red letters, SHAME! From GEMSTONE funds we had that page reproduced by the thousands with the red overprint and distributed it all over the country. It had taken me twelve years, but I had finally closed the "Nixon Deed" case to my satisfaction.

On Monday, 22 May, Bernard Barker, Eugenio Martinez, Virgilio Gonzalez, Frank Sturgis, Felipe De Diego, and Reinaldo Pico flew up to Washington from Miami and moved into the Hamilton Hotel until rooms at the Watergate became available. The Watergate penetration was scheduled for Friday night, 26 May. The intervening days were spent meeting Jim McCord and Thomas Gregory and their familiarizing themselves with the areas immediately around both McGovern's headquarters and the Watergate complex. There was a large convention in Washington at that time called "Transpo '72." It made an excellent cover for the Cuban contingent. Groups of men were moving about all the hotels in town and our group just signed the General Security Services log in the lobby of the Watergate office building and went right on up to inspect the entrance to DNC headquarters. Hunt took a soft clay impression of the lock on the front door.

McCord told me he had rented a room at the Howard Johnson's motel across the street from the Watergate, but it was on the fourth floor. To see into the DNC offices, he'd need one higher up, which he promised to get. To my annoyance he still had not obtained the listening device I'd ordered, nor, in fact, did he yet have even the small transceivers. There was some excuse for the delay on the listening device; it was being handmade to order. But the transceivers were off-the-shelf items. He explained that he had to get FCC clearance for their frequencies. That annoyed me. It's like registering a gun you're going to use in a holdup.

We made familiarization tours of both places in darkness as well as daylight so we'd know them well under operational conditions. During these meetings and tours I noticed an annoying habit in McCord. He was like Lamont Cranston, always slipping away, only to reappear when there was something specific for him to do. He hated to stay in one place very long, or to be in the company of more than a very few people. Sometimes he would just loiter in the shadows, on the sidelines, so to speak, trying hard not to be noticed. I wasn't sure whether this was the product of long clandestine service-induced caution or a lack of nerve. Because he had really been in counterintelligence more than in the collection of intelligence, I put this behavior down to nervousness and over-caution—the same thing that led him to seek FCC approval for his transceiver frequencies.

Hunt was reporting increasing nervousness in Bennett's nephew, Gregory, and I was not at all sure he'd prove to be any help in penetrating McGovern's headquarters. In that event we'd have to run a complete OPAL operation. Because of the Burns guard on the front door, the obvious entry point would be the rear door, which also had the advantage of being on the floor below. The chief problem with the rear door was that it was brightly illuminated by two clusters of floodlights. One cluster was over the rear door itself, the other farther out toward the alley where it supplemented the light from a streetlamp. I decided that the floodlights would have to be extinguished, and that it would be best to do it immediately to see whether it attracted attention and immediate replacement.

To do the job I purchased some blunt-nosed 4-mm Benjamin projectiles for the Walther, then bought four floodlamps identical to those in use at McGovern headquarters. Retrieving the Walther from my file safe, I brought it home and set up the floodlamps in the fireplace in my basement. I found that with the blunt-nosed ammunition the Walther would smash through the heavy, weatherproof glass of the floodlamps at a range of ten meters so long as the projectiles hit head-on, at a 90-degree angle. On 24 May I brought the Walther with me to the office and put it in the file safe.

When Hugh Sloan called me into his office shortly before noon the following day, 25 May, I regretted having taken the CIA 9-mm home. He displayed a suitcase filled for the most part with one-hundred-dollar bills, but a few bundles of fifties and some five hundreds were also in evidence. It was lunchtime, and he said he had to deposit $350,000 in cash at a bank at 15th and Pennsylvania—just a two-block walk past the White House. He was concerned about robbery and asked me to go along with him for protection. I agreed. With the 9-mm no longer in my safe, the only thing I had with which to arm myself was the Walther with the Benjamin projectiles. I loaded it and slipped it under my belt. Because I had no nicotine, if necessary I would shoot any would-be robber in the eye. The projectile would penetrate to the brain easily through the eggshell-thin bone at the rear of the socket and kill instantly.

Sloan and I had planned on lunch, but we didn't realize how long it would take when the bank required us to participate in the counting of the cash. Even in bills that large, it took more than an hour to get through the $350,000 to the satisfaction of the bank officer, so we were very hungry by the time we had finished. We walked back to Lafayette Park, opposite the White House, then decided to have lunch in the downstairs dining room of the Hay

Adams Hotel on 16th Street, just across the park from the White House.

Both of us went to the men's room, where Sloan was startled to see me draw the Walther. I no longer needed a loaded gun and I didn't want to put any more strain on the air seal than necessary, so I discharged the pistol into a toilet to release the pressure. It was noiseless, and I knew from my FBI experience that water slows down and stops a high-velocity projectile rapidly. We had used a water tank to recover fired bullets for comparison examinations.

I explained about the seal to Sloan, and we went in and had lunch.

On the night of 25 May we all made another tour of McGovern's headquarters area. I brought the Walther with me and, after the others were clear, Frank Sturgis and I walked through the alley to the brightly lighted area of the rear door. There, with Sturgis watching my back, I used the single-shot Walther to shoot out the three floodlights over the rear door, loading, cocking, and firing individually for each one. The *luftpistole* was silent, and all that could be heard was the breaking of the glass and the SHSsssss of the escaping gas that filled the bulbs as it flared briefly before they died.

The cluster of lights farther out proved to be a problem. A head-on 90-degree-angle shot was impossible from the ground because of an obstructing framework of steel beams supporting an air-conditioner. I'd have to get higher. I signaled Sturgis, a massively built man, and he obligingly bent over, bracing his hands on his knees, and let me use his back to climb onto the overhead steelwork. From there I shot out the last three lights. Because the light from the streetlamp didn't reach the rear door, I left it alone, hoping what light it shed would conceal the fact that the other lights had been extinguished. If they were noticed, I hoped the destruction would be laid to vandals.

As Sturgis and I walked back out the alley, I realized that I might have left my fingerprints on the steelwork.

The cool-nerved Sturgis had no objection to going back and once more acting as my mounting platform while I wiped down the beams.

On 26 May the Cubans all moved into the Watergate Hotel under assumed names, posing as a group working for a corporation named Ameritas. The DNC headquarters was in a different building in the complex, the Watergate Office Building, which was well guarded. Our survey had found that not one but two guard services afforded it protection: General Security Services (GSS), which had a man on duty all the time, and the Federal Reserve Board (FRB) guards. The FRB had space both in the basement and on the eighth floor of the office building and had recently been burglarized. While the FRB guards were not there all the time because they had to check on other FRB space on a roving basis, we found they were frequent visitors to the halls of Watergate, probably because of the burglary. The GSS guard was known to inspect the entire building following every shift change.

To get to the DNC headquarters on the sixth floor by conventional means meant walking over to the lobby where the elevators and stairwell were within easy view of the GSS guard post, where one would be required to sign in. Another route was through the garage on a lower floor and, finally, and undeground corridor that connected the hotel and the office building. The underground corridor was the first choice because it led to both the stairwell and elevator at a point two floors below the guard post. The problem was that it ran from a banquet room, the Continental Room, which also led to the inner court through an exterior door.

We had found that the Continental Room door to the corridor was equipped with an electric alarm, so we couldn't get through the banquet room after hours without first defeating it. McCord discovered that the door alarm wasn't activated until 11 P.M. That proved the key to our plan.

Ameritas told the Watergate Hotel that it wanted to

hold a dinner meeting and presentation. To allay suspicion and kill time Hunt had a multicourse banquet ordered and rented a motion picture projector and travel film to play after the dinner. The plan was to keep the meeting going until after the waiters had all cleaned up and—well tipped—left us alone in the Continental Room. We expected the DNC headquarters would be vacant well before 11 P.M. on a Friday night.

I gave Hunt the $10,000 budgeted as a contingency fund for use in case something went wrong and instructed him to keep it in a place that was not only safe but available to him at all hours. I took $2,000 in cash as an additional emergency fund, in case Hunt and I became separated, and locked it in a two-compartment wooden bank I had made when I was twelve, using the second compartment to keep the committee money separate from my own. I kept the box-bank in my bedroom dresser drawer. I paid everyone for the job in advance. McCord had set up a charging unit in the command post and was charging the nickel-cadmium batteries of the transceivers. Now one was issued to him for personal use, one for the observation post, one for Barker, and the last for Hunt and me.

McCord, typically unwilling to stay in one place or in the company of so many, excused himself from the banquet, leaving us with one extra serving. Banquet time arrived and the rest of us had a good time, even polishing off McCord's meal. The film went on as scheduled and was so boring the waiters were encouraged to clean up and leave us early. We ran the film a couple of times for the benefit of anyone looking in through the glass door to the inner court. Finally, at 10:30 P.M., with no word from McCord that the DNC offices had yet been vacated, a guard making his periodic rounds looked in and told us we'd have to leave. Everyone did, except Hunt and Gonzalez, who stayed behind to turn out the lights, hoping to receive word from McCord over the transceiver before the alarm was armed on the corridor door at 11

P.M. They hid in a liquor closet. By 11 P.M. the word from McCord had not come that the DNC was clear. A guard locked the door leading to the inner court, and when the alarm on the corridor was armed at 11, Hunt and Gonzalez were effectively locked into the Continental Room until the next day.

Gonzalez slipped out of the closet and tried but failed to pick the court door lock. A guard appeared and swept the inside of the banquet room with his flashlight through the glass door to the inner court, and Gonzalez had to go back to the closet, where he and Hunt stayed the night. The next morning Hunt, once free, came up to our room in the Watergate Hotel. He was tired from his night in the closet, but his sense of humor had not deserted him.

"Gordon," he said, laughing, "I know you like scotch, but don't ever drink it at the Watergate Hotel."

"Why not?"

"Because last night, in that goddamn closet, I had to take a leak in the worst way. I was desperate. Finally I found a nearly empty bottle of Johnnie Walker Red. It's now quite full."

"Ah," I said. "I can see Larry O'Brien now, with a puzzled look on his face, saying, 'Funny—if I didn't know this was scotch, I'd swear it was piss!'"

Hunt was still laughing as he climbed into bed to get some sleep.

Saturday night, 27 May, we tried again, waiting until after the 8 P.M. building inspection and then for McCord to radio from the observation post when the DNC was clear. Once again we didn't expect anyone to be working late, especially on a Saturday night, but once again we were wrong. The hours passed without word from Mc-Cord, and when it finally came I thought it too close to the midnight shift change and building inspection. We waited until that was accomplished and sent in the team again; Hunt and I waited to learn by radio from Barker of the successful entry.

The message never came. In about forty-five minutes

the team reappeared at the command post in the Watergate Hotel room Hunt and I shared. Barker reported failure to gain entrance, saying that Gonzalez had worked long and hard on the lock on the front door to no avail. The excuse offered was that Gonzalez had not brought the necessary tools with him from Miami. I was disgusted; then, as Barker told me how hard Villo had worked, even somewhat damaging the lock, I was worried. If the damage was noticeable, the Democrats would be alerted to the fact that an entry attempt had been made and would take the necessary precautions to prevent future penetration or to trap the entry team. I interrogated Villo about the extent of the damage but, because of his less than fluent English, couldn't satisfy myself that I understood the situation. I'd have to inspect the lock myself, and the sooner the better.

According to one of the Cubans, that would be no problem. They had just signed the guard log and gone right on up. I decided to risk it. I wasn't going to break into the place and would be carrying no tools. I took a couple of Cubans and, all of us dressed in business suits, approached the guard confidently, scribbled on the register, and went up to DNC headquarters. The lock bore the marks of tampering, but they weren't obvious. Relieved, I looked around the lobby area once, then took the elevator back to the lobby, scribbled on the log again, and returned to the command post in the hotel. There I overrode Hunt's objections and ordered Gonzalez to return to Miami the following morning for the correct tools. I didn't care how tired he was; he could sleep on the plane. We were going again the very next night. I had no intention of going back to Magruder on Monday morning to tell him that I'd failed.

Late Sunday afternoon I rejoined Hunt in the Watergate Hotel command post. Gonzalez had returned with what he assured us were the proper tools. I didn't think it wise to try to have the team sign in at the guard post again; two nights in a row would be pressing our luck.

Hunt suggested the garage-level entrance doors and Mc-Cord agreed to tape them open. It was an old maintenance man's trick. They all carry keys but to use them time after time just gets to be too much trouble. Experienced guards are used to finding doors taped open no matter how often the maintenance people are admonished. It is done *across* the lock bolt and around the edge of the doors, rather than along the inside edge of the door, for a very good reason; with the commonly carried electrician's tape, that's the only way it will work. Tape placed edgewise hasn't enough purchase to restrain the strongly spring-loaded bolt of commercial building doors. Even if it *did* work we wanted it to look like a maintenance man's routine, and they don't do it that way. Why should they? They're not trying to burglarize the place and have nothing to fear from discovery. Burglars don't tape the locks. They wedge a matchstick in between the bolt and the bolt opening, then snap it off flush. I would not have approved that method; if discovered by a guard, it's a dead giveaway; he knows immediately he has a burglary on his hands.

At about 9:45 P.M. McCord reported from the observation post that the lights had gone out in DNC headquarters and, a few minutes later, that a man had left the building. Because it was Sunday night Hunt was sure no one would be going back in later, but with the experience of the previous weekend behind us, and the fact that the Democratic National Convention was coming up soon, I thought it best to wait and see. At 11 P.M. I was satisfied. That would give our men an hour to enter (which might take a good bit of time, even with the new tools), do the electronic work, and still get out before the midnight shift change and building inspection.

To Hunt's and my delight, that's exactly how it went. McCord reported success, and Barker had two rolls of 36-exposure 35-mm film he'd expended on material from O'Brien's desk, along with Polaroid shots of the desk and office before anything was touched so that it could all be returned to proper order before leaving. I congratulated them all and we had a small victory celebration in the command post before going home. The Watergate entry had been successful. Or so I thought.

XXI

On Monday morning, 29 May, I reported to Magruder the successful entry into Democratic National Committee headquarters in the Watergate. For proof, I showed him Polaroid photographs of the interior of Larry O'Brien's office, taken by Bernard Barker. Magruder was pleased. He asked how soon he'd be getting the first reports of what was going on in there and the photographs taken of O'Brien's correspondence. I told him I'd received nothing yet, the film was being processed, and promised to get the reports to him as soon as possible.

When I had nothing from McCord by Wednesday, I asked him why. He said he'd had difficulty "finding the signals" of the transmitters but had finally found one, and he offered to take me up to the observation post to explain his difficulty with the equipment used. I took him up on it that evening, carrying my black briefcase with the initials GGL, which still contained the Walther, wrapped in a towel.

The observation post was dark. Inside was a man whom I could hardly see, and McCord introduced us monosyllabically, using aliases. As the man returned to his watching of the DNC offices across the street, McCord showed me an elaborate receiver with an oscilloscope and bandspreader. He explained that the way the system worked was very secure but, for that reason, difficult to receive. The devices he had hidden were miniature transmitters of very low power, so that they could not be picked up beyond the immediate vicinity—a protection against accidental interception. The transmitters were designed to send weak signals on a very narrow wave band. Unless highly sensitive equipment was tuned precisely to that band, the signals could not be received. That was a second precaution. In order even to *find* the signals, McCord had to tune the ultrasensitive receiver, which alone, he said, cost $8,000, with the aid of the oscilloscope. The band-spreader operated to broaden the sensitivity of the receiver to that frequency. McCord said that he had found the signal for one of his transmitters, but that the other one had so far eluded him. I thanked him for the explanation and left, inadvertently leaving behind my briefcase.

I returned for my briefcase the following evening and noticed a typewriter with paper in it. McCord gave me some typed logs of the interceptions to date. I put them in my briefcase without looking at them and asked McCord why he didn't just tape everything coming over the receiver. He replied that while he had a recorder, it had proved to be incapable of adaptation to his receiver because the resistance, stated in ohms, was mismatched. I understood that but noted that it would not preclude either taping it from a microphone rather than jack-to-jack or buying compatible equipment. McCord didn't want to run the intercepted conversations through a speaker to another microphone; for security reasons they were using headphones. He assured me that when I looked at the logs I'd see that the system was working well, that there was no need for purchase of a compatible recorder; much of what was coming over was of no intelligence value anyway, and by using the typed-log method he'd edit out the junk and save me the trouble. I told him I wanted it all; that *I'd* do any editing necessary, and we left it at that.

When I got home I looked over the logs. Whoever McCord's assistant was, he was no typist. The logs revealed that the interception was from a telephone rather than a microphone that relayed all conversation in the room, and that the telephone tapped was being used by a number of different people, none of whom appeared to be Larry O'Brien. I decided I couldn't send that to John Mitchell and had to wait until I had more product of better quality from McCord. When he was able to tune into the office microphone, I expected the product to improve.

No such luck. The next day's take was the same, and there was no indication of a second source. On Monday, 5 June, I dictated from the typed logs to Sally Harmony for transcription, editing as I went along. The material was marked "for informational purposes only," meaning that other exploitation could jeopardize the source. I didn't want Magruder or someone like him using it in such a way that the Democrats would guess that their phones were tapped and offices bugged.

I was still getting nothing from O'Brien. I spoke to McCord again, and he said he was still unable to intercept the signal from inside the O'Brien office. He attributed this failure to either of two causes: a defective transmitter or placement of the transmitter in such a way that a hidden steel beam was between it and the receiver. In that event, said McCord, the steel beam would absorb or mask the signal and there was no hope of receiving it. I knew enough about such matters from my military and FBI training to know that what McCord said could very well be true. Nevertheless it was his responsibility to overcome such obstacles; he was being paid very well for it and I told him just that, adding that if my principals were dissatisfied, I would offer them the same explanation he had given me, which might prompt them to order that the problem be corrected. In that event, I told McCord, there would be no additional entry fee paid because the job should have been done correctly the first time.

What made me so annoyed was that I believed the second transmitter to be the one for which I had given McCord $30,000 and which was supposed to be the room bug, one we could subsequently expect to give us a wealth of information once the Democratic convention was over and the candidate moved into the DNC offices for the campaign.

On Thursday, 8 June, I gave Magruder a sealed manila

envelope for delivery to John Mitchell. Inside it was another envelope with a "code word material" notice on it (indicating how it was to be handled), and inside that was the product of the interceptions from the Watergate to date. I had not as yet received the correspondence photographs from Hunt. I told Magruder that the product was only half what we'd expected because of trouble with the second transmitter and related to him what McCord had told me.

Magruder questioned me closely about the interior of the DNC offices and especially about the location of the files. He asked whether they were locked and when I told him they were, he asked whether the photographs taken included any from those files. I told him they did not because our instructions had been to photograph whatever was available while the electronic installation was being accomplished, adding that the men had gone in with only one camera. Magruder took the envelope and I left.

On Friday, 9 June, Magruder called me in again. Not to my surprise he said that the content of the logs to date was hardly worth the effort, risk, and expense we had gone to and asked me whether the defective bug could be replaced or moved so that it would function. I told him that it could, but that it would mean another entry, one that had not been budgeted.

I had received from Sloan by this time three more scheduled payments of $63,000, $12,000, and $12,000, for a total of $170,000, and I had already spent considerably more than I was supposed to according to the budget, to perform unbudgeted tasks assigned to me. The Democratic convention had not yet even begun and we had the entire campaign ahead of us. I knew that as campaigns get closer to election day there is a great deal of competition for remaining funds, and I wasn't hopeful of getting any more than my flowchart called for. I might not even get *that* if things got tight and the choice, for example, was between polling and intelligence.

I told Magruder that we intended to hit McGovern headquarters on the weekend of 17 June and would be bringing the men up anyway; that I had no hesitancy in requiring my wireman to get things working properly at no additional expense. Therefore, I added, we should be able to do it if it were just a quick in and out with a keyman and a guard in addition to the wireman. He said he'd let me know, and I told him I'd need a decision right away because of the short lead time involved. He promised to let me know on Monday.

On Monday, 12 June, Magruder called me up to his office again and annoyed me immediately by returning to the file cabinets in the DNC offices. I thought he was reneging on his promise of a decision and asking for more information to cover the fact that he'd forgotten to get it. He asked how many file cabinets there were and their proximity to O'Brien's office. I said there were many locked files, and I was telling him that they had just the common push locks, that they weren't the file safe type, when Magruder suddenly became agitated and exclaimed, "*Here's* what I want to know." He swung his left arm back behind him and brought it forward forcefully as he said, "I want to know what O'Brien's got right here!" At the word *here* he slapped the lower part of his desk with his left palm, hard. "Take all the men, all the cameras you need. *That's* what I want to know!"

There was a world of significance in Magruder's gesture. When he said "here!" and slapped that particular portion of his desk, he was referring to the place he kept his derogatory information on the Democrats. Whenever in the past he had called me in to attempt to verify some rumor about, for example, Jack Anderson, it was from there that he drew whatever he already had on the matter. *The purpose of the second Watergate break-in was to find out what O'Brien had of a derogatory nature about us, not for us to get something on* him *or the Democrats.*

Magruder didn't tell me what he either expected, or was afraid, we'd find in O'Brien's files. He instructed that we go in there with all the film, men, and cameras necessary to photograph *everything* in his desk and in those files.

This time McCord was going in merely as an unpaid electronic hitchhiker, free to leave when he was through.

Early in the week of 11 June I spoke to McCord and told him to be ready to go in and repair or move the room microphone in O'Brien's office. McCord had let me believe that he had placed a room mike. I did not yet know that the malfunctioning transmitter was on another telephone. He gave me the accumulation of logs from the operating transmitter, which was by now considerable, and I set about editing them. There was some, but still not much, intelligence contained in them, but the bulk continued to be of a personal nature from a number of people.

I told all this to Hunt. He had been in contact with the Cubans in Miami, and he reported to me that they had been successful in setting up an operation in which some of the filthiest hippie types imaginable would pose as McGovern supporters. With the aid of our Cuban hotel employee accomplices, the hippies would be able to get into the hotel suite occupied by McGovern. Acting or actually half out of their minds on drugs, in full view of the press, they would, among other acts typical of their kind, urinate on the floor.

Hunt gave me the photographs from the first entry and I put them, together with the second batch of edited logs, into the usual two sealed envelopes for delivery to John Mitchell.

On 12 June McCord sent in his assistant from the observation post to report on the current interior arrangement at the DNC offices, and he obtained the location of all the file cabinets. With pride McCord told me that his man had posed as the nephew of a former Democratic National Committee chairman and been given a guided tour. The information helped me to calculate the time involved and the amount of film required. I decided to order that fifty rolls of 35-mm be brought along by the Cubans.

Gordon Strachan called me to the White House and told me that the original submissions from the electronic surveillance were unsatisfactory. I assumed he was speaking for Haldeman so I repeated what McCord had told me of the technical problem and that we intended to correct it by going back in shortly.

On Wednesday, 14 June, I met Howard Hunt in his office. I had an appointment for a conference in John Mitchell's office on 15 June to discuss nonintelligence matters with Mitchell, Magruder, and a few others, and I wanted to be able to tell Mitchell that everything was set for the corrective and photographic mission. I told Hunt of the necessity of going back into the Watergate. He balked.

"Jesus, Gordon," he protested, "you know how much trouble it was to get in there in the first place. We've got McGovern coming up again this weekend, and we're going to hit O'Brien again in Miami or Sonesta Beach soon anyway. Looks like high risk, low gain to me."

"You're missing the point, Howard. McCord's fucked-up bug is incidental. This trip he's just a hitchhiker. What's wanted is a photo mission. They want everything in the files."

Hunt was incredulous: "*All* of them?"

"You got it."

"Jesus! There's rows of them. It'll take hours!"

"Exactly. We'll have to do it between shift changes. That'll give us four hours between building inspections. No way we can justify longer exposure than that. Tell them to bring another camera and fifty rolls of 35-mm. Thirty-six exposure rolls. That'll give us eighteen hundred pages' capacity. That ought to satisfy them."

"What about McGovern?"

"We hit him too. If we can get the DNC job done between the eight and twelve shift changes we'll do McGovern the same night. If not, the following night."

"Goddamn, Gordon, the boys'll be exhausted!"

"It's gotta be done, Howard, one way or another."

"All right. At least the McGovern entry won't take long. We'll try the typewriter again. What about compensation? Another Watergate entry wasn't in our budget."

"Everyone but McCord gets compensated at the same

327

rate. I'll do what I've been doing since the beginning—rob Peter to pay Paul."

I told Hunt that the budget and flowchart were meaningless now anyway: that, as he well knew, we were being tasked with many matters never budgeted; and that Magruder had to approve every disbursement of funds to me specifically, regardless of the fact that they had been approved as scheduled previously. Hunt knew I detested Magruder, and that the situation would have been otherwise if there had been anything I could do about it. I didn't tell him that I'd tried, in the LaRue meeting, and failed. Hunt just shook his head and said, "That wasn't our deal, Gordon."

But Hunt was a professional and used to the vagaries of superiors and coping in spite of them. We sat down and planned a second entry into the Watergate. This time, however, the two men previously posted outside as guards were eliminated to save money. Another camera and fifty rolls of film would be purchased, and the fact that this was primarily a photographic mission impressed upon Barker. McCord was free to leave when he had accomplished his corrective mission, but his participation was only incidental. Hunt and the Cubans would have the same monetary arrangement as for a budgeted mission, as would McCord for the McGovern headquarters penetration. We elected to use the previously successful garage-level entry approach.

On Thursday, 15 June, I went to the meeting with Mitchell carrying the thick sheaf of accumulated log entries sealed in two envelopes. Intelligence wasn't on the agenda, but because of Magruder's complaining I wasn't sure what to expect from Mitchell. I decided to bring the matter up myself, offering the envelope, the confirmation that the faulty bug would be corrected that weekend, and the humor of what we had planned to do to McGovern with the hippies in Miami to placate him.

I should have kept my mouth shut. Mitchell, it turned out, didn't need placating. At least until I told him of my plans for McGovern. I entered and took a seat to Mitchell's immediate right. He was reading and smoking his pipe, and, as he glanced up to acknowledge my presence, I slipped the thick envelope, bearing no markings at all on the outside, onto the right rear corner of his desk, saying, "That's for you, General."

Mitchell just nodded his head, making no move to pick up the envelope. Indeed, the entire time I was in his office he never touched it. I added, "The problem we have will be corrected this weekend, sir."

Again there was no more reaction from Mitchell than slow head-nodding.

Not willing to let well enough alone, I pressed on. "General, we've identified the exact suite McGovern's going to be using during the convention, and we've got a little surprise cooked up for him. We've got the hotel people on the payroll, so just as the press arrives for one of his interviews, we're gonna have a bunch of really filthy zonked-out hippies—not fakes, these are the real thing— swarm in there, all wearing McGovern buttons and carrying his signs." I leaned back, smiling. I had the full attention of everyone in the office, including Mitchell, who had stopped reading and removed the pipe from his mouth.

"Then," I said, "just as the television and press get their cameras going, and with McGovern standing there, helpless—the hotel people don't know about *this*, of course— every dirty hippie there is gonna whip it out and take a leak, right there in front of everybody. They'll never be able to get the stink out of the carpet so he'll have to move, and no way they'll be able to keep quiet why."

I laughed. The others laughed. Everybody laughed— *except* John Mitchell. He knew something I didn't. I knew, of course, that by this time the Republican convention had been moved from San Diego to Miami. I knew, too, that McGovern's suite was the best in the hotel. What I *didn't* know was that after the Democrats moved out and the Republicans moved in, John Mitchell would be staying in the suite just vacated by George McGovern.

Mitchell didn't laugh, he *roared*: "God*damn* it, Liddy, that's where *I'm* staying. You better *not* have any hippies pissing all over my rug!"

Mitchell was glowering at the very idea. The others froze into silence. I couldn't help it; I started to laugh. The others picked it up and soon Mitchell was laughing along with us. I participated in that brief portion of the meeting that concerned me and rose to leave. As I did, Mitchell said, with a twinkle in his eye, "I mean it, Gordon; keep those weirdos out of my hotel room."

"Yes, sir." I smiled and left to tell Howard Hunt to call off "Pissers for McGovern."

On the afternoon of Friday, 16 June, Hunt called to tell me that Barker, Martinez, Gonzalez, and Sturgis had arrived from Miami and were occupying rooms 214 and 314 at "the location," meaning the Watergate Hotel. It would take a while for the eight o'clock building inspection to be accomplished, and the chances that the DNC offices would be vacant by 8:30 P.M. weren't very good anyway, so we agreed to meet in room 214 about then, which at that time of year would be just about dark.

The last day of school in the District of Columbia, where Fran taught, was 16 June, and she had gone to a party thereafter in McLean, Virginia. I had dinner with her at home and then disappointed her by saying I couldn't help her celebrate, that I had to work late and she shouldn't wait up for me.

I took my Jeep and drove into Washington. Running a bit late, I jumped the yellow light behind the Bureau of Engraving and Printing and was pulled over by a traffic officer who gave me a verbal warning and waved me on. I continued on to Virginia Avenue, parking on the north side of the street about a hundred feet east of the Howard Johnson's motel. I walked into the Watergate Hotel, glancing up at DNC headquarters and noticing that the lights were on, and took the elevator to the second floor, where I joined Hunt and the Cubans in room 214.

The room was in disarray. Personal belongings and photographic equipment (such as special lights) were much in evidence, and Barker and Martinez were practicing rapid operation of the two Minolta cameras they had brought for their massive photographic assignment. Sturgis would assist and Gonzalez would attend to unlocking all the cabinets. This time Reinaldo Pico and Felipe De Diego were not with the team. Previously they had acted as guards, hiding outside the DNC entrance in the stairwell and just inside the door, ready to silence the building guard should he pull a surprise inspection not noticed from the observation post in time for the team to get away.

Hunt told me that Thomas Gregory had run out of guts and quit. We decided that we'd follow the same plan—the typewriter delivery with McCord the installer—relying on deceiving the Burns guard. The loss of Gregory was not considered fatal to the operation.

The men were in good spirits with Gonzalez pleasant and confident. I kidded him about having the right tools this time and he grinned. Martinez was effusive and thanked me for the new assignment. "That is what I have been saying to Eduardo, George. [I was using my CIA-furnished cover identity of George F. Leonard.] Use us. *Please* use us. We *want* to help!"

Because McCord was not yet there and I didn't want to rub in the fact that he wasn't getting an entry fee for this second penetration, I gave the men their compensation (reimbursement for time lost) and included the same amount for the McGovern job because I always felt bad about their refusal to accept direct pay. Hunt got six thousand dollars for himself, three each for Watergate II and McGovern. The difference between what he was getting and what, for example, Gonzalez was getting, bothered me. I respected those Cuban guys.

About eleven o'clock McCord came in. Typically he'd stayed away, over in the observation post, reporting once in a while by phone that the DNC was still occupied. With him he had six small transceivers, but he said that two of them were in need of a charge, something I thought an unprofessional oversight on the eve of a penetration. With no guards this time, however, it didn't matter so I said nothing. He also had with him a round white plastic device labeled "Smoke Detector—Do Not Remove." I took this to be the means by which he was going to correct what I still believed to be the room bug transmitter. He could move the device in to that "detector" and place it anywhere on the wall he wanted to be sure it was away from the steel beam that had been absorbing the signal. I thought it a good move.

McCord said that the DNC offices were still occupied, but that didn't matter either. By ten o'clock I had decided not to go until after the midnight inspection. There would have been plenty of time for McCord to do his correcting, but it would be unreasonable to expect the Cubans to be able to pick open and photograph all those files in under two hours. I took McCord aside and gave him his two thousand dollars for the McGovern job, even though it was now out of the question for that evening. I didn't want him any more unhappy than necessary about going into the DNC without pay. Disgruntled agents are a hazard to be avoided when possible.

McCord said that he'd already taped the garage-level doors by the simple expedient of going in through the lobby and down the stairwell. From the inside, of course, the door to the garage was not locked, so he simply opened it and taped it so that later the team could get into the stairwell via the garage. Not surprisingly, he now wanted to go back to the observation post. It was obvious that he was uncomfortable in the room with all the rest of us. He said he'd let us know when the DNC was clear, and I told him we'd be waiting anyway until we were sure the midnight inspection was completed. McCord, a man of few words, nodded his approval and left.

Someone brought in some Coca-Cola, but I declined it and suggested instead going across the street to the Howard Johnson's coffee shop for a snack. Hunt agreed and we strolled over, noticing as we crossed the street that the lights were still on in the DNC offices. We left about midnight to wait out the building inspection, and I noticed that the lights were still burning. Hunt went off to reposition his car.

As 12:30 A.M. came and went there was still no call from McCord in the observation post. Either the DNC offices were still occupied or McCord could not monitor the progress of the guard as he inspected the building and was waiting until he finished. We were all weary now and eager to get going. It was going to be a long night, and there was McGovern to contend with tomorrow. That thought was even more tiring. Hunt was wondering what the hell the Democrats were doing past midnight on a Friday night, and I observed that this late-night activity argued against the theory that all the action was now down in Miami. We speculated that McCord, whom we both regarded as overcautious, was waiting to be sure that the building guard was out, or that the FRB guards had not chosen this inconvenient time to make *their* roving inspection.

Our speculation was interrupted at about 12:45 A.M. when McCord phoned to say "it's clear" and that he was on his way over. All fatigue vanished as the men got themselves ready. It took McCord a good fifteen minutes to get there. He offered no explanation for the delay and I attributed it to his caution, thinking he must have walked down to the intersection, then back up to the other side of Virginia Avenue or some other such "dry cleaning" tactic. Everyone wished each other luck and the men left, moving out the door as quietly as possible in view of the hour.

Within a few minutes McCord, Barker, and Martinez were back wearing troubled expressions. McCord said that when they had gotten down to the garage-level doors they found that the tape he had put across the locks earlier had been removed. McCord said he thought it might have been a mailman who did it because there were some mail sacks in evidence. Hunt was sure it had been a guard. He wanted to abort. McCord didn't think it necessary to abort and said Gonzalez was unlocking the doors from the garage side, protected by Sturgis, so we could go forward or not, however it was decided.

Hunt who had not been enthusiastic about a second entry in the first place, thought the risk excessive. McCord, who wasn't getting paid for this one and had only a few minutes' work to do before he could leave, was for getting it over with but he was not pushing. The two Cubans were standing by, willing to abide by any decision and not offering any opinion so I asked them.

Eugenio Martinez, who is afraid of absolutely nothing, said, "Sure, George; whatever is the decision." Barker said, "I'm ready either way."

I knew Hunt's position. I took McCord aside. I knew him better than Hunt did. I wanted to get his opinion of the situation. He spoke quietly and with professional detachment. The tape had not popped off, someone had removed it. Some mail sacks were nearby. He would go with the decision either way. I asked his preference. He was, after all, one of the entry team and taking far more risk than Hunt or I. He said he thought it normal for the tape to be removed when discovered and would just as soon go in and get the job over with.

The decision was up to me. I was the leader and it was my responsibility. The others accepted that and would abide by my judgment. I knew that lock-taping was a common, if disapproved, practice of maintenance personnel in large buildings. That should not have alarmed the guard, who could be expected to remove it. I saw no reason that the guard should think anything other than that the maintenance people would have to be lectured.

I had no idea that McCord was going to retape the locks. I understood that Gonzalez would open the doors and he and Sturgis would hold them that way for the few minutes it took for a decision. Once in, the tape was supposed to be removed behind the team anyway. We had a safety valve in the observation post. When our men were inside, the offices would still be in darkness. The approach of a guard with a flashlight could be seen easily and Martinez and Sturgis could take care of any rent-a-cop. Were police called, they'd be noticed immediately when the cruisers drove up. Under all those circumstances I did not feel justified in aborting and decided to send the men in.

I left McCord and said to Howard: "Jim doesn't share your concern. He's willing to go, wants to get it over with." I pointed out that it had been a while since the tapes were put on and that if there'd been any commotion we'd have heard about it from the observation post or our men downstairs. "Everything seems quiet," I said. "All things considered, I think we should go."

I locked the door to the hotel room behind the three as they left. The team of five did go through that garage-to-stairwell door and on up the stairs—failing to remove the now-functionless tape from the door. This was fatal since it was only after finding the same door taped a second time that the guard called the police. It was now nearly 1:30 A.M., and we had a long night of waiting ahead of us. The radio call sign for the command post was simply "one," "two" was the entry team, and "three" the observation post. We had been using the telephone between the observation post and command post, but that was only safe when there were messages no more significant than "nothing yet" or "clear." For communications about the entry we had to rely on the security of the transceivers. I wanted to be sure our reception was good and not blocked by another steel beam in the Watergate office building or the hotel, so I took out a portable antenna that McCord had brought along and fastened it to the glass doors to the balcony, then jacked it into my transceiver. The television set was on low as I waited for word over the radio that the team had made the entry and gotten inside without incident. That word never came.

Just after 2 A.M. there was a transmission over the radio: "There's flashlights on the eighth floor."

It was McCord's man at the observation post. I repeated the news to Hunt. We agreed that it was probably one of

335

the two guard forces making a 2 A.M. door check. We were not concerned, believing that our team would be in darkness and not visible through the glass doors, which they would have locked from the inside behind them after Gonzalez picked the lock to gain entry. The next transmission was mine: "One to two. Did you read that?" There was no answer.

"One to three. Keep us advised."

The next transmission seemed to support our theory of a guard's making a routine check. "Now they're on the seventh floor."

There was a pause, then came the query, in a wondering tone that made its way through even the low fidelity of the transceiver: "Hey, any of our guys wearin' hippie clothes?"

It was only then that Hunt and I realized that something was very wrong.

"One to three. Negative. All our people are in business suits. Why?"

"They're on the sixth floor now. Four or five guys. One's got on a cowboy hat. One's got on a sweat shirt. It looks like . . . *guns*! They've got guns. It's trouble!"

Hunt and I were standing now. I said, "Shit!" and hit the mike switch: "One to two. Are you reading this? Come in!"

Hunt grimaced, convulsively lifted his right knee up toward his chest, then spun around to pound his right fist into his left palm.

"One to two," I repeated. "Come in. That's an order!"

That finally brought the first and last transmission we were going to receive from the entry team. A whispered voice said, simply and calmly: *"They got us."*

The observation post obeyed my prior order to keep us advised: "Now I can see our people. They've got their hands up. Must be the cops."

Hunt went out on the balcony to see whether he could see anything as the observation post continued to report: "More cops now; uniforms . . ."

336

Hunt and I began packing everything of an incriminating nature that we could find, intending to leave the room clean. Suddenly Hunt said, "Damn!"

"Now what?"

"We've gotta get out fast. I just remembered Macho's [Barker] got this room key."

We took what we had and started to leave. Hunt went over to the antenna to take it when we received a last transmission from the observation post: "What should I do now?"

Both my hands were full so Hunt answered: "Stay put. Keep the lights out and stay out of sight. I'll be right over."

Howard slipped the antenna down his pants leg, which gave him a stiff-legged gait, as we snapped out the lights, closed the door, and walked to the elevator. It was a quick trip down one floor. The door opened and we walked easily past the desk to the front door and out to the street. The place was swarming with police and squad cars; their flashing lights cast Christmas-like reflections incongruously into the warm June night. As Hunt turned right toward his car, he said, "Where's your Jeep?"

"Up ahead. On the other side of the street. Facing this way."

"Get in. I'll drive you up a few blocks and you can approach it from the other direction."

"Good idea. Thanks."

We drove east on Virginia leaving the arrest scene behind us. Crossing the first intersection, Hunt pulled over to the right and let me out. "You got the contingency fund ready?" I asked him.

"My office safe. I'll get it just as soon as I take care of McCord's man."

"O.K. Get hold of Caddy. Use the money. I'll call you tomorrow." Doug Caddy was a lawyer we both knew and always had in mind for emergency use.

Hunt made a U-turn and headed back toward Howard Johnson's while I walked across the street, then headed the same way on foot. I got into my Jeep and drove slowly past the now bustling area in front of the Watergate, turned right at the intersection, and headed home.

It was about 3 A.M. when I eased my way into the bedroom, trying not to awaken Fran. Light streamed into the room from the streetlight outside, and I could see her still form as I started quietly to undress. After a moment she stirred. I stopped moving, hoping she'd stay asleep. Hunt would, I thought, think back to the original plan for GEMSTONE—the one in which all entry people were to be untraceable and, in the event of difficulty, be bailed out under their aliases only to disappear—if necessary to Nicaragua, where Hunt had close ties with the Somoza family. I knew that wouldn't work now. Alias or not, McCord had been an FBI agent and his prints were on file in the identification division; they'd make him in twenty-four hours at the latest. Fran stirred again. "Is that you?"

"Yes."

I continued undressing. Fran has a sixth sense. Maybe all women married to the same man for fifteen years do.

"Anything wrong?"

"There was trouble. Some people got caught. I'll probably be going to jail."

Perhaps the experience of the FBI years told Fran it would be pointless to inquire further. She closed her eyes and said nothing more. Neither did I. What more was there to say?

I climbed in bed and went to sleep.

XXII

I was awakened at 5 A.M. on 17 June by the phone ringing at my bedside. I picked it up quickly, hoping it wouldn't wake Fran. It was Hunt. He was, he explained, with Doug Caddy. Caddy, said Hunt, did not feel well enough versed in criminal law and the procedures of the

Washington criminal court system to be of effective assistance. Hunt reminded me that Caddy was a labor law specialist and said he wanted to retain the services of a criminal lawyer named Rafferty.

Speaking quietly, I told Hunt that if that was Caddy's judgment it was fine with me, and it wasn't necessary for Hunt to check with me on everything Caddy wanted to do—at which point I asked Hunt what time it was, to impress upon him as gently as I could that it was especially not necessary for him to check with me at 5 A.M.

Hunt defended himself by pointing out that he knew I was a criminal lawyer and that he was used to consulting me about legal matters. Besides, said Hunt, Caddy wanted $8,500 as a retainer. Was that all right? Was it all right for him to use some of it for Rafferty? I told Howard the fee requested was reasonable. "Just a minute," he said, "Doug wants to talk to you himself."

Caddy apologized for the hour and before he could say anything more, I said, in order to place him under the restrictions of the attorney-client privilege: "Doug, the fee's fine; but I think it should include Howard and me."

"Howard's already asked me to represent him and I've agreed."

"Fine. I'm asking you to represent me, too, Doug; and anything I have to say to you comes specifically within the attorney-client privilege. Hunt's not a third party who can take it out of that. We're prospective co-defendants."

"I understand. I just wanted to get your O.K. personally on using Rafferty."

"You've got it. Tell Howard to get some sleep."

I told Caddy that I wanted Rafferty to bail out the five men arrested a few hours previously, and that I'd make up anything he used from the $8,500 fee for cash bail. I guessed it would be set at $10,000 each, which

339

would, at the usual 10 percent rate, cost a total of $5,000. There was more than double that still left in the GEM-STONE treasury in my office.

I went back to sleep until six. I had a lot to do that day and wanted to get an early start. The most important item was to get the facts to John Mitchell as quickly as possible. That meant a call to Magruder. The arrests might be on the early morning news, and I didn't want my superiors to get the word that way. I also had a lot of material in my office that was now white-hot and had to be destroyed immediately. It was 7 A.M. I thought it wise to start assuming for operational purposes that my home phone was tapped, so I drove to Bowie's Texaco Station on Livingston Road, where there were two full-closure outdoor telephone booths that were to become my after-hours communications center for Watergate damage control.

I dropped a dime in the slot and called the White House operator, that legendary corps of women from whom there is absolutely no escape. The best way for the FBI to catch a Ten Most Wanted fugitive is to ask the White House operator to get him on the phone. I didn't know Magruder's home phone, and I asked to be patched through or given the number. There was a wait, and I was advised that Magruder was with Mr. Mitchell in California, where, of course, it was 4 A.M.

With both Magruder and Mitchell out of pocket temporarily, I drove to CRP headquarters, parked in the underground garage across the street, and went to a nearby coffee shop for breakfast. The best thing to do in a situation like mine was to conform to normal patterns, and I often worked on Saturday mornings. I signed in at about 8:30 A.M. and went up to my office, closing and locking the door behind me and opening the GEM-STONE file safe.

I went through all the envelopes first, removing receipts from FAT JACK, Tom Gregory, and anything else but the cash, then went around the corner to the utility/

coffee room that housed the shredder. It was one of those few approved by the government for destruction of classified documents, cutting paper into little more than long, curling threads. The machine was slow, but absolutely sure, and I sacrificed speed for that security, feeding no more than two or three sheets in at a time.

As the morning wore on, other employees came in and I had to be more careful. I was not, however, careful enough, and as I bumped into Hugh Sloan in the hallway he eyed me and my clutch of hot trash. I had shown him the budget and he had provided me the funds for GEMSTONE, so I sought to warn him: "Our boys got caught last night. It was my mistake and I used someone from here, something I told them I'd never do." I gestured with the trash in my hands toward the shredder room. "I don't know how much longer I'm going to be able to keep this job."

Sloan looked bewildered, obviously not putting together his cursory exposures to the GEMSTONE budget with what I was saying. I let it go and continued on my way; he'd understand soon enough.

The five men in jail weren't the only ones who needed a lawyer; so did I. The best criminal lawyer I knew was my old law associate in Poughkeepsie, Peter Maroulis. Like me, he was a former prosecutor and good enough at defense to have won an acquittal in a federal case with four defendants accused of extortion in which the FBI had color movies of the payoff. Three were convicted. Peter's client, the only one in the movie, went free. I called him from the office, told him I needed help, and asked him to fly down.

The small shredder was too slow. I had confidence in my men, but I had to act on the assumption that it was just a matter of time before the FBI was coming to my office with a search warrant. I knew that there was a huge, high-capacity shredder somewhere in the committee complex, but I didn't know where. I sought out the man who would know, Rob Odle, and he directed me to it and showed me how to operate it. I didn't like Odle's shredder. It cut paper into strips the size of confetti, not threads. I'd be able to use it for a lot of peripheral stuff, but the most sensitive would still have to go into the small, slow, few-sheets-at-a-time high-security model near my office.

I became concerned about the possibility of press inquiries at the committee. I had still not seen the morning papers, but I would not have been surprised to learn that reporters were even now upstairs after our press relations people.

I went up there and found the press deputy, Powell Moore, and told him of the arrests, impressing upon him the necessity for the utmost secrecy about the identity of McCord. Moore, who had been at Justice, was no stranger to the need for discretion. But now he told me something very disturbing: John Mitchell was scheduled to hold a press conference at noon, California time. That would be three o'clock Washington time, and there was a good possibility that he'd be asked a question about the arrests at Democratic National Committee headquarters. Without foreknowledge of the events of early that morning, he'd be blind-sided by the press. I had to get word to him. By now it was almost eight o'clock in California. I needed two things: someone who could get me Magruder on the phone and a phone that was absolutely secure. That meant just one place: the Situation Room in the West Wing of the White House.

Early in my employment at the committee, the Secret Service had sought to revoke my White House pass. Through John Dean I had gotten it back. Now I was grateful as I used it to gain immediate entrance to the White House through the Old Executive Office Building, then across West Executive and up the steps to the entrance next to the Situation Room. I told the guard at the door I needed a secure phone in the Sit Room and was ushered inside. I told the White House operator I needed Jeb Magruder in California and waited. She got him.

The fact that I was at a secure phone didn't mean that Magruder was. I told him that I had an urgent message for John Mitchell that had to be delivered before his noon press conference and over a secure phone. In the Situation Room I had access to a KYX scrambler. I asked Magruder where he was, then relayed that information to the Situation Room personnel. They told me that the closest KYX to Magruder was at an Air Force missile base nearby, and I told Magruder to go there.

"*Why*? Why, Gordon, do I have to go to a missile base and use a scrambler phone? Aren't you overdoing all this secrecy stuff? I'm out here with John Mitchell. I have to stay with him. I can't just go wandering off to some missile base and ask to use the scrambler on your say-so. Be reasonable!"

Good old Magruder. If the plane was crashing he'd object to the inconvenience of putting on a parachute.

"Listen, Jeb, Goddamn it. I'm not over here in the fucking Situation Room because I haven't got a dime for a public phone. Get your ass to a secure phone and call me, or I guarantee by noon Mitchell will be building you a new one." I hung up.

Magruder called me back in a short while. He didn't say where he was calling from, but it wasn't on the KYX.

"Now what the hell's going on, Gordon?"

"Jeb, are you on a secure phone?"

"Yes, but I haven't got long. What's the problem?"

I laid it out for Magruder, telling him that five of our men had been arrested in DNC headquarters in the Watergate early that morning and that it could compromise the committee.

"You mean it can be traced?" Magruder reacted with horror in his voice. "How can that *be*, Gordon? You said . . ."

343

"Because one of them's Jim McCord, that's why. He's under an alias, but I don't know how long it'll hold up."

"You used *McCord*? Why, Gordon? *Why*? That's the question I'm gonna be asked. You said . . ."

"Listen, Jeb, this is no time for recriminations. I take responsibility, O.K.? But that's not the problem now. The problem is Mitchell's got a press conference out there at noon. He could get questions on this. He's got to know and have a statement ready or he could be sandbagged."

"But *why*, Gordon; that's what they're gonna ask me . . ."

"For Christ's sake, Jeb, there's less than an hour till that press conference. You've got to get to Mitchell and get working on that statement. I'll tell you all about it later. Now *move*."

I hung up and went back over to report to Powell Moore that I'd reached Magruder and he should be able to warn Mitchell in time to prevent disaster at the press conference. We were discussing how best to respond from the committee if he should get an inquiry when I was called to the phone. It was Magruder. He told me that he'd reached Mitchell and given him the information. I was set for another bout of sniveling, but it never came; instead he had a message for me from Mitchell. I was to find Dick Kleindienst, the Attorney General, and ask him to get McCord out of jail immediately. "Tell him 'John sent you' and it's a 'personal request from John.' He'll understand."

I didn't argue. From experience as a prosecutor I knew that the number of people involved in trying to effect a request like that would make it impossible to keep secret and, in this case especially, it could only make matters worse. But an order from John Mitchell to pass along a message was not to be disobeyed. I hung up and asked Powell Moore where I'd be likely to find Dick Kleindienst at noon on Saturday.

Moore was apprehensive. What did I want with Kleindienst? I told him of the message I had just received.

Moore looked very troubled. "I know, I know," I said, "it's not a good idea, but I've got to pass it on."

Moore shook his head in dismay but recognized that the message would have to be transmitted and was of such a kind that it would have to be done personally. He undertook to locate Kleindienst, whom he knew well from his days in the Department of Justice, and picked up the phone. Presently he announced that Kleindienst was playing golf at Burning Tree. I had never been there and asked Moore if he could give me directions. He started to, but because speed was important I thought better of it and asked him to accompany me. Moore offered to do the driving, and we left in his battered Volkswagen and arrived at Burning Tree a little after noon.

I walked immediately to the pro shop area and asked for the Attorney General. Someone said they thought he had already come in from the course and was probably having lunch. Moore and I walked into the dining area, and I spied Kleindienst seated at a table in the middle of the room, dining with others. I caught his eye and gestured to him, hoping he'd understand that I would not presume to do such a thing to the Attorney General of the United States in other than exceptional circumstances. He caught my signal and left the table, making his way to me and Powell Moore. I told him that I had a personal message to deliver to him from John Mitchell and we'd need privacy. Kleindienst looked around and nodded toward a locker area. Moore and I followed him in.

We walked to the back, where there were some chairs. Kleindienst and I sat down, facing each other. Moore stood to my left, between us. Despite the abrupt interruption of his luncheon, Kleindienst was most pleasant, made a few self-deprecatory remarks about his golf game, then asked: "What's this about John?"

I asked Kleindienst whether he'd heard of the arrests the night before at Democratic National Committee headquarters in the Watergate, and he said, "Yeah. Henry Petersen called me this morning. What about it?"

345

I spelled it out for Kleindienst. I told him that the break-in was an operation of the intelligence arm of the Committee to Re-elect the President; that I was running it for the committee and the men arrested were our people working under my direction when they were caught. I told him that they were good men who would keep their mouths shut; that all were arrested under aliases but that one, James McCord, was also on the regular committee payroll under his true name.

"Jesus Christ!" interjected Kleindienst.

"I know," I said, "that was my fault. At any rate, you see the problem."

"God, yes."

I told Kleindienst that the message I was to deliver was from John Mitchell, and he interrupted to ask if I had received it from Mitchell directly. I told him I had not; that it came through Magruder. I was very uncomfortable because I knew the message was a bad idea, so I said, "I don't know how you can do this, but I'm supposed to tell you that it's a 'personal request from John.' Anyway, he wants you to help get McCord out of jail right away—before it's found out who he really is."

Kleindienst looked stunned. Moore hadn't said a word but was shaking his head from side to side, negatively. I agreed with him and said, "I know. There's no way you can even try to do it without it getting out. Then what happens to you?"

Kleindienst exploded. "*Me?* Fuck what happens to *me!* What happens to the *President* if I try a fool thing like that? It's the Goddamnedest thing I ever heard of!"

Moore and I said nothing and Kleindienst continued: "Jesus Christ! *That's* what everybody ought to be thinking of—the President! What the fuck did you people think you were *doing* in there?"

I started to explain the mission's purposes but Kleindienst waved me off. "Never mind, never mind." His mood became subdued and pensive. "God," he said, "this is terrible. I can't imagine John Mitchell asking me to do a thing like that." Then, abruptly, his speech grew crisp again. "Well, listen. You tell whoever it was that John Mitchell knows me well enough to call me himself if he has anything more like that to say to me. And tell them I can't do it—*won't* do it. For the President's sake I'm going to handle this one just like any other case."

Kleindienst rose and I got up with him. He looked distracted. "I'd better be getting back," he said and we shook hands. Kleindienst headed back to his table, and Moore and I tried to be inconspicuous as we strolled out and walked quietly to his Volkswagen for the drive back to Washington.

"He did the right thing," said Powell Moore.

"He did," I agreed.

Kleindienst's disregard of himself and immediate thought of the President impressed me greatly. His words articulated forcefully and concisely the unspoken attitude and criterion that I had found myself applying instinctively to Watergate: "*Fuck what happens to me. What happens to the President if I do that?*"

When I returned to my office on Saturday afternoon I continued destroying my records. I found that film cassettes would not go through Odle's monster shredder; they just kept rolling against the blades.

Hunt telephoned. He wanted to know whether Caddy had got the men out on bail yet. I told him I had no information. Then he startled me: "The FBI was here. They want to interview me. Bernie (Barker) had my name in his address book."

"What'd you say?"

"I told them I'd consult my attorney and let them know."

"That's exactly what you should have said. When they come back, you tell them that on advice of counsel you have nothing to say to them. Period."

By late in the afternoon I had completed shredding the GEMSTONE files. The only thing I couldn't get into the shredder was the huge roll of blueprints for the Convention Center in Miami, but because the Republicans would be using it too, and there was no longer a plan in existence to sabotage the air-conditioning units to which the blueprints could be linked, I thought it safe to leave them in the office.

Sunday morning, 18 June, Peter Maroulis called to give me his ETA at Hyde Field. I was waiting in my Jeep as he greased his four-place Cessna onto the runway, then taxied to the aviation fuel island. A tall, powerfully built man with a Clark Kent face and glasses under thinning sandy hair, Peter Maroulis will correct anyone who refers to his ethnic extraction as "Greek" by advising sternly that he is a Spartan. He was my best friend.

"What's up?" Peter asked as we drove to my home.

"I need a favor."

"You got it."

"Don't be so quick to answer."

"I'm listening."

"I want you to defend me in what will be the biggest trial in the country if I get indicted, and I'll probably get indicted. But there's a catch."

"Which is?"

"You can't win."

"Jesus. Thanks for the vote of confidence."

"Uh, uh. You don't understand. I can't let you win. I can't defend myself. If I'm thrown in this thing, and the way things are it's very possible, I'll have to sit still, shut up, and take the weight. It's my job."

We arrived at my home and Peter said, "How 'bout a cup of coffee and you can tell me about it?"

For the next few hours I did. Peter cherishes his reputation, as would any outstandingly successful lawyer, and I couldn't have blamed him for being reluctant to go into the national eye knowing he couldn't use all his information, potential witnesses, and other normal assets in an attempt to win. The best we'd be able to do was play for error. Peter never hesitated. I was his friend and needed his help and that was that. In the afternoon I waited until he'd fire-walled the throttle on the Cessna and lifted off before I drove back to the house.

I had no sooner arrived home than Hunt telephoned to report that he had replied to the FBI as I had instructed, but that a reporter named Woodward had the information about his name being in Barker's address book. The situation was deteriorating rapidly. There was now no doubt that committee involvement would become an issue. The only bright outlook was that no matter what happened, I could stop the thing with me. All I had to do was keep my mouth shut and that was as far as the matter could go; the hearsay rule of evidence would see to that. I decided to get plenty of rest. The Watergate break-in would be the conversation subject of the day at the committee tomorrow. I had plenty of legal work to do, and the best thing I could do to avoid suspicion would be to look and act as if I were as completely mystified as everyone else.

On Monday, 19 June, I arrived at work at the usual time. I called in Sally Harmony and closed the door. I didn't have to explain anything to her; she's a very smart woman—smart enough not to ask questions. I asked her to check all her shorthand notebooks and shred any pages that had anything to do with "other than finance committee matters." Mrs. Harmony nodded her head in understanding and left.

About 11 A.M. I received a message to telephone John Dean. When I called back he said he wanted to see me in his office. I was pleased because Dean was the man who had recruited me for the intelligence arm of the committee and the logical choice to serve as damage control action officer for the White House. Now I'd be getting some decisions and assistance in getting our men out on bail. I told Dean I'd be right over.

I entered the Old Executive Office Building by the main entrance on Pennsylvania Avenue. The building had once housed the Departments of State, War, and Navy, if one can imagine a time when the Pentagon and the

State Department could fit together in one building, and I walked past the little office on the right where my mother had worked for the State Department in 1928, flashed my pass to the guard at the desk, and turned right down the hall. At the corner I turned left for Dean's office, but he was outside in the hall, waiting for me. He was nervous, saying only, "Let's go for a walk."

It was obvious that Dean didn't want to be seen with me if he could avoid it. He would be on top of the investigation, and his attitude meant I was hot. We said nothing to each other until we were outside and walking down 17th Street. There were people on the street, so we kept the conversation to the pleasantries of the day until we crossed the street and walked into the park.

Dean was dressed nattily, his overly long lightened hair flowing over his ears and down beyond his suit coat collar. A breeze swept a dust particle into my eye as we sat down, and as I held one hand over my eye to let it tear and flush out the tiny grain, Dean asked if I was O.K.

"It'll be all right in a second," I said, "it's just a little more problem than usual because I wear contact lenses."

"Do you? So do I," said Dean.

I blinked and the dust was gone. Turning to him I said: "Am I correct in assuming that you're the damage control action officer for this problem?"

Dean looked a bit puzzled by that, but said, "Yes, Gordon; you could put it that way."

"I'm not playing games, John; it's just that I have to know how much you need to know. If you're the action officer, then you need to know it all. D'you follow me?"

Dean nodded his head.

"O.K. The first thing I want to say is that I was commanding the aircraft carrier when it hit the reef. I accept full responsibility. All of the people arrested are my men. You remember the intelligence operation you recruited me for and those meetings in the AG's office? Well by the time the damn thing was finally approved we were down to a quarter million. Anyway, that's water under the bridge."

Dean was looking distinctly uncomfortable. He didn't like being reminded that he had recruited me for what I had been doing and had participated in the early discussion of what I was to do. He cut me off with: "Gordon, there's something I've got to know right away. Did anyone in the White House know you were going there—I mean specifically."

I thought for a moment, then remembered the conversation I'd had with Gordon Strachan about repairing the defective transmitter.

"Gordon Strachan," I said. "I don't know that he knew the exact day we were going back in there, but ..."

"*Back* in?"

"Yeah. Look, John, if you'll just let me lay the whole thing out for you ..."

"How about Colson? Did he know?"

"Not unless Hunt told him, and I have no reason to believe he did."

Dean looked relieved, and I continued: "Look, if they're worried over there that someone called over from the White House and said 'go in,' or 'go back in' the Watergate, you're talking to the wrong guy. Fucking Magruder sent us in there. *He* was the one pushing for it. If you'll recall, *I* was the one who was supposed to choose the times and places of entry, but the thing got ass-backwards. Even after the budget and the funding schedule finally got approved, Magruder insisted on personally approving every disbursement to me from Sloan. Now who, if anybody, was pushing Magruder from the White House, you'll have to ask him. I don't know. They certainly didn't call me. Strachan knew I was going back in, but he didn't give me the order, Magruder did."

Dean looked at me closely. "Did Magruder authorize you to use McCord?"

"No. Absolutely not. That was my mistake. You'll remember I promised there'd never be any link. I meant

351

it when I said it. By the time the program finally got approved, McCord was the only game in town and I used him. I shouldn't have. Magruder never knew about McCord."

Dean rose to leave and I stopped him. "Wait a minute, John. If you're going to be the action officer for damage control, you've got to know something else."

Reluctantly, Dean sat back down on the bench beside me. He was impatient. People were streaming out of the government office buildings across the street with their brown bag lunches and heading for the park. Our privacy would soon be gone.

"McCord's all right. He's a professional—FBI and CIA. So are the Cubans. They won't talk. But on a worst-case basis, you've got to know what they *could* say if they did."

I told Dean about the Fielding entry in Beverly Hills to get Daniel Ellsberg's psychiatric file. He turned white. "These are the same people?"

"The Cubans. Not McCord. And, of course, Hunt."

Dean's composure cracked. "Jesus," he said. Then, "Anything more?" He was almost wincing in anticipation.

I couldn't help smiling. "No. And don't worry about it. They won't talk. But I think it's imperative we get them bailed out. That D.C. jail's a hellhole, especially in summer, and they expect it. They were promised that kind of support . . ."

"What kind of support?"

"The usual in this line of work. Bail, attorney's fees, families taken care of, and so forth . . ."

Then Dean said something he later claimed he did not say. "That goes without saying. Everyone'll be taken care of." Dean's tone of voice was confident, but the look on his face was decidedly troubled. Well he might be, I thought to myself. Dean now knew that what I knew could cost Richard Nixon the Presidency. As aware of the hearsay rule as I was, he also knew that without me

352

no investigation could reach higher. *I* knew I would never talk, but he and those above him couldn't be absolutely sure of that. Except one way. It occurred to me that people who would seriously consider the use of drugs against Ellsberg and the killing of Jack Anderson might well decide to go ahead with an assassination in my case. It would be reasonable; the stakes—the sure loss of the Presidency—were immensely higher and, after all, it *was* my fault.

That raised another problem. So far as I knew, I was the only one readily available to the White House for a domestic sanctioned killing. They certainly couldn't turn to the CIA without handing Helms the keys to the kingdom. Hunt was blown. What was left to them?

What was left would be some well-motivated amateur who didn't know the rules. I didn't mind being killed, if that was thought necessary, but I didn't want some scared-to-death nonprofessional to try it at my home or anywhere else where my family could be endangered. I had visions of shotgun blasts through the kitchen window on a Sunday morning while we were all at breakfast.

By now Dean and I were walking slowly back up 17th Street. Dean had his head down, looking at the sidewalk, when I told him: "Look, John. I said I was the captain of the ship when she hit the reef and I'm prepared to go down with it. If someone wants to shoot me"—Dean's head snapped up and he stared at me—"just tell me what corner to stand on and I'll be there, O.K.?"

Dean searched my face to see whether I was joking. I wasn't, and he could see that. "Well, uh," he stammered, "I don't think we've gotten *there* yet, Gordon."

"All right. But please remember what I said."

"Believe me, Gordon, I will."

Thus assured, I changed the subject. If Dean was going to be the action officer, there were some practical things he should know about how to keep on top of the investigation. Routinely, he'd be sent FBI "letterhead memoranda" summarizing the investigation. That would be way behind the actual pace. If he pressed he might get the reports sent in to FBI headquarters by the Washington and other field offices. Those, too, would be behind the investigation; nor would they tell him the direction in which the investigation was heading. When, after World War II, the courts decided in the Judith Coplon espionage case that the defense must be given access to FBI reports, the Bureau devised a way to circumvent much of the effect of the decision. Instead of the report's containing page after page of narrative, each interview was placed on a separate form, called an FD-302. Only that form was given the defense. Further, investigative leads were placed on a separate page not given the defense. When lawyers got on to that, leads and sensitive matters were put in a "cover-letter" that accompanied the report but, because not considered a part of it, were withheld from the defense and the courts. To save teletype charges, "expedite" leads were sent on a blue form that went airmail and was called an "Airtel."

I told all this to Dean and advised him to get the Airtels and FD-302s before they were combined into a report. He thanked me, then said, "Where's Hunt these days?"

"Lying low. The reporters are after him. Why?"

It was at this moment, and not later, on the telephone after talking to Ehrlichman, that Dean said: "Well, for that reason, and what you've told me [which I took to be a reference to the Ellsberg matter], I think he'd be better off out of the country. Does he have someplace he can go?"

"Most of his family's in Europe right now, as a matter of fact. He could join them, I suppose."

"Good. Have him do that. The sooner the better."

"How soon?"

"Today, if possible."

"O.K. I'll tell him as soon as I can get hold of him."

We were nearly at the northernmost 17th Street entrance to the E.O.B. now, and Dean paused, saying: "Ah,

Gordon, I don't think it's a good idea for me to be talking with you anymore. I hope you'll understand."

I did. The White House was trying to put as much distance between itself and me as possible. That was reasonable under the circumstances.

"Sure, John. But if you're not going to be the action officer anymore, who is?"

"It'll be someone from 1701" (the committee).

"How'll I know him? I can't talk about this to just anyone."

"He'll come to you and identify himself. You'll know him."

I was a bit mystified, but it was clear that that was all I was going to get out of Dean on this or any other subject. He was standing on first one foot and then the other in his anxiety to get out of my company and back into the building. I stuck out my hand. "Sorry about the way things turned out, John."

Dean took my hand and shook it listlessly. "Yeah," he said, head hanging and, I suppose, still absorbing the full meaning of what I had told him. "It sure is a mess." I tossed him a final salute and crossed the corner diagonally to return to my office and try to raise Hunt.

With Hunt so hot I thought it best not to go over to the Mullen Company. It might be staked out by reporters. For that matter, I speculated, Hunt might be being followed. I didn't want to end up in the papers so I devised a plan to meet him that offered a chance to detect surveillance. Hunt was in when I called a little after noon. I identified myself by my operational alias, "George," and asked Howard to leave his office, turn left on the south side of Pennsylvania Avenue, and keep on walking, saying that I'd intercept him. He agreed readily.

I posted myself at the corner, reading a paper, where I could watch Hunt approach and check for a tail. He appeared alone so I moved toward him and we walked south on 18th Street. I told him my principals wanted him out of the country.

"For how long?"

"They didn't say. I guess until you cool off."

"Where?"

"Your choice. I mentioned your family's abroad; they thought your joining them a good idea."

"Damn, I dunno, Gordon; I don't like the idea of looking like a fugitive."

"That's the beauty of joining your family. It's a normal thing to do in the summer. They're already over there. Hard to make anything out of that."

"Not for *The Washington Post*. If this is another screwball idea of Magruder's . . ."

"Uh, uh, Howard. This one came from across the street."

That seemed to reassure Hunt. I asked him if he would be able to leave that day and he glanced at me sharply. "Today?"

"If you can."

"Well," he said, "I've still got that $1,500 left over from the emergency fund . . ."

"Use it," I said. It wouldn't be fair to expect Hunt to use his own funds.

Hunt agreed to go and we both expressed continuing concern for the men in jail. He suggested that the fact there was high-level interest in getting him out of the country might be a hopeful sign that things were finally getting organized and the same high-level people would do the necessary to get the boys out on bail. Then Hunt asked that I do one thing for him right away. "I'm going to need a good lawyer for myself, Gordon; I'd like you to make that top priority." I said I'd see what I could do.

Back in the office I asked Sally Harmony whether there were any messages. There weren't; I hadn't been gone that long. She told me she'd shredded all her notes and I thanked her.

"How's it going?" I asked her.

Sally grimaced. "You know what is the principal subject of conversation around here." I grimaced back and returned to my legal work. After a while the phone rang. It wasn't my line from Hunt, so Mrs. Harmony answered it and buzzed me: "John Dean."

Now what? I thought. Maybe he couldn't get out of being the action officer. I scooped up the receiver. "Hi, John. It's been a long time."

Dean wasn't amused. "Ah, Gordon; that message to Hunt. Cancel it."

"Jesus, John; I don't know if I can."

"Why not?"

"Well, I delivered it . . ."—I checked my watch—". . . about forty minutes ago and told him to leave immediately. Now, if I can reach him, fine; but if I can't, I don't think we ought to drag him back from his family . . ."

"Gordon," Dean was brusque, "Ehrlichman says cancel it."

"All right, John. I'll get right on it."

I tried Hunt's office. He was gone. I reached him at home. "Glad I got you, Howard. Signals off; you don't have to go."

Hunt was upset by this development. "Gordon, a one-eighty on a thing like leaving the country in forty-five minutes doesn't exactly inspire confidence we're dealing with people who know what the hell they're doing!"

"What can I tell you, Howard? That's the message."

"The logic of the first one appealed to me better. Besides, in another forty-five minutes they may change their minds again. Tell you what. I've got business in New York. From there I can get a domestic or international flight more easily than anywhere else. I'm going up there now."

"I can't argue with you, Howard. Keep me posted."

The day ended with no more messages from Dean, nor was I approached by anyone resembling the expected new action officer on Watergate. I went home and gave my now-rumpled suit to Frances to send to the cleaners. "I wish you'd get rid of that awful suit," she said. It was a

357

family joke that I tend to hang on to old clothes longer than the Salvation Army. I smiled, but I was thinking that now was not the time to be buying new clothes; the government might soon enough be taking care of that.

XXIII

On Tuesday morning, 20 June, I dressed in the same suit I had worn on the evening of 16 June. As I put it on, I felt something in my suit coat pocket and discovered a key to room 214 in the Watergate Hotel. I wondered what other little gems were lying around awaiting the execution of a search warrant by the FBI. I checked and found nothing. Then I remembered that because Fran liked Neutrogena and other fine soaps used in first-class hotels, I used to bring her home a bar or two from my travels. I had done so from the Beverly Wilshire and some hotels in Miami. I looked for them and found them unused. The fireplace had been cleaned for the summer and the wrappers were coated wtih a substance that would preserve them in water so I put them in my pocket to shred when I got to my office. Enroute I threw the Watergate key into the Anacostia River, where it lies buried in the mud to this day.

By Tuesday morning I had learned that money found in a search of the men arrested in the DNC offices and our rooms at the Watergate Hotel included new, sequentially numbered bills. The first thing I did when I got to the office was check my file safe and, sure enough, there were thirteen brand-new hundred-dollar bills with sequential serial numbers among the more than one hundred still in the GEMSTONE treasury.

The only way to get rid of the bills, which could provide a direct link to the committee and to me, was to shred them. But there were people in and out of the shredder room all the time—especially in the morning—because that was where we kept the coffee. While there was nothing unusual about anyone's using the shredder—that was what it was there for—someone coming in for coffee only to find me shredding hundred-dollar bills would think I'd lost my mind at the very least and word would be all over the office. I solved the problem by placing the bills between sheets of paper and feeding the expensive sandwich to the machine very carefully. Then, to be sure that the shreds of the bills would be buried thoroughly, I shredded some more trash in on top of them so they wouldn't be at the top of the bin when the shredder was emptied.

In the afternoon Fred LaRue called me. He said he wanted to talk to me privately and suggested that we go to his apartment in the Watergate complex. I laughed and told him I was game if he was and we went over there, entering by a side door to be as inconspicuous as possible. When we got inside the apartment I was surprised to find Bob Mardian. I thought he was still in California. I'd called him over the weekend to urge that he—or someone on the political committee in executive authority other than Magruder—come back in view of the flap, and he had called me back to say that despite my wishes it was Magruder who would be returning.

"Gordon, I have to talk to you," Mardian said.

"O.K., but how much I'll say to you depends. Are you the new action officer I've been waiting to hear from?"

"Yes."

We were still standing. LaRue had walked a distance away. Mardian led the way toward a lighted corner.

"All right," I said, "if you're the action officer you'll have to know it all. I'll lay it out for you: best case and worst case."

I saw a radio and suggested he turn it on against microphone surveillance. It can be filtered out by experts, but there's no sense making it easy for the opposition. Mardian sat down first and I started to follow; but before I had done more than bend my body he said, "Gimme a quarter."

I fished in my pocket and handed him one. He pocketed it and with a grin and said, "That's my fee; now I'm your lawyer. You don't have to disclose the fee, and I want your promise that under no circumstances will you ever waive the attorney-client privilege."

I promised Mardian I wouldn't, although I wondered why he went to all that trouble with LaRue there. The presence of a third party took the conversation out of the privilege, unless he viewed LaRue as a codefendant.

For the same reasons that I had insisted on telling Dean the whole story—because the damage control officer has to know it all so he can deal intelligently with the situation—I started my narrative at my meeting with Dean in Bud Krogh's office, including my insistence that Dean and Krogh take the matter up both channels for a decision about whether this was the best way I could serve the President in 1972, and brought Mardian up to date. Then I told him of the absolute confidence I had in the Cubans and McCord: of their intelligence-service backgrounds and willingness to keep silent; that they were under aliases and that John Dean had, only the day before, assured me that they'd all be receiving the usual family support and legal fees. I stressed that they should be bailed out as soon as possible and said that on a best-case basis, while it appeared my partner, Howard Hunt, had been identified, he wouldn't talk either and the matter would end there.

Before I got to the worst-case presentation, Mardian started to cross-examine me. He had, for a short while, been in charge of the now defunct Internal Security Division of the Department of Justice and had associated there with a lot of FBI types. He had no experience in criminal investigation or criminal law, but now he was playing cop: "How can you say it won't come to you? You were in the hotel room. Your fingerprints must be all over the place."

360

I assured him they were not. I hadn't left any.

"How about glasses and bottles? How about the toilet, did you use the toilet?"

I had but had followed my usual practice of using my shoe to lift the seat and flush it. Mardian, a man who finds it impossible to hide his exceptionally emotional nature, had been reacting to what I told him by throwing his head and body backward and blowing loudly through pursed lips, tossing his pencil high in the air, and other melodramatic gestures. He made it quite clear he didn't believe that I had left no prints for the FBI to find. (The Bureau took prints from me later—full palm, side and tips of fingers, etc., and never was able to find a single print of mine in the Watergate Hotel room in which I'd spent so many hours.)

I told Mardian of shredding even the California hotel soap wrappers; of shredding the thirteen sequentially numbered bills, all my GEMSTONE files, and Sally Harmony's notes. I was, I insisted, clean.

Mardian said I ought to resign. I told him that was the last thing I ought to do; it would throw suspicion on me immediately. He nodded his head in agreement at that. Then I gave him the worst-case situation: an assumption that one of the five should crack. I told him of the Fielding break-in in the Ellsberg case; of the ODESSA unit in the White House; and of Hunt's clandestine interview of Dita Beard using physical disguise from the ODESSA unit provided by the CIA.

Mardian jumped on the CIA connection and I detailed the assistance we had received from CIA; Hunt's and McCord's CIA careers; and the Cubans' long association with the agency on a contract basis. Mardian couldn't hear enough about CIA. LaRue just sat and listened, taking no part in the long conversation. Then Mardian said he'd be calling the shots from now on and the meeting was over.

Back at the office Bob Bennett, Hunt's employer and the man with whom I'd worked out the $50,000 Howard Hughes contribution, telephoned. He asked me to meet him in the bookstore on the first floor of his building, facing 17th Street. I agreed to see him there in a few minutes.

Bennett was reading when I spotted him. I moved next to him and picked up some reading material myself. As we both "read," Bennett told me that Howard Hunt was now in Beverly Hills at the home of Tony Jackson and wanted to see me. The message was to "bring money and the name of a lawyer." I decided that it would not do to add to Hunt's feelings of abandonment by ignoring his request. I didn't have a lawyer for him yet, although I hoped that Mardian would come through on that, but there was still over $12,000 in the GEMSTONE kitty, $10,000 in the file safe, and the $2,000 I had as an emergency fund at home. The least I could do was resupply Howard with some cash while he was on the run.

I had to go out to California on other committee business anyway, and I could see Hunt between Los Angeles and San Francisco and the trip, overtly for the committee, would provide good cover.

On Wednesday, 21 June, I arrived at Dulles Airport for what would be an uncomfortable trip. I didn't know what Hunt was going to tell me and thought it best to be prepared for anything, so I had $5,000 wrapped around each lower leg and held in place by elasticized calf-length socks. If my bag was inspected by airport anti-hijacking personnel, it wouldn't do to have a hundred one-hundred-dollar bills found in the possession of the finance committee counsel flying out of Washington only five days after Watergate.

Once in Los Angeles I switched the money into my briefcase in a men's room. I handled some routine committee business and then telephoned Tony Jackson. He gave me directions to his house, which I repeated to a cab driver, and I sat back for the climb high into beautiful Beverly Hills.

A Hispanic maid greeted me at Jackson's home and invited me in. In a moment Jackson himself appeared and we made small talk as he skillfully noted my demeanor and checked to see whether I was armed. Once satisfied that I was there on a friendly mission and not to kill Hunt, he said in a loud voice, "Howard, here's Gordon!" Hunt slipped from around the corner of a doorway where he'd been waiting for an all-clear signal from his old CIA colleague, Jackson.

I told Hunt that I regretted not having a lawyer for him yet but offered the encouraging news that there was now a new action officer, who was none other than the recent Assistant Attorney General of the United States in charge of the Internal Security Division, which should start things going more smoothly.

"I'd be satisfied if they'd just start going at all!" Hunt exclaimed. I gave him $1,000 cash for himself and, when he pointed out that Jackson had not only been hiding him but acting as his attorney until the committee came through with one in Washington, I gave Jackson $500 in cash as a token fee.

"Five *hundred*?" asked Hunt; "I should think it would be five *thousand*."

I didn't want to alarm Hunt further by telling him that the GEMSTONE treasury was low and I'd been given no additional funds for this mission, so I changed the subject to the Cuban families in Miami and asked Hunt to fly down there to interview and reassure Clara Barker, asking her to act as the conduit for funds for them all. He suggested that a prominent Cuban businessman who had been active in the 2506 movement—the Bay of Pigs invasion force—might be approached to start a fund for his fellow 2506 veterans and committee funds for family support and legal fees be funneled through him.

I promised Hunt I'd raise that with Mardian, and I tried to comfort him again with the thought that the millionaire Phoenix construction magnate and recent Assistant Attorney General was now in charge of Watergate damage control—what the press would soon be calling the "cover-up." Then Hunt came with Jackson as he drove me back to my hotel. Flying to San Francisco, I got some things done for the finance committee and flew back to Washington. This time my socks were less bulky; I had only $4,250 around each leg.

Early in the final week of June I learned why Mardian was so taken with what I'd had to tell him about the CIA connections of Hunt, McCord, and the Cubans and the assistance the agency had given to Hunt and me while we were part of the ODESSA unit. He called me to a meeting with Paul O'Brien. O'Brien and Kenneth Parkinson were the attorneys retained by the Committee to Re-elect the President when the Democratic National Committee filed a civil suit against it for the Watergate break-in. Mardian told me that I could speak freely because the attorney-client relationship obtained between us. He then asked me to tell everything I knew about the Watergate entry.

There followed what was to me at first an astonishing performance by Mardian. As I went over the whole thing again from my recruitment by Dean forward, Mardian went into his blowing, snorting, and pencil-throwing routine again, reacting exactly as if he were hearing all this for the first time. O'Brien sat quietly taking notes, displaying no reaction at all. I'd hate to play poker with O'Brien, I thought, but I'd *love* to get in a game with Mardian.

Then Mardian's performance became even stranger. He started questioning me, using CIA jargon, talking about "the company" and eliciting answers from me, by means of repetitious questions, which required me to mention the CIA. Then he began actually to lead me and I caught on; Mardian was trying to persuade O'Brien that the Watergate entry was really a CIA-sponsored operation. This was confirmed for me when, after I discussed the jailed men's expectations of family and legal support and Dean's assurance that it would be forthcoming, Mardian said, " 'The company' should take care of its own, don't you think?" I answered, "It always has in the past."

I couldn't for the life of me figure why Mardian wanted to deceive O'Brien, whose task so far as I knew was to defend against the civil suit by the Democrats. Mardian was an attorney and if there's anything an attorney will advise against, it's lying to one's lawyer. It makes about as much sense as lying to a physician and the effects can be just as disastrous. The irony of the whole thing was that O'Brien, I knew, had an intelligence background and was unlikely to be deceived by Mardian's performance. But Mardian was the action officer, so I went along with his game although I never actually said that the operation was CIA-sponsored. If Hunt could hear a tape of this, I thought, he'd either die laughing or flee to Nicaragua.

On Wednesday, 28 June, I was told that FBI agents were in the outer office waiting to interview me. For some days now the Bureau had been interviewing committee employees, and the order was to cooperate fully with the FBI or be fired. There was another order: all FBI interviews were to be conducted in the presence of one of the attorneys retained by the committee in the civil suit. In my case Parkinson escorted the agents into my office at the finance committee. I sat behind my desk. Parkinson sat off to my left, taking notes. The two Special Agents of the FBI, Messrs. Daniel C. Mahan and Donald E. Stukey II, sat across my desk from me.

Mahan did the talking. He came on like a wise-ass. Some FBI agents, like Lew Fain, have such engaging personalities they get an extraordinary amount of information from people who are determined to give them nothing. Others, like Mahan, can turn a cooperative witness for the government into a deaf-mute in about one minute. But there was no harm done. All I had ever intended to give the FBI was the time of day, and Mahan promptly talked me out of giving them even that. In minutes it was all over, and so was my career as counsel to the Finance Committee for the Committee to Re-elect the President.

On Thursday, 29 June, I was called to Fred LaRue's little office. I knew what was coming so I cleaned out the GEMSTONE treasury and brought the $8,500 and change with me. LaRue was thoughtful and considerate. He reminded me of the committee policy of retaining no employee who did not cooperate fully with the FBI, and I told him I was aware of it and understood what had to happen. LaRue asked me whether I wanted to resign and have the record so state or be discharged. I asked what difference it made, and he said that were I to resign, my pay would stop as of that day. Were I to be discharged, however, the law required that I be given severance pay. I thought of the desert ahead and told him I'd take the discharge and the severance pay. That done, I told him of the balance of the GEMSTONE funds I had with me and asked him what to do with it. He said, "I might as well take it," and I gave it to him, then I thought of the $2,000 I had at home and told him I'd bring it in the next day, a Friday and my last working day.

"Keep it," said LaRue in a sad voice. "You'll need it." He was right. I thanked him and left.

Friday, 30 June, I broke the news to Mrs. Harmony. She had expected it but still her eyes misted over. I asked her to help me pack. She did, then said I shouldn't have to be seen by everyone carrying out my things. She offered to come in Saturday and put them in her car so I could pick them up privately. I made one last request: that after I was gone she search the place and destroy every piece of paper that had any of my handwriting on it. I didn't want to leave any exemplars around for the FBI laboratory to use for comparison purposes—anything to slow them down. If we could get the President through the election, we'd be home free. Mrs. Harmony agreed and the FBI found nothing. The last thing she did as I left was offer to help in any way she could, and later on she was to be of invaluable assistance to Peter Maroulis, and, of course, to me. Sally Harmony is one loyal lady.

It was about noon, and I went to the office of Maurice Stans to say good-bye. By failing to inform him of my intelligence role I had, in effect, deceived him. I was now about to become infamous, and that would reflect unfavorably and unfairly upon him. Stans deserved better than that and I expected him to be furious and let me know it. Nothing of the sort happened. Maurice Stans has a temper, but he is also a most thoughtful and considerate man. Rather than chew me out he asked if I'd had lunch and, when I said I had not, he said, "Let's go."

The two of us took the elevator down to the lobby and got into his waiting Lincoln limousine. The driver made a U-turn and took us directly to the White House where Mr. Stans and I dined. He asked me no questions about Watergate and I volunteered nothing; his whole concern was for me and my family.

"Well," he asked, "what're you going to do now?"

"Keep my mouth shut and go to prison."

Stans shook his head sadly from side to side. "That shouldn't be necessary."

"Believe me, sir, it is."

Stans looked grim. His head continued its slow, negative shaking. "What about your family?"

"My wife works. She teaches school. It's not much, but it's something."

Stans looked angry. "Those people upstairs," he said, referring in his usual way to Magruder et al., "aren't worth it!"

I felt a great affection for Stans. Instead of justifiable recriminations he offered sympathy and support to one of his subordinates in trouble. Maurice Stans knew what loyalty meant, so I put it to him that way: "It's not for them. It's for the President. I've got just one asset left for the cause, but it's one no one can take away."

"What's that?"

"Balls."

Stans smiled. He was well supplied himself and knew what I meant. "Well," he said as we parted, "they won't forget you. I won't let them."

I understood him clearly. It was nothing so mundane as financial help. What Stans was talking about was a man's appreciation for another who behaves like a man, an acknowledgment that I had performed to standard and would be remembered by my peers as having done so.

Peter Maroulis flew down to see me right after the Fourth of July, and I arranged to do legal work for his practice in Poughkeepsie to earn some income. All we had was my severance pay; income from the rental of our home in Poughkeepsie; the $2,000 gift from LaRue; and Fran's modest salary as a schoolteacher in the District of Columbia. I told Peter and Fran that, on the basis of Dean's assurances on 19 June, he could expect his fee to be paid by the committee and I'd probably continue to receive my salary. Within a few days I heard more on the subject when the telephone rang and a voice that sounded vaguely familiar said: "Mr. Liddy?"

"Speaking."

"This is your publisher, Mr. Waters. I'm gonna publish your manuscript. I wanna talk to you about your royalties."

I became incensed. Legal fees and continuation of salary were one thing, but these people had somehow gotten the idea that I intended to sell them out and write a book. "Waters" was offering to pay me the same kind of money to keep quiet. It did not occur to me that this was just a continuation of the code theme used in conversations with Mrs. Hunt, whose husband was a writer. I was furious. "Wait a minute. You tell them I'll stand up no matter what! I'm not looking to make money . . ."

"Waters" cut me off. "I'm not involved in policy. All I do is deliver."

"Then deliver that message."

"I got somethin' to deliver to *you*. How soon can you get to National Airport?"

"This time of day, thirty minutes."

"Make it forty. What are you wearing?"

I described my sport shirt and the caller instructed me to enter Washington National Airport in exactly forty minutes by the Eastern Airlines entrance and walk straight ahead toward the observation area. On the left, as I walked down the steps, I'd find a suitcase with a locker key taped on its top. I was to take the key off the suitcase, go to the lockers to my right, and retrieve the package inside, then leave the premises immediately.

I did as instructed, found the key, but chose the wrong locker bank. I found the correct one quickly, removed the package, and took it home. In my bedroom I opened it up. It contained eighty one-hundred-dollar bills: $500 more than three months' salary.

I followed the case closely through the press. The three prosecutors assigned to the case were Earl Silbert, Seymour Glanzer, and Donald Campbell. Don Santarelli had introduced me to Silbert. He was polished, wore too much oil in his hair, and was obsequious in the presence of those he deemed more powerful or in higher authority. Glanzer I knew only by reputation: he was rough-cut, and had made it on sheer brains and an aggressive personality. Both were considered candidates to succeed to the office of United States Attorney. Silbert was the odds-on favorite: his diction was as polished as his hair, and he was a world-class ass-kisser. Glanzer, on the other hand, still had a heavy New York accent and wouldn't kiss ass; he preferred to kick it. Campbell I'd never heard of.

Chief Judge John J. Sirica I knew only by reputation as an embarrassment to the Republican Party. A political hack, he was one of the most reversed judges on the Washington bench.

On 20 July it was my turn before the grand jury. I could have pleaded the Fifth Amendment and that would have been that. Had I done so, however, the grand jury would have been able to proceed immediately with its investigation. With the election coming up in early November, every day counted. I decided to delay the grand jury as much as possible. To do that, and to have an accurate record of what questions I was asked and the answers I gave, I availed myself of the right to consult my attorney whenever I needed his advice. I'd listen to and answer a few questions, then go through an elaborate request to consult with counsel; leave once permission was granted formally; enter a small antechamber where Peter Maroulis and his law clerk were waiting with a tape recorder; dictate the previous questions and answers; consult with Peter on the latest question; return to the grand jury room after I'd stayed out as long as I thought I could (sometimes they'd get impatient and knock on the door) at which time the prosecutors, Silbert, Glanzer, or Campbell, would have to ask for the record whether I'd had an opportunity to consult with counsel and was now prepared to answer. I'd say I was and we'd start the whole process over again.

I had a few other tricks, too, that I'd learned while spending many an hour in a grand jury room as a prosecutor: whenever a grand juror had to leave to go to the rest room, I'd suggest the absence of a quorum. The prosecutors, sarcastically, made the mistake of inviting me to count the remaining jurors to establish for the record that there was still a quorum. I took them up on it and stood, counting slowly and methodically. Once, they asked me in exasperation to leave the room, and I refused, stating for the record that I wasn't through with my counting. When the grand jurors moaned at my tactics, I lectured them.

I argued with Glanzer about the meaning of "restricted" stock and anything else I could. When I didn't want to answer a question 1 invoked the attorney-client privilege, sometimes as the attorney and someimes as the client. When they went to the trouble of getting a release from the Committee to Re-elect, I objected on technical grounds and made them get individual releases from the subsidiary committees, signed by the appropriate officers. Finally, when they countered me by going to Sirica for a ruling that I was not entitled to invoke the attorney-client privilege, I invoked the Fifth Amendment, but not without first embarrassing Silbert before the grand jury.

I had gotten his goat by my tactics, and Silbert had made the mistake of telling Peter Maroulis that he was going to indict and convict me. I told the grand jury what Silbert had said, pointing out that he had done so without the investigation being completed and before they—the supposedly independent Watergate Grand Jury—ever had a chance to vote on it. He was treating them contemptuously, like a rubber stamp.

The prosecution then lied to the grand jurors by denying it, saying that all they had told Maroulis was that I was the "target" of the investigation, a perfectly proper notification. I pointed out to the grand jurors that I was under oath and challenged the prosecutors to repeat their denial under oath. They refused. But at the hearing before Sirica, Maroulis forced them to admit it. When I came back into the grand jury room to take the Fifth Amendment, I announced that the prosecutors had, in open court, admitted to what they had just denied to the grand jury. With that, I wished them all a pleasant day and left. I had tied up the Watergate Grand Jury for six precious days.

The prosecution countered by telling John Dean that I had "talked." It was another lie, and an old trick, but Dean, who was weak as well as inexperienced, fell for it. He figured I wouldn't be in front of the grand jury for six days saying nothing. He ultimately learned he was wrong.

While I was before the grand jury, Fran and I visited the Hunts at their Potomac, Maryland, home. I told them what I was doing in the grand jury and of my receipt of funds. Mrs. Hunt, a strong personality and the center of the Hunt family, was surprised to learn how little I had received, and Howard insisted on giving me $2,000 more from what they had received. We compared notes on the phone calls, noting the similarity of names between my "Mr. Waters" and their "Mr. Rivers." We decided they were identical. I received one more phone call from "Mr. Waters." It was to tell me that he was having difficulty, but he assured me that it would only be temporary and he'd call again soon. I never heard from him again.

It was during one of my several meetings with the Hunts

in their Potomac home that Howard took me aside to tell me that in the event our "principals" changed their minds again and wanted us out of the country with our families— or we should decide the matter for ourselves—both families could be provided temporary safety among the Cuban community in Florida long enough for a Nicaraguan National Guard transport aircraft to slip in quietly and fly us all out to sanctuary on Corn Island, courtesy of the Somoza family. I told him I would keep it in mind but would use it only if in fact we were directed to leave the country. Later, in the D.C. jail, Hunt tried to interest me in a joint venture with him and the Somozas, after we were free, to develop part of Corn Island in the Caribbean Sea.

Sometime later Dorothy Hunt asked me whether I'd ever received anything more from "Waters." When I replied that I hadn't, she said that they must have decided to cut down on the risk by dealing solely with her. She said she was unhappy with the arrangement because while she was perfectly content to take care of matters for me and the Cubans, McCord was acting strangely on the phone and she didn't trust him. She gave me $19,000, and I insisted upon returning the $2,000 pressed on me earlier. Howard and I laughed, calling it "the floating deuce." I went downstairs with Howard to his writing office, which was replete with his OSS "Fairbairn" fighting knife, a rare American Eagle-model Luger in .30 caliber, and other trophies of his clandestine past. There I gave him some technical advice about the caliber of a firearm he was describing in his latest novel and, over brandies, he expressed his reservations about the manner in which the financial commitments were being met. I thought him overly concerned because he was contrasting the performance of our principals with that of the professionals of the CIA. Hunt was disturbed further by his wife's reservations about the behavior of James McCord. I left concerned about Hunt.

My family and I kept the same telephone number. It was listed in the book and reporters often tried to interview me. I responded with a polite no comment, but the burden really fell upon Fran; I was spending a lot of time back in Poughkeepsie practicing law.

Edward Bennett William took my deposition in the civil suit by the DNC but I gave him nothing. Then, on 15 September, what we all knew was coming finally arrived. I, along with Howard Hunt, Jim McCord, and the Cuban men of the entry team, was indicted by the Watergate Grand Jury.

XXIV

Nikons clanked and Leicas whispered in the hands of backward-scuttling photographers while swarms of reporters, like so many Middle Eastern street vendors hustling microphones, milled around us as I made my way with Peter Maroulis into the United States Courthouse at the foot of Capitol Hill for my arraignment on 19 September.

The proceedings were held in John Sirica's courtroom. I was charged with two counts of burglary, two of intercepting wire communications, one of intercepting oral communications, and the one all-important charge of "conspiracy." The latter meant little more than planning to do the former, but it is always included by prosecutors when possible to deprive the defendant of much of the protection against use of mere hearsay as evidence. I used to do the same thing.

John Sirica, then Chief Judge by virtue of seniority, had assigned the case to himself only the day before, and I wanted to get a look at him. The proceedings were over so quickly, however, that all I could tell was that he was short and squat with a tendency to play to the press. My mother put up the required 10 percent of my $10,000 bail and after greeting my codefendants warmly, signing a few papers, and checking the reporting requirements with the probation office, I surrendered my official passport to the clerk of the court and went home. I recalled having read something about Sirica a few years before in *Washingtonian* magazine. It had long since been discarded but I found a copy of the September 1970 issue in the library. In an article on the Washington judiciary, Harvey Katz had reported on Sirica's careless, slipshod performance on the bench. He gave the examples of cases where Sirica was reversed:

> . . . he is reversed for the most incredible reasons. In one case, he ordered the suit transferred to the federal district court in Minnesota without having first determined whether suit could have been brought there. I was in court when he considered a similar matter. The defendant was seeking a transfer of the case to Houston, claiming that most of the witnesses were there. Plaintiff contended that there were as many witnesses and documents in Washington and New Orleans, and that the case should remain here. "All right, all right," Sirica said. "The case is transferred to New Orleans." Both lawyers had to tell him that no one wanted the case tried there. "Well, Houston, then," Sirica said. "Or wherever."

"Boy," I said to Peter Maroulis, "we drew some judge— a bookthrower with the intellect of half a glass of water."

"Count your blessings," said Peter. I knew what he meant: the combination of Sirica's ill temper, little education, and carelessness increased the chances for reversible error considerably, and that was the only chance we had. It didn't really matter though; trial was set for 15 November, and that was *after* the election.

Fran was now back at work teaching and I spent as much time as possible practicing law in Poughkeepsie. Sirica had postponed the trial to January. I kept in touch with the Hunts. They were becoming more and more dissatisfied with the way commitments to all of us were being handled. When they asked me to attend, with Peter

374

Maroulis, a meeting at the home of their counsel William Bittman, I thought perhaps they had another delivery of funds to make that would include counsel fees. I hoped so, because I had received nothing since the net $17,000 from the Hunts, and I had given that, plus the $500 I'd received over and above my three months' salary from "Mr. Waters" to Peter as a down payment on his fee.

The meeting took place on Monday evening, 27 November. Peter Maroulis and I arrived early and had a scotch with Bittman and his partner, Austin Mitler, as we waited in the den for the Hunts, who lived about a mile away.

When Howard and Dorothy Hunt arrived, it was Dorothy who appeared to be in charge although Howard did the talking. Every few words he would glance over at his wife, as if for reassurance and approval of what he was saying. He began by remarking the obvious: our principals' financial aid program, administered fitfully at best, could no longer be relied upon. The Cuban families in particular were in severe distress, and Howard was embarrassed because he couldn't keep his promises to them. He, too, was in distress because of legal fees, and McCord was acting so strangely he might well be off the reservation. All this had been made known to their contact to no avail, and now a recent approach to Howard's old comrade, Chuck Colson, had been unfruitful.

I listened to all this calmly, wondering where it would lead, when Hunt announced, "It seems to me it's now 'every man for himself,'" and he went on rapidly to suggest that the two of us collaborate on a book about our activities on behalf of the White House and reelection committee. "I'd say the bidding should start," he said, selling hard, "at five hundred thousand."

The enormity of what the Hunts were proposing took my breath away; but before I could speak, Dorothy Hunt read my face and said, "Howard, I think we'd better tell him."

Hunt nodded in assent as I asked, "Tell me what?"

Dorothy answered. "Howard and I gave you that money

from our own, because we knew how badly you needed it. None of that delivery was for you. There has never been a *cent* for you."

I was furious—not because my erstwhile superiors had apparently decided to abandon me. I had made it clear to "Mr. Waters" that my silence could be counted upon in any event, and they might understandably have taken the position that because my error of judgment had caused all the trouble in the first place I didn't deserve assistance. What infuriated me was the Hunts' bland assumption that my loyalty *was* conditional upon the receipt of money. I took a deep breath and said, "Howard, I came to Washington to do something for my country that needed to be done and I did it. I did what I did because I *believed* in it. I *still* believe in it. We won the election and Richard Nixon's got four more years to straighten this country out, and I won't be a party to *anything* that could change that. I don't know why there's been nothing for me and I don't care—" I stared at the others in the room. Only Peter was still looking at me levelly; the rest were looking down at the floor. "I just want everyone in this room to understand one thing: *I am not for sale!*"

With that I rose and, Peter following, walked out of the meeting. I never saw Dorothy Hunt again; on 10 December United Flight 553 crashed at Midway Airport in Chicago, carrying her to her death.

The directions I received to get to the funeral were poor, and by the time I found it the services were nearly over. I pulled my Jeep into the motorcade to the cemetery and sought out Howard to offer my condolences. He was obviously grief-stricken, but his years of clandestine training did not desert him. As an old CIA hand approached, Hunt glanced about and, seeing many persons close by and within earshot, he introduced us to each other loudly and elaborately, although the three of us had worked together in the past.

Fran went out of her way to make memorable what we

expected to be our last Christmas together as a family for a long time, and Peter gave me his airplane to use as I wished before the trial. I spent my last days of freedom really free: alone, high in the sky where I feel most at home.

Right after New Year's Day 1973, I was approached for an interview by a member of the staff of the Senate Commerce Committee. Bud Krogh had been nominated for Under Secretary of Commerce and the staff was preparing for his confirmation hearings. I was concerned. Were I to be placed under oath before the Senate and asked everything about my working relationship with Krogh, I would be presented with the dilemma of an oath to tell the truth on one hand and the national security of the United States on the other. The only way out would be a refusal to testify and that could only damage, if not destroy, Krogh's chances of confirmation. Were I merely to refuse to be interviewed, a clever antagonist might be able to use that, too, against Krogh. The decision, I thought, should be Krogh's. I called him at his office and was told he was out. That annoyed me. I was annoyed about something else, too, and went to see Paul O'Brien about it.

In O'Brien's office I told the counsel to the Committee to Re-elect the President that I understood the necessity for the circulation of negative stories about me in the press because I was taking the weight for Watergate and the official position that I, a Law Review graduate, former FBI supervisor, army officer, Wall Street lawyer, prosecutor, and White House aide, had gone off on my own without authority and masterminded Watergate to my employer's unwitting embarrassment wouldn't be easy to sell to the experienced Washington press corps. They had bought it because of the "wild man" image concocted from highly colored and exaggerated versions of some of my past activities; but some of the stories had no basis in fact at all and I told O'Brien I thought they were going too far. The trial was just days off; I'd be convicted, and there just wasn't any reason to continue.

O'Brien wanted to know what I was referring to specifically. I told him that a recently criticized speech I'd given to the National Rifle Association had been authorized, with content that was just a recapitulation of administration policy. I said the story to the contrary probably originated as "payback" from Rossides and Walker rather than the committee. The story that I was asked to resign from the FBI was also without foundation. I had, in fact, been told specifically by Section Chief M. A. Jones that my file was marked "eligible for rehire." As I continued to list the nonsense, such as the story that I had fired 2,000 rounds of .38 Special ammunition into the dining room wall of my home in Poughkeepsie, O'Brien cut me off with: "Well, at the trial we're going to have to knock you around a bit."

I knew Magruder would be testifying as I said, "You better control Magruder. That sonofabitch . . ."

"We have a problem with Magruder," O'Brien interrupted. "Every time we talk to him we get a different story. We don't know *what* he's going to say."

I could believe that and left the subject with "Tell him to watch his mouth. I'll be there." Then I brought up the fact that Krogh wouldn't talk to me and explained my problem. O'Brien promised to look into it and I left.

Intense preparations for the trial were going on that week. Peter Maroulis had taken an apartment in Washington, and I spent my time there or in one attorney's office or another as we sought to coordinate seven defendants.

On Thursday, 4 January, I was told I had a phone call. I took it and found it was Sandra Greene, Bud Krogh's secretary. "Hello, Gordon; I've talked with Bud and he really regrets he can't talk to you at this time because of the confirmation hearings coming up—but he hopes you would not talk to Mr. Sutcliffe (the Senate investigator who was seeking the interview) in light of the impending case. Bud believes that Sutcliffe doesn't expect a return call from you."

"O.K. Thank you very much."

That gave me the decision I wanted and I hung up. Apparently the fact I hadn't engaged in any small talk with Mrs. Greene, whom I knew, led Bud to conclude that I was offended because on Saturday, 6 January, two days before the trial was to start, I received a telephone call while in my bedroom: "Gordon, I think you'll recognize my voice."

I did. It was John Dean.

"First off, I want to tell you that Bud's really sorry he couldn't talk to you himself. It's just that with his confirmation hearing coming up, he wants to be able to testify truthfully that he hasn't spoken to you in the past year. You understand. He's really a good friend of yours and wishes you well."

"I understand perfectly. Please tell him that."

"I will. And Gordon, I want to assure you; everyone's going to be taken care of—everyone."

"Oh?" Dean was repeating almost verbatim his assurances of 19 June, but now he went into detail.

"Absolutely. First, you'll receive living expenses of thirty thousand per annum. Second, you'll have a pardon within two years. Three, we'll see to it you're sent to Danbury Prison; and fourth, your legal fees will be paid."

Boy, I thought, with the trial only forty-eight hours away, they're not taking any chances. I was pleased to receive these assurances, but on top of the bumbling performance of "Mr. Waters" or "Mr. Rivers" or whoever he was, I wasn't counting any chickens. I sought to pin Dean down: "You said, 'pardon.' You know the difference between a pardon and a 'commutation'?"

"I do, and it's 'pardon.'"

"Well, that's good to hear. But times change and things sometimes become difficult, so I want you all to remember two things. First, if it comes to a choice between continuing my salary and paying my legal fees, pay the legal fees. Peter's my friend and anything else would be unfair to him. More important, I want it understood there's no *quid pro quo* here. I'll keep quiet no matter what."

"I know that, Gordon, but I'll pass it along."

"O.K. And tell them to watch; I'll show them how to die."

I hung up the phone, picked up a felt-tipped pen, and wrote a note:

1. Living Expenses
   $30,000 per annum

2. Pardon within
   2 years

3. Danbury Prison

4. Legal Fees

On Monday morning, 8 January, Fran dropped me off at Peter's southwest Washington apartment on her way to work. I gave him the note. He studied it and said, "Interesting. What's the story?" I told him of John Dean's Saturday phone call and he handed the note back to me and said, "Better make a note of that, too."

On the bottom of the note I wrote, "Dean by phone to me at home" and gave it back to Peter. He still has it in his files.

The trial was to start at 10 A.M. with selection of the jury. Peter and I arrived early in case and we were delayed by the huge crowd of reporters and cameramen swarming around the side entrance to the courthouse. Inside, GSA guards checked our briefcases, something I thought quite reasonable at a time when the left was bombing the Capitol of the United States, universities, banks and just about everything else but the YWCA.

The ceremonial courtroom seethed with hostile humanity. It was payback time for the left and the seats were full for the show trial. We all knew it would be impossible in that atmosphere for there to be anything remotely resembling a fair trial, but that gave us one more chance for error in the crucial *voir dire*—the choosing of a jury.

Voir dire is the process of examining the prospective jurors to ensure that no one is chosen who cannot serve competently, durably, and impartially. In federal practice the judge conducts the *voir dire*, with an eye toward screening out those who, for example, for reasons of hardship could not be sequestered for the many weeks the trial might take, or who, after being exposed to pretrial publicity, already have an opinion about guilt or innocence.

Sirica started out on the right foot. He called Peter and the other counsel to a bench conference and said: "What I expect to do as to those two major points is go into my conference room with the attorneys seated around the table and call each one of those jurors in separately where we can talk to them informally, you understand, on the question of sequestration, hardships, things like that; any opinion they might have. I can do it at the bench but it is a little more comfortable if we do it in the conference room . . . sometime a prospective juror will talk more freely out of hearing of the other prospective jurors. . . . It might take a little longer but we have to be patient, we want to get a juror that will give all the defendants and the government a fair trial."

"Looks like we're in trouble," I said to Peter. "He's doing it right by the book. Either he's smarter than he gets credit for, or he's getting damn good advice."

"Looks that way," Peter agreed.

We were wrong. We were in trouble, all right, but not because Sirica went by the book. Addressing the problem of sequestration he did do it right. It was an all-day process, but he carefully interrogated each juror separately in the conference room, giving every one a chance to admit if the long separation from his or her personal life would be an unendurable hardship.

Toward the end of the day Sirica moved on to the question of pretrial publicity. The potential impact of the massive pretrial press coverage was crucial to the question of a fair trial. As McCord's lawyer Gerald Alch put it: ". . . on the area of exposure to publicity which has been, as Your Honor knows, most substantial in this case, the perfect example was yesterday when a witness came up— a juror came up—and acknowledge (*sic*) he had read something in the newspaper. Then the court asked him a question: has what you read caused you to form an opinion? And he answered no. But then on a very simple follow-up Mr. Rothblatt [the Cubans' lawyer] asked the potential juror: after reading what you read do you expect the defendants to come forward and prove what you read was false? He said yes. Which of course in my opinion disqualifies him."

So we all agreed—even the government—that individual interrogation of the jurors be pursued. During the rest of the day Sirica questioned four jurors, and three were dismissed.

The following morning Sirica began by telling counsel he wanted to stop individual conference-room questioning on publicity. "It is time-consuming and I don't think it is going to do a lot of good."

After both government and defense protested, Sirica agreed to go on with individual questioning—and did so for eight more jurors. Then over the objection of the defense, he declared that the rest of the *voir dire* would be conducted from the bench. Whereupon he asked all ninety-four jurors at once: "Are there any, among you seated in the courtroom now, you prospective jurors, who have heard anything about the case before you came into the courtroom yesterday? When I say have you heard anything about the case I include of course anything you may have heard about the case over the radio, television, or read about it in the newspapers, or anything you may have heard by word of mouth, whether you have heard it recently or whether you have heard it at an earlier time or any time?"

Sirica continued, "That is a very broad question. Now if your answer is yes, please stand."

All but three rose. Sirica looked unbelievingly at the three who remained seated and said to one of them: "You didn't read about it, hear about it on the radio, never heard about the Watergate case?"

"No."

"All right," said Sirica. "Incredible!"

The judge then turned to the ninety-one who'd said they'd read or heard about the case. He asked them en masse if they'd formed any opinions about guilt or innocence. When three responded that they had, they were dismissed. He asked the eighty-eight remaining if any couldn't ignore what they'd read, and no one responded this time. He asked if anyone had a "fairly clear recollection of the detail of the matters." None raised a hand. Thus the en masse questioning went on, with very few raising a hand, knowing, in effect, it meant exclusion from the jury. In the end eight were interrogated for one thing or another, from the bench.

The result of all this was that of the twelve jurors selected, only one had been individually examined. Defense requested individual *voir dire* on the other eleven at that point, noting it was counsel's first opportunity even to see the jurors, let alone talk to them. All defense knew about the jurors was each one's name and employment. The motion was denied. The jurors were sworn in.

So much for concern about the effects of pretrial publicity in one of the most widely publicized affairs in this country since World War II.

As an experienced criminal trial lawyer I was aware of the significance of what we were seeing. It is the key to what everyone in that courtroom observed was my attitude toward the trial: it was to be a farce.

Just as I do, John Sirica believes the end justifies the means, and in the Watergate trial he put that philosophy into practice. I certainly could not then and can not now quarrel with that. The difference between us is that I admit it openly and don't pretend to be anything other than what I am.

Sirica knuckled under to the politicians when they protested his ban on pretrial talk by the parties prior to trial, and, when *Washington Post* reporters Carl Bernstein and Robert Woodward were caught trying to subvert the grand jury by interviewing members concerning testimony, he knuckled under to the *Post*'s powerful lawyer, Edward Bennett Williams. Sirica says self-righteously in his book that he ". . . settled on a stiff lecture in open court." Baloney. He never even identified Woodward and Bernstein. In the course of that "stiff lecture in open court" he *never even mentioned their names*.

The trial itself got under way and suddenly (to the public, not to me; I had heard it was coming) Hunt and the Cubans pleaded guilty to all the charges against them. Sirica began questioning the defendants, and I laughed openly as he interrogated Eugenio Martinez. Martinez is a highly intelligent man who was a hotel and hospital owner in Cuba, and when Sirica went into his Junior G-man act, Martinez went into his "pardon-me-for-talking-in-your-face-Señor" Frito Bandito routine. It was just too much.

Because this had taken place outside the presence of the jury, and because the jurors had been sequestered—locked up in a hotel without access to news and guarded by U.S. marshals—they could only speculate on the implications when, upon returning to the courtroom, they found that more than two-thirds of the defendants had vanished. Although it wasn't hard for them to guess, and they were admonished to think nothing of it, were word to get through to them of what had happened and that got on the record, it would be grounds for a mistrial. There followed one of the most astonishing incidents in the Watergate trial, an event that has remained a secret all these years.

Following the five guilty pleas, the prosecution started

introducing its evidence, then court recessed for the day. Before proceedings resumed the next day of trial, Peter and the other attorneys were called into conference by Sirica. When it was over, Peter, his voice reflecting his astonishment and unbelief, told me what had happened. At about nine o'clock that morning one of the jurors had spoken on the telephone to his wife, and it was feared he might have learned about the guilty pleas from her and revealed them to other jurors. Had that happened, there would have been a mistrial. The one juror could always be excused and replaced by an alternate, but there were only six alternates. If the word had gotten to all twelve on the jury, that trial was over.

Sirica, properly concerned, did the correct thing. He ordered all counsel and the court reporter into the conference room so that he could interrogate the juror himself and establish for the record exactly what had happened. When everyone was settled in the conference room and the court reporter had his machine set up, he began his questioning. There was only one problem: Sirica and the juror couldn't communicate. They didn't understand each other.

In his haste to eliminate the possibility of individual questioning of the jury panel on the issue of pretrial publicity, Sirica had seated as a juror a man who could barely speak or understand the English language! The situation was so bad, Peter said, that Sirica had to ask the Cubans' lawyer, Henry Rothblatt, who speaks fluent Spanish, to act as interpreter.

Speaking in Spanish, Rothblatt was able to determine that although the juror had indeed been told of the guilty plea by his wife, he had not mentioned it to any other jurors. He was excused immediately and an alternate seated in his place.

John Sirica was now faced with a terribly embarrassing problem. Should it become known that he had, after all those objections from the defense, mishandled the *voir dire* examination to the extent that he'd put on the jury a man he'd had to use an interpreter to talk to, but who would have been expected to listen to, understand, and apply serious and lengthy instructions on the law from Sirica himself at the end of the trial—to say nothing of all the complex testimony about telephone transmitters, oscilloscopes, band-spreaders, and the like—he would stand exposed for the incredibly careless practitioner *Washingtonian* magazine had branded him two years before. Were the stakes not so high and the situation so serious, it would have been laughable, something one would expect in a Marx Brothers movie, not a United States District Court. He had to do something to save himself. Fast.

John Sirica was equal to this challenge to his threadbare reputation. He used his power as a judge to *seal the record* of everything that had transpired with respect to that entire incident. It remains officially a secret to this day; the record of this portion of the trial is still sealed. Because I knew I was going to be convicted anyway, I was able to see the humor in the incident and I laughed at it and Sirica openly in court. I really had to hand it to the old goat; neither one of us ever hesitated to use power. If the judge disputes my account of this event, I challenge him to unseal that suppressed part of the record and end his own "cover-up."

The trial went on, and I observed the prosecutors closely with a professional eye, developing a grudging admiration for Seymour Glanzer. Time and time again, as Silbert Uriah Heeped his way through the trial, every other word to Sirica modified with a fawning "if the court please" until everyone was sick of it, Glanzer would pull on his coattail, whisper in his ear, and steer him from the brink of error. No question about it, Glanzer was a hell of a lawyer. Campbell was quietly competent. Together they saved Silbert.

Sirica plunged ahead. He swallowed the perjury of Jeb Magruder whole but wouldn't believe poor Hugh Sloan who was doing his best to tell the truth. As the prosecution questioned Sloan, Peter became concerned about where a particular line of questions was leading and asked for a conference at the bench, which was, of course, out of the hearing of the jury. He asked if the prosecution were leading up to asking a question about a concern of Sloan's that might have violated the new election laws—a crime not mentioned in the indictment and therefore prejudicial and completely inadmissible. Silbert admitted that was exactly what he was leading up to. Peter objected and Sirica, correctly, upheld the objection immediately and forbade any mention to the jury of the possible crime not mentioned in the indictment.

When the prosecution had completed its examination of Sloan, Sirica sent the jury out and grilled him himself. Then, the following day, he brought the jury in and read the transcript, not only of his examination of Sloan, but of the private bench conference, *including the discussion, objections, and ruling concerning the crime not mentioned in the indictment that he had held should be kept from the jury only the day before.*

I was astonished. "Peter," I said, "I can't believe what just happened."

"Count your blessings," said Peter Maroulis. When court recessed I was elated at the error, and when Bob Woodward tried to interview me about it outside the courtroom, I said, "They've just lost their Queen," a reference to the damage the loss of that piece in chess entailed. Carl Bernstein was also a constant presence. I never gave either of them information, but I liked Bernstein; he was scruffy but impressed me as sincere. Woodward was stuffy. He had tried to interview my friend John Martin of the Internal Security Division about me, and Martin had declined comment.

"Nobody turns down Bob Woodward," huffed the newly baptized member of the Beautiful People.

"Well, then," said Martin, "let me be the first."

During the trial Spencer Oliver, the one whose phone we successfully bugged, enlisted the aid of the American

Civil Liberties Union, in the person of its Washington representative, attorney Charles Morgan, to intervene in the trial to block disclosure of what had been overheard on his telephone. Morgan and Peter Maroulis became good friends and, when Morgan obviously shared our opinion of the way Sirica was conducting the trial, Peter asked Morgan if he could get ACLU support for the defense. Morgan told Peter that the decision wasn't his, that the ACLU would have to authorize it; then he commented that although the situation was just the kind to interest the ACLU, there was no point in even asking. "If it was anyone but Gordon Liddy," said Morgan, "but not for him."

And so it went. The outcome was a foregone conclusion, and when Fran dropped me off at the corner by the courthouse on Tuesday morning, 30 January 1973, she held me and gave me an extra long kiss. I got out of the car and leaned inside.

"Take it easy, kid," I said, then closed the door and walked away as she drove off to work.

The verdict was guilty. Sirica set my bail at $100,000—cash—and refused to let me stay free pending any appeal for reduction, ordering me jailed immediately. The marshal led me behind the bench to a rear door that opened into a small holding cell and locked me in. I'd been in them many times before, interviewing suspects for the FBI or clients I was defending. This one, at least, was clean. The marshal left and I was alone.

In a few minutes the marshal was back with Peter Maroulis. We had expected this from the beginning, but I was his best friend and he had defended me—with both hands tied—and I could see that he was struggling to control his emotions. I gave him my wallet and wristwatch to give to Fran. We embraced, then I told him to quit wasting time and get working on the notice of appeal. The marshal came back in and it was time to go. As he led me to the small elevator that led to the underground detention enter, Peter called after me, "Hang in there, man!" I grinned at him.

"*Gha mautau stravrau su!*" I said, and stepped into the elevator. (Effectively untranslatable, it's the ultimate insult in Greek.)

The marshal seemed puzzled as the little steel box descended in its shaft, possibly because I was smiling. *Erica must think I'm scared to death right now,* I said to myself. What the old fool didn't know was that sending me into his crummy prison system was like the Germans sealing Lenin into a boxcar and shipping him into Russia. I chuckled out loud at the thought and the marshal looked startled. One of the most interesting times of my life had begun.

XXV

In the antiseptic basement of the courthouse in Washington, U.S. marshals maintain an office and miniature jail. There are small cells and larger "tanks." All are equipped with a steel bench molded into the glazed brick wall and a seatless toilet (one sits on the rim) with a water fountain built into the top. I was placed alone in a small cell. There I took off my suitcoat, turned it inside out, folded it into a pillow, and stretched out on the steel bench for a nap.

At the end of the court day, when all the defendants being held in the District of Columbia jail had been returned to the basement, we were brought into a room and required to undergo a "strip search." I was familiar with the routine from my own police work. We stripped, placed our clothing in neat piles where we could keep a wary eye on it, and stood naked in two lines before a pair of marshals.

As each man's turn came the marshal would command: "Arms up," at which the man being searched would lift his arms to show that he had nothing concealed under them; "Hands through your hair," directing a rough combing motion through one's hair to dislodge anything hidden there; "Lift your stick," and one raised one's penis to show there was nothing there; "Balls," raised in turn for the same purpose; "Turn around and spread 'em," and the searched man turned his back to the marshal, leaned forward and spread his buttocks with his hands to display his anus; finally, "Lift 'em," and each foot was raised in turn to display its sole.

We redressed and lined up again. A marshal fitted a "belly chain" around each prisoner's waist leaving a link in front. The prisoner was then handcuffed, with the cuff chain slipped through the belt chain link. All of us were then led out into the underground garage and loaded into a bus that had been modified by having heavy steel mesh welded over all the windows and a steel mesh barrier with a padlocked door placed between the prisoner seating area and the driver and guard area in the front. An electric motor rolled the garage door overhead, and the bus drove off to southeast Washington. A few minutes later I got my first look at the D.C. jail.

In 1973 the District of Columbia Asylum and Jail, to give it its correct name, was 104 years old. It was built of brick and steel. From a five-story-high rotunda, cellblocks reached out in opposite directions. It served as a state penitentiary for the District of Columbia. It was not merely a holding place for accused persons; there were sentenced men there, including those doing life or awaiting death in the electric chair situated conveniently in the "penthouse" on the roof. The previous summer there had been violent riots when the temperature inside exceeded 105 degrees for days on end. The place was in such a state of neglect, disrepair, overcrowding, and filth that a lawsuit was pending to have it declared unfit for human habitation and, indeed, after I left it for the last time, the officials in charge of it admitted that it was *not* fit for human habitation. It was so ruled and condemned by the courts and has since been for the most part torn down.

The bus pulled up to a wire-mesh gate at the rear of

he prison. The horn was blown, the gate swung open
lectrically, and the bus eased into a courtyard befouled
vith pigeon droppings that had accumulated for a century.
'urtive cats hunting the ever present rats and mice darted
side as the bus emptied. Prisoners called to their friends
s we lined up to be admitted inside: "Hey, Leroy! Mova-
ucks gotcha 'gan, huh?"

"Yeah, bum beef, man."

"I know whatcha talkin' bou'. You seen Marybelle?
Vhat that bitch doin'?"

In here, people were all neighbors and it was like old
ome week. I couldn't understand most of what was being
aid. It was all in black dialect, and I didn't speak it. (I
ave since, of necessity, become fluent.)

The entry procedure was careful. A door opened elec-
rically and a marshal entered the jail with our "paper-
vork": orders of commitment without which no one would
e admitted any more than he would be released without
he appropriate writ. That done, we were admitted to
n antechamber where, once the door was closed and
ocked behind us, a marshal released us from our chains
nd handcuffs. James McCord was the only other white
nan in the group. A marshal positioned himself by the
;ate and, as our names were called alphabetically, we
vould step to the gate, be frisked by the marshal, and
ermitted to enter yet another antechamber; this one
ormed a hallway along the outside of "control," the
entral nervous system of the prison that housed the
urveillance television monitors and the all-important
'count" figures, the number of bodies for which the watch
:ommander would be held responsible upon his relief at
he change of shift.

Since *L* and *M* are next to each other in the alphabet,
AcCord and I were admitted to the antechamber almost
ogether. We stepped up to the window of "control,"
vhere a guard had our commitment papers and a photograph. He checked our identities visually and nodded us
over toward the benches along the opposite wall. We sat

and waited for all the men to go through the same pro
cedure.

When all of us were inside the second antechamber, a
guard appeared at the other end, behind an electrically
operated sliding steel-barred gate. The gate slid open and
the guard led us down a long hallway to another locked
door. A buzzer was pushed and that door opened. We
marched a few yards to yet another locked door. It was
opened and we were admitted to another bench-filled
antechamber. There we waited as once again our names
were to be called.

We were now at a stock feature of every prison in the
country; "R&D" for Receiving and Discharge. A guard
appeared and called out: "Any man who slept here last
night, line up over here!" That was to move out those men
who were already assigned cells and were just returning
from a court appearance.

When the regulars had been admitted, it was the turn
of the new prisoners. We were called in, alphabetically,
one by one. The concrete floor was painted with markings
resembling those for street traffic control. It was very hot.
We were in a basement area, and steam, water, and waste
pipes ran overhead so low it was sometimes necessary to
duck under them. To the left the floor marking directed
one to a small island where a prisoner trusty took inked
fingerprint impressions. We then moved along to another
station where we deposited and were issued a receipt for
any valuables. From there one undressed, deposited, and
was issued a receipt for his civilian clothing worn into
prison. Nearby there were two yellow feet painted on the
floor; the position from which one went through the strip
search routine once again.

To the right and down stairs was a steamy subbasement
where we were each issued a towel, a bar of old-fashioned
yellow lye soap, and a sheet and a blanket which we rolled
together. Then we proceeded to the showers.

Once through the delousing spray, each of us was issued
a set of clean but ragged underwear, blue work shirt, and

pair of denim dungarees. Neither of the latter fit, nor were they new. They were, however, laundered. The trusties all wore new, well-tailored shirts and dungarees. For the going rate of cartons ("boxes") of Kool cigarettes (the brand preferred by blacks in that prison above all others) one could, I learned later, have tailored clothing or anything else; drugs; a "fuck boy" or "punk" for homosexual gratification; home-brewed alcohol; a weapon; or, for two cartons of Kools, one's enemy murdered.

Once dressed in prison garb, we reported to a bench table behind which sat one of the few literate trusties. He had a typewriter and a general information form:

"Whatcha name?"

"Where ya live onna street?" (address)

"Whatcha do onna street?" (occupation)

"Whatcha make onna street?" (highest hourly wage)

This went on to include the name and address of the closest relative to be notified in the event of "emergency" —very practical; people were always being killed or maimed—and other basic information. The trusty had a tough time with me because it was difficult for us to communicate. It took some time, for example, for me to learn that he wanted to know how much money I earned, and he couldn't cope with an annual figure; the form didn't provide for anything but an hourly wage. So I gave him what I charged when last I'd practiced law—a hundred dollars an hour—and he didn't believe me. We passed that and went on to:

"How long wuzjhu 'n skoo?" By which I finally figured out he wanted to know the extent of my education. When I told him I had a doctorate in law he couldn't handle that either. The form was designed to record only years of schooling, so I added it up for him and answered "twenty." He looked at me as if I were some sort of god and then immediately accepted the figure of a hundred dollars an hour as my earning rate. Finally he figured out who I was. He screwed up his features and asked: "You Watagate?"

"Right."

"You Liddy?"

"Right again."

"You really know Nixon?"

"Yup."

My interrogator shook his head in wonderment, and I moved on to the next station where I was photographed, front and profile, with the date and my new D.C. jail number.

Processing completed, we were led through more labyrinthine locked doors, stairs, and passageways up to a small mess hall. It was lighted dimly. We received a starchy meal that I consumed quickly because the hours-long process of getting out of the basement in the courthouse and into the D.C. jail had left me quite hungry. The experience was proving fascinating. The meal consumed, we were led to our assigned places of confinement.

For McCord and me it was Cellblock 1. We approached the steel door that led to it from the small cellblock control room, where a guard sat before a wallboard maintaining his count, and the door swung open to admit us.

As it did there burst from behind a wave of high-pressure sound. The five-story interior of the cellblock, four rows of human cages jammed two or three to a cage stacked vertically on one side of an open floor, and an equally high brick wall on the other side created a huge cavern through which shouts, screams, screeches, and moans echoed and reechoed into an unintelligible roar like that of a stadium crowd following a touchdown in some hellish arena from the imagination of Dante.

McCord and I were led down the catwalk of the first tier. The shower area came first, then the individual cages. These were the "deadlock" cells; one stayed in them twenty-four hours a day, being fed through an opening in the door wide enough to admit a metal tray. Once a week one was permitted a quick shower under guard. Anti-white racial remarks followed us from the depths of the cages as we passed them. They were not meant for us as

394

individuals; I don't believe the wretched denizens of those filthy holes had any idea who we were; it was enough that we were of the hated white race—something rarely seen in the D.C. cellblocks.

We were assigned the last cell on the first tier. It was opposite a stairway leading upward to the other rows of cages. The barred door slid open automatically, we entered, and the door slid shut behind us with a clank.

There was a double bunk in the 6' × 8½' cell. It left us little room. A metal desk and seat were welded to the wall. Like the walls themselves and the low ceiling, it was solid steel covered by some fifty coats of paint applied over a century of time. At the rear was a basin from which water could be drawn at the heavy push of either of two spring-loaded metal buttons, and in the corner was a solid ceramic toilet without seat. From a recess near the ceiling on the back wall glowed a feeble light bulb. A roll of toilet paper sat on the metal desk. Two thin mattresses lay on the wire network of the double-bunk frames. Most of the springs were missing and the wire was secured to the frame for the most part by twisted pieces of scrap that seemed to have been salvaged from old coat hangers.

McCord and I surveyed our new home. He had been here before, of course, from the time of his arrest until release on bail. He was older than I, so I suggested he take the lower bunk and he accepted it gratefully. We made up our beds one at a time to keep out of each other's way.

"Is it always this noisy?" I asked McCord.

"It quiets down about two o'clock in the morning. Breakfast is about 4:30, then everyone goes back to sleep until about eight. Then they turn on the radios and televisions."

"The what?"

"That's where a lot of the noise comes from. Look up there. See them?"

McCord was at the bars in the front of the tiny cell. He made room for me and I looked up toward where he was pointing, at the five-story brick wall. In the space between the dirty translucent windows I saw a brown television set and a loudspeaker I had noticed when I entered.

"You can't see them all from here," said McCord, "there're four televisions; so everyone, no matter which end of the tier or how high up, can see at least one of them. Same thing with the radio speakers. The speakers are all on the same station, some local black music thing. Unless there's basketball or something, the televisions are usually on four different channels. Makes it impossible to understand what's being said unless you're directly across from one, and even then it's hard. Just adds to all the noise. Everything's turned up to maximum gain."

Over the steady roar McCord and I agreed that we might have been placed in the same cell so our conversation could be monitored by a bug. We agreed not to mention anything about Watergate that occurred before the trial. McCord started to exercise, running in place at the front of the cell. I was tired. I mounted to the top bunk, took off my dungarees and shirt, folded them into a crude pillow (none was provided), stretched out, and pulled the blanket over me loosely. Through the bars I could see the stairwell directly across the catwalk from me. On it a piece of paper was Scotch-taped. It was hand-lettered crudely with a broad, black Magic Marker and read:

ALL YOU NIGGERS

GOT BOWELS

BRING EM BACK

I was wondering what that was all about when I fell asleep.

I awoke at what must have been after 2 A.M., because it was quiet. I was warm and had pushed the blanket down from my naked body. Something was tickling me on my chest and belly. Then I felt something on my face. The light at the rear of the cell had been extinguished through a remote switch, but there was still some light filtering through the bars from the catwalk used by patroling guards. I looked upward and saw hoards of cockroaches running across the ceiling. From time to time several would drop off onto my body. I raised up and chased them away with a sweeping motion of my hand, brushed myself off, and checked my bed as best I could. Recalling with some little comfort that cockroaches don't bite, I went back to sleep.

McCord had been right about breakfast. We were awakened by the crash of large metal containers being brought into the floor area. I looked out and saw that there were tables and chairs. At one end there was a long table upon which were set big thermal cans. After a while there was the sound from above of a row of metal bar doors rolling open in unison with a thump and prisoners ran down the stairway opposite my cell on their way to breakfast. They appeared to be released and returned tier by tier. Presently a trusty came to the door of my cell with trays for McCord and me. On them were metal bowls, several small packages of a popular dry cereal, army-style powdered eggs, and a greasy sausage. The bowls had been half-filled with milk and, I found, a great quantity of refined sugar spooned into them, apparently on the assumption we'd want it. It made the milk syrupy sweet and I resolved to avoid stirring it the next time. By the time I wolfed down the eggs and sausage the trusty was back with a large pitcher.

"Gimme ya bowl ya want coffee."

I rinsed it quickly to get rid of the sugar and held it out to him. He filled it with a black coffee that was good. As I was sipping it, he nodded toward the sign on the stairwell and said, "Don't hold out d'bowl, man. We short."

That solved the "bring back your bowels" mystery. After breakfast McCord and I took turns running in place, bending, and doing jumping-jack exercises in the crowded space, then I got back on my bunk to let McCord use the toilet and, later, he did the same for me.

McCord started to speak bitterly of Magruder. He had seen a photograph of Magruder and his family in a newspaper with a story saying Magruder intended to return to California to seek the Republican nomination for Governor. I laughed at the very idea, but McCord took it seriously and was furious. Then he got on the subject of Sirica. He believed him mentally unstable, or so he said, and was certain our conviction would be overturned on appeal. He urged that I have any friends I could muster investigate Sirica's past for evidence of irrational acts. He said something about sending Sirica a typewriter, which to this day makes no sense to me, and I began to think McCord was becoming unhinged by the pressure of events and imprisonment. Next he went into detail about telephoning the Chilean and other embassies, railing at the government for denying that his calls had been intercepted by wiretaps. "You were in the FBI," he'd say vehemently, "*you* know they tap those embassies."

I told McCord he was right and that I knew very well that we wiretapped almost every foreign embassy in Washington, friend or foe, and in the case of some, such as the Soviet, take movies of everyone who goes in or out. I tried to point out to McCord that it was unrealistic for him to expect that the United States government would admit to such a practice. He was unbelieving. For all his exposure in the FBI and CIA to the way of the clandestine world, McCord actually believed that the United States government wouldn't lie. He was utterly naïve on the subject. As the days wore on he turned more and more bitter and I tried to avoid conversation with him, by either sleeping during the day or feigning to, and by exercising to the extent possible. A trusty under sentence of death for rape and murder came to the bars and we played chess. He was one of the only blacks who did not seem to resent my whiteness. The others, as they passed my cell on the way up or down stairs, invariably had a sneering racial remark to pass, especially

398

after it got around that McCord and I were "Watergate," i.e., Nixon men.

McCord was not always present. I assumed he was receiving family or legal visits. That, too, helped me to avoid conversation with him after I grew tired of his bitterness, which was, in my opinion then and now, unjustified and based on an unrealistic view of the world. It has been since alleged that McCord was a "double agent" who sabotaged the second Watergate break-in and betrayed his comrades. I don't believe that at all. What I think led to his sending the letter he was soon to give John Sirica was the increasing bitterness he experienced. I believe it finally led him to believe that the United States government was in conspiracy against him, and that the only prominent government figure who wasn't a part of the conspiracy was John Sirica, who was too aberrant to be trusted by the rest of the government. I think he even felt betrayed by his beloved CIA, and that his actions were the result of an at least temporarily obsessed man. McCord was also very religious, and I think he experienced a feeling of estrangement from his God and jumped at the chance to become once more a "good Christian" back on what the conventional wisdom was telling him through the media was the side of the angels.

Toward the end of the approximately one week I was there in the D.C. jail immediately after my conviction, I began to get tired of the racial slurs. I knew I shouldn't let it bother me, but I felt an increasingly strong desire somehow to respond, a product, I suppose, of my intensely competitive nature. There were virtually no options. I couldn't challenge anyone to a fight; I was in deadlock. Responding in kind would have been childish and reduced me to their level. Still, I had to do *something*.

My chance came one morning when it was my turn for a shower. McCord was off someplace when the guard came to the cell door and asked if I wanted a shower. When I said I did he nodded, said "get ready," which

I took to mean undress. He left to operate the control which would unlock my cell. When the door opened, I picked up my towel and bar of yellow soap and started walking, naked, down the catwalk toward the other end where the shower area was. What I didn't realize was that I was offering severe offense to those whose cells I passed. The problem was my nakedness. Prison etiquette demanded that I wrap the towel around my waist. That never occurred to me; I had, after all, spent years in athletic locker rooms with other men, to say nothing of my years in the army.

But in the D.C. jail, I was thought to be flaunting my sexuality. There I was, walking past them, offensively naked—and *white*. The catcalls came in a storm from the locked cells as I walked past them. "Honky!" I heard. "White movafuck!" *They* were angry because, as one voice I heard put it: "White movafuck ain' showin' no respek fo d'Brothas!" *I* was angry at all the racial remarks.

Even though the radio speakers and televisions hadn't yet been turned on for the day (something that was at the whim of the guard) the noise was deafening as I started my shower. I seethed. Then an idea hit me. They wanted race? *I'd* give them race! My mind reached back thirty-five years, deep into my childhood. In my head the shortwave of my mother's old Emerson snapped on. The music started and I started to sing, sing as I hadn't in years. I roared out into the chaos about me the anthem of the nation whose psychotic obsession with race sent millions of those believed inferior to their graves:

"*Die Fahne hoch!*" I sang, "*Die Reihen dicht geschlossen . . .*"

A curious phenomenon occurred. The roaring noise started to abate.

By the time I reached the second verse of the "Horst Wessel Song," my voice was the only one in the entire cellblock. I don't believe there was a man there who understood one word of what I sang. But they got the message.

XXVI

I was in the D.C. jail with McCord only a week when I was abruptly released to the custody of two U.S. marshals who handcuffed, chained, and placed me into the rear of an automobile between two junkies and leg-ironed me to them. In this posture I was driven north toward the federal prison in Danbury, Connecticut. The marshals got lost in Westchester County. I recognized where we were because we happened to be near the Westchester County airport, which I'd flown in and out of a number of times. I suggested it was as good a place as any to stop and let the three of us go to the bathroom. The marshals refused to remove any of the chains, including the leg irons, so the three of us jammed into a tiny men's room and took turns at the one urinal trying not to splash the others' feet.

The prison at Danbury was different from the D.C. jail in two fundamental ways. First, it was clean. In all the time I was there I never saw a cockroach. The second difference was more profound. In the short time I had been at the D.C. jail my exposure to the guard force had been slight because I was on deadlock. The few I observed were just trying to see to it that they had the same number of bodies at the end of the shift as were turned over to them when they came on duty. Their attitude was "live and let live." They had a filthy job in a filthy place and no illusions of any essential difference between themselves and their prisoners except that they got to go home at night. The guard force at Danbury, however, appeared to think they were morally superior to their charges, were there to "correct" them, and actually thought they had a chance of doing so. This attitude manifested itself right at the beginning, in the Receiving and Discharge section, when we went through the initial strip search routine. As I bent over and parted my buttocks for the anal inspection, the guard sneered, "I hope you don't mind my looking up your asshole, Mr. Liddy."

I straightened up, turned around, and looked him in the eye as the other prisoners stared at my breach of discipline—I hadn't been given permission to move—and said: "Doesn't bother me in the slightest. *You're* the guy who earns his living looking up assholes, not I. Just don't ever try to get *me* to look up *your* asshole."

The guard turned purple but kept his remarks to himself as I completed the routine and went through the rest of the R&D procedure.

Because I was unsentenced and liable to many years in prison, and Danbury, unlike the maximum-security D.C. jail, was rated only medium-security, I could not by regulation be admitted to the general population. Instead I was given prison garb dyed a deep brown to distinguish it from that worn by sentenced prisoners and put into the maximum-security cellblock, which was known officially at that time by the euphemism "New Hampshire East." In New Hampshire East the cages were slightly smaller than those of the D.C. jail and made of masonry with only the barred door and front of the cells of steel. They were stacked four tiers high. I was not, however, on deadlock in the upper tier "hole" but free during the day to roam the tier floor area. My fellow prisoners were also unsentenced, there to relieve overcrowding at the Federal Detention Center at West Street, Manhattan, now defunct. Most were black. There were a few Hispanics and some whites. The charges against us ranged from the serious and violent such as armed robbery and assault down to drug abuse and counterfeiting. It was there that I met my first Black Muslims since my days in the FBI. One was assigned to my cell. He had come in with a number of others and asked me politely if I would mind his switching to a cell with another of his faith because he prayed five times daily and might disturb me. Like all Black Muslims I ever encountered in four and a half years in prison, he was immaculately clean, neat, and respectful of those who offered respect to him. I ended up in a cell by myself.

My situation and mood were expressed in a letter to Peter Maroulis on 8 February 1973:

Dear Pete:

All well here. Am in same size cell, maximum security etc. and not permitted to mix with the general prison population as I have not as yet been sentenced. Conditions are, however, an improvement over my prior accommodations.

I know you must be engulfed in the accumulation of regular business now that the trial is over, but if you could manage a visit it would be helpful as, in spite of assurances that our apprehensions are groundless, there are matters I am reluctant to entrust to the questionable integrity of the mails.

The persons one meets in prison can be fascinating. My current chess partner is the son of the wartime SS Gestapo Commander of Brussels. We get on famously. He knows more songs than I do, and shower time sounds like the invasion of Poland.

The typewriter is permitted to be used for legal correspondence only, so please explain the absence of letters to Frances and my parents. [Despite reams of samples of my handwriting given the FBI under court order, they had been unable to make a single identification because I employed one of my alternate styles. In case of retrial, I didn't want to give them any more.] You might pass on my mailing address to

*them when you get the chance, along with my love
and reassurances as to my wellbeing.*

*I trust that by now you have heard from Ireland.
[A code reference to the color green, signifying cash.
I was concerned that Peter be paid. He was, at about
that time, handed a paper bag by an unidentified
caller. It contained $20,000 in hundred-dollar bills
toward his fee.] . . .*

*My maximum security status prevents me from
receiving newspapers and magazines, but it is permissible for you to send me Xerox copies of clip-
pings, and I would like to know what has been going
on. When and if my money is forwarded from D.C.
I will be able to purchase magazines by order to the
commissary (I am not allowed near it) but most
offered are of the motorcycle fan club variety.*

>*My address is:*
>*G. Gordon Liddy*
>*No. 25106*
>*Pembroke Station*
>*Danbury, Connecticut, 06810*

>*Many thanks, amigo,*

>Gordon

My good spirits notwithstanding, I knew I faced an
attempt to force me to testify after legal immunization
and, I was sure, a heavy sentence from Sirica; it was
clear he had as little use for me as I had for him. In the
FBI, I had read a psychological study circulated among
agents in training. It concluded that in the case of a subject sentenced to prison, the ideal time to interrogate him
was *not* immediately following incarceration. According
to the study, the spirit or psychological strength of the
newly imprisoned person described a curve that sloped

downward for a maximum of six weeks, then climbed upward as adjustment was made to new circumstances, and leveled off at the same place it began. The study recommended that interrogation be held off until about the sixth week of imprisonment, when the psychological strength of the person in question was at its nadir.

Although I felt no depression coming on, it made sense to be careful. I decided to tune up my will so as to be ready for anything. The first thing I did was limit my food intake to six hundred calories per day. This induced sharp hunger. Because it stayed with me day and night, the discipline was excellent and worth the severe weight loss. To keep up my strength I increased the number of pushups I did daily from one to two hundred (in sets of one hundred) added jumping jacks, jogging along the exterior of the cells, and sit-ups. My mood remained steady. I was getting along with all the other prisoners. Things were going very well, too well, I decided. I needed more stress to bring my will to maximum power. I turned to my old reliable method of ordeal by fire. This test would have to exceed all others in destruction of tissue and time of severe pain.

I selected a particularly strong-willed black bank robber named "Tex" with whom to engage in a battle of wills. Ready with a box of wooden matches, I got him into a discussion of the subject and pressed him to the point where he expressed disbelief and challenged me. Because I had been warned never again to indulge in that practice near or on finger joints and my palm was already burned out, I had to go back to where I started years before: my forearm. The scars there were light.

"Strike a match," I said to Tex, and locked my eyes into his. He struck it and held it out, not knowing what to do next. I put the unburned outside of my left forearm directly over the flame. As the fire burned through my flesh and melted it back into a blackened depression, a look of horror came over Tex; but he stayed with it. The match burned down and scorched his fingers before

405

he dropped it. I grinned at him as he looked at the burn unbelievingly, then looked ill, got up, and left.

The pain was not as severe now because all the nerves in the roughly oval 1½″ × 2″ area had been destroyed. There was just a deep ache in the center with the severe burning sensation confined to the less destroyed circumference. The wound needed attention and would have to be reported to get it. I summoned a guard, showed it to him, and told him that a box of matches had been set off under my arm as I played chess with a smoker who was careless. I declined, of course, to identify the nonexistent smoker. The burn was recorded and treated in the prison hospital. It was so deep I had endangered the tendons that operate the wrist. Finally satisfied that my will remained invincible, I was ready.

Sentencing was set for 23 March. I went south by automobile in the custody of a U.S. marshal, who gagged my black fellow prisoner with adhesive tape as he sat handcuffed, chained, and shackled because he refused to be "respectful" or silent. In Washington I was lodged once again in the D.C. jail. On 23 March I was brought again to the basement of the U.S. courthouse.

As I entered Sirica's courtroom for sentencing at 10:15, I was sleepy. Whenever there is a court appearance scheduled, the U.S. marshals like to have the person arrive at about 8:30 A.M. The procedure is so cumbersome and time-consuming that they have to wake the prisoner in the jail at about 4:20 A.M., so I had already been up for six hours. I sat at the end of the defense table and greeted my fellow defendants warmly, including James McCord, who sat just to my left.

Sirica entered and, after we had all been seated and the rumble of the jammed courtroom had died down, he announced that he had a "preliminary matter" to attend to. He then announced that he had received a letter from McCord and went through an Academy Award bit of business with the sealed envelope before starting to read it aloud to the hushed courtroom.

As it became obvious from what Sirica was reading that McCord had gone bad, I looked over at him. He was slinking farther and farther down in his chair. He noticed my look and leaned toward me saying, "This will help you and the others." I ignored him. I had no use for an informer. The letter read, Sirica declared a recess abruptly and left the bench. The courtroom erupted as press personnel ran for the phones outside. I was disappointed and disgusted by McCord, but not surprised or concerned; he had, I decided, finally flipped out completely. The letter itself gave no details but was, rather, a promise to talk in return for a lighter sentence; but because he could testify to nothing that wasn't hearsay at best, the damage was only apparent, not real. Only Hunt or I could do real damage—Hunt because of his direct participation in ODESSA operations and his working relationship with Colson. Only I, however, could take Watergate any higher.

So it was with equanimity that when Sirica reappeared to sentence the Cubans and me—having hastily canceled McCord's—I rose to hear him have his say. He sentenced me first. As he said in his book, Sirica had "given up on Liddy." My part in his scheme to coerce grand jury and Senate hearing testimony from the convicted defendants was to serve as an example of what the others could expect if they failed to cooperate with the several investigations then in progress.

As Peter Maroulis stood next to me ordering his notes in a request for leniency he insisted upon for purposes of the record, I checked the microphone on the rostrum by tapping it with my finger and it made a thumping sound through the speakers, to Sirica's added annoyance. Peter gave it his best effort as I waited; then Sirica asked if I had anything to say. "Nothing at all, Your Honor," I answered. I hadn't even wanted Peter to say anything.

Sirica then launched into his speech, carrying on and characterizing the Watergate operation as "sordid and despicable," then sentencing me to twenty years in prison and a fine of $40,000. He went on to note for effect that I (or anyone sentenced to a flat twenty years) would not become eligible for parole until I had served a minimum of six years and eight months, and the sentence was promptly misreported as six years eight months to twenty years. It was, however, recorded correctly by the Bureau of Prisons as a flat twenty years.

As Sirica pronounced sentence, there was much sucking in of breath among the audience but I was pleased. He had gone so far overboard that whether or not Dean's promise of a pardon ever materialized, I knew the sentence would never stand. Sirica had blown it. Twenty years for a first offense B and E of a nondwelling with nothing taken and no resistance to police was ridiculous and would be recognized as such when things cooled off.

I returned to my seat. Hunt and the four Cubans rose and Sirica addressed them. To coerce cooperation with the government, he misused his power to sentence provisionally to maximum terms while supposedly awaiting additional presentence investigation. The clear implication was that the maximum sentences from "Maximum John" could be expected to remain unmodified in the event of noncooperation with the prosecutors and the Senate. Sirica made no bones about it, saying to the four Cubans and Hunt:

> I am making no promise of leniency—but the sentence I will impose will depend primarily on whether or not you cooperate fully with the permanent subcommittee on investigation of the United States Senate. . . .

> I fully expect you to cooperate absolutely, completely and entirely with whoever from that subcommittee, whether it is a Senator or whether it is a staff investigator. Whoever it is who interrogates you, you will openly and honestly testify. . . .

I recommend your full cooperation with the Grand Jury and the Senate Select Committee. You must understand that I hold out no promises or hopes of any kind to you in this matter but I do say that should you decide to speak freely I would have to weigh that factor in appraising what sentence will be finally imposed in this case. Other factors will of course be considered but I mention this one because it is one over which you have control and I mean each one of the five of you.

Although by sentencing me finally, rather than provisionally like the others, Sirica made it obvious to any lawyer that he was excluding me from consideration as a potential informer, that might not have been understood by the press and other laymen in the audience. For that reason I appreciated Sirica's addressing the others by name and limiting his urgings to cooperate specifically to "each one of the five of you" (Hunt and the four Cubans). That made it clear to the world that he harbored no hope at all that I might turn informer and cooperate to save myself. I took it as an unintended but welcome compliment from my enemy.

Danbury, Connecticut, is just forty minutes away by automobile from Peter Maroulis's office in Poughkeepsie. We had a lot of work to do together in drafting the appeal, so he asked Sirica to recommend to the Bureau of Prisons that I be incarcerated at Danbury and Sirica agreed. I was returned to maximum security in the D.C. jail and waited to be transported back to Danbury. That was not to be for a long time.

I was no longer in "deadlock" in Cellblock 1. For the past few days I had been lodged in a vast dormitory that was adjacent to Cellblock 4. It was on the third floor and featured broken windows through which an occasional pigeon would enter and fly around frantically, eventually to be either freed or killed according to the whim of the prisoner who captured it. There was an adjacent "recreation room" with an old black-and-white television mounted high on a wall in front of rows of pewlike benches. In the rear of the room was a Ping-Pong table and to the right of the entrance a commissary from which candy and sundries were sold for tickets representing currency. The real currency, however, was cigarettes and, sometimes, homosexual intercourse.

My cot was along the right-hand center row near the opening to the recreation room. My possessions—toilet articles, a plastic brush and comb, and a few magazines brought with me from Danbury—were in a brown paper bag that I'd put under my cot when I left for court that morning. As I approached my cot upon returning, I was aware that most eyes were upon me; and when I saw it I understood why. In my absence my brown paper bag had been rifled. It lay where it had been tossed contemptuously, on top of my cot. The other prisoners awaited my reaction to this breach of the most fundamental of prison taboos, the violation of my territory.

Privacy is so rare in a prison that space that is not really private is treated as if it were. Had I a cell, it would be called my "house," my private space, and the rule about how to treat trespassers was: "you find him there, you leave him there." It translates to knocking the intruder out at the very least but, more usually, killing him. In the absence of a cell, the area immediately surrounding one's cot or mattress on the floor constitute's one's "house." My house had been invaded.

I inventoried the paper bag. Everything was there except my green plastic hairbrush. It was clear that the invasion and theft were meant to be symbolic, a test rather than a genuine attempt at theft. My reaction was of the utmost importance. I started by asking my neighbors—almost all of them black but a few decrepit white winos who hardly knew where they were—if anyone had seen who had taken my hairbrush. Most just shook their heads

410

coldly, refusing to "rat," but one asked me loudly, for the benefit of the others, what I'd do if I knew.

"Take it back," I answered. That was the right answer, but the man then denied any knowledge of the identity of the thief. That was on Friday, 23 March.

On Saturday I was able to buy some commissary tickets and was standing in line about to take my turn at the window when the next test came. A rather substantial man walked up to me and said, "Man, buy me a pack'a Kools." He was scowling in an attempt to "Bogart" or intimidate me. Had I gone along with it, I'd have ended up buying something for everyone in the dormitory.

"No," I said.

"Why not? You rich. You got money."

That gave me the opening I was looking for. It was not enough to decline and be willing to fight. I wanted to take the initiative. I knew I was going to have to fight one or more of these guys soon anyway, and *I* wanted to start it. This guy was big, but he looked slow and he had assumed a posture intended to show contempt and dominance. He had his hands on his hips, both feet nearly together for added height and was leaning forward from the waist in what he hoped would appear an ominous and threatening manner. His weight was unbalanced to the front. Without moving my hands I could have broken his knee with my right leg before he could react.

"Because I'm not running a bank here. And if I were I wouldn't lend to you. I don't like your credit rating."

That put the burden on him. He had to fight or back off. The man stood there for a moment while I tensed my right leg. Then he grinned, shook his head, and walked off mumbling "cheap movafucka." No one else asked me for anything, but the real test was still to come. I kept walking up and down the aisles, watching for my hairbrush. On Monday, 26 March, I found it.

It was morning. Again I felt all eyes upon me and looked around. A young black man of my approximate height (5′ 9″) and perhaps a few pounds heavier, was brushing his hair elaborately with my hairbrush. His cot was over against the inside wall. As I watched he put the brush down carefully on his cot and walked away. I had no idea whether he was the man who stole it or had just been selected because of his size as my prospective opponent, but I knew that the time had come.

I walked over to the young man's cot, invaded his territory, and picked up the brush. I stayed there in his "house" as I examined the object ostentatiously, then put it, handle down, into the rear pocket of my prison dungarees and walked away. In a moment the young man was behind me, following me down the aisle saying,

"Hey, man; you can't do that, man. You went in my house an' took my brush!"

"Wrong, mister. I went in your house and took *my* brush."

"Hey, man, you got t'give that back!"

"Sorry, fella. You want it, you take it."

I had stopped at the rear of the dormitory and faced him.

"Then take off them glasses," the young man said. The D.C. jail was so septic I had reverted to glasses from contact lenses, which must be kept clean to prevent infection.

With my right hand I removed my glasses and was sliding them into my left breast pocket when the right cross came. The kid was fast, but when I had looked down toward the pocket it caused him to miss and he struck my left ear. He followed up with a good left jab that hit me flush on the nose. It was the last punch he landed.

I had started this fight, and I had nothing against the young man. The others had crowded around to watch and were not interfering; to injure him seriously was not justified, so I boxed. I caught the kid in the mouth with a left jab and sent him back about three feet. The next several minutes were spent parrying wild hooks and crosses with relative ease and backing the kid up with my left. I missed his solar plexus with a right to the body and caught him in the ribs. At that moment a guard arrived and broke it up, charging us both with fighting. To my astonishment I found that I was bleeding copiously from the left ear. There was also a small amount of blood from the bridge of my nose. Both my opponent and I were sent to the prison hospital where we were examined separately. The physician who treated me was black. He said that I had a neatly sliced ear and he stitched it up expertly. That increased my puzzlement; the man I fought had had no knife. Another black man then took my medical history and, when I had difficulty understanding his dialect and kept responding "I beg your pardon?" "what?" and "excuse me?" to his questions, he noted in my file that I was partially deaf.

A guard came up and asked me what had happened. I declined to say, whereupon he demonstrated that he knew all about it anyway by demanding the hairbrush. He said he knew we had fought over it and to prevent further trouble neither one of us was going to have it. I never did get it back.

When I returned to the dormitory the atmosphere had changed markedly. A big black man walked up to me, smiling, and said, "You all right, Liddy. Now we know your heart don't pump no Kool-Aid." I smiled back and asked about my cut ear. I still couldn't understand how that had happened.

He smiled knowingly and said, "Kid had a fightin' ring."

"What's that?"

The most common weapon in the D.C. jail, it seemed, was a "fighting ring." It consisted either of a ring with an open setting, the stone having been pried out to leave the prongs exposed and able to cut when a blow was delivered with the fist (as had occurred in my fight that morning) or a ring specially made in the basement maintenance shop. One of those adorned the ring finger of the man I was talking to. It was silver-colored polished steel made from pipe and tapered to a broad top, which was filed into a series of ostensibly decorative stepped flat plains with sharp corners and edges able to cut with ease.

"Where'd you get that?" I asked.

"Dude downstairs. You want one? I'll send him to ya."

"What do they go for?"

"A box." (One carton of cigarettes.)

"Yeah. I'd like to have one made." And I did. I've still got it.

The guard reappeared and told me to report to R&D; the marshals wanted me for a court appearance. When I arrived at the courthouse, Peter Maroulis was waiting for me. He said I was to be taken before the grand jury again.

This time things went quickly; I invoked the Fifth Amendment and was returned to jail. When I got there I found that I had been transferred out of the dormitory—probably as an official precaution following the fight—into Cellblock 4, third floor. This was a happy development. First, it meant that I would have my own cell and be able to walk the floor at will except during the night when we all were locked in, and during the two daytime "count" periods when we were required to remain motionless. Second, CB4 third floor was where my codefendants Hunt, Barker, Martinez, Gonzalez, and Sturgis were being held. It was like old home week. The Cubans were particularly well liked by the other prisoners, and there was plenty of contraband food as well as other amenities like a pillow, a good blanket, and, wonder of wonders, a bathtub.

I was assigned the cell near the television room. It was of masonry with a steel door, had a window through which came fresh air, and fewer rodents and roaches—far fewer than the heaving masses of insects in CB 1, and there was even army surplus insecticide available. The only problem was that to affect the roaches one had to use so much of the potent insecticide there was a question which of us would die first.

I conferred quickly with Hunt. He explained that he was feigning cooperation with the grand jury, would not mention any ODESSA matters, and just kept referring to me as the source of his hearsay. No damage, he assured me, would be done by his testimony. He asserted that he had the Cubans briefed thoroughly and there would be no problem from them.

Hunt was in good spirits. He told me that he had received word through Colson that he would be pardoned and asked what I had heard on the subject. I told him of Dean's assurance of a pardon in two years. Hunt was shocked. "Two years?" I reassured him that the figure was specifically applied to me. In all likelihood, I speculated, because I had been cast as the top man, Hunt and the others would be released earlier than that.

"When?" Hunt asked.

"Well, I don't *know*, Howard, but I wouldn't be surprised if you and the boys had a Merry Christmas."

"Merry Christmas!" Hunt huffed, "A Happy Fourth of July would be more like it!"

That was so breathtakingly unrealistic that I began to worry about Hunt. What would happen when the Fourth of July came and went and he was still here? But he moved on to another subject, wanting to know what, if anything, I had received since the last money Dorothy had given me. I told him that Peter Maroulis had received $20,000 as a fee last month. Hunt protested bitterly about how little he had gotten in support and legal fees, never mentioning $75,000 he had received just a short while before. What could I assure him of now?

"Nothing, Howard. We're in the same boat."

"Hardly."

"What do you mean by that?"

"Well, I just assumed that with that GEMSTONE money in the till, after everything blew you'd take care of number one."

415

I was furious. "Howard," I said icily, "I do not steal from my clients." I walked away from him to cool off and when I looked into his cell a bit later I saw him sitting like an Indian fakir on his cot, mumbling. He called it "transcendental meditation." I called it starting to crack. If Hunt went bad, the President had a serious problem. I began thinking about a way to solve it.

On Friday, 30 March, I was hauled before John Sirica again. Silbert and Glanzer informed the court that I had invoked the Fifth Amendment again. He promptly granted me "use" immunity and ordered me to return to the grand jury and testify. Back I went and once more refused to talk, then went into the little antechamber again to confer with Peter Maroulis. Silbert and Glanzer knocked on the door and said they wanted to talk to me. Peter let them in and sat to my left. I sat on a desk top, in my shirt sleeves, feet dangling over the side.

The two prosecutors must have sensed my contempt for Silbert and respect for Glanzer because they went into the old good cop, bad cop routine with Glanzer the good guy. At first I was amused. These guys seemed to forget I knew more about this routine than they did. Then Silbert began coming on strong about how long they were going to keep me in jail; that I'd be in there so far they'd have to pipe daylight to me; that I should by now have an idea of what the D.C. jail was like, and that was just the beginning, and so on. I became angry.

Glanzer started to tell me how a cooperative witness wouldn't even have to go back to the D.C. jail that night, but I wasn't listening. I unbuttoned my left sleeve. Maroulis saw me do it and made a move to dissuade me. He had guessed what I was going to do. Coldly I brushed even Peter aside. My eyes fixed Glanzer's. It was to him I wanted to make my point; I couldn't care less about Silbert.

"I don't think you understand yet," I said, turning back my sleeve and starting to unroll the gauze bandage from my left forearm, "with whom you are dealing."

Glanzer's eyes followed the unraveling of the bandage as if my upraised arm were a cobra in striking position. Then the last of the gauze fell away from the three square inches of seared flesh. The sight was hideous. A mass of yellowish white dead flesh was close to the point where it would slough off. Surrounded by an angry red ring of less badly burned tissue, the sticky mess glistened wetly in the purplish glow of the overhead fluorescent light.

I shoved my forearm toward Glanzer's startled face. He recoiled in horror as I said, "*I am not subject to coercion!*"

XXVII

On 3 April a furious John Sirica held me in contempt of court. In his rage he held specifically that the D.C. jail was an appropriate place to confine me until I either broke and talked or the grand jury was dismissed. The maximum term for which I could be so confined was a year and a half and he suspended the running of my twenty-year sentence until I had served the contempt time. The net effect was that I now had a sentence of twenty-one and a half years. Sirica was technically correct but factually wrong; I had no contempt for the United States District Court, only for him. We were now even: John Sirica had held me in contempt as a matter of law, and I held *him* in contempt as a matter of fact.

Following my sentencing for contempt I was taken to the courthouse basement again to await the completion of court business for all prisoners so we could be bused together back to the jail. The difference was that I was now no longer placed in a holding cell by myself, but in one of the two large "tanks." They held not only prisoners who had come from the jail but newly sentenced men going there for the first time—at least for this case.

That evening we were loaded onto the bus and began

the trip back to jail. The marshal locked the gate to the prisoner section with a padlock after we were all seated, handcuffed two by two. No sooner were we out on the street than the trouble started. One of the additions to the bus was a "sissy" or male homosexual of the passive variety. Such persons are always referred to in prison by the feminine "she."

"She" was attacked immediately by a number of other prisoners. The marshals dared not unlock the gate to intervene and so were helpless to prevent the strong-arm robbery that took place right before their eyes. The bus just kept on rolling as the victim screamed as "her" wallet was taken and money in it passed around. "She" quieted down after being slapped repeatedly in the face and told to "Be still, bitch!"

When my "share" of the money was handed to me I declined. That was taken as a sign of weakness by another new man who was seated on the aisle opposite the seat I shared with a very fat young man. I sat in the window seat. As the others watched covertly, the new man got out of his seat and, by extending his arm and pulling on the arm of the prisoner he was handcuffed to, slipped far enough over to reach around behind me and snatch off my glasses. I had been so busy watching the robbery of the sissy I hadn't seen the man make his move. Now he was back in his seat, posturing with my glasses on his face. As the only white man in the bus with the exception of one of the marshals, I, not the sissy, suddenly became the focus of open attention.

"Excuse me," I said to the fat fellow I was cuffed to as I rose and started to clamber over him.

When I got astride him and pulled my left leg up and back, my thigh pushed his head over and he protested, "Hey, man, whatcha doing?"

"I'm sorry," I said, "I won't be a minute. I'm going to take the outside of this foot and kick that gentleman across the aisle right under his right ear. It'll make a noise when his spine cracks. If you listen, you'll be able to hear it."

418

Fatty's eyes rolled. "Why you wanna do that, man?"

"To kill him, of course. Then I'm going to take back my glasses."

There was no way that the glasses thief could escape because he was cuffed to the man in *his* window seat. As my leg cocked all the way back to deliver the lethal blow, he whipped off the glasses and handed them to me saying,

"Here, man. Can't you take a joke?"

"I don't look upon it as funny."

Another prisoner who knew me from the jail said, "Don' fuck with ol' G. Gordon, man, he *knows* somethin'!" ("Knows somethin'" meant "possesses fighting skills.")

Despite the presence of the guards as witnesses, I'd have had to kill the man had he not returned the glasses. Failure to do so would have meant that I could never go to sleep again in jail. Like sharks in a feeding frenzy, the strong devour the weak quickly in prison. Nothing ever happened to those who robbed the sissy. Such things are just part of everyday life in prison.

Back at the D.C. jail I settled in for a long stay. A week before, John Dean had asked through Peter Maroulis that I give him a statement that he had no prior knowledge of Watergate. I declined. What was happening, of course, was that Dean was starting to crack under pressure but I misinterpreted the signal; I thought it might be a test of whether I would talk under any circumstances, or a sign of general White House unease that the Watergate investigation was continuing after the trial. I recalled that Dean had responded to my offer to permit my life to be taken by saying that we had not yet reached that point. That led me to the thought that the White House might be concerned that Hunt might really talk to the grand jury. They could monitor that through his attorney. Dean knew, because I had told him during our post-Watergate meeting in the park nearly a year ago, that Hunt could give direct evidence against the White House in the Ellsberg matter. It was possible that Dean might now suggest to the President that we had finally arrived at the point where *Hunt* would have to be killed. In that event it was reasonable to expect orders to execute such a decision. It behooved me to be ready.

By now I knew that the fee for a killing in the D.C. jail was two "boxes." I'd be an immediate suspect were Hunt to be killed, so it would have to be a contract sanction and I'd have to arrange an airtight alibi. That would be easy: just have myself put back in deadlock prior to the event. It wouldn't do, however, to go around soliciting Hunt's execution. Prisons are filled with informers. For that reason I sought the advice of a gangland figure I knew and could trust.

My friend was sharp and as soon as I began to broach the subject, he nodded his understanding but jumped to the conclusion I was referring to McCord, now free on bond. He offered immediately to have McCord shot. I had to explain that I appreciated his offer but had someone else in mind. McCord, I knew, could not hurt the White House, and I'd never receive orders to kill him, if for no other reason than that it wouldn't occur to my superiors that I could accomplish that task from inside a maximum-security prison. (For all the press accounts about how ruthless the Nixon White House staff was, they were really rather naïve.)

I explained carefully to my friend that I had *not* yet received orders to kill Hunt, and that under no circumstances was he to be harmed without my specific authorization, which I would not give in the absence of unequivocal orders from my superiors. That was a condition he could certainly appreciate, and he agreed to respect it readily. That precaution out of the way, we decided quickly upon the method. Hunt received special meals because of his history of ulcers. In the parlance of the D.C. jail it was a "diet tray," and it was served to him in his cell rather than in the CB4 mess hall on the first floor. Should I be ordered to kill Hunt, he would be served a special meal indeed. It would contain a lethal poison.

On Sunday, 15 April, the day John Dean was secretly

telling Silbert and Glanzer what I had told him of the ODESSA entry into the office of Dr. Fielding in Beverly Hills, Peter Maroulis received a telephone call at his home from Assistant Attorney General Henry Petersen. The message was:

> A report had been received by the Government that Gordon Liddy is not cooperating because of a misguided sense of loyalty to the President. The President when informed of this asked Petersen to contact his counsel and tell Mr. Liddy that the President expected all parties in this to cooperate, subject only to the reservation that no one wants to create the impression that Gordon Liddy or anyone else is being pressured by the President of the U.S.

Peter wrote it down verbatim on a roll-pad mounted on the wall next to his kitchen phone and came to see me immediately. We decided to get a reading on the real meaning from John Mitchell, and Peter visited him in New York on Wednesday, 18 April. Mitchell told Peter that the message meant just what it said. With that unhelpful advice, Peter conferred with me again and I zeroed in on the phrase, ". . . subject only to the reservation that no one wants to create the impression that Gordon Liddy or anyone else is being pressured by the President of the U.S." as the real message, and I instructed Peter to pass the word that I would remain silent.

In the meanwhile Hunt was going back and forth to testify before the Watergate grand jury and returning daily to report to me and the Cubans that he was only telling them what they already knew. On Wednesday, 2 May, however, Hunt came back in an agitated state and called us all together to a meeting for his report, rather than briefing me privately first as had been his practice. I didn't like this development and suspected the worst. We met in the small "card room" that the Cubans occupied at the end of the cellblock. Hunt waited until we were all seated before he spoke, leaning forward with a worried look on his face.

"There's no sense holding out any longer," Hunt began, "they know everything."

"What do you mean, 'everything'?" I interrupted.

"I mean they've got it all. They know all about the Beverly Hills entry. They've got the ODESSA files."

"How do you know?" I asked.

"They showed them to me."

"O.K. So somehow they got the ODESSA files. Why help the bastards?"

"Gordon, I may as well tell you now. I'm not holding out any longer. There's no point to it. I'm cooperating with the prosecutors."

I stood and moved back from Hunt's side as if from a loathsome thing. I started to say something, thought better of it, and walked out. I have never spoken another word to Howard Hunt.

It occurred to me that I might receive orders to silence Hunt at any moment. I got hold of a guard and asked to be placed in deadlock immediately. It would be a simple matter to send a coded message to my friend to poison Hunt, even from the depths of "the Hole," as deadlock segregation was called by the prisoners, and just as simple for my supervisors to get the message to me. I waited, but because the message never came, Hunt lives.

The Cubans never cracked. They "testified" before the grand jury but never identified me, acknowledging only that there was a man other than Hunt present in Beverly Hills during the Fielding entry. Hunt, however, spilled his guts and within three weeks the five of them were transferred to the federal prison at Danbury as a reward. I was then released from deadlock status and lived for a time as a regular prisoner in Cellblock 1 on the fourth tier. I was the only white on the tier and possibly in the entire cellblock. We were permitted to go downstairs to the first floor, one tier at a time, for meals and, on good days to spend forty-five minutes in the CB2 yard. It was covered with cinders, and I spent most of my time outdoors running around the yard and doing pushups.

I returned one day from the yard to find a newspaper clipping tacked to the small bulletin board on the wall outside my end cell. The text described me as an antiblack racist. I left it there. When one of the blacks I knew well asked me why I didn't take it down, I said, "You guys know me. Let the sonofabitch who put it up there take it down." It was gone after the evening meal.

From time to time I gave my fellow prisoners legal advice. The first occasion was when someone told me he was offered "immunity" by the prosecutors. I asked him to repeat carefully what he could remember of the offer. It was clear that it was "use" immunity and worthless, a ploy based upon a case called *Murphy* v. *The Waterfront Commission*. I told the man to hold out for *transactional* immunity, the only kind with any meaning.

I had been reluctant to permit my children to visit me in the gloomy conditions of the rotunda of the D.C. jail, but Fran insisted. They took turns at the telephone through which I communicated from the glass booth that separated prisoners from their families. The children looked well. All were competitive swimmers and were doing well in the Prince Georges County, Maryland, public schools, which were, at the time, excellent, not yet having been destroyed by forced busing. I told the boys, the three youngest, that although they were not yet grown, the three of them *together* equaled a grown man and as such they were to take my place in defending their mother and sisters and being the man of the house. All three accepted this new obligation solemnly. Visits were for a maximum of thirty minutes and theirs was soon over.

Fran told me privately something that cheered me considerably. The very day that I first went to prison, an unmarked car arrived at the front of the house soon after she returned from work. In it was an officer of military intelligence who inquired after her well-being and left a number where he could be reached in the event of necessity. Fran was to understand that she was not alone. This communication, I learned later, had nothing whatever to do with the White House. The intelligence community was looking after one of its own. Our neighbors, Fran assured me, were wonderful; they were virtually all military officers' families and treated Fran like the wife of a prisoner of war.

In late April I learned that for one seeking privacy and confidentiality the last place in the world to look for it is in the Marine Midland Bank of Southeast New York. Fran had rented safe deposit and storage space in its Poughkeepsie branch, and Marine Midland told Jack Anderson. The next thing Fran knew the Ervin Committee had served her with a *subpoena duces tecum* for examination of the contents of the footlocker she stored in the bank. At that time there were rumors galore that I was being paid off by the Committee to Re-elect. Fran heard that I had a tin box of cash buried in the backyard (probably because that's where we bury our dead cats and dogs when they've been run over in the street), and I was also supposed to have a huge fortune buried somewhere in Virginia. Apparently Anderson and the committee thought they'd find a huge cash hoard in the footlocker.

Senate investigator Scott Armstrong—the future exposer of the fact that Supreme Court justices are human and put their robes on one arm at a time—arrived in Poughkeepsie in May to watch as the power of the Senate and the big mouth of the Marine Midland Bank forced Fran to open the chest. Surprise! No money. Just some firearms Fran thought dangerous to have around the house in my absence and an old demonstration kit I'd borrowed from Bob Berberich of the Poughkeepsie police force for drug lectures that Fran didn't think belonged in the house either. End of scoop.

On 4 June I was told to report to R&D and escorted by a guard through numerous locked gates to the basement where I could dress in my civilian clothes. Then I was turned over to two U.S. marshals. They put me in a car without telling me that the Senate had obtained a writ commanding my presence to testify before the Ervin Committee, then conducting an anti-Nixon inquisition before the nation's television cameras, complete with moralistic posturings from the likes of Lowell Weicker. No one went before the camera before he had been thoroughly interrogated in secret; the inquisitors didn't want to be embarrassed by surprise answers from witnesses; it wouldn't look good on television. For that reason I was brought to a basement on Capitol Hill where Senator Ervin and his staff were gathered. Peter Maroulis met me there, and Ervin asked me please to stand and raise my right hand. I did. The Senator then intoned, "Do you solemnly swear to tell the truth, the whole truth, and nothing but the truth so help you God?"

I said no. The good Senator's eyebrows started working up and down so hard I thought they'd fly right off on their own power.

Staff mouths hung open; no one had ever done that to them before. Peter Maroulis then explained that he had counseled me not to testify because to do so might prejudice any retrial I might win upon appeal, but the fact of the matter was that I wouldn't have testified anyway. It was my idea to refuse to take the oath to tell the truth. They weren't going to interrogate me without my being under oath, and it saved all the formal who-struck-John of going through the Fifth Amendment after every question—a very efficient and respectful way of telling the Ervin Committee to go piss up a rope. I was out of there in minutes, but I'll say this for Ervin: he respected my position and the committee didn't recommend to the Senate that I be held in contempt.

On 15 June I was served with a summons and complaint in a lawsuit brought by Spencer Oliver against me and about every other Republican in Washington. It demanded damages amounting to $5,050,000. The Democratic National Committee had filed a similar suit in June 1972 that was still pending. I wasn't concerned. The Committee to Re-elect the President was the principal defendant and its lawyers were defending. I was sure that both suits would be settled eventually at no cost to me, so I just filed a denial to avoid a default judgment and opened a file looking forward to reading all the motions that would be going back and forth. If I thought of anything else that should be done, I'd do it, filing in my own behalf.

On 10 July I was sued by Elmer Davis, a California convict who had allegedly confessed to the Ellsberg break-in in a deal with Beverly Hills police to clear a lot of burglaries on their books after having been caught red-handed at one of them. Davis wanted $2,000,000 for being made a "scapegoat." This sort of thing continued until I was a defendant in a dozen different lawsuits and counterclaims arising out of Watergate seeking from me a total in excess of $56,000,000. I defended myself in all of them and when the last, Jack Anderson's, was dismissed on 4 April 1978, I had the satisfaction of knowing that in six years of litigation over all those millions of dollars, I had lost not one cent and had a hell of a lot of fun.

The Anderson case was the most enjoyable. It was brought on a novel theory in what I believed was an attempt not to win the $22,000,000 demanded, but to gain information and publicity for Anderson's column. Watergate had, after all, embarrassed Anderson. For a would-be big-time muckraker, all he'd been able to accomplish was the publication of some stolen grand jury minutes, negative stories about me, and the fiasco of Fran's innocent footlocker. Had he been able to force me to say anything, even by way of denial, it would have been a moral victory for him. I was determined to frustrate him, so instead of filing an answer, I filed a motion to dismiss for lack of jurisdiction over the subject matter and failure to state a claim upon which relief could be granted. So long as that was pending I could not be compelled to answer. I never had to. Anderson tried to invoke a spurious claim of journalistic privilege when questioned during a deposition, and the judge threw his suit out of court.

On 20 July I was taken before the special subcommittee on intelligence of the House Armed Services Committee. They were engaged in the destruction of the covert activities branch of the CIA and in causing damage to the FBI, later completed by Senator Church, and they wanted me to help them by testifying. I would have no part of it and repeated my refusal to take the oath as I had before the Senate. This time I was cited for two counts of contempt of Congress, the House of Representatives voted in favor of the resolution, and I was indicted.

During the summer of 1973 in the ancient D.C. jail's maximum security Cellblock 1 there was a battle of wills between John Sirica and me. I accepted that challenge. The temperature in my fourth-tier cell sometimes reached 104 degrees, according to guards who complained, and fans were brought to the far end of the tier in a futile attempt at relief. The moist heat, compounded by the stench of sweat, feces, vomit, and urine, seemed to be just right for the roaches, and there was a population explosion among them. Rats and mice flourished. The din was deafening and I fashioned earplugs of wet toilet paper, which were of limited effectiveness. When the cell was locked I'd play chess with my neighbor by reaching through the bars to a board on the floor between our cells. I couldn't see my opponent but I could see the board.

Sometimes there was trouble and the whole block would be locked in as a preventive or punitive measure. When that happened, the din increased. Screams would be heard as the guards came to a "troublemaker's" cell: "They're breaking my fingers! Help me, God!" The cellblock would go wild. It was jammed. With a rated capacity of 608 prisoners, up to 1,200 men were packed in that jail. They could no nothing to help their tortured fellow prisoner, and their rage boiled over. The only forms of protest they knew were self-defeating. Cells would be set afire and, as the mattresses burned, acrid smoke filled the cellblock and added to the stifling 100-degree-plus atmosphere. To keep from smothering I covered my face with a wet towel and breathed through it shallowly, lying motionless on my back so as to require a minimum of oxygen.

One memorable time, as a helpless prisoner below screamed under a beating by the guards, the entire cellblock—all but mine packed two or more to a tiny, hot, ovenlike cell—started shouting in rage. Then someone began to pound on the metal walls of his cell. The booming resounded throughout the block because the all-metal stacked cages were like a huge accumulation of steel drums open on one end, stacked and welded together. The idea caught on and others started to pound. Then it became rhythmical as the men synchronized the beating of their fists against the steel walls. Louder and louder grew the slow, powerful drumming as the beat reverberated back and forth throughout the cellblock, blotting out the sound of the radio and television speakers still blaring inanely into the cavern while the prisoner was tortured and his fellows stormed in helpless fury. Finally, someone thought to roll over on his back in his bunk and start to pound his cell wall with both feet together. The sound took a quantum increase in volume as others realized what he was doing and joined in. The effect was like being inside a five-story steel drum pounded on by a hundred drummers with sledgehammers, all striking in unison. The whole world seemed to reverberate until nothing else could be heard, not the screams of the beaten prisoner, not the television and radios at full volume, nothing. Nothing but the overwhelmingly powerful beat of that terrible drum as hundreds of caged souls poured out an unremitting stream of rage into the hellish, superheated atmosphere, all united in one emotion, an all-consuming incandescent hate.

By midsummer I was back in Cellblock 4, third floor. The living conditions were better but the food situation worse. The CB4 mess hall was on the ground floor, and as I stood in line at the serving counter something wet dropped onto my tray. I looked up and saw that raw sewage was dripping onto the serving counter. I stopped eating that food in order to protect my health and instead subsisted on fruit (mostly apples) and dry cereal that I stole from the mess hall in the morning. It came in little one-portion boxes. A contact in the hospital gave me an empty plastic jug that had held thousands of aspirin tablets, and I cut the bottom off another smaller one, laboriously with a plastic knife, to make a bowl.

I stored the cereal in my cell and got up during the night to protect it from rodents, which could gnaw through the boxes easily. Once I chased a mouse out of my cell and it ran into the cell across the hall. The prisoner there chased it back, claiming it was *my* mouse. This friendly game kept up until I was able to kill the mouse and end the argument.

There was always a lot of stolen sugar around the cellblock, but I didn't use it. The real problem was milk. I made a deal with a prisoner who worked in the repair shop for an electric fan and mounted it in my window with an elaborate rig of stolen rubber bands to provide circulation during the hot weather. But my cell was still so hot that milk stored in my aspirin jug soured quickly. To solve the problem I employed elementary physics. I stole a scrub bucket, half-filled it with water, and placed the jug of fresh milk in it, weighing the jug down to keep it from floating. Over the jug I draped a terry-cloth towel, all its ends down in the water. Capillary action drew water up through the towel covering the jug. I took down my fan, put it in front of the pail, and had an effective evaporative cooler that kept my milk fresh. Milk, cereal, and fruit made up my diet for a long time. My weight went down to 137 pounds, but I kept from getting sick from the sewage-fouled mess-hall food.

Another contribution to sustained health was regular exercise. Inside I used a pail of water for a remarkably versatile weight-lifting routine taught me by other prisoners, and outside I continued my running during the

429

forty-five minutes a day we were permitted in the CB4 yard. Despite the fact that I was well known to my fellow prisoners by this time, there was always someone new who, together with a few others, wanted to see whether I could be intimidated. A typical method was to walk ahead of me, in the same direction I was running, and as I approached, step "accidentally" into my path in an effort to force me to go around. I never went around. I just dropped my shoulder and, using, momentum, brushed whoever it was out of the way. I could play the "accident" game too, and I always said "sorry" as I did it. It was accepted as a fair test, fairly met, and no one offered to fight me over it. Some, however, did manage to think up more imaginative tests.

On a hot morning at 10 A.M. the sun-baked walls of the small yard radiated heat as I ran around its circumference, following a trail I had worn in the grass by mile after mile of running, day after day. As I neared the end of my laps I was passing in front of the slope leading up to the cellblock itself. Many prisoners sat there taking the sun. In the middle of the slope was a concrete stairway leading up to the entrance to the cellblock. Because the steps formed seats it was the most desirable place to sit and, as such, was occupied by a guard. He was obviously uncomfortable wearing a uniform and policeman's cap in all that heat. The slope formed a crude grandstand for the little drama that was to be played.

As I ran along the front of the "grandstand" I noticed that at the far end there was an object directly in the middle of my path. Getting closer, I could see that it was a dead rat. A big black man sat on the slope in front of the rat, grinning. I figured that it was his rat and he hoped I'd either stop running altogether before I came to it or, at the very least, go around it.

As a white man from an upper-middle-class background of what must have seemed wealth to my impoverished black fellow prisoners, it figured my sensibilities would not be inured to facts of life common to black ghettos—facts such as rats.

I smiled. This guy's rat, all puffed up from poison and decomposition, was bigger than the one I had partially devoured to finally cure my fear of rats so many years ago, but it was nothing compared to the wharf rats that infested the piers I played on in the late 1930s. As I approached the rat, I altered my stride so that I landed on it squarely with my right foot.

The impact popped the rat's intestines out its anus and, with a little squirting sound, bloody fluid oozed from its mouth. I kept on going, made another circuit, and came down on the rat again, harder. The rodent, having lain dead in the sun for a while, reacted to this second blow by expelling gases of putrefaction. I went around one more time and sprinted to the spot where I usually stopped, at the beginning of the slope, then started walking round the track to cool off and regain my breath.

When I arrived at the rat I reached down and picked it up by the tail. Walking over with it to the prisoner I believed had put it there, I stood next to him as he sat on the slope, the rat hanging by its tail in front of his face. Now *he* was on trial as all eyes were upon us, save those of the guard who was studiously avoiding what was going on.

"Sorry, friend," I said pleasantly, "I'm afraid I fucked up your rat. But I really didn't see him in the path there till just now. Here." I held the rat closer toward him. He shrank back from its stench.

"Hey, man! That ain't my motherfuckin' rat! What made you think that my motherfucker?"

"Nothing. Just thought it must be, since you were sitting here right in front of it. If it's not yours, whose is it?"

"Man, *I* don't know whose is th' motherfuckin' rat! This here's a jailhouse, right? Thas a jailhouse rat. Everthin' in the jailhouse belong to the Man, 'cludin' you an' me. Give the motherfucker to the Man!"

He said it while pointing to the guard, who was still staring straight ahead, seeing nothing. Nice recovery, I thought, and headed over toward the guard. There must have been seventy men in the yard, but not one was moving or saying a word. All were watching to see what I would do now, many smiling in the same appreciation as I at the way the black prisoner had put the ball—rather, the rat—back in my court.

I came up on the guard from the right rear and slowly lowered the rat down right in front of his face.

"Excuse me, officer," I said, respectfully, "I found this dead rat. It seems to be a health hazard. What should I do with it?"

The guard was no rookie. He knew what was going on, and he had a place to maintain in that jungle, too. He kept looking straight ahead and said, "Educated man like you oughtta know what t' do wit a dead rat, Liddy. Throw the motherfucker away."

"Sounds reasonable," I said and, ignoring the trash barrel, walked down the steps and across the yard until I was about fifteen feet from the high wall. Still holding the rat by the tail, I swung it in a giant circle and hurled it over the wall toward the area where another guard patrolled whenever there were prisoners in the yard.

"Way t' go, Liddy! *Fuck* the rat!" someone shouted and the tension dissolved in a roar of laughter. Grinning I threw them all a salute and went over to the fountain to get a drink of water.

As the summer wore on, I became a trusty. A newly created law library for prisoners had to be set up, and I was asked to do it. I was happy to, and I soon had the place functioning. I did what I could for the other prisoners, giving them both legal and practical advice—the latter usually tipping them off to the tricks either prosecutors or court-appointed lawyers were trying to play on them to induce guilty pleas, and I filled many a "porpoise paper."

For the uninitiated, as I was at the time, a request for help with a "porpoise paper" can be baffling. "You know, man," I was told. "You a lawyer! One of them papers in the form of a porpoise." Then it dawned on me. What the poor guy was trying to get me to help him with was a motion filed *in forma pauperis*, a Latin legal term meaning "as a pauper."

Since I was once more practicing law, life was as pleasant as it can be in the D.C. jail. As Fran would say, "You can get used to hanging if you do it long enough." But problems did arise from time to time, sometimes with quite unintended consequences, which brought home to me how very careful I had to be in conversation with my new friends in the prison. The most forceful example occurred late in August.

A young white man was assigned a cell in my tier, CB4, third floor. No sooner had he arrived than he started hanging around my cell, trying to make conversation. I became suspicious of him for a number of reasons. First, he apparently was assigned immediately upon arrival to CB4, third floor, which was preferred housing in the D.C. jail. That just doesn't happen in a prison. One waits his turn. The young man told me that he was a Quaker who had been arrested for some antiwar disturbance on the White House grounds and had refused to pay the modest fine imposed, preferring instead to go to the D.C. jail. That didn't make much sense either. Then he asked me, "What are you in for?" and I made an excuse to leave and asked one of my friends to check him out.

My friend came back the next day and said, "I don't know what he does now, but the dude say he a reporter. He tol' some people he works or usta work for *The Washington Post*."

Alarm bells went off in my head. It would be just like some young, idealistic, leftist reporter for the *Post* to try to steal a march on Woodward and Bernstein by getting a firsthand story from me. Even though I wasn't going to

433

talk to him, the mere fact that he was in a cell on my tier with access to me would lend credence to any story he might write.

"Damn!" I exploded. "That's all I need."

Then, as if speaking of Becket as a "turbulent priest," I said, "*Jesus*, I'd like to get that sonofabitch transferred off this tier," and walked away.

That, I would learn, was a mistake. I did not yet understand the depth of loyalty and appreciation I had generated among many of my fellow prisoners by helping them. Do them a favor or an injury, honor requires them to repay it, and they were constantly looking for some way to do so.

Just how much of a mistake I had made in thinking out loud was brought home to me a few days later when I noticed that the young man wasn't around and inquired after him. He was, I learned, in the hospital.

"What happened?" I asked.

"Tore his ass."

That was all the answer volunteered. Further inquiry would have been a breach of etiquette, and it wouldn't do to appear too concerned about the fate of the young man, nor too curious. By the same token I had to find out what had happened to him. If someone had slugged him saying something like "That's for lookin' to snitch on Liddy" and the guy *was* with *The Washington Post*, I could expect an uproar in the press. There would, I knew, be an official report of any incident that caused someone to be hospitalized. My next move was obvious: get hold of the official report. I'd have to bag the records office.

That might sound difficult, but it wasn't. The records office was right next to the area where sick call was held. Like all prisons, the place couldn't be run without convicts, and many were assigned to the records office. Officials were used to seeing convicts in there. I went on sick call and, when I got near the head of the line, bribed a couple of guys to create a diversion while I slipped into the records office.

434

If you act as if you own a place and know exactly what you're doing, others assume it to be the fact. Within minutes I had located the file, removed the report I wanted, copied it on the Xerox machine, and was out of there.

Back in my cell I examined the report. It speaks for itself in describing not only what happened to the young man, but what was common in the place John Sirica designated specifically as an appropriate place to confine me for contempt of court for refusing to turn informer. (I have deleted the inmate's name from this report.)

DEPARTMENT OF CORRECTIONS

DETENTION SERVICES

AUGUST 24, 1973

Memorandum

To   : Mr. A. Washington, Superintendent
            (Acting) Detention Services

Thru   : The Associate Superintendent, Operations

Thru   : The Senior Captain

Subject : STATEMENT OF SEXUAL ASSAULT

Re   : [   ]

Inmate [   ] #[   ], was interviewed by the writer on August 23, 1973, in the Captain's Office, D.C. Jail.

This interview was conducted in the presence of Lieutenant J. Eaton and Officer D. Robinson. In reference to the alleged sexual attack on Inmate [   ] on August 22, 1973, the subject gives this version of the incident:

Inmate [   ] contends that he returned to Cell Block #2 after a Rotunda visit, at 8:30 PM, August 22, 1973. As he was approaching his cell (229), he observed about a dozen inmates at the far end of the range. He entered his cell, (which was already open and remained open) and began writing a letter. At this point, four (4) inmates entered his cell, pushed him in a corner and demanded him to engage in oral and anal sex with them.

Inmate [   ] states that he did not immediately comply with their demands, and they began to beat him about the head with their hands. He did not fight back, he states, because of his religion and his beliefs, nor did he yell out, because he was fearful for his life.

Inmate [   ] contends that ten or twelve inmates forced him to submit to acts of fellatio and sodomy for one and a half hours. When he became nauseated, they released him and allowed him to sit on the bunk. Using this opportunity, he dove through the open cell door and darted to the range gate and collapsed.

During this same interview, Inmate [   ] alleges to have been sexually assaulted on one other occasion. This earlier incident, he asserts, occurred August 21, 1973, in Cell Block #2, First Range, West, during the Inside Recreation Period. Inmate [   ] claims that he was lured into a cell ". . . they wanted to talk to me," was assaulted forty or fifty times by thirty or thirty-five inmates.

Inmate [   ] contends that he can positively identify only two inmates in either of the alleged assaults, stating that [   ] #[   ] and [   ], #[   ], on August 21, 1973 and August 22, 1973, did sexually assault him, beat him with fist, covered his head and face with sheets, and let other inmates unknown to him to commit sexual assaults on him.

For the record, it should be noted that Officer E. Todd, on August 22, 1973, at approximately 11:00 AM, reported to the Captain's office an unusual amount of inmate traffic around Inmate [ ]'s cell. Inmate [ ] at that time was housed in CB-4, in a Third Floor cell. Officer Todd suspected, although he could not substantiate the fact, that Inmate [ ] was participating in some sex activity because of the attention given him by other inmates, and felt that if he remained in the Unit, he would be attacked by numerous inmates.

The writer and Lieutenant Sutphin interviewed Inmate [ ] and discussed at length, with him, the reason for his transfer to a Maximum Security Cell Block. Inmate [ ] was transferred to CB #2, Population, single cell status.

Submitted for your information and the record.

Clinton Cobb
Captain
Shift #2

XXVIII

Everybody wanted to get into the Watergate act, including the District Attorney of Los Angeles County. He indicted John Ehrlichman, Bud Krogh, David Young, and me for the Fielding entry in Beverly Hills on a charge of burglary under California law. Howard Hunt testified against us to the California grand jury that brought the indictment; so did the Cubans, but they didn't say anything. Young got out of it on a federal grant of immunity. In the middle of September 1973, U.S. marshals picked me up at the D.C. jail for transport to Los Angeles to face the charge.

The first leg of the trip was short; we went directly to the Alexandria, Virginia, jail. It must have been standing there when my mother's family owned that part of the country because the cell I was placed in had for a toilet a recess in the masonry wall at the bottom of which was an open hole. Below that was an open sewer. Peter came to the jail to explain what was going on; Fran paid a final visit, and the next morning the marshals and I boarded a commercial jet for Los Angeles.

I was lodged in the Los Angeles County jail, where, after a supervised delousing shower and the affixing around my wrist of a plastic band, I was led away. I glanced at the band. It had the number 2596–931 embossed on it, plus the letters "H.P.—K.A." The number I understood. I asked the deputy who was escorting me what the letters stood for and he answered, "High-powered. Keep Away." It meant that I was to have no contact with other prisoners under any circumstances.

They meant it. An entire wing of the jail hospital had been cleared, and I was placed in the last room on the hall. It was windowless except for a peephole in the steel door. Inside a fluorescent light protected by a steel grill burned overhead day and night. From time to time the peephole would slide up from the outside and a deputy would peer in to be sure I was still there. Meals were served to me. The emphasis was on Mexican food, for which I'd luckily acquired a liking in the days I used to go into Juárez from Fort Bliss as a cadet.

The light burned constantly, and I began to have difficulty keeping track of the time of day. I didn't trust the type of meal served as a reliable indicator because that could be manipulated. The problem was solved when I noticed that there was an ant colony infesting the area near the toilet. The ants had regular hours that appeared to coincide with local time. When, according to the ants, it was time to go to bed, I tied a black sock over my eyes as a blindfold and went to sleep. On 19 September I wrote to Peter Maroulis:

Arrived today safely and without incident on writ of Habeas Corpus ad Prosequendum. U.S. marshals confirmed arraignment AM tomorrow, 20 September, at which time I shall advise court that you are attempting to arrange counsel pro bono publico, but request appointed California counsel in the interim or, failing pro bono, for the duration of the prosecution.

Local officials (Jail) here courteous, positive in attitude. I am isolated in hospital room apparently in sincere effort to avoid possibility of incident. Result, however, classic KGB/KAFKA. . . .

Two things helped me maintain my orientation: visits by my court-appointed attorney, Charles Gessler of the Los Angeles Public Defender's office, and my fellow prisoners. I knew no one in the Los Angeles County jail, but the fact that I had defied all three branches of the United States government, executive, judicial, and legislative, in refusing to become a "rat" had preceded me. Sometime during the endless hours there was a lifting of the peephole and soft knock on the door. I went to the hole and saw a prisoner on the other side. He looked furtively from side to side, trying to spot any guards before they spotted him and he said hurriedly: "We know who you are. We got the word you're O.K. Need anything?"

"No, but thanks."

"How about a good milk shake, with eggs and ice cream?"

"Sounds great, but how're you going to get the door open?"

"Don't need to. I gotta go. I'll be back."

And he was. Again the lifting of the peephole and the soft knock. When I came to the door he pointed toward the floor and disappeared from the peephole. There followed a noise at the floor along the bottom of the door. I squatted down and in a moment a piece of plastic slid

439

under the door through the thin crack between it and the floor.

"Pull on it!" came the hoarse whisper from under the door. I did and the plastic turned out to be one corner of a clear plastic bag.

"Hold it!" I stopped pulling.

There was more sound, a gurgling this time. Then the plastic bag, most of which was now on my side of the door, began to fill with a thick fluid. After it was fat with the liquid there was more rustling and then a whispered, "Pull!"

I pulled and the rest of the bag, now knotted to retain the content on my side of the door as I pulled the still flat and empty portion toward me, came all the way through the crack.

"Drink it; it's good! I gotta go. Be back later for the bag."

My benefactor vanished as swiftly as he had appeared. I looked at the bag. It could have contained poison, but I had come to trust my fellow prisoners. Although this man was Hispanic, the blacks had taught me how much the poor appreciated a white man who would help them. To the impoverished and semiliterate, an education such as mine was viewed as godlike because of the power it represented. I could take on "The System" on its own terms and best "The Man" at his own game. I had never accepted so much as an apple from a prisoner for my help, and as prisoners were transferred from one prison and one prison system to another, that fact had spread among the prison population of the nation like a cold in a subway train. I lifted the bag and drank.

Peter Maroulis reacted immediately to my being held in such conditions, and within two weeks I was transferred to the federal prison at Terminal Island, off the coast in Los Angeles Harbor at San Pedro. There the warden placed me in isolation again.

My father was a man very slow to anger but when he

440

did he used all the power of his extraordinary mind, personality, and experience. He flew with Peter to California and requested an appointment with the warden of Terminal Island. The warden fled, leaving a female associate warden to face my father. After he and Peter punctured several ridiculous rationales with logic, it was decided there had been a mistake and I was released to the general population of the prison.

It was rare that my father was able to visit me, but he did so a few times in the D.C. jail and now in Terminal Island. I marveled at how well he handled visiting his son in prison. I might just as well have been a boy at summer camp again, for all the bars and other penal trappings seemed to mean to him. Typically, there was not one word of rebuke. Quite the contrary, my father supported my refusal to incriminate my former associates. A superb lawyer himself, he had nothing but contempt for John Sirica's professional ability; during his visits he and I and Peter would discuss case law that might be helpful in the argument of appeals; he even attended the argument of the appeal of the Ellsberg case, the Court of Appeals displaying courtesy by permitting him to sit inside the bar. Other than such professional conversations, my father limited himself to assuring me of the health of my mother, wife, and children.

Years later, when I was free and he dead, I commented on his seeming imperviousness to what I had assumed must have been very alien circumstances and surroundings for a man with multiple knighthoods, a former mayor of our town, and eminent member of the bar. It was then my mother said to me, "You still don't know, do you?"

"Know what?"

"The first time your father was ever in a prison wasn't to visit you. It was to visit his father, at Sing Sing, when he was fifteen years old."

In California, I thanked my father for his help in person and Peter by letter dated 15 October 1973:

Peter:

Just want to say 'thank you' amigo, and tell you not to worry about me.

My only instruction is that you spare six for pall-bearers. As for the remainder, kindly do the usual.

Charles Gessler turned out to be a remarkably good lawyer. He quickly noted that under the law of California at that time, burglary was defined as the breaking and entering of a dwelling place in the nighttime with intent to commit a crime therein. There was no question of the breaking, the entering, the dwelling (there was an apartment on the floor above), or that it was in the nighttime. But where, Gessler wanted to know, did the California penal law say that photographing a document (what the prosecution said we intended to do in there) was a crime? The prosecution went crazy trying to get around that one. They speculated that we must have used lights and, therefore, must have stolen some of Dr. Fieldings electricity, but they couldn't prove even that.

In the meanwhile I stayed at Terminal Island, assigned to the recreation office as one of the clerks. I started working out with the other clerk, a good friend who hated weight-lifting as much as I loved it. He paid a black man who had operated a health club in civilian life to drag him out of bed to the "iron pile." The black guy could bench-press 400 pounds and kept his end of the deal with glee.

I joined the famed writing class run by ex-prisoner and noted screenwriter Bob Dellinger who brought best-selling authors into the prison as guest lecturers. There I struck up a friendship with a classmate from the woman's prison, situated on the same island. She was rated nationally at chess and I played her by mail. Meanwhile I continued my efforts on behalf of other prisoners with legal problems. Here's how I recorded the windup of the year 1973 at the time.

3 December 1973

Dear Peter:

Little news, but I am happy to report that the master has not lost his touch. Did a federal sentence modification appeal for a chap and got results within one week—immediate freedom! Score one more for the Archfiend!

Gordon

13 December 1973

Dear G———:

Sorry we didn't have more chance to chat after class. To answer your question more fully, it never occurred to me to leave the country to begin life anew elsewhere, nor does your inquiry prompt any inclination to do so in the future. I love this country; it is the greatest and most powerful in the world and I have been serving it in one capacity or another for most of my adult life. Besides—running from trouble is not my style.

Gordon

(over for chess)

17 December 1973

Dear Peter:

Please don't let my present circumstances throw a pall upon your Christmas. Thanks to your efforts I am out of the hole and very well indeed. I am now 155 pounds (up from 137) and today bench pressed 195 lbs. . . .

Gordon

It was a remarkably happy Christmas and New Year, considering the circumstances. My sister and brother-in-law gave Fran $1,000 so she could visit me for a week during her Christmas vacation, and Peter flew out to spend Christmas Eve with us. Going into 1974 I was at a physical and mental peak.

Terminal Island prison was fascinating in the people I met, things I was able to do, and events I observed there. Once out of the hole and in the general population I lined up with the rest at the mess hall and sat wherever was convenient. The population was about one-third white, one-third black, and one-third Hispanic. The men seemed to gravitate naturally toward their own race in the mess hall, and that's the way we sat; but if a man of a different race sat at one's table, that was fine too. Some tables, however, were filled with close friends who always sat together. I hadn't been there long before I noticed one of them. It stood in the best location in the mess hall, in a corner, where everyone's back was protected, in an elevated area with a commanding view of the entire place. The table was always piled high with fresh fruit and the finest of foods.

One winter day, as I was looking about for a place to sit, I was tapped on the shoulder and a prisoner nodded toward the table in the elevated corner. One chair was empty. "Sit over there," said the prisoner, "you're welcome." I went over and as I did the others rose and greeted me warmly. "From now on, you sit here," said Salvatore Bonanno.

His nickname was Bill and I was soon to meet him again as a classmate in Bob Dellinger's creative writing class. Bill Bonanno himself had been the subject of a best-selling book, *Honor Thy Father* by Gay Talese. We became good friends. Huge associates sat at the surrounding tables, and no one approached who wasn't invited.

At Christmas Eve dinner Bill asked me whether I planned to go to midnight mass in the chapel and I told him I did not.

444

"I hear you can sing," he said, smiling; "the right kind, like in church."

I admitted I could sing but said it had been a long time since I'd been in a church—to sing or for any other purpose. Bill nodded and changed the subject.

At about 11:50 P.M. that night I was sitting with some friends. The dormitories were still unlocked for the night because the evening count had been postponed for Christmas Eve. I felt a presence and looked up to see two huge figures towering over me. They were men who sat regularly at tables flanking Bonanno's.

"*We're* all goin' t' midnight mass. *We're* all gonna sing with Mister Bonanno. What're *you* gonna do?"

I peered upward at those giants standing at either side of me and said, "Looks like *I'm* going to midnight mass to sing with Mister Bonanno."

The two behemoths smiled. "We figured you musta forgot," said one, looking at his watch. "We knew you wouldn't wanna keep the priest an' Mister Bonanno waitin'."

At the party Bill gave after midnight mass he threw his arm around me and announced: "I *knew* anyone whose mother's name was Abbaticchio hadda be O.K.; right, boys?" As they all laughed he added, "What I like about this guy, it's the only kinda singing he knows."

The authorities were always leery of me, yet at Terminal Island, once we got the matter of my being in the general population straightened out, they gave me little trouble. Things were not always good times and sunshine at T.I., and during the cold, rainy winter there was a mass strike. As it went on, anyone talking to me in the yard was photographed with me from the rooftops by guards.

When the prison was once more secured, the guards came in force in the dorms in the middle of the night wearing helmets and carrying shields and truncheons to take away those that informers had fingered as leaders of the strike. One of those removed slept in the bed next to me, and I expected to join him but they left me alone. The

445

others were made to run naked in the cold across the rain-swept yard to board a bus for other prisons.

Terminal Island had its share of the normal goings-on in any prison: drugs, corruption, and homosexual triangles. One morning I awoke to find the young man in the bunk three rows away from me awash in blood. His throat had been cut from ear to ear. No weapon was ever found. He was due to be released in six weeks. Because the death rate was becoming embarrassing to the administration—it averaged a murder every ninety days while I was there—his death was ruled a "suicide." Laughingly we all called it a "suicide with help."

The education department at Terminal Island was the only good one I observed in the many prisons of my experience. Once, when a college professor, who had taken a flyer on a marijuana venture, was released on bond after starting a class in world history, I was asked to continue it. I agreed, provided I be permitted to start the course all over again and teach it my way. I did, and the prisoners told me no one had ever leveled with them before on the way the world really worked and they now understood it for the first time. By the time I had gotten to the Middle Ages, class size had doubled and members of the administration often came to hear my lectures. There were a lot of unintended laughs.

"All right, men, here we have Catherine de Medici, Queen of France, with one son who's an idiot, another who's sick, and a third who's a fool; so she's got to run France herself. And she's got the Huguenots in rebellion and here she is, an Italian girl in France and in trouble. What does she do?"

A hand went up. "Well, the thing t'do in a situation like that is, if y' can, y' whack out the big machas on the other side."

There was a murmur of approval at this analysis.

"O.K. What's the best way to do that?"

"Well," suggested another student, "da *best* way is t' set up a sitdown; catch 'em all in one place an' waste 'em."

446

Another murmur of approval.

"All right," I said, "let's see what Catherine did. She invited all the Huguenot leaders to a banquet to talk over their differences. A lavish sit-down. Then, just as they're all seated, back go the drapes and in come the guys with the swords and crossbows. Zap! Every one of the son of bitches is wasted."

Up jumped a burly man of Italian extraction accused by the government of belonging to a group noted for its organization. He slapped his cloth cap on his desk top and exclaimed, "*God*damn; I *knew* a good Italian broad like that would know what to do!"

One of the most interesting persons I have ever known I met at Terminal Island. Somewhat disguised (which, for obvious reasons must be continued), I used him as the model for the character T'ang Li in my novel, *Out of Control.* A pure Mongolian, he was a red-belt master of the High T'ai Chi Tiger-style martial art. I was attracted to him by sound. One day, as I walked the yard, I heard a steady series of what sounded like heavy-caliber pistol shots resounding around the walls. It came from the direction of the heavy bag hanging in the rear of the yard. Curious, I walked toward it. I had never heard any of the many boxers who used the bag hit it anything like that hard.

As I closed on the bag the sharpness of the sound grew in intensity, and finally I detected another sound immediately preceding the powerful "crack!" It sounded like a flag flapping furiously in a gale, almost a ripping sound. To my astonishment I saw a fifty-year-old Oriental hitting the heavy bag backhand with his bare fist. His arm and hand moved so fast his sleeve was making the ripping in the wind sound. Then he hit it a series of blows with fists and elbows with blinding speed and finished with a high, leaping kick that almost took the bag off its chain. The man was surrounded by a number of others, all Oriental (one, I learned, an American Indian), who deferred to him. I knew some lethal moves that I'd learned

447

in the army and the FBI, but I'd never seen anyone move like that, including the best of my instructors.

I noted that the man used weights to maintain his remarkable physique and slowly I got to know him. He was interested in firearms, and after some conversation he realized that I knew as much more than he about gunfighting as his knowledge of martial arts exceeded mine. We worked out at the weights together, and finally I suggested that it might be mutually advantageous to exchange instruction. He hesitated, then took me aside and told me that he had never imparted such knowledge to an Occidental and, despite our friendship, was not sure he ever should. He paused and studied me quietly. Finally he spoke. "You are a very violent man. I can see it in your eyes."

"I control it."

"You must. If you ever use what I teach you to take advantage of the weak, I'll find you wherever you are and kill you myself."

I knew he meant it. He wore long-sleeved shirts buttoned at all times to conceal the tong tattoos on his wrists. As a child, both his thumbs had been broken deliberately by his father in two places, then tied back so that they grew into recurving hooks that were nearly useless for gripping but rigid as steel and able to tear out a throat or disembowel a man with a single backward stroke.

In the recreation office, with the door closed and locked against outsiders, I taught my friend slowly and patiently all I knew about gunfighting. Slowly and painfully he instructed me in his art. He taught that the outcome of every battle is decided in the minds of the opponents before the first blow is struck. His ability to concentrate was such that his muscles became incredibly hard, his body seeming to swell and strain from within. Even though he was pulling his blows they came close to shattering my bones, and when I blocked his arm or leg it was like hitting a concrete post. I showed and explained to him my burn scars and he understood immediately, suggesting that it was that degree of concentration that was needed to produce the transformation of flesh and bone into steel and concrete. He was a truly remarkable man and from him I learned in months of concentrated effort not only exceptional physical feats but, more important and lasting, an even deeper appreciation of the extraordinary power of the human will.

By March of 1974 the District Attorney of Los Angeles had been re-elected, and no one could get around Charlie Gessler's defense so the locals made a deal with the feds for a face-saving exchange: the Fielding entry defendants would be released by California with all charges dismissed so they could be tried in Washington for the alleged violation of Dr. Fielding's civil rights by breaking into his office. The theory was that it had somehow intimidated Dr. Fielding in the exercise of his civil rights, even though he didn't know at the time who had done it, and believed the police when he was told it was a junkie in search of drugs. But in those days no one cared whether anything made sense or not. Richard Nixon was still President of the United States and anything went. Once again it was back to the D.C. jail.

My job as law librarian at the D.C. jail was now held by someone else, so I was assigned to work as a clerk in the classification and parole office in the Rotunda, which also served as a visiting room. Because I was once again a trusty, Fran was permitted to sit across from me at a metal table when visiting rather than forced to view me through shatterproof plastic and speak to me on a phone. She visited me the maximum three times a week, stopping off at the jail on her way home from Langdon elementary school in northeast Washington.

On one of these visits, I told Fran that she was still a young, goodlooking woman and that if she wanted a divorce for a new start in life, I'd understand. She shook her head and answered with a smile, "No thanks. The devil you know is better than the devil you don't."

449

The new job was pleasant. With the exception of the chief of classification and parole—one of the few whites remaining in the system—the personnel were all black and they made an honest effort to be fair and compassionate in their dealings with the prisoners there. If I had to have dealings with any prison personnel, I would choose those over any group in the Federal Bureau of Prisons with whom I have ever come into contact. The black personnel of that office were, perhaps because they came from the same community as those with whom they dealt, not infected with a sense of moral superiority and seemed genuinely to care about the prisoners, treating them like people rather than "cases." They had nothing to do with me because I was here for civil contempt rather than serving my twenty years so I could observe their performance objectively.

The building was in such bad condition that sections of masonry were falling away and an overhead shield of scrap lumber protected us all from injury from the falling debris. We joked about any of us ever getting out of there alive.

On 1 April, at 11:35 A.M., I was told to report to R&D to don civilian clothes. At 1:10 P.M., still not knowing what was going on, I was turned over to three U.S. marshals who whisked me away by car. When I asked to see their writ they admitted they had none; I was being removed from prison illegally.

The marshals drove me to the Congressional Hotel on Capitol Hill, where I was asked to sign in at a security desk. I did, adding to my signature the words "under protest." I was then ushered into a room occupied by a young lawyer named Cates. He was on the staff of the House Judiciary Committee. It was considering the impeachment of President Nixon and he wanted to question me about the Fielding entry in Beverly Hills. I declined. "Boy," said Cates with a sigh, "I wish you'd talk. I'd sure like to be the guy who got G. Gordon Liddy to talk!"

"How about settling for the guy who got G. Gordon Liddy a sandwich?"

"Huh?"

"Listen, you dragged me out of prison illegally, without a writ, and brought me here for questioning without even notifying my attorney. That wasn't bad enough. You made me miss the noon meal, such as it is."

The young man looked worried and asked the name of my attorney. I gave him Peter's name and phone number, and he called, telling Peter that I had refused to answer questions about the Fielding entry. Peter was patient with his young colleague: "I'm not surprised that Gordon won't answer questions about the Fielding case. You guys just indicted him on it. He goes to trial in June."

"*We* indicted him?"

"You're part of the United States government, aren't you?"

"Yeah, of course."

"Well, who do you think indicted him, East Germany?"

"Yeah, yeah. I can see your point."

"Look," said Peter, "he's not going to talk to you. You've got him there illegally without a writ and . . ."

"We just wanted to ask him some questions."

"Without a writ? Tell you what: *I'd* like to ask him some questions, too. When you're finished, why don't you send him up here?"

"Uh, yeah. I see your point."

"Look," said Peter, "why don't you just get him a nice sandwich, take him back to the jail and we'll forget all about it?"

"Right. And thanks." Cates hung up and turned to me. "What kind of sandwich would you like?"

Thus ended my experience with the Judiciary Committee. Thanks to Peter I got a good ham and swiss on rye out of it. The committee got zilch.

On 10 May a one-day trial on my two-count indictment for contempt of Congress was held in the United

States courthouse before Judge Pratt. The facts were not in dispute, only questions of law, so a jury was unnecessary. Peter protected the record and I was found guilty, waived a presentence investigation, and asked to be sentenced immediately.

Judge Pratt was no John Sirica. He is an intelligent, educated, and experienced man with judicial temperament and, it developed, a sense of humor. Because I was already doing twenty-one and a half years there was little point in trying to sentence me to anything more than something for the record, and Judge Pratt knew it. He gave me a year, suspended it, and put me on a year's probation. Downstairs I went to the office of the Chief Probation Officer where he slid a form in front of me and said, "Sign here."

"You don't mind if I read it first?"

"No, no. Go ahead. It's just routine."

He was right. The paper was a routine probation agreement in which, among other things, the probationer agrees in writing to refrain from association with other felons. "I'm sorry," I said, "I can't sign this."

"What? Why not?"

"Because I'd be in violation of the terms of my probation by six o'clock this evening."

"Huh?"

"If I sign this, I'm agreeing not to associate with any known felons, right?"

"Yeah."

"Well, when I get back to the D.C. jail this evening, I'm going to start right in associating with a thousand felons. All day, all night, twenty-four hours a day, seven days a week. What do we do about that?"

"Oh, Jesus. Look, Mr. Liddy, I can't go up and tell the judge that. Would you mind writing that down so I can bring it to him?"

"Sure."

Back up we went to the courtroom. Judge Pratt, trying hard to keep a straight face and almost succeeding, remarked, "There is something to what you say." He then reduced my probation to one hour and ordered the marshal to hold me for that hour in the small cell behind the courtroom. "And don't let any other felons near him while he's there." Judge Pratt smiled. So much for contempt of Congress.

The Fielding entry trial that started before Judge Gerhard Gesell in the same courthouse on 26 June, however, was something else again. Judge Gesell, too, was about as far removed from Judge Sirica as a Porsche 911 SC from a clapped-out Volkswagen. I disagreed with him politically, philosophically, and on some matters of law, but Gerhard Gesell, by breeding, education, experience, and temperament was a judge to be respected, and anyone who had observed my demeanor in his courtroom and that of John Sirica noted the contrast.

The first order of business turned out to be a novel guilty plea by Chuck Colson. He came into the courtroom and I tossed him my usual salute. Colson appeared distracted. Well he might. He pleaded guilty to conspiracy to obstruct justice by spreading a derogatory press account about Daniel Ellsberg. There was no such crime; they all just made it up, and Colson, now in the throes of religion, pleaded guilty to it and turned government witness. When I realized he had undergone conversion I observed to Peter that ". . . everyone who ever knew this guy is in trouble. If he'd run over his grandmother for Nixon, imagine what he'll do for Jesus."

The trial was a classical battle between branches of the federal government. Judge Gesell forced the executive branch, in the person of President Nixon, to hand over evidence in the interest of a fair trial. When it came my turn, however, he was to prove less effective. Many of the witnesses expected to testify for the government had testified before Congress and, under rule 3500, the defense was clearly entitled to transcripts of that testimony for purposes of cross-examination. Judge Gesell duly issued the subpoenas for us to Congress; but when Congress chose to ignore them—the same thing it was up in arms about the executive branch's doing—the judicial branch, in the person of Judge Gesell, proclaimed itself powerless to compel the legislative branch to abide by the law. I watched all this with knowing amusement, by now thoroughly acquainted with the Watergate double standard, and finally refused to allow Peter to take the issue to the Supreme Court as he wanted very much to do; there was enough bad law coming out of Watergate.

On 12 July, after a trial that seemed to feature as a witness everyone who was anyone, including Henry Kissinger, and some comic moments when Dr. Fielding got started testifying and even Judge Gesell had difficulty shutting him up as he rambled out of control, the jury found us guilty. On 31 July Judge Gesell sentenced me to one to three years in prison, to run concurrently with my twenty-one and a half. For all practical purposes it was no sentence at all, but I was now a veteran convict with a record of nine felonies.

I returned to my job at the D.C. jail, but now I had something more to occupy my mind; *Harper's* magazine had asked me to write for publication a letter to my wife giving my views on what was going on in the country at the time and some thoughts on the raising of our children. It was a chance to earn $5,000 for Frances and I jumped at it. Both Fran and the children helped with the research. To further stave off boredom, I started growing a beard.

On 9 August President Nixon resigned. He had been insufficiently ruthless in not destroying the tapes. Had he done so, he would have served out his term. I had, at least, the knowledge that my silence had helped bring him more than two additional years as president, and I was pleased when President Ford issued his controversial pardon. It would take years, I knew, to wind the hysteria down, but with the possibility of doing anything more to Richard Nixon removed, the psychotic Nixon-hate would run out of fuel eventually, and I'd have a shot at getting out of prison when the majority came back to its senses and saw things as they were, rather than through the distorted looking glass of the television screen and some major newspapers. In the meanwhile the great Watergate flywheel set in motion by the news media and engaging the energies of so many unreconstructed liberal Democrat lawyers obeyed the laws of inertia and continued to spin.

On 12 October I was brought by marshals to the office of the Watergate Special Prosecution Force to meet James Neal. He, too, wanted a crack at trying to persuade me to turn informer and testify at the continuing trials of my former superiors and associates. I thought that strange. By now, I was certain, everyone on the other side must have understood that the last thing I was going to do after coming this far would be to turn informer. I wondered if there was some other, undisclosed, reason for my being brought to Neal's offices.

The marshals ushered me into the building. I must have looked quite out of place among the crisply dressed young attorneys. Although I weighed 155 and had as recently as the previous March bench-pressed 245 pounds, I was bearded and wearing the same grimy-collared shirt stored in the basement of the D.C. jail that I'd worn every day of my two last trials, and my suit bore the wrinkles of eighteen days in court.

We threaded our way through the halls until someone told the marshals that Peter would be with me shortly. I was to go right on into Neal's office. I walked in and the door was shut behind me. When I looked at the figure sitting behind the desk I couldn't believe my eyes. It wasn't Jim Neal. I had been shut in the room alone with John Dean.

I stood stock-still, trying to figure out this development. Here was the perfect opportunity to kill Dean. A pencil was lying on the desk. In a second I could drive it up through the underside of his jaw, through the soft-palate and deep into his brain. Had someone set it up? If so, why now? President Nixon was out of office. I had received no orders to kill Dean and certainly wouldn't be presumed so irresponsible as to do so on my own initiative; his death might hurt, through reaction, the trial chances of Mitchell, Ehrlichman, Parkinson, and Mardian. I decided to consider that my being shut up alone in the room with Dean had just been an incredible error.

Thoughts similar to mine must have been going through Dean's head. He had jumped up with a look of stark fear to find himself trapped behind the desk. There was no way out except through me. I let him suffer for a moment, then said: "John. I don't think they knew you were still in here."

Dean stammered in relief. "Gee, uh, Gordon, uh, how are you?"

"Not bad, considering the circumstances. How's yourself?"

"Oh, good, good, fine!"

"I'll wait outside."

"No, no. I was just leaving." Dean scooped up some papers, scurried around the desk, and swept past me to the door and out on a nearly dead run. I sat down and moments later Peter Maroulis followed Jim Neal into the office.

Neal was to the point. He told me he disagreed with my not talking but said he had to admit that he saw something admirable in it, then added that with President Nixon now out of office and my having been abandoned to my fate by my erstwhile superiors, he could see no more point to it. He noted that I had now served nineteen months and that were I to cooperate, he didn't see the necessity of my spending another night in prison. He thought I owed it to my family, for whom he expressed high regard, to consider his offer.

I liked Neal. He appeared to me to be a sincere man who just happened to be on the other side of the fence politically. In that spirit, I declined his offer politely, but he refused to take my no for an answer, asking me to think it over and consider carefully what he said. I agreed

456

to do so and, on 25 September, after explaining my position to Fran, I wrote the following letter:

Hon. James Neal
Associate Prosecutor
Watergate Special Prosecution Force
United States Department of Justice
1425 "K" Street, N.W.,
Washington, D.C., 20005

25 September 1974

Dear Mr. Neal:

Recently, you asked that I re-evaluate a decision, taken two years ago, which led me to decline to appear as a witness before a Grand Jury of the United States District Court for the District of Columbia; the United States Senate and the United States House of Representatives, to testify on matters encompassed generally by the term, "Watergate."

I have completed such review, which included a careful consideration of the arguments you presented. I have concluded, however, that for the reasons expressed to you both by my counsel, Peter Maroulis, and by me, that my original decision was correct. Accordingly, I must advise you that, should I be summoned as a witness in the forthcoming trial of Messrs. Haldeman, Ehrlichman, Mitchell, et. al., by either the prosecution or the defense, I shall decline, respectfully, to testify.

I know that you appreciate the fact fully, but for record purposes let me state that should it be necessary, I am prepared to demonstrate a third time the futility of attempting to force me to violate the principles by which I live.

457

*Thank you for the courtesy you have displayed
continuously in contacts with my counsel, my family
and with me.*

Sincerely yours,
G. Gordon Liddy

G. Gordon Liddy, No. 175-292
Cell 208, Cellblock 4
D.C. Jail
200 19th Street, S.E.,
Washington, D.C., 20003

A week later, the year and a half for contempt Sirica
had given me for refusing to talk ran out. Peter applied
immediately for bail pending disposition of my long-
standing appeal of the original Watergate verdict and, to
my surprise, it was granted. On 2 October 1974, after
twenty months in prison, I was again a free man.

To be alone, Fran and I took a trip to the Outer Banks
of North Carolina; then I appeared with Mike Wallace
on CBS's *60 Minutes*, splitting the fee 60/40 between my
obligations to Fran and my children for support and Peter
for legal services.

A friend was retiring from a career in military intelligence, and I was invited to the ceremony, held at a
guarded military post. There I was greeted warmly by
intelligence generals and asked to speak. I did, stressing
the necessity of fidelity to the code of the intelligence
officer. Applause and praise greeted my remarks, and
among my finest memories of Watergate shall always be
the hours spent among those splendid men.

The errors at the original Watergate trial were serious,
but I wasn't optimistic about winning the appeal; the
courts are swayed by public opinion, and I doubted that
anyone wanted to reopen the Watergate can of worms
just to give me a new trial. *Carpe diem* seemed the most
appropriate motto in the circumstances, and I made the

most of my brief span of freedom. In the four months fate was to allot me before returning to prison to serve my twenty-year sentence I enjoyed my wife, children, family, and friends; I lived as I flew: mixture full rich, throttle to the firewall. Then the fun was over. The Court of Appeals denied my appeal, invoking the "Catch-22" of criminal law, *Chapman* v. *California*: error of constitutional dimension notwithstanding, there's enough evidence of guilt for the error to be deemed "harmless." In prison it's called the "if they wantcha they gotcha" rule and on Monday, 20 January 1975, Chief Judge George Hart said "gotcha." He ordered me to turn myself in at the Danbury prison within forty-eight hours.

XXIX

Beards were not permitted at the Danbury prison, so on the morning of Wednesday, 22 January, I shaved it off in the home of Peter Maroulis. He arranged with the warden to have the front door manned and ready so that when he drove me up to it, I could enter immediately, avoiding the expected horde of reporters.

We arrived on time but the front door was locked. I waited as the press swarmed around me until a guard came out and led me to another entrance in the front wall a hundred feet away that opened into the Receiving and Discharge office. The pack of reporters separated us quickly and I walked rapidly trying to catch up. A reporter tripped over some cables and fell. Another planted himself in front of me; he wasn't going to let me by until I said something. I gave him a right forearm blow, low across the stomach and he, too, went down. Finally I gained the R&D door and was let in.

"Goddamn, Liddy," said one of the guards, "you're the first guy ever knocked someone down to get *into* this place!"

459

Because I had been sequestered from the general population of Danbury the first time I was there as an unsentenced prisoner, I wasn't very familiar with the place. Now I saw that it was a mirror image of the prison at Terminal Island. The WPA had marched across the country in the 1930s building prisons from the same set of plans. The front of the place contained a hospital and administrative offices. A wing down the left contained cellblocks and dormitories. The right wing was another set of dormitories, a theater, and mess hall. The rear was sealed off by a dormitory over a laundry, more administrative buildings, a commissary, and barbershop. A sally port led into a small rear yard housing the power plant, garbage disposal, and shop offices. To the rear of that was "industry," where they made electrical wire harnesses, and a glove factory. A huge water tower dominated everything. The principal yard was the great rectangle formed by the walls of the buildings. The prison was classified as medium-security.

The now familiar processing went quickly, and I was assigned to "Massachusetts House" as the first-floor dormitory housing those assigned to "orientation" was called. It was jammed. Designed for about fifty prisoners, there were nearly a hundred packed in there. Lines formed at the few toilets at some times of day, and it could be very uncomfortable.

There is always a solution to a problem if one has imagination. I visited the office and stole a piece of official stationery, the typical "optional form No. 10" headed, at the top left:

United States Government
MEMORANDUM

In appropriate bureaucratese I wrote a memo from "The Associate Warden Programs" to "All Concerned." Subject: Venereal Disease.

The memorandum noted the alarming increase in venereal disease among prisoners newly admitted to Danbury and ordered that pending their successful treatment, one toilet be posted V.D. ONLY and all those identified as suffering from venereal disease be restricted to the use of that one toilet. While the guards weren't looking, I posted the memo on the bulletin board, then made a cardboard V.D. ONLY sign, and posted it over the far toilet. For about a month, until the hoax was discovered, I never had trouble finding a toilet when I wanted one.

Things went smoothly at first, but on Sunday, 9 February, one of the guards looking to make a name for himself accused me and another prisoner of eating a contraband sandwich. He claimed to have observed this dangerous activity from a spot where to do so would have been all but impossible, then offered me the choice of "extra duty" with a mop or a "shot"—slang for a disciplinary report, something like an indictment.

The shot, I knew from my experience at Terminal Island, was the basic institutional fear mechanism. It could lead to solitary confinement; increased custody restriction; restriction of mail, visiting, and other privileges; set-off of parole date; and other unpleasant consequences. I was being offered a choice of letting this cretin get his rocks off making me mop the floor or accepting the uncertain results of a shot. The psychology of the incident was clear; so was the counterpsychology: "Mister, I'm doing twenty years in this joint. I'm not eligible for parole until 1981 and you'll *have* to let me out in '94. Shots mean nothing to me. For your information I was eating a Triscuit, not that you could have told a sandwich from a watermelon from where you were. Get somebody else to mop; I'll take the shot."

The kangaroo court that follows every shot gave me a "warning and reprimand" and the guard was furious at my open defiance. Any kind of loss in a contest with a prisoner is considered very serious by prison guards; it threatens their shaky self-image. They're supposed to be the good guys; yet they live on the verge of poverty, in-

461

side they are psychologically weaker than the "bad" guys, drive clunkers, and go home at night to plain-looking wives. It galls them no end when the Cadillacs and Mercedeses glide up to disembark beautiful women into the visiting room, each wearing a guard's yearly salary on her finger or around her neck. And when the woman is white and the prisoner black, they go right out of their minds. Looked down upon universally in the community, the guards could not tolerate any loss of face *inside* the prison.

Faced with this loss, the guards struck back, employing an old trick I had heard of at Terminal Island. I wrote to Fran regularly, as well as to other friends from the past. One of the letters was to a woman I had known. At the nightly inspection and reading of mail one of the guards held the letter back until my next letter to Fran came out from me. He then switched letters and envelopes.

When Fran got the wrong letter, she understood the guard's tactic immediately and it made her furious. The first thing she did was to call Peter to alert him to the tampering with the mails.

While this was going on I received word that my father, seeking to spare my mother the chore of picking him up at the end of his commute from New York City because of a heavy snowstorm, had elected to walk the more than a mile home through the snow in spite of the fact that he was living on nitroglycerin for his heart and was seventy-five years old. It was a gentlemanly gesture typical of the way he lived his life, and that's what it cost him that Wednesday, 12 February 1975. He never made it home.

With obvious relish the captain of the guards told me as I sat across from him in his office that I would be permitted to attend only the actual funeral and that in the custody of two guards. I asked to use his phone.

"Help yourself."

I called Peter Maroulis and explained the situation to him, then said: "Peter, there is no way I am going to my father's funeral under guard and let my mother go home alone afterward. These people need some guidance, fast. Burn a favor; call in an IOU; do anything you have to. Just do it."

"I'll take care of it."

The captain was grinning when I left. The rules were clear. I had a twenty-year sentence and that meant close custody and that meant two guards, and I was lucky to be going at that. He had a winner.

So he thought. While I was in the mess hall having an early lunch the following day a "caseworker" rushed up to me. "Mr. Liddy, please come to my office right away to sign your furlough papers. We've got to get you out of here by *noon!*"

"I'm not going anywhere with guards."

"No, no. Your custody's been changed to 'community.' You're going by yourself. You can stay at your mother's. You don't have to be back here until Sunday night at eight o'clock. How much money from your commissary do you want to take with you?"

Peter never told me how he did it; he just did it.

The funeral was what one would expect for a man who had achieved knighthood, was an ex-mayor, and loved by everyone who ever knew him.

That Peter had been able to handle the problem of the guards didn't change the fact that they had tried. Fran was up for the funeral with the kids and let me know in short words how angry the switched letter had made her. "Something should be done about them doing that," Fran had said, "trying to break up families like that is sick." She was right.

A great joy came over me as I drove back. I am happiest in battle, and I was going to war. My thoughts wandered, and the next thing I knew a traffic cop was pulling me over for a moving violation.

"May I see your license and registration please, sir?"

I took out my Danbury prison furlough paper. On it was my photograph, prison number, and all the details of what I was doing out of prison. The officer studied it

463

a moment, then handing the paper back to me, he said, "Take it easy, Mr. Liddy, O.K.?" snapped me a salute, and waved me on.

I'm old school. I believed that when one goes to war it ought to be declared, so I made an appointment with the warden. When I entered his office he had the associate warden for Programs—the man who had day-to-day operational control of the prison—in there with him. I told them of the letter switching. They denied it, as I had expected.

"Gentlemen," I said, "you're on notice. You fuck with me at your peril. All I wanted was to be let alone to do my time. But you and your underlings chose to shoot. Well that's fine. Because unlike anyone else you've ever had in here, I can shoot back. And I've got the heavy artillery."

I stared at the associate warden, a man named Max Weger infamous among the prisoners for his unfairness toward them. He walked around like a peacock in polyester leisure suits with white plastic stack-heeled shoes and matching belt that made him the envy of every pimp in the prison. "I'm not going after your men, mister; I'm going after you. And I'm going for your throat."

I turned on my heel and walked out. Weger followed me into the hall as the warden sat open-mouthed behind the desk.

"What do you mean?" Weger asked, "What are you going to do?"

"You'll find out when I've done it, when it's too late."

I knew that the two of them would consider what I'd said in light of their recent experience in having received orders to change my custody and send me to my father's funeral alone on a three-day furlough. They'd be expecting something political, from Washington. The administration was, after all, still Republican. They were as wrong as they could be. This was a personal war, and I intended to fight it myself.

The first thing any commander needs in war is information on the capabilities and intentions of the enemy. I also wanted to know their weaknesses. Any prison is a close little community, a microcosm susceptible to all the weaknesses of the flesh and spirit to be found in larger communities everywhere. I intended to conduct psychological warfare, my will and intelligence against theirs. They had tried to disrupt my family. I would cause them grief for that. I knew the world of the bureaucrat to a degree they never would. I intended to hurt them in their careers by seeing to it that every mistake they made came back to haunt them. There is nothing a bureaucracy fears more.

To do all that I needed information, intelligence. I had all the time in the world and I intended to use it to build a full-capability intelligence organization. In the meanwhile I would gain the confidence of my fellow prisoners by running a first-rate legal assistance program. There would be no charge for my services, but when I needed help I knew that gratitude would prove invaluable. For the moment, though, I was left to my own resources. I noted that nothing was accomplished at Danbury without the use of prisoners. That included maintaining the electrical system and internal telephone repair. I saw a prisoner walk into the administrative offices section with a tool kit on his hip and, dangling from his belt, a Western Electric model 1011-8 lineman's telephone test handset equipped with alligator clips. It was the one known to Bell system workers as the "Butinsky." I grinned as the poetic justice of the opportunity hit me. My next move was obvious. It was beautiful. I was going to wiretap the sons of bitches.

The ideal place to wiretap in Danbury prison was the junction board but that was out of the question. It was up front in the administrative area, near the captain's office, next to the control center, and always padlocked securely when not under supervised use. I had no business in that area, and my presence there would have been noticed immediately. The lines, on the other hand, were easy to spot and trace. There were a lot of telephones,

465

only some of them capable of being used for making an outside call. I determined that the handset, a tightly controlled item, was available, but only for very short periods during working hours. That was sufficient. I noted that the prison administrators were on the phone frequently, and my plan was simply to tap in to likely lines briefly but persistently, taking potluck.

All prisoners were liable to search by any guard at any time. Usually they were looking for a sandwich being smuggled out at the mess hall. Fortunately it was the dead of winter and I had been issued a bulky, shapeless, homemade outer jacket. It was ugly, and all prisoners preferred first the navy pea coat, then the army surplus field jacket with liner. It was the new men, like me, who were stuck with the homemade Mother Hubbard. Its saving grace was that it concealed the outline of the handset stuck in my waist. If I were caught with the forbidden device in a search, what did I care? I was doing twenty years.

My system worked well and in a remarkably short time I knew who among the staff was having sexual intercourse with the wife of what other staff member; who was telephoning the Bureau of Prisons in Washington to undermine his superior behind his back; details of a dispute between the guards' union and the administration; and who was jealous of and suspected his wife of infidelity. That was all I needed.

Shortly thereafter, one man, whose wife was faithful now but had been promiscuous before wedlock became convinced that said wife was still rolling over for almost everyone and it drove him crazy. False transfer rumors caused some to lose sleep for weeks, while others agonized that their petty thefts had been discovered and an investigation was imminent.

But all that was kid stuff. I just did it to keep them off balance while I sought the lever to really take them apart. I almost had it once when men I recruited reported that a guard had sold off a batch of prisoners' winter clothing. I heard about it too late. A prisoner had confronted the guard with the receipt and in exchange for it he got the clothing back. It was then that I called people together and pointed out how much more devastating could have been an indictment for theft of government property to say nothing of the embarrassment to the careers of the warden and associate warden for being so lax that such theft by their own men could be accomplished under their noses. I extracted a promise that anything like that in the future would be brought to my attention immediately. With their help I accumulated valuable materials from the warden's and other administrative offices that we were able to borrow and copy on the Xerox machine.

Some of the things I did were just plain fun. When the maintenance department head neglected to fix a leaky faucet that was keeping me awake, I got an empty one-gallon can from the kitchen and put it under the faucet. As the hot water trickled into it, I timed the flow, then calculated how many thousand gallons of water was being wasted from that faucet, how much the electricty cost to pump it into the water tower, and the cost to heat it all. I then wrote a suggestion memorandum to the associate warden for operations, stating how much money and precious "O.P.E.C. fuel oil" could be saved the government by repairing that faucet; then suggested that all other faucets in the prison be checked immediately. With copies designated everywhere, the poor maintenance man, near retirement, was foaming at the mouth. My faucet was fixed immediately. Another time I found a dead bat in the power house. I sent it to the safety and sanitation officer with the memorandum suggesting an autopsy to see whether or not it had a communicable disease. All these things had to be taken seriously and answered; once something has been made a matter of written record in a bureaucracy, it cannot be ignored. It drove them nuts.

But I was after bigger game. These were the people who put a young kid to work in a front-end loader that wouldn't be permitted on any job site in the country because of its archaic and dangerous design. While a guard

467

ran around in panic, it slowly crushed the kid's neck. A convict brushed the guard aside, picked up a sharp tool he was forbidden to touch, and cut the hydraulic hoses to relieve the pressure. By that time it was too late. The young man had been decapitated. The administration just hosed off the blood and put somebody else in that deadly machine. Another time they remodeled the dormitories. In the course of that they nailed shut the fire door. When fire broke out, the trapped convicts used the guard telephone in the dorm in a frantic effort to reach the control room to report the fire. The response of the guard in the control room was to tell them that prisoners were forbidden to use that phone. Then he hung up and let them burn. A horrified fire chief from a nearby town was denied entrance to fight the fire. Furious, he drove his engines through the fence in an effort to save the trapped and screaming men. It was too late for five of them. They burned to death. That's the kind of people I was making war against.

The administration maintained a network of informers in the prison, so I built up my own organization slowly and carefully, taking great care against the possibility of penetration by an informer for the warden. In the meanwhile John Sirica denied my motion for a reduction of sentence. On 20 June I had sought it on the theory that the original sentence had been handed down consistent with the then position of the government that I was the most senior person responsible for Watergate. Since that time the government, in the trial of Mitchell and the rest, had taken the position that I was anything but the most senior man involved, and yet I had nearly three times the sentences of Messrs. Haldeman, Ehrlichman, and Mitchell. And adjustment was in order.

In his Memorandum Opinion and Order turning me down, Sirica noted correctly that I was unrepentent and then carried on about the fact that I had refused to talk, despite the fact that I had served a year and a half—most of it in the notorious D.C. jail—for that refusal. Still, the press would be watching and on the issue of my refusal to inform, Sirica's position was weak. I hadn't been given a temporary sentence conditional upon cooperation with the prosecutors or the Senate, like Hunt and the four Cubans; mine was final, the example held up to the other five. That his exhortations to cooperate were directed to them and not to me he made quite clear when he summed it up for them on 23 March, 1973:

> For these reasons I recommend your full cooperation with the Grand Jury and the Senate Select Committee. You must understand that I hold out no promises or hopes of any kind to you in this matter but I do say that should you decide to speak freely I would have to weigh that factor in appraising what sentence will be finally imposed in this case. Other factors will of course be considered but I mention this one because it is one over which you have control and I mean each one of the five of you.

Nothing could be clearer than the last sentence of that paragraph.

But in his decision Sirica wanted to contend that all those urgings to cooperate were directed to me, too. As he put it in his Memorandum Opinion and Order turning me down:

> Yet, despite this admonition by the Court and the fact that the Court subsequently gave consideration to the other defendants on this basis, this defendant chose to continue to refuse to cooperate with the government investigations.

How to get around what he said on 23 March? Easy. Just falsify the record. When Sirica quoted himself in his Memorandum Opinion and Order, here's how that last sentence came out:

Other factors will, of course, be considered but I mention this one because it is one over which *you have control* and I mean each and every one of you.

Look at it again. ". . . each one of the five of you" has become ". . . each and every one of you." It's no mistake; the italics for "you have control" were admittedly added for emphasis. The change was deliberate. John Sirica falsified the record.   ..

Moreover, the old fool actually attached as an appendix to his Memorandum the original court transcript of the sentencing proceeding, and buried in it is the line as he in fact uttered it. In preparing his Memorandum he must have looked right at it, doctored it for his purposes in the new opinion, and then later forgotten he was giving the lie to himself by attaching the original. Those who have a hard time believing that anyone can be that dumb can look it up for themselves. The citation is 397 F.Supp. pages 949 and 963.

One mustn't be *too* hard on the old fraud, however. Consider the circumstances. He's a bit slow and was caught in a bind. On the other hand, how *does* one characterize the behavior of a federal judge who uses his power to seal the record to cover up his mistake in seating a juror who cannot speak English well enough to answer his questions without an interpreter? Of a United States District Court judge who deliberately doctors the record of his own court to support a false position he has taken on the facts in an official opinion and order of the court? Two words with a familiar ring come to mind: *sordid* and *despicable*.

By the autumn of 1975 I had the administration of the Danbury prison at each other's throats and was ready to launch a full offensive. Experience disclosed that the Bureau of Prisons printed up "Policy Statements" that ostensibly required the wardens of prisons under bureau jurisdiction to conduct themselves in ways that would at least appear to be reasonable. These statements were given out to legislators and the press when prisoners complained of abuses, and the press especially was too eager to believe that what the statement commanded was the way the prisons were actually being run. In fact the statements were a sham. Wardens had a free hand and treated the prisoners arbitrarily, paying only lip service to the statements of policy. The Bureau of Prisons could not care less.

Two prisoners, Richard Dale Stover and Raymond S. Miley, had brought an action in the United States District Court, New Haven, Connecticut, seeking to compel the warden to obey the Bureau of Prisons policy statement with respect to legal mail. By October 1975 it was getting close to trial. Stover was a bright young man but not a lawyer. He asked me for help and I saw my opportunity. I was preparing a suit of my own to compel the warden to obey the Bureau of Prisons rules with respect to solitary confinement. At Danbury any guard who wanted to throw a prisoner into solitary could do so at will. Even if the facts were so clear that he were later found not guilty by the kangaroo court, the man typically had suffered for days in solitary anyway. It gave guards enormous power over prisoners, and I was determined to strip them of it.

With Stover's permission I applied to the court to join our causes. It was granted. I asked for and received permission to prosecute the case myself. The Legal Services Division of the Yale Law School under Professor Dennis Curtis provided the facilities I needed to supplement the gross deficiencies of the law library at Danbury, and on 5 May 1976 a writ of mandamus was issued against the warden and those officials acting under his supervision.

The victory rocked the prison. The hated guards had been defeated in court. New prisoner recruits were brought into my organization, and Dick Stover was able to get statements from many who had heretofore been afraid of the guards, sure they could never be defeated by prisoners. Finally, I was able to recruit guards themselves as informers against the administration. Satisfying as that victory was, I wanted Weger. He played right into my hands, seeking to evade the judgment of the court. The old warden retired and the new one wouldn't even speak to me, turning around and going the other way when I walked toward him. The effect on the morale of the guards, already low because of the internal dissension I had provoked or exacerbated, was severe. The warden was running from a prisoner! It was unheard of. Then I struck again, bringing suit to have the new warden held in civil contempt of court for failure to abide by the court order Dick Stover and I had won. I demanded and received a hearing in federal court and put the warden himself on the stand. Now he couldn't escape me and I smiled as I moved in, sweeping my arm to indicate the courtroom, and said: "Welcome to *my* yard!"

Although knowing an objection would be sustained, I sought to introduce into evidence written charges of lack of training made against the warden by his own guards through their union. I was precluded, but not before I got what I was really after: to show the warden papers from his own desk; to let him know that I had the power to reach out and take anything I wanted in that prison.

The warden was mortally embarrassed. Present in the courtroom was a lawyer from the Bureau of Prisons, his associate warden, and top officers. When the judge took over the questioning, the unnerved warden agreed that many of the acts described in our affidavits were violations of policy—in effect tossing Associate Warden Weger to the wolves. I smiled at Weger. It was 19 August 1976. It had taken me more than a year and a half, but I had made good in my promise to "go for your throat," and I drew my finger across my throat to remind him. Weger responded typically: he insisted upon testifying as a witness and then tried to justify what he had done, in effect contradicting his superior. From that moment Max Weger was finished at Danbury.

By noon, word of the fact that I had put the warden on the stand and he had given up Weger reached Danbury. By the time I had returned, gone through R&D, and was on my way back to my quarters everybody had heard the electrifying news.

It was after working hours when I approached the rear of the grandstand from which softball and other games in the prison yard are watched. I was greeted and hailed by passersby for the victory, even though it was as much the result of the efforts of Dick Stover as of mine. About thirty black prisoners were congregated behind the grandstand and on nearby benches. When the black men saw me, they grinned and raised their fists in salute, shouting, "Hey, Hey!" The closer I got the more excited they became and when I was upon them some were on their feet, right arms and fists outstretched, shouting. A feeling of immense power came over me. The martial music and roaring crowds that thundered through the shortwave forty years before rang through my mind again with undiminished strength as I answered the blacks' salute with the one I'd learned before the American flag so long ago in 1938: my right arm shot out, palm down, and was answered by a roar of approval. In that moment I felt like a god.

XXX

As far back as April 1975 a man named Bill Braswell, of Charlotte, North Carolina, whom I had never met, started a campaign for my release from prison with the distribution at his own expense of bumper stickers reading FREE GORDON LIDDY. Then one of my neighbors, Jim Gavin, whom I had also never met, started another movement and the two were joined. Gavin was an ex-Marine, former congressional aide, and now Washington representative for the giant conglomerate Tenneco. He knows how the system works and he started to organize. William F. Buckley, Jr. was kind enough to lend his name to the committee, and soon Fran was appearing on national television, and letters started to pour in to the White House backing my release.

Not long afterward a prisoner on furlough from Danbury on his own initiative approached the famed Boston lawyer and best-selling author George V. Higgins and asked him to help me. Higgins, quite properly, told him that if I wanted his help I could ask for it and pointed out that I was already represented by counsel. A mixed-up story got into a Washington newspaper, and I invited George down to get the matter straightened out before things got out of hand. We found each other at opposite poles politically but with a shared sense of humor that was enough to frighten conservatives and liberals alike. That did it; with Peter Maroulis's blessing Higgins, who had represented among other notorious figures Eldridge Cleaver, took on another. Me. He started seeking support for clemency among those I considered "the other side." Peter Maroulis submitted a petition to Gerald Ford, and it, and I, sat it out through the election of 1976.

Meanwhile, back at the Danbury prison, the administration looked upon me with fear and loathing in about equal measure. When the Department of Justice requested a "Progress Report" on me in connection with my request for commutation of sentence, the prison authorities saw a chance to at least get me out of Danbury, something they would otherwise not have been able to do because I had a twenty-year sentence. They weren't about to recommend clemency for their enemy—but a transfer was something else again. Under "Evaluation" the report referred to all the trouble I had caused them with understatement: "He is a strong willed, capable individual who does, at times, try to influence the actions of others through intimidation," and went on to recommend that ". . . he be transferred to a camp type facility at this time to complete the remainder of his sentence."

The intent was clear: to get rid of me they wanted to ship me off to Allenwood, Pennsylvania.

The campaign to free me boomed on. I was now being

474

referred to in editorials as "The Man in the Iron Mask," and columnist after columnist was backing my immediate release. Thousands of signatures on petitions were being collected by the organization Jim Gavin had put together and in response to Fran's remarkably effective appearances on television as far away as Canada. George Higgins was bringing in some of the biggest names in the country, but on 2 December I learned in a letter from him that he had gone too far: "Terry Lenzner is pondering the best way to feel out John Sirica. . . ."

I stopped reading and sent the following message to George:

> FUCK SIRICA. STOP LENZNER. STRONG LETTER FOLLOWS.

In that letter, dated 8 December, I said ". . . there is a limit. That limit is John Sirica. I'll do the full twenty before I'll authorize an approach to him, or sit still for an unauthorized approach. I'm serious. Stop Lenzner."

George Higgins stopped him. And when *The New York Times* later supported my release editorially, he sent a telegram of his own:

> MY PROFOUND SYMPATHIES ON THE ENDORSEMENT OF OUR CAUSE IN TODAY'S TIMES. I KNOW HOW EMBARRASSED YOU MUST BE.
>
> GEORGE

On 3 January 1977 I was advised that the Federal Bureau of Prisons had approved my transfer to the Allenwood prison camp, my ninth place of incarceration since January 1973. I was on my way in forty-eight hours. After a stopover at the Federal Detention Center in Manhattan, we went on to arrive at a frozen, filthy, overcrowded dump. The place was so crowded that the newer prisoners slept on cots in the hallways next to single-sheet glass walls covered with ice. My bunk was across from the ice machine—an incongruous touch, I thought. It labored and chugged to the accompaniment of all-night television echoing from the TV room around the corner, where four insomniacs insisted on keeping it at maximum volume. I disabled the ice machine, but that didn't stop the television.

After ten nights of asking politely that the television be lowered so I could get some sleep, I filed a request for administrative action asking the television be limited to from 6 A.M. to 11 P.M. My request was ignored. The next night it was 12 degrees Fahrenheit and windy, but I moved my cot outdoors anyway, leaving a note for the guard so that he'd know where I'd gone when he came around for "count." He found me outside.

"Liddy! What the hell are you *doing* out here?"

"Well, until you woke me up I was sleeping in the nice fresh air. What the hell did it *look* like I was doing?"

"Man, you can't *do* that! Nobody's *ever* done that! You gotta go back inside!"

"Nope. Can't sleep inside with that damn television on all night. I'm not going back in until it's off."

"I'll turn it off. Please. You can't stay out here."

"O.K. On your assurance that the television stays off I'll move back in."

The man was as good as his word and I kept mine, getting my first night's sleep in ten days. The next day a new camp rule was promulgated restricting television playing to reasonable hours.

All hell broke loose. As I wrote on 27 January to my friend Judith Mears, one of the lawyers of the Yale Legal Services Center:

> . . . *the camp is polarized between those who love me for belling the cat and those who hate me for asserting that my right to sleep is superior to their claim of privilege to view cartoons at all hours at maximum volume. I now sleep with a contraband ax-handle. I love it. As Kipling said:*

476

"Four things greater than all else are,—
Women and Horses and Power and War."

Love,

Gordon

I had gotten the weapon, a stout handle with a piece of
jagged, rusted metal still attached to one end, by jumping
the fence into a restricted area and taking it from behind
a tool shed. Things got worse before they got better, and
I decided I needed something more easily wielded. From
the power plant I obtained a short length of steel pipe and
from the kitchen a table knife. I sharpened the table knife
on cement, the way I had a similar one at Danbury when
I learned from the authorities that an informer had told
the FBI there was a contract out on me and I declined
official protection in favor of my own method.

I was assigned to work in the kitchen, and when I'd
come back in the evening, I'd find my mattress either
burned or soaked. I got a new mattress and slid it under
a nearby vacant one, used it to sleep on at night, and replaced it with the burned and wet one every morning. The
nitwits who were trying to bother me never caught on and
kept burning and soaking the same mattress. When that
didn't drive me to ask for a transfer out of the dorm,
whoever was behind all the foolishness transformed it into
a serious matter by stealing my locker. It had my legal
papers in it. Now I had to do something.

I had a friend in the same dormitory whom I knew from
Danbury. He had been trained by the French in counter-
terrorist work in Algeria. Together we picked out the most
likely suspect and watched his habits to establish his pattern of activities. As this was going on, an old Italian man
undertook to learn what he could for me. The whole business offended him because my enemies wouldn't come out
and fight. The word started to go round that whoever they
were, they were yellow.

My friend and I planned to kidnap and interrogate our

477

suspect, whose loose talk had now confirmed that he knew the location of the stolen property. Before we could take the first step to put our plan into operation, the necessity for it disappeared. The pressure on my enemies grew to such an extent that to combat accusations of cowardice from other prisoners, they passed the word that they were going to attack me on the night of Thursday, 3 February 1977. I was determined to fight it out and knew well that I'd have to kill. I telephoned Peter Maroulis to tell him so that he could testify as to my prior knowledge that my life was in danger, and he suggested that I put it in writing in a letter to him for use in evidence in a plea of self-defense in case of a murder prosecution. I sat down and wrote:

> Peter L. Maroulis, Esquire
> Counsellor-at-Law
> 104 Hooker Avenue
> Poughkeepsie, N.Y., 12601
>
> *Thursday, 3 February 1977*
>
> Dear Peter:
>
> *This will serve as the writing you suggested I send to you in our telephone conversation this evening.*
>
> *In short, a situation, not uncommon in prisons, has arisen here in which I believe I may be called upon imminently to defend myself from attempted lethal attack. To do so effectively may well require that I use at least equally lethal force, and that may result in the death of my assailant or assailants.*
>
> *I believe that any such assault will be by persons who are armed and I have, accordingly, armed myself.*
>
> > *Arma virumque cano!*
> >
> > Gordon

P.O. Box 1000
Montgomery, Pa., 17752

There are few guards at Allenwood; it is not that type of facility, and even fewer are on duty at night. They have a large area to patrol and cannot really control the place in the late evening and early morning hours. One guard on duty that night who knew (as did everyone) of the planned attack, begged me to accept protection by spending the night in the hospital. He had been a Hungarian Freedom Fighter, immigrating to the United States after his country was invaded by Russia in the 1950s.

I put it to him this way: "If I run now, where do I stop? You of all the people should understand the results of weakness."

"But it's different, what happened in Hungary. That was between whole countries!"

"The principle is the same."

"Please. I cannot protect you. You may die."

"I don't want your protection. I can protect myself better than you can. If I die, I won't be alone." I showed the guard my weapons. I was smiling.

"You enjoy this!"

"Yes."

"It's true what they say. You are a fascist!" And off he went.

I lay down and arranged the covers over me lightly. I was fully dressed except for shoes so I needed only a blanket to keep warm. I had no intention of sleeping. In my right hand, lying alongside the right side of my body under the blanket, was the big ax-handle. That was the side that faced the open hall. I could sweep that handle out in a second and knock two men off their feet by striking directly at their knees. In my left hand was the knife, and the pipe was under my pillow. I was ready.

It was then that a second guard approached me. He asked if I wanted to go to the hospital to sleep, and when I declined he just nodded his head and said, "I didn't think you would."

"Don't worry about me," I said, "worry about them." I showed him my weapons and he shined his light on them, then looked up at me with a smile and said: "Shoot straight." I knew what he meant. Don't leave anyone alive as a witness. It was good advice and I intended to follow it.

The night wore on and the attack never materialized. No one wanted to be the first to die. They were afraid, never having learned what I taught myself as a boy: defeat the fear of death and welcome the death of fear.

At dawn it was all over. My enemies were in universal disgrace as cowards. In a dramatic about-face I was told by intermediaries that I would be given the location of my property if I would promise no reprisals. I agreed, got back my property, and that was that.

Only once did I serve time with someone I had myself prosecuted and sent to prison. At Allenwood I heard there was a black prisoner named Butch Anderson there. I had prosecuted a black drug addict by that name in the early '60s and sent him to state prison in New York. If he were the same man, he would be doing time on a different charge, but it made sense to find out just who he was and, if the same man, to keep an eye on him. I ran a little operation to obtain and copy his record. Sure enough it revealed he was the same man, yielding a photograph, his birthdate, residence, full information on his current offense and sentence, and so forth. I kept him under surveillance, but he caused no trouble at all. In turn, I left him alone.

On 11 February Fran, Jim Gavin, and George Higgins were received at the White House by Counsel to President Carter Robert Lipschutz. He was sympathetic, spent forty minutes listening, and promised action on my petition for executive clemency. Fran described Lipschutz as "kind and a real gentleman" and she was very encouraged.

While I waited I reestablished, on a much smaller scale, my intelligence organization using men transferred in from Danbury. More than anything else it was to keep my skills from becoming rusty, and just for fun I determined that the safe in the Control Center contained the following firearms: ..

Three Colt Police Positive revolvers in .38 Special caliber. Check the serial numbers and you'll find one is 470798.
One Colt Official Police revolver in .22 long rifle caliber. It has serial number 12670.
Five Colt Official Police revolvers in caliber .38 Special. One of them has serial number 716052.

If Allenwood was easy, it could also be funny. When warmer weather occasioned my cutting the grass at a cemetery on the grounds and an allergic reaction put me into the Lewisburg penitentiary hospital for a week to clear the fluid from my lungs, I returned to my old job as clerk in the kitchen. It consisted of typing up the daily, weekly, and monthly menus from the master that came from Bureau of Prisons headquarters in Washington. The master just read, for example, "peas." I was instructed to make that "fresh June peas." For "potatoes" I was to type either "oven-baked" or "fluffy mashed" potatoes and so on. It was harmless.

At about that time the Jewish prisoners won a court action requiring that those wishing to observe Jewish dietary laws be given a kosher kitchen and be permitted to prepare their own food. This infuriated the virulently anti-semitic guard force in general and kitchen staff in particular. I was given the new kosher menus to type and, following the usual practice, gave them "fresh June peas," "oven-baked potatoes," and so on. I did, that is, until the steward told me to stop. "Plain peas," he said, "are good enough for Jews. They don't need anything else."

I went to the Jewish guys and apologized, saying they couldn't have "oven-baked" and things like that on their menu anymore and told them why. They laughed so hard I thought they'd die, one saying: "The bastards would put *us* in the oven if they could, and they won't let us say

481

that's where we bake the potatoes? I'd write a letter to *The New York Times*, but they wouldn't believe it!"

There were only about thirty-five Jews in the whole camp and they stuck together. One of them decided to make an issue of the menu description just for the principle of the thing and they won. I was told angrily to put on the kosher menus ". . . whatever they wanna call their damn Jew food!"

The kosher menu was more limited than the non-kosher, so I did my best to make up attractive adjectives for them. When I substituted for "tomatoes" "Delicious Kosher Tomato Surprise," the kosher cook came over to me and said: "Goddamn, Liddy, what the fuck is that? I never heard of it!"

"Just cook them any way you want, and when you serve them, say, 'Surprise! Tomatoes!'"

On 12 April 1977 President Carter reversed Judge Sirica yet again and commuted my twenty-year sentence to eight "in the interests of justice." The only negative reaction was from Sirica and the Soviet Union, Sirica grumbling petulantly in the Washington press and TASS blasting Carter for the commutation on 14 April. I was now eligible for parole and a hearing was set for June.

One of the Jewish prisoners, a man called Jerry, became a good friend of mine. He had been an organizer for the International Ladies' Garment Workers' Union and was a fine amateur musician and a professional photographer. Jerry and I would take long walks and feed on conversation. He was a brilliant man who had gone into business for himself, lost a sum unfairly on a government contract, and recovered the exact amount in what was deemed by the courts an illegal scheme. When the situation in the mess hall, and other prisoner grievances mostly attributable to severe overcrowding and the ridiculous attempts of simpleminded prison authorities to try to "rehabilitate," boiled over into a food strike, I was elected by my dormitory as a bargaining representative. Jerry was elected by his dorm, and another Jewish man, a lawyer from New

York, was among the dozen finally chosen. That was too unwieldy for effective bargaining, and we ended up selecting from among ourselves five men: Jerry, the lawyer, a black, a Hispanic, and me. The strike was settled peacefully, but the administration resented it. I was called in by the captain and told that I was expected to decline such requests in the future, with the hint that failure to do so might affect my chances for parole adversely.

In June I was given a hearing by representatives of the Parole Commission and told that their guidelines made me eligible for immediate release. Because of my notoriety, the case was referred to the full commission for a decision and on 12 July I was scheduled for release on 7 September. All I had to do now was enjoy the Pennsylvania countryside for the summer and look forward to visits by Fran on weekends. A big cross-country race was scheduled for Labor Day, and I started training for it by running miles every day in addition to my workouts in the weight room. I should have known it couldn't last; trouble has a habit of finding me and I have the habit of embracing it when it does.

The superintendent of Allenwood tried faithfully to live up to his word in the negotiations that led to settlement of the food strike, but his concessions were resented by the red-necked guard force. A new assistant superintendent was assigned, a black man named Pringle. He came from Danbury with a bad reputation among the prisoners, and as soon as one superintendent went on vacation in August, Pringle abrogated part of the settlement agreement. The result was another strike. This one would be much harder to settle because the prisoners now had no confidence in the word of the prison administration. Once again I was approached to be a negotiator for my dorm, although the men said that in view of the fact that I had a parole date they wouldn't blame me for declining. But the captain had threatened me and that is always a mistake. I agreed immediately. So did Jerry and we were back in business as negotiators.

What the men were doing was not against the regulations of the camp. Had they refused their work assignments, it would have been, but no one is obliged to eat a particular meal. All they wanted really was to talk to someone from "Washington." For those who haven't been to Washington and thus don't know that officials from D.C. are no less anti-Jewish, anti-black, or anti-Hispanic than the rest of the country, because that's where they all come from, "Washington" spells hope for reasonableness. I knew better and so did Jerry, but we couldn't persuade the prisoners. The Bureau of Prisons sent up a regional commissioner from Philadelphia, but that wasn't Washington. No settlement.

The superintendent came back from vacation, but by that time Pringle had done his damage. Finally the Bureau sealed the place off and early in the morning removed me and several others in chains on the assumption that we were the leaders of the strike, Pringle telling the press that I had intimidated 400 men in the camp into it. The Bureau then poured in hundreds of shield-and-truncheon-carrying guards in an attempt to get the remaining men to eat. Many did. The rest were thrown into the hole at the Lewisburg penitentiary with me. When my Allenwood living quarters were searched my ax-handle and pipe were found but the knife was not. I was charged with possession of weapons.

At Lewisburg things had come full circle. I had served four years—over a hundred days of it in solitary—and was now the "oldtimer" who instructed the others in how to exercise and otherwise make it "in the hole." I was tried before the kangaroo court and sentenced to forfeiture of "good time," an automatic result of which would be loss of my parole date. I wasn't worried. I could always get another, and I looked forward to being in the general population at Lewisburg. The warden there was a man who boasted of his power, and I wanted to do to him what I had done to the warden of Danbury—in spades. It would

484

be a superb challenge, and this time I would have some really hardened convicts to work with.

It was not to be. I was told that the Lewisburg warden had taken the position that there was no way they were going to turn *me* loose in *his* prison; I had come from Danbury and I could damn well go back there. In days I was on my way, and you have seldom seen anyone sadder to see someone than the authorities at Danbury when I was brought back in there. I was put in the hole immediately and given another kangaroo hearing for good measure to keep me there while the Parole Commission took action.

When the hearing was over I used the weapon I had been saving for more than four years for just such an eventuality. I had placed on file a writing that said I would not speak to the press under any circumstances. I asked that it be canceled and for a copy of the form necessary to be filled out when one requests a meeting with the press. I knew I could get Barbara Walters and her equivalents from CBS and NBC up to see me with camera crews on a moment's notice, so I listed them in the form, telephoned Peter Maroulis, then turned in the form. The official held it as if it were red-hot: "You're finally gonna talk about Watergate?"

"No, my friend, I'm going to talk about the fire you had here when I was gone in which your guard, the same one I know had as many as sixteen administrative remedies filed against him in one day, refused to take a call from a dormitory full of men that was on fire. A fire that killed five men. I'm going to talk about the machine you're still using out back that cut the head off that poor kid. I'm going to talk about what happened to the guy you let a medical technical assistant operate on to remove a growth instead of having the doctor do it. The guy whose cancer spread because the growth was malignant and the M.T.A. didn't get it all. You know, little things like that."

I think it was about thirty minutes later that I was told that the superintendent of Allenwood had reviewed my

485

sentence and found it too harsh. I would lose no good time. The Parole Commission would be so notified. It was not expected that there would be any delay at all in my release. In the meanwhile, welcome back.

I grinned at them and made another phone call to Peter. He made another himself and then wrote the following letter:

PETER L. MAROULIS
ATTORNEY AT LAW
104 HOOKER AVENUE
POUGHKEEPSIE, N. Y. 12601

———

(914) 471-6050

August 25, 1977

Mr. Allan Turner
Federal Correctional Institution
Pembroke Station
Danbury, Connecticut 17752

Re: Interview with Media Pool

Dear Mr. Turner:

This letter will confirm this afternoon's telephone conversation with you in which I related to you that Mr. Liddy is postponing his interview with the Media Pool from Monday, August 29, 1977, (at Danbury), to September 8, 1977, (at Washington).

Very truly yours,

Peter L. Maroulis

PLM:in
cc: G. Gordon Liddy, Esq.

I celebrated this victory by entering the open-mile run in the prison's Labor Day games held on Monday, 5 September. I was curious to see how my physical condition had been affected by my time in the hole at Lewisburg and Danbury. I managed to do the mile in 5:30, but no victory this time: I came in third.

Because President Carter had not commuted my $40,000 fine, I still had one formality to get through before I could be released from prison. I had declared myself a pauper months before and filed a financial statement with the Department of Justice. The FBI investigated the matter and a hearing was scheduled for 6 September in the U.S. Magistrates Court at Williamsport, Pennsylvania. There the government disclosed that the FBI had discovered that my Korean War G.I. Life Insurance had a cash value of $3,000. It was surrendered to the court and I was ordered freed the following day. I still owed the $37,000, but I was no longer bound by Sirica's order that I stay in jail until I paid it.

At 3 A.M. on 7 September the press started to arrive and camp on the steps of the Danbury prison. Fran arrived at 8, and after parking her car—actually my son's '71 Pinto —she was ushered inside to wait for me. I was packed and ready to go. By now the press corps numbered more than a hundred. I waited on the front steps for Fran to drive the Pinto around because although I had a valid license, I was not yet covered by insurance. One of the reporters asked me where we intended to go, and I called from memory the name of an old Norwegian folk tale, "East of the Sun and West of the Moon." Another asked me how it felt to be out of prison and I replied in German, "What does not kill me, makes me stronger."

Fran couldn't move the car because of the crowd so I went over to her, put my gear into the trunk, closed it with some difficulty, and off we drove.

As Fran turned left out of the prison driveway, I saw a lineup of cream-colored Ford Granadas, all bearing New York state NYP license plates identifying them as press cars. They peeled off to follow. We got out to the highway and they were still with us. I told Fran to drive slowly as they moved ahead, filming through the rear windows; I thought that after they'd gotten their film they'd go away and leave us alone. No such luck.

When at least three of the Granadas were still with us as far south as New Rochelle, New York, I forgot that Fran was not one of my men and snapped: "Lose 'em!"

The poor girl tried, but she's just not cut out for that sort of thing—she kept signaling her turns courteously and, of course, they were all over us like a blanket. Finally, I'd had enough.

"Pull over."

"What?"

"You heard me, pull over. We're putting in the first team."

"But you're not even insured!"

"Don't argue with me. Goddamn it, pull over!"

Fran pulled over and we exchanged seats. "Now," I said to her, "let's see if these guys want to play." I tore away from the curb and turned left against a red light. The press guys had come to play all right and stayed right with me. I took them all over Westchester, the Bronx, and back into Westchester and they were *still* with me. "Damn it," I said to Fran, "I know they've got more cylinders and radios but *nobody* stays with me when I don't want him to. There's something wrong here. Hang on; I'm gonna see what we're up against!" I put the Pinto into a high-speed four-wheel drift across traffic and up into a dirt road leading into a cemetery, then did a one-eighty to see what was coming after me the other way.

"There's the problem!" I said to Fran, pointing out four Granadas and another make lined up after us, "there's *five* of the sonsofbitches!"

It was a challenge I couldn't resist and I took off, hitting over 70 mph through city streets, going through red lights deliberately, and taking turns at the limit of adhesion. By

488

the time I got into Jersey there were only two tails left and Fran, scared out of her wits, was crying uncontrollably.

Those last two guys were good, and the extra power and radios made them even better. But I was on home ground now. I grew up here. I took them down a side street with a partially concealed unimproved road leading off to the left. It looked like a driveway but gave out onto an intersection with three different directions to choose from. That's where I lost them. Just to make sure, I tore through about five more red lights, then slowed to calm Frances. As she wept I remembered that I always used to sing to Fran on long drives, and we were going all the way to Washington. I chose one of my favorites from *Cabaret*, whose lyrics I had modified to suit myself:

> . . . *the babe in his cradle is closing his eyes*
> *the blossom embraces the bee;*
> *but somewhere a voice says, 'arise,* arise!'
> *tomorrow belongs to me.*

A feeling of triumph surged through me. I was free and on my own terms. Blowing the reporters off the road was symbolic of my victory over Sirica and his allies in the press and all three branches of the federal government. In my mind a mighty chorus joined me as I finished singing:

> *America, 'merica, show us the sign*
> *your children have waited to see!*
> *The morning will come when the world is thine;*
> *tomorrow belongs to thee!*

Fran was wiping her cheeks with her handkerchief now. She looked over at me, eyes still wet with tears. "God, after all these years, you haven't changed at all!" She blew her nose lustily, then sighed, "I don't suppose you ever will." I grinned over at her:

"Bet your ass, kid!"

489

EPILOGUE

Readers might be interested in the results of the considerations that led me to ask Fran to become the mother of my children, and of the effect of Watergate upon their lives.

Our eldest, Alexandra (we call her Sandy), found herself ready to go to college with her father in prison, mother working, and no money. She entered the University of Maryland and earned her way by becoming a licensed commercial vehicle operator and driving a diesel bus at night, armed with a baseball bat. Now twenty-one, she is finishing her nursing studies at the College of New Rochelle, New York, where she is captain of the swimming team and well on the way toward her goal as an officer in the United States Navy Nurse Corps.

Grace, twenty, is a computer science major and language minor (French and Russian) at the University of Maryland, where she became vice-president of her dormitory. She earned her tuition working in a dress shop, and NASA is interested in having her work at the Goddard Space Flight Center even before she graduates.

In 1978 I watched as Jim, then seventeen, about six feet tall and 170 pounds, won the Washington metropolitan area CCSA senior breast stroke championship. He went on to be a scholarship student at Pennsylvania's fine Mercersburg Academy, contributing $1,000 per year to his tuition from summer earnings, making the honor roll, varsity swimming and water polo teams, and becoming chairman of the student body.

Our youngest, Raymond, hopes to follow his brother Jim to Mercersburg after having won varsity letters in both cross-country running and wrestling in his freshman year at Bishop McNamara High School in Maryland.

Between Jim and Ray in age is Tom. In 1975, just after John Sirica refused to reduce my sentence in a much publicized opinion, Tom entered the Washington metropolitan areas CCSA swimming championships in thirteen-and-under breast stroke. It was held at the Congressional Country Club in Bethesda, Maryland, and because of the vast number of competitors, took three days to get to the finals. As Tom progressed through the elimination races over those three days, his name was frequently heard by the crowd over the loudspeaker and there was much whispered speculation about whether he could be "related to *that* Liddy."

On 3 August, as the last race was about to be held, Tom lined up behind the starting blocks with the other finalists and started to strip off his warm-up suit. Unlike the others, however, Tom left on one last item of clothing besides his bathing suit, and when he mounted the block the tense crowd gasped at the inscription in bold red letters across his novelty T-shirt:

Property of
WATERGATE BUGGING TEAM

Now the crowd knew who he was, all right. As the starter called "swimmers ready," he stripped off the shirt, took his mark, and at the gun dived into the water. He came out the champion. Tom went on to become a scholarship student at Washington's outstanding St. Albans School, where he swims varsity, won the Interstate Athletic Conference breast stroke championship, and became president of his class.

Tomorrow belongs to them.

POSTSCRIPT TO THE 1991 EDITION

Not one word of the original edition of *Will* has been changed.
According to one of the authors of *Silent Coup*, the now-definitive
account of Richard Nixon's fall from office, this book was the key
to unraveling the truth about Watergate and, as such, should be
preserved intact. But *Will* is not just a book about Watergate. It
relates a lifelong journey from physical and psychological
weakness to strength, and a philosophy based on that journey. It is
a journey and philosophy that, according to the many letters I
have received in the past ten years, has changed uncounted lives,
so much so that in some bookstores the book has been displayed
under the heading "Inspirational" rather than "Biography." It has
been turned to in time of need by persons as remarkably different
from me as the late John Lennon.

Readers will note that in *Will* I approached my task of writing
from the perspective of what historians call a "primary source,"
relating only what I did, saw and heard. By that method I
discharged what the late Stewart Alsop characterized as my debt
to history. The new Postscript to this edition is different. I am
commenting upon a secondary source. There have been many in
the years since Watergate, of course, but this is the only one I have
deemed worthy of comment. I do so because the extraordinary
revelations in the book *Silent Coup* demand it, and have
engendered in me, once again, a sense of obligation.

WATERGATE REVISITED

The disembodied voice startled me: *"If you'd like to make a call, please hang up and try again."* It was late in October, 1988, and I was standing in my living room with a telephone receiver in my left hand and, in my right, a piece of paper that bore the telephone number 466-5544. Beyond the picture window in front of me lay my lawn, seawall and the Potomac River, but all I could see was the man whose telephone number I held and was about to call. He was sitting behind his desk, exactly as he was the last time I laid eyes upon him sixteen years ago, believing as I had until just days before that my intelligence operations at the Committee to Re-elect the President, including the Watergate break-ins, had been undertaken with his full knowledge and approval. Now I knew that to be false. Embarrassed, I punched in the number and prepared to apologize to John Mitchell.

My telephone call had been arranged. It had to be. At the very suggestion that he speak to me, John Mitchell had balked: "Good God, the last time I talked to Gordon Liddy, I went to jail!"

Mr. Mitchell was warm and gracious to me on the phone. He knew he had been the victim of lies, but he knew they hadn't come from me. I had remained silent. He forgave me for that—even after reading *Will* and realizing that in it I had told the truth and, had I testified to the same things years before, his chief accusers, John Dean and Jeb Stuart Magruder, would have been exposed as perjurers and his prosecution blown out of the water.

I concluded the conversation by thanking him for not "throwing me out the window," as he was reported to have suggested when asked why he didn't "throw Liddy out of your office" when I had presented the GEMSTONE plan to him on 27th January 1972. It was good to hear him laugh and realize that, despite what had been done to him, there wasn't a hint of bitterness in his voice. On the contrary, as he thanked me for my call, there was a kinship and

493

camaraderie in his tone that I shall always cherish—for, ten days later, John Mitchell was dead.

My telephone call to Mr. Mitchell had been arranged by Len Colodny, a liberal Democrat who had then been researching Watergate for three years with his partner Bob Gettlin, having started with a first step obvious to everyone except the Watergate Committee of the Congress, the Watergate prosecutors, the major news media and the academic establishment now teaching "the lessons of Watergate" at endless history, government, journalism and political science classes: they read the accounts and testimony of the same witnesses, given at varying times and venues, and found that they often differed materially. Six years of investigation and research later, their book, *Silent Coup*, has demolished the accepted version of all that transpired under the rubric "Watergate"—the central portion of which even *I* had believed.

Let's get one thing straight right now: I'd do it all again (the entry into the office of Daniel Ellsberg's psychiatrist for national security reasons, and the political intelligence operation to advance the cause of the re-election of a president whom I was serving) without hesitation *in the same circumstances that I believed obtained the first time around*—general disintegration of the social order—and with the same authority *I believed* I then possessed, i.e., when asked to do so by the president's closest confidant and highest-level (cabinet member) advisor. Unfortunately, while the reasons I performed the former operation were valid, I have learned from *Silent Coup* that one of those of the latter were *in*valid, and based upon a central lie: John Dean's misleading me into believing that my participation, my plans, and their execution, were all at the express wishes of John Mitchell. How Dean pulled that off was an exercise in sleight-of-hand worthy of The Amazing Randi himself. Follow the middle card:

As readers of *Will* will know, John Dean approached me in November, 1971, to recruit me to run the political intelligence operations of the 1972 Republican presidential campaign, something he wanted to be "... much better, much more sophisticated, than Jack Caulfield's SANDWEDGE proposal," for the implementation of which he offered "half a million for openers." I demurred unless I was assured of the approval of my current boss, John Ehrlichman, and my future boss, John Mitchell. Only when I later received those assurances through Bud Krogh did I agree. I was to become the General Counsel of the Committee to Re-elect, an ideal cover for what I understood to be my principal responsibilities, the intelligence operation I was to plan and run.

Next, Dean introduced me to Jeb Magruder at the Committee to Re-elect. We discussed election law advice needed by Magruder while I was wearing my General Counsel hat, and intelligence matters while wearing my other hat. Then I clashed with him over the issues of title and pay.

At my request, Dean then arranged a meeting between himself, Magruder, Mitchell and me to get the pay/title issue settled and discuss election law and intelligence matters. The meeting was held on 24th November and, although we got through the first two items, and Dean later testified that we discussed the third, *Mitchell cut the meeting off before a word was said about intelligence*. Nevertheless, Dean instructed me to proceed immediately with organizing and preparing an intelligence plan to present to Mitchell.

On 27th January 1972, Dean and Magruder were present as, with the aid of elaborate, CIA-prepared charts, I presented to Mr. Mitchell what I told him was the service requested through John Dean. I expected enthusiastic response from Mitchell to what Dean had led me to believe he had asked of me. Instead, at the end of the meeting, a decidedly *un*enthusiastic Mitchell ordered me to burn my charts *personally*. It was an order that, years later, Dean took credit for, but—believe me—it was Mitchell. Rarely have I been so embarrassed.

The meeting over, Dean interpreted Mitchell to me as wanting a "...less broad-gauged program" and agreed with Magruder that I ought to "...cut it back." I did, and on 4th February was ready to present a revised program to Mitchell costing only half as much as the first one. Again in the presence of Dean and Magruder I did so. This time all I could get back from Mitchell was an equally unenthusiastic "I'll think about it," and an agreement with Dean that the decision should come to me through "completely unofficial channels." Again I cut the proposed budget in half, submitted it through Magruder and awaited a decision.

This time I finally got what I *thought* was Mitchell's approval. The "unofficial channel" demanded by Dean turned out to be Bob Reisner, relaying a message from Magruder that I had a "go on your project." Still believing I was working for Mitchell and, through him, the president, I pressed on, responding to requests for investigation relayed by Magruder and organizing the implementation of the GEMSTONE plan I had been assured had Mitchell's imprimatur. On one occasion I addressed a report to Mitchell and, to my surprise, it came back with a request for additional information written on it and initialed, not by Mitchell, but by *Dean*.

Finally, at the end of April, I received, again through Magruder, the order to go into the Democratic National Committee headquarters in the Watergate office building, targeting party chairman Lawrence O'Brien for electronic surveillance. I planned accordingly. My men got in, placed the listening devices, but got nothing from O'Brien, who wasn't there, and nothing of real intelligence value from whoever was. Nevertheless, I addressed a summary of the intercepts to Mitchell and forwarded it through Magruder. I got the feedback through Magruder, too. It was, understandably, negative.

I saw Mr. Mitchell twice more. On 7th May, at a briefing by General Alexander Haig on the Vietnam war, and again on 15th June when, in spite of my trying to broach the subject of my intelligence operations by discussing a prank to be played on Senator McGovern, then segue into the proposed solution to the poor electronic surveillance product, Mitchell shot down my planned prank with such force I just left the envelope with the latest intercept logs on the edge of his desk and left. I didn't see or speak to John Mitchell again until my telephone conversation with him just before he died. And I can assure you that during that conversation, he didn't approve my GEMSTONE plan either. Bob Woodward, of course, is probably out at the Arlington National Cemetery right now, interviewing Mitchell for his next book, in which Mitchell will admit he approved everything and, when asked why, will be quoted as saying, *"I believed."*

Magruder has since had a book written for him in which he describes in detail an alleged meeting at CRP headquarters at which Mitchell chastised me for the poor electronic intercept product. There never was such a meeting. Mitchell, too, has denied it and, fortunately for the truth, his daily appointment and telephone logs show no such meeting.

So that's how it was done: Dean invoked Mitchell's name to me, then danced me past him at a meeting at which we didn't get to intelligence matters, and I was sold. After the next meeting, at which I was told to burn my charts, Dean told me that meant to just reduce the scope, and was backed up by Magruder (whom a group of people in Columbus, Ohio, gullible enough to have bought the act of a Jim and Tammy Bakker, later accepted as their new pastor, and the whole city swallowed as its ethics commissioner).

Another meeting ended in another failure and Magruder, whom Dean had persuaded me spoke for Bob Haldeman, sent me back into the trenches again. Mitchell, seeing all this being fronted by Dean, read Haldeman and the White House and kept trying to make me and my plans go away. Finally, we learn now from *Silent Coup*, Magruder buckled under the pressure from Dean and, through Reisner, gave me the go-ahead. He didn't mention Mitchell; I just *assumed* Mitchell's approval. (Were I to have agreed to testify and, under oath, been asked whether I had John Mitchell's direct approval, I would have had to say no—that in my direct dealings with him he either disapproved or was noncommittal.) The stage was now set for Watergate and what followed: a parade of press and politics-driven, suppressed evidence, and perjury-predicated prosecutions and public hearings, proclaimed by the perpetrators thereof as: *"the system worked."*

Recall now that the morning after the abortive Watergate break-in I learned from Powell Moore that John Mitchell was scheduled for a press conference in California at noon, Pacific time. I telephoned Magruder, briefed him on the situation and asked him to inform John Mitchell so that Mitchell wouldn't be blind-sided by the press at the conference.

Magruder swore under oath, in testimony used to convict John Mitchell, that after receiving my call and having Fred LaRue brief Mitchell on the arrest of the men in the Watergate, he was called into the meeting and was present while Mitchell began the "cover-up" by instructing Bob Mardian to telephone me with orders to go to Attorney General Kleindienst and ask him, in the name of John Mitchell, to get James McCord out of jail.

We now know from *Silent Coup* that John Mitchell had nothing to do with my approach to Kleindienst. Magruder has admitted that he telephoned *John Dean* and that *he and Dean* cooked up the bogus order to me from Mitchell to see Kleindienst. Magruder has also now admitted that, as I wrote in *Will*, it was *he,* not Bob Mardian, who telephoned me with the false message. Moreover, the authors of *Silent Coup* have demonstrated that simple arithmetic applied to time zone changes renders impossible the false stories Dean and Magruder told to both the investigating committee and the prosecutors. Yet, despite the denials of those falsely accused and the mathematical impossibility of the accusations, the committee and the prosecutors pressed on with their personal agendas—agendas which did not include interest in facts not supportive thereof. Deliberately they closed their ears to the denials of the accused and refused to do the grammar-school sums that would have demonstrated the obvious perjury they welcomed into the record in their pursuit of the reversal of the election of Richard Nixon.

On Monday morning, 19th June, John Dean telephoned me and asked for a meeting. We met in the park behind the White House where Dean affirmed to me that he was the damage control action officer and, therefore, entitled to all information about the failed operation. Once he had it, he could report to the president all facts concerning an event that could bring down the administration. I gave them to him, responding to his questions as to who knew what, mentioning specifically that Haldeman staff member Gordon Strachan knew that we were going back into the Watergate. Then, because the president had to know what is called in Washington jargon "the worst case scenario," I told him of the classified Ellsberg investigation, including the surreptitious entry into Dr. Fielding's office in Beverly Hills, because it had been accomplished by essentially the same team and could conceivably come to light. I instructed Dean how to obtain the necessary FD 302 forms and "airtels" from the FBI to keep abreast of the

Bureau's investigation. Dean was more than up to that. As *Silent Coup* makes clear, he didn't just keep abreast of the investigation; with the information I had given him, he effectively *controlled* it.

Having digested all the information I provided, Dean ordered Howard Hunt out of the country. Then he told me that he was no longer the action officer. It is clear now, from reading *Silent Coup*, that Dean was more interested in learning how much *I* knew of the operation than he was in the knowledge of others. I expected Dean to report what I had told him to the president immediately. He didn't. He didn't tell the president until *nine months later*. Dean turned my damage report to the president into "A Message to Garcia." There was, of course, a reason: As I have just learned from *Silent Coup*, Dean knew more about Watergate than anyone else because it was *his* operation, and the last person in the world he wanted to know that was the President of the United States, Richard Nixon.

When Dean ordered me to send Hunt out of the country, I assumed that the only reason he didn't order me to leave along with him was the fact that I held the high-profile position of General Counsel of the Finance Committee to Re-elect the President. It is now obvious why I was not included in the order: In the time-honored tradition of intelligence services, Dean had been using me, not as the operations officer, but as the cut-out. The real ops officer was Hunt; and his principal, the man who conceived and commanded the Watergate operation, was John Dean. John Mitchell and Richard Nixon had nothing whatever to do with it.

It was Hunt, therefore, not I, who possessed the knowledge so dangerous to Dean: that the real target of the operation was not Lawrence O'Brien or his office, but the three-office complex occupied by R. Spencer Oliver, his secretary Ida Maxine Wells and the nearly-always-vacant office of the Chairman of Democratic State Governors—and, in particular, that the specific target of the second break-in was the locked desk of Maxie Wells. What Hunt knew, and I did not, was that there was a call-girl service being offered visiting firemen by the Democratic National Committee headquarters, through an inside contact, using the facilities of a prostitution ring run out of the nearby Columbia

Plaza apartments by a madam named Heidi Rikan, under the alias Kathy Dieter. Moreover, Hunt knew that the true mission of the Cuban cohort was to follow a map that he had given to Eugenio Martinez that led to and marked the desk of Maxie Wells, the secretary of R. Spencer Oliver and, using a key to the desk also given by Hunt to Martinez, extract the contents therefrom and give them to Hunt for delivery to Dean.

What *Dean* knew was that Philip Bailley, a man recently indicted for white slavery, had been caught by police with an address book—a copy of which Dean had asked for and obtained from the prosecutors—that contained the names and code names of some of the Columbia Plaza hookers, and *also* contained the name, and code name, of other of his legal clients and acquaintances, including another woman who just happened to be the roommate of the madam: Maureen Biner, code name "Clout"—soon to become, through marriage, Maureen Dean.

Hunt denies this. He says I told him the object of the mission was to obtain contribution records, from a safe in Larry O'Brien's office, which would show that the Democratic Party had received campaign contributions from Fidel Castro's Cuba. Baloney. I never received nor passed on such instructions, never heard of a safe in O'Brien's office and none was there. And look at the rest of the evidence:

The observation post set up in the Howard Johnson's Hotel across Virginia Avenue couldn't even *see* the office of Larry O'Brien. Equally out of the way and unobservable was the office of the treasurer, Robert Strauss, in whose complex any contribution records would most likely be kept. They certainly wouldn't be kept in the desk of the secretary of the Executive Director of the Association of State Democratic Chairmen, R. Spencer Oliver. The observation post was chosen to, and did, look directly into the three-room complex where the telephone tap (obviously removed *before* the second break-in) was placed so that the conversations of those for whom prostitution dates were being made could be recorded, along with their stated sexual preferences, and where, also, the prospective "Johns" could be photographed with a camera equipped with a telephoto lens I saw on a tripod inside the

500

observation post when I was brought there on an inspection trip by James McCord.

In support of the above, there is the statement of Eugenio Martinez that Howard Hunt gave him a key to Maxie Wells' desk, and a map marked with its location, with the understanding that he was to remove the contents of the desk for delivery to Hunt. Martinez' statement is in turn confirmed by the recovery of the key and map from him by the police at the time of his arrest.

These facts explain the assertion by prosecutor Earl Silbert that "Hunt was trying to blackmail Spencer and I will prove it." He did not, of course, because the American Civil Liberties Union intervened and prevented the disclosure of what was learned through the wiretaps. And, of course, in any move against the Democrats, Hunt would have been acting as Dean's agent.

Admittedly, anything Silbert says must be taken with a grain of salt. Prior to trial, my lawyer, Peter Maroulis, demanded from the prosecution any "Brady material," so named after *Brady vs. Maryland*, the U.S. Supreme Court case requiring the prosecution to give the defendant any evidence in its possession of an exculpatory nature. Nevertheless, Silbert deliberately withheld the existence and contents of FBI reports revealing that immediately after the arrest of my men inside the Democratic National Committee headquarters, personnel of the famed FBI Laboratory checked all of the telephones in all of the offices and found that *none of them were bugged*. (See Appendix.) It is hard to think of anything more exculpatory than that in a wiretapping prosecution, yet Silbert withheld it. (We know from *Silent Coup* that the bug had been removed prior to the second entry.) My men were carrying more bugs because I was being led to believe that the purpose of going in again was to place new ones, not to retrieve the contents of Maxie Wells' desk. Note that Silbert also did not tell us that Martinez had had a map leading to Wells' desk, as well as a key to it.

Silbert was out to win, one way or another, and the law be hanged. (He is quoted in the *Columbia Journalism Review* as referring to the United States Supreme Court's Brady rule as a mere "legalism," a position it would be interesting to listen to him defend before the Bar Association.) I have no problem with Silbert's "anything to win" attitude; it mirrors my own. It is his trademark moral posturing that would gag a maggot.

All of the forgoing explains something else. Recall that Dean promised me in our walk in the park that the usual bail money, attorney fees and family support would be provided to my captured men. He repeated the assertion to me when he telephoned me at my home on the eve of my trial. Yet, as Tony Ulasewicz has confirmed, the Cubans and I received little by way of the promised support (and kept our silence because it was unrelated; a matter of principle and not a quid pro quo) while Hunt, it turns out, received hundreds of thousands of dollars, for which he at least has had the decency to stay bought—to this day he hasn't given up Dean.

Consider: The Cubans accepted orders only from Hunt. They distrusted McCord and wouldn't have taken orders from him. They respected me, but knew that the chain of command was from me to Hunt to them. I never heard of Oliver, Wells, her desk, a map or a key. I relayed to Hunt the target I received from Magruder—Larry O'Brien. But, as we have seen, the Cubans didn't go near O'Brien's office. They were captured in the Oliver/Wells/Governors area, with Martinez having a map and a key to Wells' desk. Who could have issued countermanding orders to Hunt? The only man who knew, from his relationship with the roommate of the madam, where to look and what to look for, was John Dean. And Hunt knew Dean had recruited me and was above me in the chain of command. It was *Dean's* operation, through Hunt. And Silbert *knew* it was Hunt. Notice, although the name of the case was *The United States of America vs. George Gordon Liddy, et al.*, and I was being trumpeted in the press by the prosecution as the ringleader, Silbert didn't exclaim "*Liddy* is trying to blackmail Spencer...." Nor did he say "*Liddy and Hunt* are trying to blackmail...." He said "*Hunt* was trying to blackmail...." because he knew damn well what was going on and that I wasn't in on it.

In the years since the first publication of *Will* I have spoken before

502

tens of thousands of people throughout much of the world. I always have a question-and-answer period, and one of the most frequently asked questions is, "Have your experiences, especially in prison, left you bitter?" I'll tell you what I told them: Bitterness can only be experienced if one simultaneously indulges oneself in self-pity—probably the most useless expenditure of psychic energy I can imagine. Moreover, when one adds up my life's experiences to date, were I to complain, no one should listen. We all get dealt a bad hand or two and, from time to time, it may include marked cards. One accepts the good hands with the bad, playing them all as best one can.

As for the card sharps, in time they are all exposed for what they are: what goes around comes around. It may have taken years but, thanks to *Silent Coup*, it has come around with a vengeance for Dean, Magruder, Hunt, Silbert, Ritchie, Haig, Woodward, the Watergate special prosecution teams and congressional committee. I just wish John Mitchell were alive today to see his enemies become his footstool.

"What goes around comes around" works the other way, too. Shortly after my release from prison I was inducted as a life member of the Special Operations Association. Some members go back to the days of operations behind the lines in Nazi Germany; one extraordinary woman survived horrible torture by the Gestapo when she was only sixteen. I was nominated for my membership by a Major General of the United States Army, and the nomination was seconded by a winner of the Congressional Medal of Honor. On 15 September 1980, I was inducted into The Honor Legion of the Police Department of the City of New York. And on the very night that President Reagan hurled American air power against Muammar Ghadaffi, I was at the United States Military Academy at West Point where, in the presence of the Commandant and the Superintendent, I addressed the two most senior classes of the Corps of Cadets and received from them one of my most cherished possessions: a cased cadet officer's sword.

God and the American people have been very good to me, and I am deeply grateful. Most of all, for:

503

ALEXANDRA (SANDY)

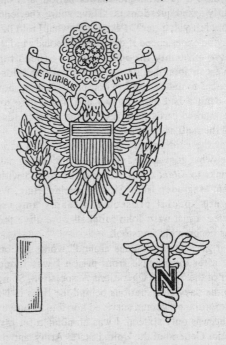

First Lieutenant, United States Army Nurse Corps Reserve.
Primarily Nurse IV, Neuro-rehabilitation specialist.

Graduate: The College of New Rochelle, B.S. (Nursing Science)
          The Catholic University, M.S. (Nursing Science)

GRACE

Graduate: The College of New Rochelle, A.B.

Grace earns her living as a computer expert, which enables her to pursue her art. She is an accomplished weaver of tapestries in the manner of Aubusson and Gobelin in France.

SALI
(Daughter-in-Law)

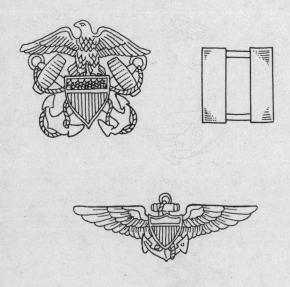

Graduate: Andover and the University of Florida, A.B.

Sali is the daughter of the late famed Navy test pilot, Lt. Commander Bud Gear, who died on active duty in the Vietnam war leaving a widow and six children, the youngest being Sali. Today Sali is a Naval jet aviator, carrier qualified in the A-4 attack jet. She wears her father's golden wings and old leather flying jacket.

A superb pilot (the A-4 is one of the two aircraft featured in the motion picture, *Top Gun*) Sali is also an accomplished horsewoman and trainer of thoroughbred jumpers.

BRYAN
(Son-in-Law)

Gunnery Sergeant, United States Marine Corps

University of Indiana, A.B. Music
The Catholic University, M.A. Music

Every inch a Marine, Bryan is First Trombone in the United States Marine Corps Band, "The President's Own," and plays in several symphony orchestras.

JIM

Lieutenant, United States Navy. Naval Special Warfare Officer. SEAL. All information as to assignment, billets or accomplishments classified or otherwise not available.

Graduate: The Mercersburg Academy and Fordham University, B.S. Varsity Swimming and Water Polo, Vice President Fordham College Student Government.

As a college student, Jim received the Excelsior Award of the Captain's Endowment Association, Police Department, City of New York, in that "on 9 September 1983 he did assist the victim of a brutal crime and pursue and arrest an armed dangerous felon at personal risk to his own life."

1983—Captain, U.S. Team South, Olympic Sports Festival—Water Polo
1986—Captain, U.S. Team South, Olympic Sports Festival—Modern Pentathlon
1987—All Navy Modern Pentathlon Champion

TOM

Captain, United States Marine Corps Reserve. More than three years active duty as an infantry officer.

Graduate: St. Albans School and Fordham University, A.B. President of his class. Varsity Water Polo.

Studied Indonesian and Pacific Rim economics at the University of Jakarta.

Languages: English, French, Indonesian, Malay.

Explorations: Interior of Iceland; Egypt and (alone) the jungle in the interior of New Guinea. Gained entrance to East Germany in 1982; interviewed by KGB.

As a college student, Tom received the Excelsior Award of the Captain's Endowment Association, Police Department, City of New York, in that "on 9 September 1983 he did assist the victim of a brutal crime and pursue and arrest an armed dangerous felon at personal risk to his own life."

Tom is now in his third and final year at The Fordham Law School.

RAY

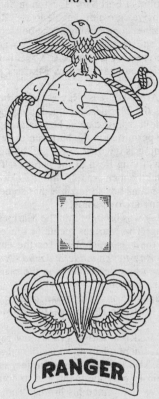

Captain, United States Marine Corps Reserve. Airborne. Ranger. Three years active duty. Infantry. Graduate: The Mercersburg Academy and Fordham University, A.B.

In 1989, while leading a Marine infantry platoon on patrol in Panama, Ray was injured severely in the course of explosive ordnance disposal. The blast burned off his face, much of the flesh of his left hand and forearm and some of his right hand. His men, who did not expect him to live, brought him out of the jungle for medical evacuation by air to the United States.

Ray was brought directly to the famed burn center at the United States Army hospital at Fort Sam Houston in San Antonio, Texas. While in the intensive care unit, unable to see, Ray heard some of the medical personnel complaining of the boisterous behavior of a squad of Marine enlisted men in a recovery ward. They were all that survived the crash of a Marine CH-53E helicopter in Korea which killed their lieutenant, fellow Marines and burned them badly in flaming fuel.

According to Army sources, Ray asked to be transferred into the same ward as the Marines. Swathed completely in bandages, Ray couldn't be told from Adam as he was brought in.

No visitors are permitted in the burn center before noon. That's because the morning is devoted to the scrubbing of dead, burned skin from the raw, living flesh of the patients. The pain involved is excruciating and the men are told that it's okay to scream. They do. And those screams are so terrible that sometimes the people doing the scrubbing are overcome.

Shortly after Ray was brought into the Marines' ward it was his turn for scrubbing. The Marines mentally braced themselves for his screams. To their astonishment, for the entire time he was being scrubbed, *Ray never made a sound.* Awed, the enlisted Marines asked the army personnel who the man was who didn't scream while being scrubbed.

"That man," came the answer, *"is a Marine officer."*

The enlisted Marines immediately adopted Ray as their lieutenant.

Ray was mustered out with a brand-new face, which was a substantial improvement when one considers that he used to look like his father. He still required minor surgery on his left hand to be able once again to play the piano and to continue composing his own music. Ray had joined his brother Tom at Fordham Law School and was in his first year when war broke out in the Persian Gulf. Arguing that "I may not be able to play the piano well, but I can sure squeeze a trigger," Ray volunteered to return to active duty, requesting a combat assignment. On 14 February 1991 he was back in uniform, where he remains as of this writing.

Today belongs to them.

UNITED STATES GOVERNMENT

Memorandum

TO : Mr. Conrad   DATE: 10/2/72

FROM : W. W. Bradley

SUBJECT: JAMES WALTER MC CORD, JR.; ET AL.
BURGLARY OF DEMOCRATIC PARTY
NATIONAL HEADQUARTERS, 6/17/72
INTERCEPTION OF COMMUNICATIONS

1 - Mr. Felt
1 - Mr. Bates
1 - Mr. Bolz
1 - Mr. Conrad
1 - Mr. Bradley
1 - Mr. Miller

    Memorandum of 9/29/72 from Mr. Bolz to Mr. Bates relative to the above-entitled matter attaches a memorandum from Assistant U. S. Attorney (AUSA) Earl Silbert to Assistant Attorney General Henry E. Peterson dated 9/28/72. AUSA Silbert in his memorandum deals with the electronic device recovered from the telephone of Spencer Oliver on 9/13/72 and sets forth his belief that the recovered device is the original device which permitted Baldwin to overhear conversations. Silbert sets forth five reasons which he believes lead to his conclusion. Laboratory is requested to review and reply.

    Review shows that none of the reasons are conclusive or compelling and that only the first reason advanced by Silbert is technical in nature and based on reported technical facts. The remaining four reasons are questionable or speculative in nature, and in at least one instance (#5) totally in error. The specific reasons cited by Silbert and Laboratory comments relative to each one set out below using Silbert's numbering.

REC-28 139-4089-1455

    1. SILBERT: The device recovered operated at 120 MHz. Baldwin was receiving at 118.9 MHz, well within the range of the device. The three devices in the possession of those arrested operated two at 110, one at 114 MHz, not at all as clearly within the range of the receiver at 118.9, particularly the two operating at 110.

    LABORATORY COMMENT: The frequency on which the recovered device originally may have operated, if at all, cannot be accurately determined since it was inoperative at time of recovery. It was made operable by replacing a defective transistor, after which the unit operated on 120 MHz. While this is closest of the four mentioned devices, this fact is not conclusive because

EX-111   NOV 10 1972

RAM:lgh
(7)

CONTINUED - OVER

59 NOV 16 1972

1-Xerox made for OPR
5/20/74

(a) there is no evidence to our knowledge that limits the original device tuned in by Baldwin to one of the four recovered (It is our understanding that two men escaped from the premises the night of discovery) (b) the original operating frequency of instant device cannot be determined; and (c) after repair, the operating frequency is not on the frequency reportedly received.

2. SILBERT: To assume that one of the three devices recovered upon arrest was the one used on Oliver's telephone assumes that the defendants removed it. I see no reason to assume that. A more or at least equally logical assumption is that they were going to put more taps on, not take those they had in out. Clearly, they were going to put the bugging device in. Why not the taps?

While the Oliver tap was not O'Brien, they apparently had considered it to be producing useful information. There was, accordingly, no reason to remove it while putting in other taps.

LABORATORY COMMENT: Reason appears speculative. We do not know the basis validating the assumption "Clearly, they were going to put the bugging device in." Laboratory tests of the batteries associated with the bugging device showed that some were partially run down. This would not be the normally expected condition for a new installation of batteries. However, more in point, the absence of a device in Oliver's phone at the time of the security check does not necessarily carry with it the assumption that one of the devices found in possession of defendants was the one heard by Baldwin.

3. SILBERT: The location of the tap in the telephone is totally consistent with Baldwin's explanation of how the telephone calls were intercepted - only three specific extensions, one at a time.

LABORATORY COMMENT: Questionable reason. Summary Bureau report dated 8/20/72 made available to Laboratory states on page 12 that Baldwin in his monitoring discovered that he could overhear telephone conversation on four extensions of one phone at the office of Oliver. General Investigative Division advises that Baldwin's interviews tend to indicate he believed he was monitoring conversations of secretaries and others from telephones which were extensions of Oliver's phone. The instant device, as installed at time of recovery would not permit this type of operation.

Memorandum to Mr. Conrad
RE: JAMES WALTER MC CORD, JR.; ET AL.
BURGLARY OF DEMOCRATIC PARTY
NATIONAL HEADQUARTERS, 6/17/72
INTERCEPTION OF COMMUNICATIONS

    4. SILBERT: I cannot imagine anyone planting a device in the Democratic headquarters after Watergate, particularly on Oliver's telephone. It is too ludicrous.

    LABORATORY COMMENT: Speculative reason. At least two other possibilities suggest themselves on the basis of reported information:

    (a) Bureau Summary report dated 9/20/72 shows on page 11 that some intercepted conversations dealt with marital problems. Marital problems are a well recognized basis for attempted wiretapping.

    (b) Democrats or sympathizers, feeling they had unusually good issue in the "burglary" and wiretapping incident, could have decided to make a more recent "installation" and call attention to it in order to keep the pot boiling. Baldwin had previously disclosed approximate frequency and fact Oliver's phone was involved. WFO wire dated 9/15/72 sets out that Oliver's office cognizant of at least part of this information. Moreover, O'Brien has recently publicly alleged his office was bugged.

    In this regard it is of possible significance that the device found on Oliver's phone on 9/13/72 was completely unlike the devices found in possession of defendants at time of arrest.

    5. SILBERT: I think the FBI missed it because the location of Oliver's office in the Democratic headquarters is such that it is almost the last place one would expect a tap to be placed - nowhere near O'Brien's office or anywhere else of importance.

    LABORATORY COMMENT: Totally erroneous reason. Laboratory's search was not keyed to relative location. Indeed, Laboratory technical personnel, in addition to knowing of attempted penetration by arrested defendants, also considered possibility Democrat sympathizers might make additional installations to exacerbate the situation, and therefore all rooms and all phones were considered highly suspect and were thoroughly searched.

*By false trouble report. In this regard WFO wire 9/30/72, advises telephone repairman attempted to observe malfunctions reported by secretary with negative results. WFO suggests possibility reported malfunction had never occurred.

- 3 -

Memorandum to Mr. Conrad
RE: JAMES WALTER MC CORD, JR.; ET AL
BURGLARY OF DEMOCRATIC PARTY
NATIONAL HEADQUARTERS, 6/17/72
INTERCEPTION OF COMMUNICATIONS

SUMMARY: While we recognize the appeal, from a prosecution standpoint, of the situation postulated by AUSA Silbert, no facts known to us at present support the presence of a listening device on Oliver's telephone at the time of the security check. There is no evidence to our knowledge that the device heard by Baldwin was heard by anyone after the arrest of the defendants. On the contrary, a check of the telephones by competent and experienced technical personnel, looking specifically for this type of device, showed no such device to be present at the time of the search. In this regard, Supervisor W. G. Stevens who was in personal charge of and took part in the search has previously stated that the device was large enough to be readily seen by physical search, and that based on the search conducted, he is positive that the device was not on the phone at the time of the search. Further in this regard, it is noted that the physical security of the Democratic National Committee space was such as to make subsequent access for the purpose of installing devices relatively easy. WFO wire to the Bureau dated 9/15/72 on page 6 states DNCH maintained no limitation to access to offices after normal duty hours until about midnight when premises secured.

ACTION:

If approved a response to Assistant Attorney General Peterson will be prepared along the above lines.

-4-

INDEX

522

527